FORENSIC SCIENCE AND THE LAW

FORENSIC SCIENCE AND THE LAW

Dr. Anne Wade

SOCIETY Publishing

www.societypublishing.com

Forensic Science and the Law

Dr. Anne Wade

Society Publishing
4164 Lakeshore Road
Burlington, ON L7L 1A4
Canada
www.societypublishing.com
Email: orders@arclereducation.com

ISBN: 978-1-77956-460-3 (Hardcover)

ABOUT THE AUTHOR

Dr. Anne Wade has been a researcher and a professor in the Criminal Justice field for over 30 years. She currently holds a position as a Provost/CAO in a University, and Director of Research at another university. She holds an Ed.D. in Educational Leadership and a Ph.D. in Public Safety Leadership/Criminal Justice. Her research interests are in Criminology, Victimology, and the Human Services. She is married to Wesley Wade. She is an artist, writer, researcher, professor, and university administrator.

TABLE OF CONTENTS

List of Figures .... *xi*

List of Tables .... *xix*

Preface .... *xxi*

Chapter 1 Introduction to Forensic Science and the Legal System 1

Introduction 2

1.1. Overview of Forensic Science 2

1.2. History of Forensic Science 6

1.3. Various Fields of Forensic Science 14

1.4. Legal System 34

References 42

Chapter 2 Crime Scene Investigation 43

Introduction 44

2.1. Crime Scene Investigation Basics 45

2.2. Crime Scene Management 63

References 85

Chapter 3 Forensic Biology and DNA Analysis 87

Introduction 88

3.1. Forensic Biology 90

3.2. A Brief History of Development of Forensic Biology 95

3.3. Overview and History of DNA Typing 97

References 108

Chapter 4 Forensic Chemistry and Toxicology 111

Introduction 112

4.1. Concept of Forensic Chemistry 112

4.2. Role of Vibrational Spectroscopy in Forensic Chemistry 117
4.3. Alcohol 128
4.4. Toxicology 132
4.5. Action of Poisons 140
References 150

Chapter 5 Forensic Anthropology and Odontology 155
Introduction 156
5.1. Definition, AIM and Scope of Forensic Anthropology 157
5.2. Biological Profiling of Skeletal Remains 163
5.3. Evolution of Forensic Anthropological Methods of Identification 171
5.4. Forensic Odontology: Bite Mark Analysis 180
5.5. Importance of Dental Records in Forensic Odontology 192
References 199

Chapter 6 Forensic Pathology 201
Introduction 202
6.1. Overview of Forensic Pathology 202
6.2. Cause and Manner of Death 209
6.3. Autopsy 210
6.4. Death Investigation 250
References 264

Chapter 7 Forensic Psychology and Psychiatry 269
Introduction 270
7.1. The Science of Forensic Psychology 270
7.2. Psychological Profiling and Criminal Behavior Analysis 282
7.3. Forensic Psychiatry 289
7.4. Forensic Psychiatry: Contemporary Scope, Challenges, and Controversies 296
7.5. Clinical Characteristics and Self-Harm in Forensic Psychiatric Patients 304
References 315

Chapter 8 Digital Forensics 319
Introduction 320
8.1. Basic Concept of Digital Forensics 320
8.2. Digital Forensic Investigation Models 340
8.3. Research Methodology in Digital Forensics 344
8.4. Challenging Aspects of Digital Evidence 351
References 354

Chapter 9 Forensic Document Examination 357
Introduction 358
9.1. Questioned Document 358
9.2. Handwriting Comparisons 360
9.3. Printed Documents: Typewriters, Computer Printers, Electrostatic Copiers 366
9.4. Other Examinations Performed by Document Examiners 369
References 380

Chapter 10 The Interface of Forensic Science and the Law 381
Introduction 382
10.1. The Role of Forensic Experts in Court 382
10.2. The Role of an Expert Witness in a Trial 394
10.3. Admissibility of Forensic Evidence (Daubert and Frye Standards) 399
10.4. Ethical Issues in Forensic Science 408
10.5. Criminal Justice and the Law 418
10.6. Future Trends in Forensic Science and its Impact on the Legal System 420
References 426

Index 429

LIST OF FIGURES

Figure 2.1. Des Moines police officers secure a crime scene related to a double homicide on Nov. 2, 2016, in Des Moines, Iowa

Figure 2.2. Forensic specialists of the German police secure the crime scene after a deadly knife attack on May 10, 2016, in Grafing

Figure 2.3. The inward spiral search

Figure 2.4. The outward spiral search

Figure 2.5. The parallel search

Figure 2.6. The grid search

Figure 2.7. The zone search

Figure 2.8. Powders and brushes at the CBI latent-fingerprint lab

Figure 2.9. This cast is a student sample. According to Mr. Clayton, footprints found at a crime scene seldom produce such perfect specimens

Figure 2.10. Crime scene security log

Figure 2.11. Stages of the criminal event

Figure 2.12. Physical evidence of crime

Figure 2.13. Exhibit log document

Figure 3.1. Forensic biology

Figure 3.2. Brief history of development of forensic biology

Figure 3.3. Illustration of the interactions between the three components of the criminal justice system

Figure 3.4. Overview of biology, technology, and genetic components of DNA typing using short tandem repeat (STR) markers

Figure 4.1. Classification of poison

Figure 4.2. Physical state of poisons

Figure 4.3. Medicolegal classification of poison

Figure 5.1. Mandible

Figure 5.2. The pelvic girdle

Figure 5.3. Lower limb bones

Figure 5.4. The first two columns illustrate the landmark locations in the inner and middle ear segments of the petrous part of the temporal bone used in this research. The third column illustrates the measurements between the landmarks in the inner and middle ear segments. The measurements are color-coded according to the legend located between columns 2 and 3

Figure 5.5. The first two images (labelled slices E&F) illustrate the locations of the landmarks around the contour of the petrous part of the temporal bone. The third image illustrates the measurements between the landmarks around the contour of the petrous part of the temporal bone. The measurements are color-coded according to the legend located between the second and third images

Figure 5.6. The first two columns illustrate the remaining landmark locations in both the inner and middle ear, and the contour segments of the petrous part of the temporal bone. The third column illustrates the measurements between the measurements that extend between the landmarks of the inner and middle ear, and the contour of the petrous part of the temporal bone. The measurements are color coded according to the legend located between columns 2 and 3

Figure 5.6. Sample test array

Figure 6.1. Scene investigation is one of the most important aspects of a death investigation. Depending on the jurisdiction, forensic pathologists may or may not participate in this aspect of the investigation, although most will visit at least an occasional scene, particularly if asked to do so by police or investigators. In this case, a forensic pathologist supervises as an elevator shaft accident victim is extricated by fire department personnel

Figure 6.2. The external examination is a very important part of a forensic autopsy. In some cases, particularly in homicide cases with multiple injuries, the external examination requires much more time than the internal examination. In the example shown, a case with multiple injuries, including blunt force, sharp force, and gunshot wounds, the external examination took several hours to complete

Figure 6.3. The internal examination allows the forensic pathologist to identify diseases and injuries at autopsy, and to collect tissue samples and certain types of evidence. In this case, showing the internal appearance of the chest, after removal of the chest plate and the anterior (front) part of the pericardial sac, a markedly enlarged heart is evident. The structure to the left of the heart in the photograph is the right lung. Immediately below the lung is the right side of the diaphragm

Figure 6.4. Microscopic examination may be a very important part of a forensic autopsy, particularly in cases where the cause of death is a natural disease process. In this photograph, a forensic pathologist is viewing slides under a light microscope

Figure 6.5. Microscopic section of normal thyroid gland

Figure 6.6. An infant brain that has been "fixed" in formalin for several weeks following autopsy. The brain shows signs of swelling or "edema."

Figure 6.7. The ability to perform and evaluate x-rays is a necessary part of the forensic autopsy. X-rays are primarily utilized to locate projectiles (bullets), to evaluate injury, and to aid in identification. This is an example of a normal postmortem chest x-ray

Figure 6.8. A forensic pathologist participating in a videotaped deposition. A court reporter documents the proceedings

Figure 6.9. Testifying in court proceedings, including criminal and civil trials, is an important part of the role of a forensic pathologist

Figure 6.10. A forensic pathologist participating in a deposition along with attorneys from both sides of the case

Figure 6.11. The scene of a rape-homicide. The attending pathologist must record the posture, state of clothing and general relationship of the victim to the surroundings, but limit the examination at the scene to avoid any interference with the vital process of obtaining trace evidence. Rectal temperatures should not be taken until all swabs are completed, usually in the mortuary. Temperatures can be taken in the ear or deep nostrils, though with severe head injuries (as here) even this must be done with care

Figure 6.12. Scene of a homicide-suicide where the locus of bodies should be widely marked off by tape to restrict access, and the actual body protected by a shelter from the weather and unauthorized onlookers

Figure 6.13. At a scene of crime, the position of the body at the time of an assault can sometimes be clarified by observing the direction of blood splashing that may have been thrown off a weapon or bloodstained hands. Blood striking vertically causes round or crenellated circles, while blood hitting at an angle is lance-shaped with the narrow end facing the direction of travel. There is often a preceding drop of blood in advance of the major splash, forming an 'exclamation mark' stain

Figure 6.14. External examination must note every feature; here there is obvious abdominal distension in a battered child with facial bruising. The intestine had been ruptured by a blow, and oxygen administered by the ambulance crew escaped to distend the peritoneal cavity

Figure 6.15. Post-mortem artifacts on the body of a homicide victim. These are due to defibrillator paddles applied in a hospital casualty department

Figure 6.16. Full external examination is vital, including the interior of the mouth. Here a large number of amylobarbitone capsules offer a presumptive cause of death, though analytical confirmation is still required

Figure 6.17. (a, b) Typical examples of the many anatomical diagrams available for the recording of external findings at autopsy

Figure 6.18. Examination and photography of injuries; after full preliminary examination and forensic sampling, the area is cleaned, shaved if necessary, and photographed with a scale adjacent to the injuries

Figure 6.19. Where there are numerous similar lesions, it assists the clarity of the autopsy report if numbers used during photography match those listed in the autopsy protocol

Figure 6.20. Scene of crime officers recovering trace evidence from hands before a homicide autopsy. The pathologist must offer the rest of the team every facility to complete their work before he begins his dissection

Figure 6.21. Autopsy incisions: (a) standard midline, (b) 'V-shape' and (c) subclavicular

Figure 6.22. The minimum instruments needed for performing an autopsy. Any further items may be useful but not essential

Figure 6.23. White shining fat droplets (chylomicrons) in mesenterial lymphatic vessels suggesting postprandial state

Figure 6.24. Toxicology kit issued by the home office forensic science laboratories. Contained in a plastic bag are a large liver tub, a smaller stomach tub, two universal (30 ml) containers, one rubber-capped fluoride vial for blood alcohol, and a syringe and two needles

Figure 6.25. Angled saw-cuts for removal of skull-cap to avoid slippage during reconstruction

Figure 6.26. Investigators should obtain copies of all medical records associated with a decedent's death. These can be particularly helpful to the forensic pathologist when medical therapy introduces artifacts that can be confused with true injuries. In the example shown, an emergency department diagram shows the exact location of injuries observed prior to implementation of medical therapy, which introduced numerous artifacts

Figure 6.27. A very important part of the initial investigation of a death is the scene investigation. In this scene photograph, the exact location of the decedent's body is documented prior to moving the body

Figure 6.28. A scene photograph showing the condition of a motor vehicle following a fatal collision. Photographs such as this can be very helpful in understanding the forces involved and the injuries sustained

Figure 6.29. Overall scene photographs are useful in providing documentation of the general conditions of the scene of death. Even though the death in this instance occurred inside the house, the photograph of the outside of the home provided important information about the death scene

Figure 6.30. A photograph showing the decedent before his body was moved. Also visible is a container of a toxic substance on the top of the bookshelf. Toxicologic analysis for the specific substance within the blood of the decedent confirmed that the death was due to the poison

Figure 6.31. Paper bags were placed on the hands of this homicide victim by the death investigator at the scene in order to preserve any trace evidence present on or about the hands

Figure 6.32. Gently vacuuming a body at the scene may ensure that important trace evidence has been secured prior to moving the body

Figure 6.33. The presence of a blood-soaked area on the pavement adjacent to the decedent (seen at the top of the photograph) at this scene indicates that, at one time, the gunshot wound victim was probably facedown on the pavement at that location. The death investigator was able to confirm with emergency medical services (EMS) personnel that the victim was in fact facedown at that location when they arrived. The decedent is in his present location as a result of EMS workers rolling him onto his back to certify life extinct

Figure 6.34. Trace material at a scene may include blood on the ground or on bushes and vegetation. All of this may be lost if there is rain or with the passage of time, hence the need for early securing, protection, and evaluation of possible crime scenes

Figure 6.35. A photograph showing the appearance of a decedent as first seen by the investigator at a death scene. In this case, it was important for the death investigator to interview the family members who discovered the body, as well as police and emergency medical workers in order to determine if the body had been moved, if the shirt was already raised when the decedent was found, and if the pants were partially down as they appear in this photograph

Figure 6.36. Scene evaluation shows a decedent lying on her back with lethal stab wounds. The knife in her hand had been placed there in a clumsy attempt to make a homicide look like a suicide

Figure 6.37. A large collection of blood next to a decedent was associated with self-inflicted rectal trauma from the shoe horn that was found next to the body

Figure 6.38. When at a death scene, it is important for investigators to observe areas away from the body. This is a photograph of the bathroom of a decedent found dead in another room. The dried red fluid in the bathroom was not blood, but was vomitus (gastric contents) containing abundant medication, leading investigators to suggest the possibility of an overdose

Figure 6.39. A young female decedent found dead in bed with her deceased mother

Figure 6.40. A woman found dead in bed with her deceased daughter

Figure 6.41. Initially, it was feared that the mother and her daughter were killed by another person; however, there were no signs of injury to either body and no signs of forced entry or disturbance at the scene. Another thought was that they may have succumbed to carbon monoxide poisoning or some other environmental hazard, which would possibly put others in the apartment complex at risk of injury or death. Examination of the refrigerator contents at the scene, however, revealed a "milkshake" in a glass jar, which had a "medicinal" odor. Further examination of the mother's computer revealed that she had concocted the "milkshake" and given it to her daughter to kill her, prior to committing suicide. Autopsy toxicology results revealed lethal levels of barbiturates in each decedent. The case thus represented a familial murder suicide

Figure 6.42. The discovery of medications at a death scene (shown on a table) should prompt the death investigator to collect the medication containers, record the information on the containers, count and record the contents of each container, and secure the containers until final disposition. In some cases, final disposition will involve analysis of the contents by a drug laboratory. In most cases, final disposition involves eventual safe, proper, witnessed, and documented destruction of the contents

Figure 6.43. If a weapon, such as a gun, is present at a death scene, it is important that the weapon be secured and made safe, while maintaining any evidence that may be present on or near the weapon

Figure 6.44. Postmortem animal predation may cause significant damage to bodies left outdoors and make the assessment of antemortem wounds difficult. Note especially the absence of tissue around the face and the left leg, the result of animal feeding. Also of note are other significant decompositional changes, including dark discoloration and mummification of the skin

Figure 6.45. Bodies that have been dumped outdoors in isolated locations may be skeletonized prior to discovery. During the process of decomposition animal predation may result in body parts and bones being scattered over considerable distances

Figure 6.46. Serial killers may choose isolated areas to dispose of bodies as in this case from South Australia where the bodies of a number of young women were dumped in an area of featureless saltbush plain

Figure 6.47. A body in a hidden location may not always indicate concealment after a homicide. In this case, the decedent had taken a cab to an isolated beach where he had crawled under a rock overhang and then shot himself in the head

Figure 6.48. An example of a portion of a four-page death investigation form used in one jurisdiction

Figure 6.49. An example of the size of medical records that sometimes require review by a forensic pathologist

Figure 8.1. The principal purpose of digital forensics

Figure 8.2. Digital forensic methodologies

Figure 8.3. History of digital forensics

Figure 8.4. Evidence transfer in the physical and digital dimensions helps investigators establish connections between victims, offenders, and crime scenes

Figure 8.5. Authentication of digital evidence

Figure 8.6. Developing digital forensics resources

Figure 8.7. Forensic models

Figure 9.1. A handwriting comparison. The questioned document is a bank check

Figure 9.2. A signature comparison

Figure 9.3. A typewriter comparison. The arrows point to unusual features of certain letters made by the typewriter in question. The features show up in both the known and questioned type writings

Figure 9.4. Obliteration. (a) A portion of a patient's medical record with an entry obliterated. (b) The same record photographed with infrared light

Figure 9.5. Erasures. Original documents read “6% interest.” (a) A pencil erasure. (b) A typewriter erasure. (c) A chemical erasure

Figure 9.6. The use of an Electrostatic Detection Apparatus (ESDA). This is a note given to a bank teller during a robbery. ESDA reveals what was written on the piece of paper above the note in the pad of paper on which the note was written

Figure 9.7. Charred writing. Through the use of infrared light, the figures made with the ink fluoresce against the charred background

Figure 9.8. Thin layer chromatography of inks. Lanes one and three are standard black, ballpoint pen inks. Lanes two and four are each different black inks

Figure 9.9. (a) The degradation of methyl violet. Each degradation causes the replacement of a methyl group with a hydrogen atom, resulting in the loss of 14 mass units. (b) An artificial aging study of methyl violet dye in a blue, ballpoint pen, by tracking with laser desorption mass spectrometry

LIST OF TABLE

Table 5.1. Differentiating features and points between ethnic groups
Table 5.2. Differentiating features between male and female for sex determination
Table 5.3. Age Determination in male and female
Table 5.4. Stature estimation using gleser formula
Table 5.5. Steps involved in bitemark recording
Table 7.1. Models for the delivery of mental health care to mentally disordered offenders
Table 7.2. Functions of NSSI (mean ISAS values) in forensic psychiatric patients
Table 7.3. Psychosocial and clinical risk factors of self-harm (NSSI & suicide attempts)

PREFACE

Forensic science is a multidisciplinary field dedicated to the meticulous examination and interpretation of evidence collected from crime scenes, employing a diverse array of scientific methodologies. It encompasses specialized sub-disciplines within criminal investigation, each playing a crucial role in synthesizing evidence to construct a coherent narrative. Particularly in forensic medicine, the importance of forensic science is underscored, especially in postmortem examinations aimed at elucidating the cause and manner of death in deceased individuals. Central to this endeavor are autopsies, which serve to meticulously investigate the physiological and pathological characteristics of the deceased.

Forensic pathologists, in collaboration with forensic scientists, conduct comprehensive examinations utilizing advanced equipment such as microscopes, cutting-edge imaging technologies, and digital histopathological techniques. Their extensive medical expertise enables them to perform detailed analyzes, revealing critical insights into the circumstances surrounding the individual's death. This interdisciplinary collaboration ensures a holistic understanding of the deceased's condition, highlighting significant observations pertinent to the factors contributing to their demise.

This book, *Forensic Science and the Law*, is a comprehensive exploration of the intersection between forensic science and the legal system, spanning 10 detailed chapters. Beginning with an Introduction to Forensic Science and the Legal System in Chapter 1 outlines the foundational principles and methodologies of forensic science in the context of criminal and civil investigations. Chapter 2 covers Crime Scene Investigation, elucidating the meticulous procedures and techniques employed to secure, document, and analyze evidence crucial to solving crimes.

Forensic Biology and DNA Analysis, covered in Chapter 3, explores the pivotal role of genetics and molecular biology in identifying individuals and linking suspects to crime scenes through DNA profiling. Chapter 4, Forensic Chemistry and Toxicology, examines the analysis of chemical substances and toxins in forensic investigations, addressing their implications in criminal cases and public health.

In Chapter 5, Forensic Anthropology and Odontology delve into the study of human remains and dental evidence, offering insights into identifying individuals, determining age, and uncovering clues vital for investigations. Forensic Pathology, as discussed in Chapter 6, provides a detailed examination of the processes involved in determining the cause and manner of death, crucial for legal proceedings.

Chapter 7, Forensic Psychology and Psychiatry, explores the intersection of mental health assessments and criminal behavior analysis, shedding light on the psychological factors influencing legal cases. Digital Forensics, detailed in Chapter 8, examines the retrieval and analysis of digital evidence from computers and electronic devices, essential in modern criminal investigations.

Forensic Document Examination, covered in Chapter 9, explores the analysis of handwriting, signatures, and documents to establish authenticity and detect forgery in legal contexts. Finally, Chapter 10, The Interface of Forensic Science and the Law, examines the ethical, legal, and societal implications of forensic science applications, emphasizing the role of forensic experts in courtroom proceedings and the evolving landscape of forensic science regulations.

This book provides a comprehensive overview of forensic science's diverse disciplines and their integration into legal contexts, making it an essential resource for students, professionals, and anyone interested in understanding the intricate relationship between science and the law.

–Author

CHAPTER 1

INTRODUCTION TO FORENSIC SCIENCE AND THE LEGAL SYSTEM

Contents

Introduction.. 2
1.1. Overview of Forensic Science.. 2
1.2. History of Forensic Science.. 6
1.3. Various Fields of Forensic Science.. 14
1.4. Legal System.. 34
References.. 42

INTRODUCTION

Forensic science is the application of scientific principles and techniques to solve crimes and aid the legal system. This multidisciplinary field encompasses various branches of science, including biology, chemistry, physics, and computer science, to analyze physical evidence collected from crime scenes. The goal is to uncover facts that can support investigations and provide concrete, scientific-based findings that can be presented in court. Forensic scientists play a crucial role in criminal investigations by examining evidence such as DNA, fingerprints, bloodstains, ballistic reports, and digital data. Their work often involves meticulous laboratory analysis, data interpretation, and sometimes providing expert testimony to explain the significance of their findings to a jury.

The legal system is a structured framework that establishes and enforces laws to maintain order, resolve disputes, and protect citizens' rights. It comprises various components, including law enforcement agencies, courts, and correctional institutions, each playing a vital role in upholding justice. The legal system operates under established laws and regulations, which are interpreted and applied by judges and legal professionals. The courts, including civil and criminal courts, serve as arenas where legal disputes are adjudicated, and justice is administered. Prosecutors represent the state or government in bringing charges against individuals or entities, while defense attorneys advocate for the accused. The legal system's primary aim is to ensure fairness and equality, providing a mechanism for addressing grievances and delivering justice in a systematic, transparent manner.

The intersection of forensic science and the legal system is where science meets law. Forensic evidence can significantly influence the outcome of legal proceedings by providing objective data that can corroborate or refute testimonies and other forms of evidence. This collaboration ensures that the criminal justice system can make informed decisions based on scientific analysis, enhancing the accuracy and reliability of verdicts. Forensic scientists must adhere to strict protocols and ethical guidelines to maintain the integrity of the evidence, and their findings must be communicated effectively to be understood by legal professionals and jurors. This synergy between science and law underscores the importance of forensic science in modern legal systems, contributing to the pursuit of truth and the administration of justice.

1.1. OVERVIEW OF FORENSIC SCIENCE

The use of a wide range of sciences to address issues of interest to the legal system is known as forensic science, or simply forensics. This could have to do with a criminal case or a civil lawsuit. Beyond its applicability to a legal system, forensics more broadly refers to the recognized scholarly or scientific methodology and standards that determine the truth about an event, an artifact, or another physical object (like a corpse). In this way, the idea is similar to the idea of authentication, in which there is a non-legal interest in establishing whether an item is what it claims to be or is said to be. The Latin adjective forensis, which means "of or before the forum," is where the word "forensic" originates.

The link between legal and medical scientists is being created by forensic science. The fields of science that make up these subjects give scientists and legal experts a common ground. According to Peter White, the term "forensic science" has two distinct meanings: a narrower meaning and a wider meaning. This broad interpretation includes civil cases involving negligence and agreement violations as well as criminal prosecutions in the broadest sense, as well as safeguards for customers, the environment, and physical conditions and protection at work. However, in common usage, the term refers more specifically to the application of science by the police and courts as evidence in order to resolve disputes in criminal investigations and subsequent trials.

Midwest Forensics Resource Center at the U.S. Dept. of Energy has defined Forensic Science as:

"Forensic science is the application of natural sciences to the procedures of law. In practice the subject of forensic science draws its Principles and Methods from the subjects like physics, chemistry, biology and other science subjects."

California Criminalistics Institute has defined forensic science as:

"Forensic Science is the application of the methods and techniques of the basic sciences to legal issues. Forensic Science is a very broad field of study. It includes Crime Laboratory Scientists, sometimes called Forensic Scientists or, more properly, Criminalists, work with physical evidence collected at scenes of crimes."

The application of natural sciences to legal matters is known as forensic science. Physics, chemistry, biology, and other scientific dare all connected to forensic science. In order toTo administer criminal justice, it entails recognizing, identifying,ividualizing, and evaluating physical evidence. It'sIt is one of the most dynamic, captivating, modern, and thrilling fields of study that helps identify crimes and offenders.

1.1.1. Nature of Forensic Science

Since forensic science applies principles from practically every scientific field to legal issues, it is not a singular field of study. At first, every technique used in forensic science was taken from other scientific fields; however, over time, forensic science has grown and developed into its own field. Additionally, it has given rise to a number of branches that are essentially forensic science subfields. In essence, only forensic science is responsible for the fields of finger printing, anthropometry, track marks, documents (particularly those involving the analysis of handwriting), and forensic ballistics. The advancements in digital photography, voice analysis, odor analysis, serology, and pattern recognition research gave this field of study a boost. The most important development of the 20th century has been the identification of human beings through DNA profiling. The advancement in the aforementioned field has led to the application of technology to both plants and animals.

The two main pillars of forensic science are that:

i. It is multi-professional; and

ii. It is multi-disciplinary

Forensic scientists rely on the investigating officer on the one hand, and present counsel and the judge on the other, in order to properly administer justice when using forensic science. The investigator must possess specialized knowledge in gathering evidence. In a similar vein, both the judge and the attorney need to have a general understanding of science in order to relate the scientific evidence to the other pieces of evidence. One notable feature of this science is its comprehensive approach, which necessitates the establishment of extensive Forensic Science Laboratories with experts from all disciplines, equipment suitable for all branches, extensive libraries, and other essential amenities.

1.1.2. Scope of Forensic Science

Because forensic science is such a broad and varied field, it is currently a vital component of the criminal justice system. India's current state of crime investigation and criminal prosecution is pretty bleak. A great deal of trials in India result in acquittals. For it, we have both official and unofficial statistics. The official figure is approximately 90%, while the unofficial figure is significantly higher. In India, criminal investigations and the prosecution of those responsible for the crime are inadequate. Even in shocking crimes, a sizable number of offenders could not be brought to justice, and a small percentage of trials result in an acquittal; as a result, both the number of offenders and the severity of crimes are steadily rising. The primary cause of these frequent acquittals is the use of antiquated investigative techniques that leave room for several ambiguities. Therefore, scientific methods of investigation are crucial for actual research. The following reasons have made the use of science in criminal justice dissemination necessary:

1. **Societal Vagaries:** The changes taking place in society are profound and happening quickly. India has seen significant transformation, going from an imperial colony to a democratic republic. Every aspect of life has been impacted by the modern revolution, including communication and transportation. However, this revolution has not only had a positive impact but has also had a negative one. For example, satellite communication, which on the one hand aids intelligence agencies, has also proven to be beneficial to criminal organizations. It is easy for a terrorist organization with American roots to train disciples or followers in India.
2. **Obscurity:** The criminal was able to evade being arrested and punished right away after committing a crime thanks to changes in transportation and the shift in society from rural to urban areas. With the aid of cutting-edge technology, the criminal can quickly conceal himself in any part of the city or travel thousands of miles from the actual location where the crime was committed. Today's society is indifferent to the facts of what is occurring in his neighborhood. Aristotle once thought of man as a social animal, but today's man is self centered. He doesn't even know the person who lives next door, especially in cities. Therefore, in the even hat a neighbor is murdered, the killers come to light only after the bodiyes decomposes and releases an offensive stench.
3. **Technical Know How:** The common man's technical knowledge has grown, which has also refined criminal tactics. To counter these sophisticated tactics, modernized and refined methods of combating the crime in question must also be developed.
4. **Extensive Arena:** The criminal law's operational domain is expanding incredibly quickly. In the past, criminal activity was primarily local and involved the use of antiquated techniques, but these days, it is not uncommon to encounter both national and international criminal activity. The fields of financial fraud, drug trafficking, and forgeries are all very broad and rapidly developing.
5. **Better Evidence:** Experts typically evaluate physical evidence in an impartial manner; for example, if a fingerprint is discovered at the scene of a crime, it is assumed to belong to a single person. Should that individual turn out to be the suspect, he needs to explain his presence at the scene. In a similar vein, a bullet recovered from a deceased person can only be linked to one gun. Should this firearm turn out to belong to the accused, he bears responsibility for its role in the offense. Such proof can never be refuted.

1.2. HISTORY OF FORENSIC SCIENCE

History is not an isolated list of dates, but the story of events and people. Advances in any area of study come from previous ideas and discoveries, and sometimes from other areas that seem to be unrelated. And so it is with forensic science. For example, the development of spectroscopy by Kirchhoff and Bunsen in a German lab almost 150 years ago created a way to identify different drugs. Here are other highlights in the history of forensic science:

About 500 CD	A bead and wire abacus is the first computer.
About 200 CD	According to legend, Archimedes determines density of a suspected gold crown using its weight and how much water it displaces.
BE 66	Emperor Nero murders his wife and presents her head on a dish to his mistress, who identifies the head as Nero's wife by two discolored front teeth.
142	Gunpowder is first described in China.
904	The Chinese first use gunpowder in warfare as incendiary projectiles called "flying fires ."
1132	Gunpowder is used in thick bamboo to fire clay pellets; bamboo later replaced by bronze, and clay replaced with iron balls.
1149	King Richard I of England created the job of coroner to investigate questionable deaths.
1216	The first written mention of the composition of gunpowder in Europe by Roger Bacon.
1248	The Chinese book Hsi Duan Yu describes how to distinguish a drowning victim from one who has been strangled. Also mentioned is a stabbing solved by observing flies attracted to blood on the killer's sickle.
1300	Portable, handheld "cannons," or gonnes, are developed.
1514	The earliest known use of blood spatter evidence is a trial in London in which the defendant, Richard Hunne, had been jailed for heresy and was then convicted of suicide, post mortem.
1540	Rifling appears in firearms.
1598	Fortunatus Fidelus is the first to practice forensic medicine in Italy.
1609	Francois Demelle published the first treatise on systematic document examination.

1628	Birth of Italian Marcello Malpighi, credited with noticing patterns in the skin of fingers.
1642	Blaise Pascal, at age 18, builds the first numerical calculating machine.
1668	Analysis of blowfly infestation of rotting meat allows Francesco Redi to refute the hypothesis of "spontaneous generation" of maggots.
1670	The first high-powered microscope is constructed by Anton Van Leeuwenhoek of Holland.
1732	Luigi Galvani discovers that the human nervous system transmits information electrically; this is the basis of current "lie detection" equipment.
1735	Carl Linnaeus, also known as Carl von Linné, publishes the first edition of Systema Naturae in the Netherlands. He is often called the "Father of Taxonomy" for his introduction of a system of hierarchical classification.
1776	The body of General Joseph Warren, killed at the Battle of Bunker Hill, June 17, 1775, is disinterred from a mass grave and identified by Paul Revere, who had made his false teeth.
1784	The first documented case of physical matching occurs when an Englishman is convicted of murder because the torn edge of a wad of newspaper in a pistol matches a piece remaining in his pocket.
1810	First recorded use of questioned document analysis involving a chemical test for a particular ink dye.
1810	The first detective force, the Sûreté, is established in Paris.
1813	Mathiew Orfila, considered the father of modern toxicology, publishes his book on the subject. Poisoning was a popular way of dispatching people.
1816	A farm laborer is convicted of murder based upon impression evidence.
1832	Charles Babbage invents his "Analytical Engine," the forerunner of modern computers.
1835	Scotland Yard, London's detective force, is the first to use bullet comparison to catch a murderer.
1836	James Marsh discovers a very sensitive chemical test to detect arsenic compounds.
1836	The first multishot pistol is developed by Samuel Colt. By the time of his death in 1862, he had made and sold almost a million guns.

1840	Forensic toxicology is first used to convict Marie Lafarge, by using the Marsh test, of poisoning her husband with arsenic.
1841	Edgar Allan Poe's short story, The Murders in the Rue Morgue, is the first detective story using forensic science, influencing future authors including Arthur Conan Doyle.
1847	The earliest examination of hairs in a criminal investigation in the murder of the Duchesse de Praslin.
1850	For the first time, a murderer is convicted in the United States based on dental evidence.
1852	Earliest reported case involving fiber analysis where the fibers of the victim's clothes matched those on the murder weapon.
1853	Soil on suspect's boots matches that at the crime scene
1855	First use of forensic entomology to estimate postmortem interval (PMI) by a French doctor, Bergeret d'Arbois.
1856	William Herschel, working in India, uses thumbprints on documents to identify workers.
1859	Gustav Kirchhoff and Robert Bunsen develop the science of spectros-copy.
1863	The first presumptive test for blood is developed, using the fact that hemoglobin oxidizes hydrogen peroxide.
1863	One of the earliest recorded cases involving simple fi rearms identi-fication occurs during the United States Civil War, when Confeder-ate General Stonewall Jackson is fatally wounded on the battlefield. Examination of the caliber and bullet shape determines that the bullet could only have been fi red by one of his own men: The Confeder-ates used a 67-caliber ball projectile, whereas the Union forces used a 58-caliber minie ball.
1879	Frenchman Alphonse Bertillon develops a system to identify people using body measurements.
1880	Scotsman Henry Fauld, working in Tokyo, uses fingerprints to exoner-ate an innocent burglary suspect.
1886	Paul Vieille invents a smokeless gunpowder called Poudre B which revolutionizes the effectiveness of small guns and leads to more reci-pes.

<table>
<tr><td>1887</td><td>Arthur Conan Doyle publishes his first Sherlock Holmes story, A Study in Scarlet.</td></tr>
<tr><td>1888</td><td>American George Eastman invents the first handheld camera. He calls it the “Kodak” camera and retails it for $25.</td></tr>
<tr><td>1888</td><td>Chicago is the first U.S. city to adopt the Bertillon system of identification.</td></tr>
<tr><td>1889</td><td>Alexandre Lacassagne publishes a text on matching bullets to individual gun barrels.</td></tr>
<tr><td>1892</td><td>Francis Galton, a nephew of Charles Darwin, publishes his book on fingerprints and their use in solving crimes.</td></tr>
<tr><td>1892</td><td>Argentina becomes the first country to replace the Bertillon system of measurements with fingerprints when Juan Vucetich solves a particularly gruesome murder using bloody fingerprints.</td></tr>
<tr><td>1894</td><td>Alfred Dreyfus is convicted of treason in France based, in part, on mistaken handwriting identification by Bertillon.</td></tr>
<tr><td>1894</td><td>Doctor Jean Pierre Mégnin presents his theory of successional insect waves inhabiting a corpse.</td></tr>
<tr><td>1895</td><td>Two Canadian researchers start a number of systematic entomological studies on human corpses.</td></tr>
<tr><td>1896</td><td>Edward Henry develops the prototype fingerprint classification system now used in Europe and the United States.</td></tr>
<tr><td>1898</td><td>Photomicrographs of two bullets allow individualization of the minutiae.</td></tr>
<tr><td>1900</td><td>Scotland Yard adopts the Galton–Henry system of fingerprint identification.</td></tr>
<tr><td>1900</td><td>Austrian Karl Landsteiner identifies human blood groups. In 1930 he receives a Nobel Prize for this work.
<table>
<tr><th>Blood Type</th><th>Antigens</th><th>Antibodies</th></tr>
<tr><td>A</td><td>A</td><td>B</td></tr>
<tr><td>B</td><td>B</td><td>A</td></tr>
<tr><td>AB</td><td>A & B</td><td>None</td></tr>
<tr><td>0</td><td>None</td><td>A & B</td></tr>
</table></td></tr>
<tr><td>1901</td><td>Paul Uhlenhuth develops the precipitin test, which distinguishes between human and animal blood. The test is used in the murder conviction of Ludwig Tessnow in the same year.</td></tr>
</table>

1902	Harry Jackson, a burglar, becomes the first Englishman to be convicted solely on the basis of fingerprints.
1903	Two convicts with the same name and same anthropometry (Bertillon) measurements are found in Fort Leavenworth prison. Two years later, their fingerprints are found to clearly distinguish between them.
1903	The New York City Police Department has started to create fingerprint fi les of arrested persons. This system is adopted by the New York State prison system two years later.
1903	Russian botanist Mikhail Tswett invents chromatography.
1904	Edmond Locard formulates his famous principle, "Every contact leaves a trace."
1904	Presumptive test for blood is developed based on benzidine, a new chemical developed by Merck.
1905	President Theodore Roosevelt establishes the FBI.
1906	Bite mark evidence is fi rst used in an English court to convict two hungry burglars using teeth marks found in cheese at the scene.
1907	The first recorded instance of fi red cartridge casings being evaluated as evidence in an investigation of a brawl involving U.S. soldiers at Brownsville, Texas.
1910	The first police crime laboratory is started in Lyon, France, by Edmond Locard.
1910	Victor Balthazard publishes the first comprehensive study of human and animal hair. He also uses photographic enlargements of bullets and cartridge cases in an attempt to connect an individual bullet to a particular weapon.
1910	American Albert Osborne publishes the seminal treatise Questioned Documents.
1915	Italian Leone Lattes develops a method for determining the blood group of dried bloodstains.
1920s	Luke May, one of the first American criminalists, pioneers' striation analysis in tool mark comparisons.
1920s	Russian paleontologist Mikhail Gerasimov develops a method to re-construct facial appearance from a skull. He is later popularized as the character Andreev in the detective novel Gorky Park.

1920s	German investigator Georg Popp uses botanical and soil identification in solving a crime.
1921	The first lie detector is built by John Larson, a University of California medical student.
1922	A Nobel Prize is awarded to Englishman Francis Aston for developing the mass spectrometer.
1923	The Los Angeles Police Department establishes the first police laboratory in the United States.
1923	In the court case Frye v. United States, polygraph test results are ruled inadmissible, bringing about the concept of "general acceptance," or evidence accepted by the scientific community.
1925	The comparison microscope for use in bullet comparison is perfected, and its use is widely publicized in the Sacco and Vanzetti trial of 1926.
1929	The infamous St. Valentine's Day Massacre occurs when seven gangsters are gunned down. Examination of all firearms-related evidence dispels the rumors that police were involved.
1932	The FBI crime laboratory is created.
1935	In Scotland, blowfly larvae provide a vital clue in the murders of Dr. Ruxton's wife and maid.
1937	Walter Specht finds that the chemical luminol glows in contact with latent blood.
1940	Landsteiner and Wiener describe Rh blood groups.
1940	The Complex Number Calculator, the first digital computer, is demonstrated at Bell Labs.
1941	Voiceprint identification is first studied at Bell Labs in New Jersey.
1946	The Electronic Numerical Integrator and Computer, ENIAC, is dedicated. It contains 18,000 vacuum tubes in cabinets 8'×100,' weighing 80 tons. It can do 5,000 additions and 360 multiplications per second.
1948	The American Academy of Forensic Sciences (AAFS) meets for the first time in Chicago and soon publishes the Journal of Forensic Science.
1948	Keith Simpson launches the science of bite mark analysis (forensic odontology) when he examines bite marks on a dead woman.

1952	British researchers Martin and Synge receive the Nobel Prize for their invention of gas-liquid partition chromatography, a powerful method of analyzing mixtures of drugs and poisons.
1954	R. F. Borkenstein, a captain in the Indiana State Police, invents the Breathalyzer for field sobriety testing.
1955	De Saram publishes careful and detailed measurements of body temperature decrease in executed prisoners to determine time since death.
1955	The murder trial of Dr. Sam Sheppard publicizes blood spatter evidence, and inspires several movies, television programs, and books.
1957	The growth stages of skeletal bones are identified by Americans Thomas Mocker and Thomas Stewart, forming the basis of forensic anthropology.
1959	James Watson and Francis Crick discover the DNA double helix.
1960s	Maurice Muller adapts the Ouchterlony antibody antigen diffusion test for precipitin testing to determine species.
1960	Gas chromatography is used for the forensic identification of petroleum products.
1961	Hungary becomes the first country in Europe to carry out research on the subject of lip prints.
1967	The FBI inaugurates the National Crime Information Center (NCIC), the first national law enforcement computing center with information on wanted persons and stolen vehicles, weapons, and other items of value.
1969	The Association of Firearm and Tool Mark Examiners (AFTE) is formed.
1972	Body armor made of Kevlar is introduced. It is currently credited with saving the lives of more than 2,000 police officers since inception.
1972	Dr. William M. Bass starts the Forensic Anthropology Center, otherwise known as "The Body Farm," at the University of Tennessee.
1973	Canada's Royal Canadian Mounted Police (RCMP) finish computerizing their fingerprint files.
1975	The Federal Rules of Evidence are enacted.
1976	Gas chromatography–mass spectrometry (GC-MS) is first evaluated for forensic purposes.

1977	The Fourier transform infrared spectrophotometer (FTIR) is adapted for use in the forensic laboratory.
1977	In Japan, investigators accidentally discover that superglue reveals latent fingerprints.
1977	The Internet is born.
1977	A limited computerized scanning mechanism is first used to develop a database in forensic science by the FBI's Automated Fingerprint Identification System (AFIS).
1978	Britain's Yorkshire Ripper case highlights the value of computers in investigating serial killings and leads to the development of "psychological profiling" techniques in the following decade.
1979	Bite mark evidence is a key in convicting serial killer Theodore "Ted" Bundy.
1981	IBM introduces its personal computer (PC) for use in the home, office, and schools.
1982	The term serial killer is first used to describe a killer who kills repeatedly and obsessively, on separate occasions.
1984	Professor Alec Jeffreys discovers that each human being has unique DNA, except in the case of identical twins.
1986	The polymerase chain reaction (PCR) DNA replication technique is developed specifically for forensic use by Cetus Corporation.
1987	DNA profiling is used to identify Colin Pitchfork as the murderer of two girls in England and to exonerate someone previously suspected of the murder. Three months later, the same techniques are applied to convict Tommy Lee Andrews for a series of sexual assaults in Florida.
1989	In the United States, Gary Dotson becomes the first person to have a conviction overturned on the basis of DNA evidence. Dotson had served eight years of a 25- to 50-year sentence for rape.
1990	Author Patricia Cornwell's first novel, Postmortem, is published. It features good forensic science, as do more than ten of her subsequent books.
1990	The first prosecution under the federal computer crime statute is for a release of a "worm" into the Internet by a graduate student.

1991	A computerized, automated imaging system is introduced for comparing marks of bullets and shell casings. It is called the Integrated Ballistics Identification System, or IBIS. The following year, a similar system, called DRUGFIRE, is introduced in the FBI.
1992	DNA short tandem repeats (STR) are used in forensic DNA analysis.
1993	In the court case of Daubert v. Merrell Dow, the court changes the standard of admission of scientific evidence.
1995	eBay is founded by a French-born Iranian computer programmer.
1996	Computerized searches of the AFIS fingerprint database are implemented by the FBI, using both live scan and card scan devices.
1996	Mitochondrial DNA typing is admitted in a U.S. court for the first time.
1998	An FBI index of DNA profiles called NDIS (National DNA Index System) is incorporated with CODIS (Combined DNA Index System).
1999	AFIS is further refined to form IAFIS, Integrated Automated Fingerprint Identification System.
1999	IBIS and DRUGFIRE are combined to form the National Integrated Ballistics Identification Network (NIBIN).
2001	The USA PATRIOT Act of 2001 allows for the search and seizure of computers.
2002	CODIS enables the first match between NDIS and a DNA profile from Florida, resulting in an arrest and conviction.
2007	The largest AFIS repository in America is operated by the Department of Homeland Security's U.S. Visit Program, containing over 63 million persons' fingerprints, primarily in the form of two-finger records.
2007	There are now approximately 400 crime labs and nearly 40,000 people involved in forensic science in the United States.

1.3. VARIOUS FIELDS OF FORENSIC SCIENCE

Various fields of forensic science that help in criminal investigation including Forensic Entomology, Forensic Toxicology, Ballistics, Forensic Chemistry, Forensic odontology, Forensic Anthropology, DNA Profiling, Fingerprinting, Forensic Engineering, Forensic Psychiatry, Document Examination.

1.3.1. Forensic Entomology

Forensic entomology, the study of insects in a legal context, is a fascinating and crucial sub-discipline of forensic science. It involves the use of insect biology to gather information for criminal investigations, particularly in cases of suspicious death. This field provides valuable insights into the post-mortem interval (PMI), the time elapsed since death and can also offer clues about the circumstances of death and potential relocation of remains.

The history of forensic entomology can be traced back to the 13th century when Chinese lawyer and death investigator Song Ci documented its use in his book "Collected Cases of Injustice Rectified." Song Ci described a case where flies were used to identify a murder weapon, demonstrating an early understanding of the relationship between insects and decomposition. However, it wasn't until the 19th century that forensic entomology began to gain recognition as a scientific discipline. French entomologist Jean Pierre Mégnin made significant contributions by studying the patterns of insect succession on decomposing bodies, laying the groundwork for modern forensic entomology.

In contemporary forensic investigations, forensic entomologists primarily focus on two groups of insects: flies (*Diptera*) and beetles (*Coleoptera*). These insects are among the first to colonize a decomposing body, with flies often arriving within minutes of death. The life cycles of these insects, particularly blowflies (*Calliphoridae*), are well-documented and predictable, making them valuable indicators for estimating PMI. For example, blowfly eggs hatch into larvae within a day, and the larvae pass through several stages (instars) before pupating and emerging as adult flies. By examining the developmental stages of the insects found on a body, forensic entomologists can estimate the time of death with remarkable accuracy.

The process of determining PMI using insects involves several steps. First, forensic entomologists collect samples of insects from the body and the surrounding environment. These samples are then identified to species level, as different species have distinct developmental timelines. The ambient temperature and environmental conditions are also recorded, as these factors influence insect development. Using this information, forensic entomologists can create a timeline of insect colonization and development, which is then used to estimate PMI.

Forensic entomology is not limited to estimating PMI. Insects can provide a wealth of additional information about a crime scene. For instance, the presence of insects that are not native to the area where the body was found can suggest that the body was moved after death. Additionally, the presence of drugs or toxins in a body can affect insect development, and forensic entomologists can analyze insect tissues to detect these substances. This can provide crucial information about the cause of death or the presence of foul play.

In some cases, forensic entomology can also help determine the circumstances of death. For example, if a body is found indoors but contains insects typically found outdoors, it may indicate that the body was initially decomposing outside before being moved. Conversely, if a body is discovered outdoors with no signs of insect activity, it may suggest that the body was kept in a sealed environment for some time before being exposed to the elements.

One notable case that highlights the importance of forensic entomology is the investigation of the death of Caylee Anthony in 2008. In this case, forensic entomologists were able to provide critical evidence by analyzing the insect activity on Caylee's remains. The presence of certain fly species indicated that the body had been decomposing for several days before being discovered, which contradicted the timeline provided by the defendant. This evidence played a key role in the prosecution's case.

Despite its value, forensic entomology faces several challenges. One major challenge is the variability in insect development rates due to environmental factors. Temperature, humidity, and other conditions can significantly influence the life cycles of insects, making it essential for forensic entomologists to have accurate environmental data. Additionally, the presence of multiple species on a body can complicate the estimation of PMI, as different species may have overlapping developmental stages. To address these challenges, forensic entomologists often rely on controlled experiments and extensive field data to refine their estimates.

Another challenge in forensic entomology is the potential for contamination or misinterpretation of evidence. For instance, insects may be introduced to the body after it has been discovered, either by investigators or through natural means. This can lead to inaccurate conclusions if not properly accounted for. To mitigate this risk, forensic entomologists follow strict protocols for collecting and preserving insect samples, ensuring that the evidence remains uncontaminated and reliable.

The future of forensic entomology holds promising advancements. With the advent of molecular techniques, forensic entomologists can now use DNA analysis to identify insect species with greater accuracy. This is particularly useful in cases where traditional morphological identification is challenging, such as when dealing with immature stages or damaged specimens. Additionally, advancements in genomics and transcriptomics are providing insights into the genetic basis of insect development and behavior, which can further enhance the accuracy of PMI estimates.

Furthermore, the integration of forensic entomology with other forensic disciplines, such as forensic anthropology and pathology, is becoming increasingly common. This interdisciplinary approach allows for a more comprehensive analysis of a crime scene, combining multiple lines of evidence to reconstruct the events surrounding a death. For example, forensic anthropologists can provide information about skeletal remains, while forensic pathologists can offer insights into soft tissue injuries. By working together, these experts can create a more complete picture of the circumstances of death.

Education and training are also essential for the advancement of forensic entomology. As the field continues to grow, there is a need for more specialized training programs and courses. Universities and institutions are increasingly offering forensic entomology courses as part of their forensic science curricula, providing students with the knowledge and skills needed to pursue careers in this field. Additionally, professional organizations, such as the American Board of Forensic Entomology, offer certification programs to ensure that practitioners meet high standards of expertise and professionalism.

Public awareness and understanding of forensic entomology are also crucial. The portrayal of forensic entomology in popular media, such as crime television shows and documentaries, has helped to raise awareness about the field. However, it is important for the public to recognize the limitations and complexities of forensic entomology, as well as the rigorous scientific methods employed by forensic entomologists. Misconceptions or oversimplifications can lead to unrealistic expectations or misunderstandings about the role of insects in criminal investigations.

Ethical considerations are also an important aspect of forensic entomology. Forensic entomologists must adhere to strict ethical guidelines when collecting and analyzing insect evidence. This includes obtaining proper consent when working with human remains, respecting the dignity of the deceased, and ensuring the accuracy and reliability of their findings. Additionally, forensic entomologists must be aware of the potential impact of their work on legal proceedings and strive to maintain objectivity and impartiality in their analyzes.

1.3.2. Forensic Toxicology

Forensic toxicology, a specialized branch forensic science that, is dedicated to the study and analysis of biological samples to detect and quantify drugs, alcohol, poisons, and other toxic substances. This field plays a critical role in criminal investigations, legal proceedings, and public health by determining the presence and impact of these substances on human physiology and behavior. Forensic toxicologists use their expertise to interpret toxicological data and provide crucial insights into cases involving drug overdoses, poisonings, impaired driving, and suspicious deaths. The history of forensic toxicology dates back to ancient civilizations, where poisons were often used for political assassinations and criminal activities. However, it was not until the early 19th century that forensic toxicology emerged as a formal scientific discipline. One of the pioneers of this field was Mathieu Orfila, a Spanish chemist and toxicologist who published the first comprehensive treatise on poisons and their effects on the human body. Orfila's work laid the foundation for modern forensic toxicology by establishing systematic methods for detecting and analyzing toxic substances.

In contemporary practice, forensic toxicology encompasses several sub-disciplines, including post-mortem toxicology, human performance toxicology, and forensic drug testing. Post-mortem toxicology involves the analysis of biological samples from deceased individuals to determine whether toxic substances contributed to or caused their death. This sub-discipline is crucial in cases of unexplained or suspicious deaths, where toxicological findings can provide critical evidence to support or refute potential causes of death.

Human performance toxicology focuses on the effects of drugs and alcohol on human behavior and performance. This sub-discipline is particularly relevant in cases of impaired driving, workplace accidents, and sports doping. Forensic toxicologists in this field analyze blood, urine, and other bodily fluids to detect the presence of impairing substances and assess their impact on an individual's ability to perform tasks safely and effectively.

Forensic drug testing, another important sub-discipline, involves the analysis of biological samples to detect the presence of illicit drugs, prescription medications, and other controlled substances. This type of testing is commonly used in legal and regulatory contexts, such as probation and parole monitoring, employment screening, and compliance with drug-free workplace policies. Forensic toxicologists use sophisticated analytical techniques, such as gas chromatography-mass spectrometry (GC-MS) and liquid chromatography-tandem mass spectrometry (LC-MS/MS), to identify and quantify trace amounts of drugs in biological samples.

The process of forensic toxicological analysis involves several key steps, starting with the collection of biological samples. Commonly analyzed samples include blood, urine, saliva, hair, and tissues from organs such as the liver and kidneys. The choice of sample depends on the specific case and the substances being investigated. For example, blood and urine are commonly used for detecting recent drug use, while hair analysis can provide a longer-term history of substance exposure. Once the samples are collected, forensic toxicologists employ a variety of analytical techniques to identify and quantify toxic substances. Initial screening tests, such as immunoassays, are used to detect the presence of a broad range of drugs and their metabolites. These tests are highly sensitive and can quickly identify potential substances of interest. Positive results from screening tests are then confirmed using more specific and accurate techniques, such as GC-MS and LC-MS/MS. These methods provide definitive identification and quantification of the substances, allowing toxicologists to produce reliable and legally defensible results.

Interpretation of toxicological findings is a complex and critical aspect of forensic toxicology. Toxicologists must consider various factors, including the concentration of the substance, the individual's metabolism, the time elapsed since exposure, and the potential interactions with other substances. For example, the presence of a high concentration of a drug in the blood may indicate recent use or overdose, while lower concentrations in the urine may suggest past use. Additionally, toxicologists must be aware of the potential for false positives and negatives, as well as the limitations of the analytical methods used.

One notable case that highlights the importance of forensic toxicology is the death of musician Michael Jackson in 2009. Jackson's death was attributed to acute propofol intoxication, a powerful anesthetic that was administered by his personal physician. Forensic toxicologists played a crucial role in the investigation by analyzing blood and tissue samples to determine the concentration of propofol and other substances in Jackson's system. Their findings provided key evidence that led to the conviction of the physician for involuntary manslaughter.

Forensic toxicology also plays a vital role in public health and safety. For instance, toxicologists are often involved in investigating mass poisoning, chemical spills, and environmental contamination. Their expertise is essential in identifying the toxic agents involved, assessing the extent of exposure, and determining the potential health risks to affected populations. In such cases, toxicologists work closely with other experts, such as epidemiologists and environmental scientists, to develop strategies for mitigating the impact of toxic substances and preventing future incidents.

Despite its significance, forensic toxicology faces several challenges. One major challenge is the continuous emergence of new psychoactive substances (NPS), also known as designer drugs. These substances are often synthesized to mimic the effects of traditional drugs while evading legal regulations. The rapid proliferation of NPS poses significant difficulties for forensic toxicologists, as they must constantly update their analytical methods and reference databases to detect and identify these novel compounds accurately. Another challenge is the potential for contamination and degradation of biological samples. Forensic toxicologists must follow strict protocols for the collection, storage, and analysis of samples to ensure their integrity and reliability. Factors such as improper storage conditions, sample mishandling, and environmental exposure can lead to the degradation of toxic substances, making accurate analysis more challenging. To address these issues, toxicologists employ rigorous quality control measures and advanced preservation techniques to maintain the stability of samples.

Advancements in technology and analytical techniques are continuously shaping the field of forensic toxicology. The development of high-resolution mass spectrometry (HRMS) and advanced chromatography methods has significantly enhanced the sensitivity and specificity of toxicological analyzes. These technologies allow toxicologists to detect and quantify trace amounts of substances with greater accuracy and precision. Additionally, the integration of bioinformatics and data analysis tools has improved the interpretation of complex toxicological data, enabling more comprehensive and informed conclusions.

Education and training are fundamental to the advancement of forensic toxicology. As the field evolves, there is a growing need for specialized training programs and courses to equip future toxicologists with the knowledge and skills required for their profession. Universities and institutions offer forensic toxicology courses as part of their forensic science curricula, covering topics such as pharmacology, analytical chemistry, toxicokinetics, and legal aspects of toxicology. Professional organizations, such as the Society of Forensic Toxicologists (SOFT) and the International Association of Forensic Toxicologists (TIAFT), provide certification programs, continuing education, and networking opportunities for practitioners in the field.

Ethical considerations are paramount in forensic toxicology. Toxicologists must adhere to strict ethical guidelines to ensure the accuracy, reliability, and impartiality of their analyses. This includes maintaining confidentiality, obtaining proper consent when handling biological samples, and avoiding conflicts of interest. Toxicologists must also be aware of the potential impact of their findings on legal proceedings and public perception, striving to present their results objectively and without bias.

1.3.3. Forensic Psychiatry

Forensic psychiatry is a specialized branch of psychiatry that intersects with the legal system, focusing on the assessment, treatment, and understanding of individuals involved in legal matters. This field plays a crucial role in both criminal and civil cases, providing expert evaluations, testimony, and treatment for individuals with mental disorders who are involved in legal proceedings. Forensic psychiatrists combine their knowledge of psychiatry with an understanding of legal principles to assist courts, attorneys, and other stakeholders in making informed decisions about issues such as competency, criminal responsibility, and risk assessment.

The history of forensic psychiatry dates back to the 19th century when the legal system began recognizing the importance of mental health in determining criminal responsibility and competency to stand trial. One of the landmark cases in the development of forensic psychiatry was the trial of Daniel M'Naghten in 1843. M'Naghten, who suffered from paranoid delusions, assassinated the British Prime Minister's secretary, believing that he was acting under divine instruction. His case led to the establishment of the M'Naghten Rule, a legal standard for determining criminal insanity based on the defendant's ability to understand the nature of their actions and distinguish right from wrong. This case highlighted the need for psychiatric expertise in legal proceedings and laid the groundwork for the development of forensic psychiatry as a distinct field.

In criminal cases, forensic psychiatrists are often called upon to evaluate a defendant's mental state at the time of the offense, their competency to stand trial, and their potential risk of reoffending. These evaluations are critical in determining whether a defendant can be held legally responsible for their actions or if they should be diverted to mental health treatment instead of incarceration. For instance, in cases where a defendant is found not guilty by reason of insanity (NGRI), forensic psychiatrists provide expert testimony to support the claim that the defendant was unable to understand the nature or wrongfulness of their actions due to a severe mental disorder.

Competency evaluations are another key aspect of forensic psychiatry. Competency to stand trial refers to a defendant's ability to understand the legal proceedings and assist in their own defense. Forensic psychiatrists assess whether a defendant has the cognitive and emotional capacity to participate meaningfully in their trial. If a defendant is found incompetent, they may be ordered to undergo treatment to restore their competency before the trial can proceed. This process ensures that defendants receive a fair trial and that their mental health needs are addressed.

Forensic psychiatry also plays a significant role in civil cases, particularly those involving issues of guardianship, child custody, and personal injury claims. In guardianship cases, forensic psychiatrists assess an individual's capacity to make decisions about their personal and financial affairs. These evaluations are essential in determining whether a guardian should be appointed to manage the individual's affairs. In child custody cases, forensic psychiatrists evaluate the mental health of parents and children, providing recommendations to the court about the best interests of the child. Personal injury claims often involve assessments of psychological harm resulting from accidents or traumatic events, with forensic psychiatrists providing expert testimony about the impact of such injuries on an individual's mental health and functioning.

Risk assessment is another crucial component of forensic psychiatry. Forensic psychiatrists evaluate the potential for future violence or dangerous behavior in individuals with mental disorders. These assessments are used in various contexts, including parole hearings, civil commitment proceedings, and workplace evaluations. For example, forensic psychiatrists may be asked to assess the risk of reoffending in a convicted offender seeking parole or to evaluate the potential danger posed by an employee with a history of violent behavior. Accurate risk assessments are essential for protecting public safety and ensuring that individuals receive appropriate treatment and supervision. One notable case that highlights the importance of forensic psychiatry is the trial of Andrea Yates in 2001. Yates, a Texas mother, drowned her five children in a bathtub, believing that she was saving them from eternal damnation. Her case drew national attention and sparked a debate about the intersection of mental illness and criminal responsibility. Forensic psychiatrists played a crucial role in her trial, providing expert testimony about her severe postpartum psychosis and its impact on her actions. Yates was initially convicted of murder, but her conviction was later overturned on appeal, and she was found not guilty by reason of insanity in a subsequent trial. This case underscored the complexity of assessing mental illness in legal contexts and the importance of forensic psychiatry in ensuring just outcomes. Despite its significance, forensic psychiatry faces several challenges. One major challenge is the potential for bias and the pressure to align with the interests of the retaining party, whether it be prosecution or defense. Forensic psychiatrists must maintain objectivity and provide unbiased evaluations and testimony, even when faced with adversarial legal contexts. Ensuring impartiality and adhering to ethical standards are essential for maintaining the credibility and integrity of forensic psychiatry.

Another challenge is the stigma associated with mental illness, which can influence legal decisions and public perception. Forensic psychiatrists must navigate societal biases and misconceptions about mental disorders, advocating for the fair treatment of individuals with mental health issues in the legal system. Educating the public, legal professionals, and policymakers about the complexities of mental illness and its impact on behavior is crucial for reducing stigma and promoting justice.

1.3.4. Ballistics Forensic

Forensic ballistics is a crucial branch of forensic science that deals with the analysis of firearms, ammunition, and the impact of projectiles to help solve crimes. This field involves the examination of the behavior and effects of bullets, the identification of firearms used in criminal activities, and the determination of the trajectory and origins of gunshots. Forensic ballistics plays an essential role in criminal investigations, providing critical evidence that can link suspects to crime scenes, reconstruct events, and support legal proceedings.

The history of forensic ballistics dates back to the early 20th century, with significant advancements driven by the need to solve firearm-related crimes. One of the pioneers of this field was Calvin Goddard, an American forensic scientist and physician who is often referred to as the "father of forensic ballistics." Goddard's work in the 1920s and 1930s established the use of the comparison microscope for matching bullets and cartridge cases to specific firearms. His contributions laid the foundation for modern forensic ballistics by demonstrating that firearms leave unique marks on bullets and casings, which can be used to identify the weapon used in a crime.

Forensic ballistics is divided into three main areas: internal ballistics, external ballistics, and terminal ballistics. Internal ballistics focuses on the processes that occur within a firearm when it is fired, including the ignition of the propellant, the pressure generated, and the movement of the bullet through the barrel. External ballistics deals with the behavior of the bullet as it travels through the air, including its trajectory, velocity, and stability. Terminal ballistics examines the interaction of the bullet with the target, including the penetration, expansion, and fragmentation of the projectile upon impact.

A key aspect of forensic ballistics is the examination of firearms and ammunition to determine their characteristics and potential links to criminal activities. Firearm examination involves analyzing the type, model, and condition of a firearm, as well as its functionality and safety features. This examination can reveal important information about the firearm's history and usage. For example, the presence of modifications or alterations can indicate attempts to alter the firearm's performance or conceal its identity.

Ammunition examination involves the analysis of bullets, cartridge cases, and other components to identify their make, model, and characteristics. Forensic ballisticians use a variety of tools and techniques, including microscopy, chemical analysis, and ballistic gelatin testing, to study the physical and chemical properties of ammunition. This analysis can provide valuable information about the type of firearm used, the manufacturer of the ammunition, and the potential source of the ammunition.

One of the most important techniques in forensic ballistics is the comparison of bullets and cartridge cases to determine whether they were fired from the same firearm. This process involves examining the unique markings left on bullets and casings by the barrel, firing pin, and other parts of the firearm. These markings, known as ballistic fingerprints, can be compared using a comparison microscope to determine if they match. A match can link a specific firearm to a crime scene, providing crucial evidence in criminal investigations.

Ballistic fingerprinting relies on the principle that every firearm leaves unique marks on the bullets and casings it fires. These marks are created by the rifling in the barrel, the firing pin, the extractor, and other components of the firearm. By comparing these marks, forensic ballisticians can determine whether a bullet or casing was fired from a particular firearm. This technique was famously used in the St. Valentine's Day Massacre investigation in 1929, where Goddard's analysis helped identify the firearms used in the crime.

Another critical aspect of forensic ballistics is the determination of bullet trajectories. By analyzing the angles, distances, and impact points of bullets, forensic ballisticians can reconstruct the events of a shooting and establish the positions of the shooter and the victim. This information is essential for understanding the circumstances of a crime, such as determining whether a shooting was accidental or intentional, identifying the number of shots fired, and corroborating or refuting witness statements.

Trajectory analysis often involves the use of mathematical calculations, computer simulations, and physical models to map the path of a bullet from the firearm to its final resting place. Forensic ballisticians consider factors such as bullet drop, air resistance, and deflection when reconstructing trajectories. In some cases, laser trajectory analysis is used to visualize the path of a bullet and identify potential points of origin and impact. This technique can be particularly useful in complex crime scenes with multiple gunshots or in cases where bullets have ricocheted or fragmented.

Gunshot reside (GSR) analysis is another important tool in forensic ballistics. When a firearm is discharged, it releases a cloud of microscopic particles containing metals such as lead, barium, and antimony. These particles can settle on the hands, clothing, and surrounding surfaces of the shooter and nearby individuals. Forensic scientists can collect and analyze GSR samples to determine whether someone has recently fired a gun or been in close proximity to a discharged firearm. GSR analysis can provide valuable evidence in cases where the suspect denies firing a weapon or where multiple individuals are present at the scene of a shooting.

Forensic ballistics also involves the examination of bullet wounds and the analysis of the damage caused by projectiles. Forensic pathologists and ballisticians work together to study the characteristics of bullet wounds, including entry and exit wounds, the presence of stippling or tattooing, and the trajectory of the bullet through the body. This analysis can provide critical information about the distance, angle, and caliber of the firearm used, as well as the nature of the injuries sustained by the victim.

One notable case that highlights the importance of forensic ballistics is the assassination of President John F. Kennedy in 1963. The investigation into Kennedy's death relied heavily on ballistic evidence, including the analysis of bullet fragments, the examination of the rifle used by Lee Harvey Oswald, and the reconstruction of bullet trajectories. Forensic ballistics played a crucial role in determining the number of shots fired, the positions of the shooter, and the sequence of events during the assassination. The findings of the ballistic analysis were instrumental in the conclusions reached by the Warren Commission, which investigated the assassination.

1.3.5. Gun Ballistics

Gun Ballistics is the study of projectiles from the time of shooting to the time of impact with the target. Gun ballistics is often broken down into the following four categories, which contain detailed information on each category:

- Internal Ballistics, (sometimes called interior ballistics) the study of the process originally accelerating the projectile, for example the passage of a bullet through the barrel of a rifle;
- Transitional ballistics, (sometimes called intermediate ballistics) the study of the projectile's behavior when it leaves the barrel and the pressure behind the projectile is equalized;
- External Ballistics, (sometimes called as exterior ballistics) the study of the passage of the projectile through space or the air; and
- Terminal Ballistics, the study of the interaction of a projectile with its target, whether that be flesh (for hunting bullet), steel (for an anti-tank round), or even furnace slag (for an industrial slag disruptor).

1.3.6. Forensic Anthropology

Forensic anthropology is a specialized subfield of physical anthropology that applies the science of human osteology (the study of bones) to legal contexts, particularly in the identification of skeletal remains. Forensic anthropologists play a crucial role in the recovery and analysis of human remains, helping to establish the identity of deceased individuals and the circumstances surrounding their death. This field integrates methods and techniques from archaeology, anatomy, and anthropology to aid criminal investigations, mass disaster responses, and human rights investigations. The roots of forensic anthropology can be traced back to the early 20th century, but it gained significant recognition and development during the mid-20th century. One of the pivotal figures in its early development was Dr. Thomas Dwight, often considered the "father of American forensic anthropology." His work in the late 19th and early 20th centuries laid the groundwork for many of the techniques and principles used in the field today. However, it wasn't until the establishment of the American Academy of Forensic Sciences (AAFS) and the subsequent formation of the Physical Anthropology section in 1972 that forensic anthropology emerged as a distinct discipline.

Forensic anthropologists are often called upon to assist in various types of cases, including homicides, accidental deaths, and cases of missing persons. Their expertise is particularly valuable when dealing with decomposed, burned, or skeletonized remains, where traditional identification methods such as fingerprinting or visual recognition are not feasible. The primary tasks of a forensic anthropologist can be summarized into four main areas: recovery of remains, identification of individuals, determination of cause and manner of death, and estimation of time since death.

The recovery of remains is a critical aspect of forensic anthropology. Forensic anthropologists are trained in archaeological techniques to ensure that remains are excavated and collected in a systematic and meticulous manner. This involves mapping the location of remains, documenting the context in which they are found, and using appropriate tools to avoid damaging the bones. Proper recovery techniques are essential to preserve the integrity of the evidence and to prevent contamination. In many cases, forensic anthropologists work alongside law enforcement, forensic pathologists, and other specialists during the recovery process.

Identification of individuals from skeletal remains involves a multi-step process that includes the analysis of biological profiles. A biological profile consists of estimations of age, sex, ancestry, and stature, as well as the identification of unique features or pathological conditions that may assist in identification. Determining age at death can be done by examining the development and degeneration of bones and teeth. For example, the fusion of growth plates in long bones and the wear patterns on teeth can provide clues about an individual's age.

Sex estimation is typically based on the examination of sexually dimorphic features, which are physical characteristics that differ between males and females. The pelvis and skull are the most commonly analyzed bones for this purpose. The pelvis, in particular, exhibits significant differences between males and females due to its role in childbirth. Male pelves tend to be narrower and more robust, while female pelves are wider and have a larger pelvic inlet. The skull also shows differences in traits such as the size of the brow ridges, mastoid processes, and the overall robustness of the cranial features.

Ancestry estimation involves analyzing morphological traits that are more prevalent in certain population groups. While this aspect of forensic anthropology is more complex and less precise than age and sex estimation, certain features of the skull and dentition can provide information about an individual's ancestral background. For example, characteristics of the nasal aperture, cheekbones, and dental arcade can be indicative of specific ancestral groups.

Stature estimation is based on the measurement of long bones, such as the femur, tibia, and humerus. Regression formulas, derived from population-specific data, are used to estimate an individual's height. These formulas take into account the relationship between the length of long bones and overall body height.

In addition to the biological profile, forensic anthropologists look for unique features or markers that can aid in identification. These may include healed fractures, surgical implants, dental work, and congenital anomalies. For example, a healed fracture with a distinctive pattern or a surgically implanted device with a serial number can provide crucial information that may help identify the deceased.

Determination of the cause and manner of death is another critical function of forensic anthropology. While forensic pathologists typically determine the cause of death, forensic anthropologists contribute by identifying trauma to the bones that may indicate foul play, accidents, or other circumstances. Trauma analysis involves examining bones for signs of fractures, cuts, bullet holes, or other marks that can provide insights into how an individual died. The timing of these injuries, whether they occurred perimortem (around the time of death), antemortem (before death), or postmortem (after death), is crucial in reconstructing the events leading to death.

Perimortem injuries, which occur around the time of death, can often be distinguished by the presence of certain characteristics in the bone. For example, perimortem fractures tend to have clean, sharp edges and may show signs of radiating fracture lines, indicating that the bone was still fresh and pliable when the injury occurred. In contrast, postmortem damage usually appears more irregular and lacks these radiating lines, as the bone becomes more brittle after death.

Estimation of the time since death, also known as the postmortem interval (PMI), is another essential aspect of forensic anthropology. Determining PMI involves analyzing taphonomic changes, which are the processes that affect remains after death. These changes include decomposition, weathering, scavenging, and other environmental factors. Forensic anthropologists assess these factors in conjunction with other evidence, such as insect activity and plant growth, to estimate how long an individual has been deceased. While this estimation can be challenging and is often imprecise, it provides valuable information for narrowing down the time frame of death.

Forensic anthropology also plays a vital role in mass disaster and human rights investigations. In mass disaster scenarios, such as plane crashes, natural disasters, or terrorist attacks, forensic anthropologists are part of multidisciplinary teams that work to recover and identify victims. Their expertise in handling fragmented and commingled remains is crucial for ensuring that each individual is accurately identified and returned to their families. The identification process often involves collaboration with forensic odontologists, DNA analysts, and other specialists to provide comprehensive and accurate identification.

In human rights investigations, forensic anthropologists contribute to the documentation and analysis of evidence related to war crimes, genocide, and other atrocities. They assist in the excavation of mass graves, the identification of victims, and the documentation of trauma and other evidence that can be used in legal proceedings. The work of forensic anthropologists in these contexts not only provides answers to families and communities but also supports the pursuit of justice and accountability for human rights violations.

One notable case that highlights the importance of forensic anthropology is the investigation of the mass graves in Bosnia and Herzegovina following the Bosnian War in the 1990s. Forensic anthropologists played a crucial role in the exhumation and identification of thousands of victims of the Srebrenica massacre, where over 8,000 Bosniak men and boys were killed by Bosnian Serb forces. The work of forensic anthropologists in this case helped to provide evidence for war crimes prosecutions and bring closure to the families of the victims.

Despite its critical contributions, forensic anthropology faces several challenges. One major challenge is the potential for environmental and taphonomic factors to complicate the analysis of skeletal remains. For example, exposure to the elements, animal scavenging, and soil conditions can alter the appearance and condition of bones, making it difficult to interpret findings accurately. Forensic anthropologists must be well-versed in taphonomic processes and consider these factors when analyzing remains.

Another challenge is the potential for bias in the interpretation of skeletal evidence. Forensic anthropologists must strive to maintain objectivity and avoid drawing conclusions based on preconceived notions or external pressures. Adhering to rigorous scientific methods and ethical standards is essential for ensuring the accuracy and reliability of forensic anthropology findings. Advancements in technology and research are continuously enhancing the field of forensic anthropology. The use of 3D imaging and printing, for example, allows for the creation of accurate models of skeletal remains, which can be used for analysis, education, and court presentations. DNA analysis, in conjunction with traditional anthropological methods, has also improved the ability to identify individuals from skeletal remains. Mitochondrial DNA (mtDNA) analysis, in particular, is valuable for cases involving degraded or limited samples, as mtDNA is more abundant and stable than nuclear DNA.

1.3.7. Forensic Odontology

Forensic odontology, also known as forensic dentistry, is a specialized branch of forensic science that utilizes dental expertise to assist in legal investigations. It involves the examination, evaluation, and comparison of dental evidence, primarily teeth and dental records, to establish the identity of human remains and assist in criminal investigations. Forensic odontologists play a crucial role in cases where traditional methods of identification, such as fingerprints or DNA, are unavailable or insufficient.

The history of forensic odontology dates back to the late 19th century, with significant advancements and recognition during the 20th century. One of the pioneering figures in the field was Dr. Oscar Amoëdo, a Cuban dentist who, in 1898, published a paper on the use of dental records for identification purposes. His work laid the foundation for the use of dental evidence in forensic investigations, demonstrating the uniqueness and durability of dental features that could aid in identifying individuals.

Forensic odontology encompasses several key areas of expertise and application:

1. **Identification of Human Remains**: One of the primary roles of forensic odontology is the identification of deceased individuals based on their dental records. Dental records, which include detailed information about a person's dental history, treatments, and conditions, serve as a valuable source of comparative data. Forensic odontologists compare ante-mortem (before death) dental records, such as dental charts, X-rays, and photographs, with post-mortem (after death) dental remains found on a body. Unique features such as dental restorations, missing teeth, and dental anomalies can be crucial in establishing a positive identification.
2. **Age Estimation**: Forensic odontologists can also assist in estimating the age of an individual based on dental development and dental wear patterns. In cases where other forms of identification are lacking, dental age estimation can provide valuable information to narrow down the identity of the deceased.

3. **Bite Mark Analysis**: Forensic odontology is involved in the analysis of bite marks found on victims of crimes, such as sexual assaults or cases of physical assault. Bite marks can be found on skin, food items, or objects at a crime scene. Forensic odontologists analyze the characteristics of the bite mark and compare them with dental impressions or models of potential suspects to determine a match. This analysis can help establish a link between a suspect and a crime scene or victim.
4. **Dental Trauma Analysis**: Examination of dental trauma, such as fractures or injuries to the teeth or jaw, can provide insights into the circumstances of injuries or deaths. Patterns of dental trauma can sometimes indicate the type of force or object involved in an assault or accident, assisting in the reconstruction of events.
5. **Expert Testimony**: Forensic odontologists often provide expert testimony in court proceedings, presenting their findings and interpretations to assist judges, juries, and legal professionals in understanding the significance of dental evidence. Their testimony can be crucial in cases where dental evidence forms a significant part of the prosecution or defense strategy.
6. **Mass Disaster Victim Identification**: In mass disasters, such as airplane crashes, natural disasters, or terrorist attacks, forensic odontologists play a vital role in the identification of victims. Dental remains are often well-preserved compared to other body tissues, making dental records and dental identification essential tools in the identification process. Forensic odontologists work closely with forensic pathologists, anthropologists, and other specialists in multidisciplinary teams to ensure accurate and timely identifications.
7. **Research and Development**: Forensic odontology also involves research and development to improve techniques, standards, and methodologies used in forensic investigations. Advancements in dental imaging technology, such as digital radiography and three-dimensional (3D) imaging, have enhanced the capabilities of forensic odontology in recent years. These technologies allow for more precise comparisons and analyzes of dental evidence, contributing to more accurate identifications and assessments.

One of the notable cases that underscored the importance of forensic odontology is the Ted Bundy case in the 1970s. Bundy, a notorious serial killer, was linked to multiple homicides through bite mark analysis. Forensic odontologists compared impressions of Bundy's teeth with bite marks found on victims, providing crucial evidence that helped convict him in several murder cases. Despite its significance, forensic odontology faces challenges and limitations. One challenge is the subjective nature of bite mark analysis, which has been criticized for its unreliability and potential for bias. Research efforts are ongoing to improve the scientific basis and objectivity of bite mark analysis through standardized protocols and validation studies.

Another challenge is the variability in dental records and the availability of ante-mortem data for comparison. In some cases, individuals may not have comprehensive dental records or may have undergone dental treatments in different locations or countries, making it challenging to obtain complete and accurate information for comparison.

Ethical considerations are paramount in forensic odontology. Forensic odontologists must adhere to strict ethical guidelines to ensure the accuracy, reliability, and impartiality of their analyses and testimony. This includes maintaining confidentiality, obtaining proper consent when working with dental records or human remains, and avoiding conflicts of interest.

Education and training are fundamental to the practice of forensic odontology. Specialized training programs and courses provide future forensic odontologists with the knowledge and skills required for their profession. Universities and institutions offer forensic dentistry programs that cover topics such as dental anatomy, forensic dental pathology, bite mark analysis, and courtroom procedures. Professional organizations, such as the American Board of Forensic Odontology (ABFO), provide certification programs, continuing education, and networking opportunities for practitioners in the field.

1.3.8. Forensic Chemistry

Forensic chemistry is a specialized branch of forensic science that applies chemical principles, techniques, and methodologies to legal investigations and criminal justice. It involves the analysis and interpretation of chemical evidence found at crime scenes or related to criminal activities. Forensic chemists play a crucial role in identifying substances, linking suspects to crime scenes, and providing scientific evidence for legal proceedings.

1. **Key Areas and Applications of Forensic Chemistry:**

i. **Drug Analysis**: Forensic chemists analyze controlled substances, such as drugs and narcotics, to determine their composition, purity, and quantity. This information can help law enforcement agencies identify drug trafficking operations, prosecute drug-related offenses, and understand drug trends in communities. Techniques used include chromatography (e.g., gas chromatography, liquid chromatography), mass spectrometry, and spectroscopy.

ii. **Trace Evidence Analysis**: Trace evidence refers to small, often microscopic, materials found at crime scenes, such as fibers, paints, glass fragments, and gunshot residue. Forensic chemists analyze these materials to identify their composition and origin, which can provide valuable clues about the events that transpired and help link suspects to crime scenes. Advanced techniques like scanning electron microscopy (SEM) and Fourier-transform infrared spectroscopy (FTIR) are commonly used in trace evidence analysis.

iii. **Arson and Explosives Investigation**: Forensic chemists investigate arson cases by analyzing fire debris and residues to determine the presence of accelerants (e.g., gasoline, kerosene) used to start fires. They also analyze explosives and explosive residues to identify the type of explosive material and trace its origin. Techniques such as gas chromatography-mass spectrometry (GC-MS), and X-ray diffraction (XRD) are utilized in arson and explosives investigations.

iv. **Toxicology**: Forensic toxicology involves the analysis of biological samples (e.g., blood, urine, tissue) to detect and quantify drugs, alcohol, and other toxic substances. Forensic chemists determine the presence of these substances and their concentrations, which can provide crucial information about impairment, cause of death, or exposure to harmful substances. Techniques include immunoassays, high-performance liquid chromatography (HPLC), and gas chromatography.

v. **Forensic Serology**: Serology in forensic chemistry focuses on the analysis of bodily fluids (e.g., blood, semen, saliva) found at crime scenes. Forensic chemists use immunological methods to identify and classify these fluids, which can help establish links between suspects, victims, and crime scenes. Techniques such as enzyme-linked immunosorbent assay (ELISA) and forensic DNA analysis (for DNA profiling) are essential in serological investigations.

vi. **Environmental Forensics**: Forensic chemists analyze environmental samples, such as soil, water, and air pollutants, to investigate environmental crimes (e.g., illegal dumping, pollution incidents). They identify and quantify pollutants using analytical techniques to determine their source and impact on ecosystems or human health. Environmental forensics often involves collaboration with environmental scientists, regulators, and law enforcement agencies.

2. Techniques and Tools Used in Forensic Chemistry:

i. **Chromatography**: Gas chromatography (GC), liquid chromatography (LC), and thin-layer chromatography (TLC) are used to separate and analyze complex mixtures of substances.

ii. **Mass Spectrometry**: Mass spectrometry (MS) is employed to identify and quantify substances based on their molecular weight and fragmentation patterns.
iii. **Spectroscopy**: Techniques such as infrared spectroscopy (IR), UV-Vi's spectroscopy, and nuclear magnetic resonance spectroscopy (NMR) are used to analyze the chemical structure and composition of materials.
iv. **Microscopy**: Scanning electron microscopy (SEM) and optical microscopy are used to examine trace evidence and analyze microscopic features.
v. **Spectrophotometry**: UV-Vi's spectrophotometry is used to measure the absorption of light by substances, providing information about their concentration and properties.

3. **Challenges and Considerations:**
    i. **Sample Integrity**: Maintaining the integrity of forensic samples is crucial to prevent contamination and ensure accurate analysis. The chain of custody protocols are followed to document the handling and transfer of evidence.
    ii. **Complexity of Evidence**: Forensic chemists must deal with diverse and often complex types of evidence, requiring expertise in multiple analytical techniques and interdisciplinary collaboration.
    iii. **Legal and Ethical Standards**: Adhering to legal standards and ethical guidelines is essential in forensic chemistry to ensure the validity and reliability of evidence presented in court.
    iv. **Advancements and Research**: Continuous advancements in analytical techniques and research are essential to improve the sensitivity, accuracy, and speed of forensic chemical analysis.

1.3.9. DNA Profiling

DNA Typing (previously referred to as "DNA fingerprinting" or "Geneting Typing" is probably one of the most important advances in the field of forensic science in the recent years. 22 DNA Proofing has become a well-known technique used in criminal and other legal cases due to the massive publicity generated by high profile cases, TV crime shows, and films.

DNA typing has the following applications:

- Establishment of paternity and maternity
- Establishment of biological relationships for immigration purposes, kidney transport etc.
- Detection of cases of child swapping
- Identification of rapist in rape cases including gang rape cases
- Identification of mutilated remains as in case of bomb blasts, murder, mass disasters.
- Wildlife identification• Detection of bacteria and other organisms that may pollute air, water, soil, and food
- Authentication of consumables such as wine.

1.4. LEGAL SYSTEM

The legal system is the framework of rules and institutions within a society that governs the behavior of its members and resolves disputes. It encompasses various components, including laws, courts, law enforcement agencies, legal professionals, and correctional facilities. Understanding the legal system requires an exploration of its origins, structure, functions, and the interplay between different legal traditions and systems.

1.4.1. Historical Development of Legal Systems

1.4.1.1. Ancient Legal Systems

The origins of legal systems can be traced back to ancient civilizations, where the first codified laws were established to maintain order and justice. Notable ancient legal systems include:

- **The Code of Hammurabi (c. 1754 BC):** One of the earliest known legal codes, established by the Babylonian king Hammurabi. It consisted of 282 laws covering various aspects of society, including property rights, family law, and criminal justice.
- **Ancient Egyptian Law:** Based on the principles of Ma'at (truth, balance, and order), ancient Egyptian law emphasized justice, fairness, and the protection of the weak. Legal decisions were made by judges and overseen by the pharaoh.
- **Roman Law:** Roman law laid the foundation for many modern legal systems. The 12 Tables (c. 450 BC) were the first set of laws publicly displayed in Rome. Roman law evolved over centuries, culminating in the Corpus Juris Civilis (Body of Civil Law) compiled under Emperor Justinian I in the 6th century AD.

1.4.1.2. Medieval and Early Modern Legal Systems

During the medieval period, legal systems in Europe developed under the influence of feudalism, the Catholic Church, and the revival of Roman law:

- **Feudal Law:** In feudal societies, laws were based on customs and the relationship between lords and vassals. Disputes were often resolved through local courts presided over by lords or their representatives.
- **Canon Law:** The Catholic Church developed its own legal system, known as canon law, which governed ecclesiastical matters and had significant influence on secular law in medieval Europe.
- **Common Law:** In England, the common law system emerged during the 12th century. It was based on customs and judicial decisions rather than written codes. The Magna Carta (1215) established key legal principles, such as the rule of law and the right to a fair trial.

1.4.1.3. Modern Legal Systems

The modern era saw the development of more structured and codified legal systems, influenced by Enlightenment ideas and the rise of nation-states:

- **Civil Law:** Civil law systems, based on comprehensive written codes, developed in continental Europe. The Napoleonic Code (1804) in France served as a model for many civil law systems worldwide.
- Common Law: The common law system continued to evolve in England and spread to other English-speaking countries, including the United States, Canada, Australia, and India.
- **Mixed Legal Systems:** Some countries, such as South Africa and Scotland, have mixed legal systems that incorporate elements of both civil and common law traditions.

1.4.2. Structure of Legal Systems

Legal systems vary widely across different countries, but they typically share common structural elements:

1.4.2.1. Sources of Law

1. **Constitutions:** Constitutions are the supreme laws of a country, establishing the framework for government and the rights of citizens. They provide the foundation for all other laws and often include provisions for their amendment.

2. **Statutes:** Statutes are laws enacted by legislative bodies, such as parliaments or congresses. They cover a wide range of issues, including criminal law, civil law, administrative law, and commercial law.
3. **Regulations:** Regulations are rules issued by administrative agencies to implement and enforce statutes. They provide detailed guidance on how laws should be applied in practice.
4. **Case Law:** Case law, or judicial precedent, is the body of law created by judicial decisions. In common law systems, courts rely heavily on precedents set by higher courts to ensure consistency and predictability in legal rulings.
5. **Customary Law:** Customary law consists of practices and traditions that have been accepted as binding by a community. It plays a significant role in some legal systems, particularly in indigenous and traditional societies.

1.4.2.2. Branches of Law

1. **Public Law:** Public law governs the relationship between individuals and the state. It includes constitutional law, administrative law, criminal law, and international law.
2. **Private Law:** Private law regulates relationships between individuals and entities. It encompasses civil law, contract law, property law, family law, and tort law.
3. **Criminal Law:** Criminal law defines offenses against the state or society and prescribes punishments. It aims to deter and punish criminal behavior while protecting public safety and order.
4. **Civil Law:** Civil law deals with disputes between private parties. It includes areas such as contract law, property law, family law, and tort law. The primary goal of civil law is to provide remedies and compensation to those harmed by others' actions.

1.4.2.3. Court Systems

1. Trial Courts: Trial courts are the first level of the judicial system, where cases are initially heard and decided. They include civil courts, criminal courts, and specialized courts (e.g., family courts, labor courts).
2. Appellate Courts: Appellate courts review decisions made by trial courts. They do not conduct new trials but evaluate whether legal errors were made that could have affected the outcome of the case.

3. **Supreme Courts:** Supreme courts are the highest judicial authority in a legal system. They have the final say on legal matters and often serve as the court of last resort for appeals.
4. **Specialized Courts:** Some legal systems have specialized courts to handle specific types of cases, such as constitutional courts, administrative courts, and military courts.

1.4.2.4. Legal Professionals

1. **Judges:** Judges are responsible for interpreting and applying the law in court cases. They ensure that trials are conducted fairly and make decisions based on the evidence and legal arguments presented.
2. **Lawyers:** Lawyers, or attorneys, represent parties in legal proceedings. They provide legal advice, draft legal documents, and advocate on behalf of their clients in court.
3. **Prosecutors:** Prosecutors are lawyers who represent the state in criminal cases. They present evidence and arguments to prove the guilt of the accused.
4. **Defenders:** Defense attorneys represent individuals accused of crimes. They ensure that their clients receive a fair trial and protect their legal rights.
5. **Legal Scholars:** Legal scholars, or jurists, study and analyze legal systems, principles, and practices. They contribute to the development of legal theory and provide guidance on complex legal issues.

1.4.2.5. Law Enforcement Agencies

1. **Police:** Police agencies are responsible for maintaining public order, preventing and investigating crimes, and enforcing laws. They play a crucial role in the criminal justice system by apprehending suspects and gathering evidence.
2. **Prosecutorial Agencies:** Prosecutorial agencies, such as district attorney's offices, oversee the prosecution of criminal cases. They work closely with law enforcement to build cases against defendants.
3. **Correctional Facilities:** Correctional facilities, including prisons and jails, house individuals convicted of crimes. They aim to rehabilitate offenders and protect society by restricting their freedom.

1.4.3. Functions of the Legal System

The legal system serves several essential functions in society:

1. **Maintaining Order:** One of the primary functions of the legal system is to maintain order by establishing clear rules and procedures for resolving disputes. By providing a structured framework for addressing conflicts, the legal system helps prevent chaos and anarchy.
2. **Protecting Rights and Liberties:** The legal system safeguards individual rights and liberties by ensuring that laws are applied fairly and consistently. Constitutions and human rights laws protect fundamental freedoms, such as freedom of speech, the right to a fair trial, and protection against discrimination.
3. **Administering Justice:** The legal system administers justice by holding individuals accountable for their actions and providing remedies for those harmed by others. Criminal law punishes offenders, while civil law compensates victims and resolves disputes between private parties.
4. **Promoting Social Change:** The legal system plays a crucial role in promoting social change by addressing issues of inequality, discrimination, and injustice. Landmark court decisions and legislative reforms have led to significant advancements in civil rights, gender equality, and environmental protection.
5. **Providing a Mechanism for Dispute Resolution:** The legal system offers a formal mechanism for resolving disputes through courts and alternative dispute resolution methods, such as mediation and arbitration. This helps prevent conflicts from escalating and provides a peaceful means of addressing grievances.
6. **Regulating Behavior:** Laws regulate behavior by establishing standards of conduct for individuals and organizations. They define acceptable and unacceptable actions, providing a basis for societal norms and expectations.
7. **Supporting Economic Activity:** The legal system supports economic activity by creating a stable and predictable environment for businesses and individuals. Contract law, property law, and commercial law facilitate transactions, protect investments, and ensure the enforceability of agreements.

1.4.4. Legal Traditions and Systems

Legal systems around the world are influenced by different legal traditions, which shape their structure, principles, and practices:

1.4.4.1. Civil Law Tradition

The civil law tradition, also known as the Romano-Germanic tradition, is based on comprehensive written codes and statutes. Key characteristics include:

- **Codification:** Laws are systematically organized into codes, such as the Civil Code, Commercial Code, and Penal Code.
- **Role of Judges:** Judges apply the law as written in the codes, with limited discretion to interpret or create new legal principles.
- **Sources of Law:** Primary sources of law are statutes and codes, with judicial decisions having less authority compared to common law systems.

Civil law systems are prevalent in continental Europe, Latin America, and parts of Asia and Africa.

1.4.4.2. Common Law Tradition

The common law tradition, also known as the Anglo-American tradition, is based on judicial decisions and precedents. Key characteristics include:

- **Precedent:** Courts rely on previous judicial decisions (precedents) to guide their rulings in similar cases, ensuring consistency and predictability.
- **Role of Judges:** Judges have greater discretion to interpret the law and develop legal principles through case law.
- **Sources of Law:** Primary sources of law are statutes, case law, and judicial interpretations, with a significant emphasis on judicial decisions.

Common law systems are prevalent in the United Kingdom, the United States, Canada, Australia, and other English-speaking countries.

1.4.4.3. Customary Law Tradition

Customary law is based on the practices and traditions of a community. Key characteristics include:

- **Oral Traditions:** Customary laws are often passed down orally and may not be codified in written form.
- **Community-Based:** Legal decisions are made based on community norms and values, with an emphasis on reconciliation and restorative justice.
- **Flexibility:** Customary law is adaptable and can evolve with changing societal norms and practices.

Customary law systems are prevalent in indigenous and traditional societies in Africa, Asia, and the Pacific.

1.4.4.4. Religious Law Tradition

Religious law is based on religious texts and principles. Key characteristics include:

- **Divine Authority:** Religious laws are believed to be divinely inspired and are interpreted by religious scholars and authorities.
- **Integration with Secular Law:** In some countries, religious law operates alongside secular legal systems, influencing personal status matters such as marriage, divorce, and inheritance.
- **Sources of Law:** Primary sources of law are religious texts, such as the Quran, Bible, and Torah, and religious jurisprudence.

Religious law systems are prevalent in countries with strong religious traditions, such as Islamic law (Sharia) in Muslim-majority countries.

1.4.4.5. Mixed Legal Systems

Mixed legal systems combine elements of different legal traditions. Key characteristics include:

- **Hybrid Structure:** Legal systems may incorporate aspects of civil law, common law, customary law, and religious law.
- **Adaptability:** Mixed legal systems can adapt to the diverse legal needs and cultural contexts of a country.
- **Sources of Law:** Legal sources may include written codes, judicial decisions, customary practices, and religious texts.

Examples of countries with mixed legal systems include South Africa, Scotland, and India.

1.4.5. Legal System Challenges and Reforms

Legal systems face various challenges and undergo continuous reforms to address evolving societal needs:

1. **Access to Justice:** Ensuring equal access to justice for all individuals, regardless of socioeconomic status, remains a significant challenge. Legal systems must address barriers such as high legal costs, complex procedures, and lack of legal representation.
2. **Judicial Independence:** Maintaining judicial independence is crucial for the impartiality and fairness of the legal system. Threats to

judicial independence, such as political interference and corruption, must be addressed to uphold the rule of law.

3. **Technology and Innovation:** The rapid advancement of technology presents both opportunities and challenges for legal systems. Legal professionals must adapt to new technologies, such as artificial intelligence, digital evidence, and cybersecurity, while ensuring the protection of privacy and data security.

4. **Human Rights and Social Justice:** Legal systems must continue to address issues of human rights and social justice, including discrimination, inequality, and access to basic needs. Legal reforms and advocacy are essential to protect vulnerable populations and promote social justice.

5. **Globalization and International Law:** Globalization has increased the interconnectedness of legal systems, leading to the development of international law and cross-border legal cooperation. Legal systems must navigate the complexities of international treaties, trade agreements, and human rights conventions.

6. **Alternative Dispute Resolution:** The growing demand for alternative dispute resolution methods, such as mediation and arbitration, highlights the need for flexible and efficient mechanisms to resolve conflicts outside traditional court processes.

REFERENCES

1. Ashbaugh, D. (1999). *Quantitative-Qualitative Friction Ridge Analysis: An Introduction to Basic and Advanced Ridgeology*. CRC Press.
2. Balthazard, V. (1911). De l'identification par les empreintes digitales. *Comptes Redus des Seances de l'Academie des Sciences*, *152*, 1862–1864.
3. Collier, P. A., & Spaul, B. J. (1990). Information Systems Forensics. *Journal of Information Technology,* *5*(3), 134–140. http://dx.doi.org/10.1177/026839629000500303.
4. Dror, I. E., & Morgan, R. M. (2019). A Futuristic Vision of Forensic Science. *Journal of Forensic Sciences, 65*(1), 8–10.
5. Hemanth, K., Tharmavaram, M., & Pandey, G. (2020). History of Forensic Science. In *Technology in Forensic Science: Sampling, Analysis, Data and Regulations*.
6. Herschel, W. J. (1916). *The Origin of Finger-Printing*. Oxford University Press. ISBN 978-1104662257. Archived from the original on 25 July 2011. Retrieved 15 January 2014.
7. Iorliam, A. (2018). History of Forensic Science. In *Fundamental Computing Forensics for Africa* (pp. 3–16). SpringerBriefs in Computer Science.
8. Prego-Meleiro, P., García-Ruiz, C., Sanz-Pareja, M., Recalde Esnoz, I., Quintanilla, M. G., & Montalvo, G. (2022). Forensic intelligence-led prevention of drug-facilitated sexual assaults. *Forensic Science International, 337*, 111373.

CHAPTER 2

CRIME SCENE INVESTIGATION

Contents

Introduction 44

2.1. Crime Scene Investigation Basics 45

2.2. Crime Scene Management 63

References 85

INTRODUCTION

Identification and retrieval of tangible evidence mark the start of the investigation at the scene. Presenting all of the findings to the court of law comes after the results of the analysis and development of the recovered physical evidence, documents, and witness statements. All staff members, from initial responders to final information users, should possess sufficient knowledge of the forensic process, including identification, recovery, collection, preservation, transportation, and appropriate documentation to uphold the chain of custody. As the initial point of contact, crime scene investigation is a procedure designed to document the scene as well as identify and gather all tangible evidence that may be needed to solve the case.

The actual site or location where the incident occurred is known as the scene of crime or place of occurrence. When police officers arrive at a crime scene, they usually start the investigation there first. First responding officers are the members of the police force who arrive at the crime scene first (FRO). The crime scene and its evidence are appropriately guarded by the first responding officer (FRO). The ability of the first responding officer to correctly identify, isolate, and secure the evidence (s) is critical to the success of the entire investigatio toTo secure the crime scene and stop evidence destruction, a restricted boundary can be established. This can be accomplished by utilizing crime scene tape, rope, or barriers. The first responding officer (FRO) is responsible for enforcing the prohibition against allowing any person who is not absolutely necessary to enter the crime scene after it has been secured. This also means keeping high ranking personnel from entering the scene who are not there to investigate or collect evidence. Those "lookers" will only contaminate the scene.

One or more locations of occurrence may be involved in an incident's investigation. At another location, there might be multiple secondary or tertiary crime scenes in addition to the primary crime scene. Everywhere (it could be a car, an indoor space, etc. All of these locations are crime scenes because that is where the incident took place, where the evidence of the crime was found, or where the incident was linked to a specific incident. In essence, a crime scene is the location (s) where the crime has occurred or where possible evidence of the crime has been found. A crime scene is more than just the place where the crime was committed. The location or locations where relevant evidence related to a specific crime may be found or recovered are also considered crime scenes in that case. All of these crime scenes should be thoroughly examined during an investigation to discover the real story behind the incident. Even the most difficult crime scenes can be successfully investigated with experience if a successful crime scene investigator applies this methodical and logical approach. Every crime scene is different. The scientific process of investigating a crime scene entails measuring, photographing, and documenting the scene, gathering and packaging tangible evidence, and then reconstructing the scene. During the examination of the crime scene, the chain of custody for the evidence must be properly maintained.

Throughout the entire crime scene investigation process, the first responding officer—typically a police officer—plays a crucial role. Maintaining the integrity of the crime scene and the evidence is the police officer's first duty. The policeman is also in charge of promptly documenting the crime scene and all of the evidence found there. "Adequate training on handling evidence at SOC is crucial to successfully carry out these activities, as most first responders are not forensic personnel." In cases where there is a possibility that the evidence will be lost, contaminated, or destroyed, the first responding officer must perform certain basic recovery procedures prior to the arrival of the crime scene investigators. The duties of the first responding officer may need to go beyond preservation and documentation in cases where there is no chance that the crime scene will be processed by crime scene investigators.

2.1. CRIME SCENE INVESTIGATION BASICS

Crime scene investigation is where logic, science, and law converge. The process of processing a crime scene is laborious and time-consuming. It entails carefully recording the scene's circumstances and gathering any tangible evidence that might shed light on the incident or identify the perpetrator. There is no typical body of evidence, a typical crime scene, and typical investigative methodology.

A CSI may use tweezers to remove hair from a victim's jacket without disturbing the fabric too much to shake off any white powder (which may or may not be cocaine) in the sleeve folds, collect dried blood from windowpanes without letting his arm touch the glass in case there are latent fingerprints there, and use a sledge hammer to break through a wall that appears to be the source of an awful smell. However, the actual physical evidence is only one component of the story. The conviction of the criminal is the ultimate objective. The CSI is therefore thinking about all the steps required to preserve the evidence in its current form, what the lab can do with this evidence in order to reconstruct the crime or identify the criminal, and the legal issues involved in making sure this evidence is admissible in court while he scrapes off the dried blood without smearing any prints, lifts several hairs without disturbing any trace evidence, and smashes through a wall in the living room. The investigation of a crime scene begins when the CSI unit receives a call from the police officers or detectives on the scene. The overall system works something like this:

- The CSI arrives on the scene and makes sure it is secure. She does an initial walk-through to get an overall feel for the crime scene, finds out if anyone moved anything before, she arrived, and generates initial theories based on visual examination. She makes note of potential evidence. At this point, she touches nothing.
- The CSI thoroughly documents the scene by taking photographs and drawing sketches during a second walk-through. Sometimes, the documentation stage includes a video walk-through, as well. She documents the scene as a whole and documents anything she has identified as evidence. She still toucheshing.
- Now it'sit is time to touch stuff — very, very carefully. The CSI systematically makes her way through the scene collecting all potential evidence, tagging it, logging it and packaging it so it remains intact on its way to the lab. Depending on the task breakdown of the CSI unit she works for and her areas of expertise, she may or may not analyze the evidence in the lab.
- The crime lab processes all of the evidence the CSI collected at the crime scene. When the lab results are in, they go to the lead detective on the case.

The division of labor between field and laboratory work is approached differently by each CSI unit. Crime scene investigation, also known as crime scene analysis, refers to what happens at the scene of the crime, while forensic science describes what happens in a lab. A forensic scientist is not a CSI. Certain CSIs only operate in the field, gathering evidence and transferring it to the forensics lab. In this instance, the CSI still needs to have a solid grasp of forensic science to identify the unique significance of different kinds of evidence in the field. However, these jobs frequently overlap.

Joe Clayton works for the Colorado Bureau of Investigation (CBI) as a primary crime scene responder. In addition to having 14 years of field experience, he is an authority in specific forensic science fields. Clayton clarifies that his involvement in the laboratory analysis differs based on the kind of evidence he retrieves from the crime scene.

Once the evidence is turned over to the laboratory, I might be involved in the actual "bench work," depending on what scientific analyzes are required or requested. I am skilled in photography, trajectory determination, serology (blood and bodily fluids), and blood pattern identiftion (blood spatter). I'mI am also knowledgeable about a lot of other topics, like firearms, fingerprints, and disputed documents.) that could help me on the scene. I may be required to use one or more of my specialized disciplines at the scene as a primary crime scene responder CBI. Even though I wouldn'twould not test a firearm's functionality here at the lab, my job at the crime scene would be to gather the gun and assess its possible value as evidence.

Crime scene investigationa massive undertaking. Let'sLet us start at the beginning: scene recognition.

2.1.1. At the Crime Scene Recognition

A CSI doesn'tdoes not just show up at a crime scene and begin gathering evidence. Understanding the scope of this specific investigation and creating a methodical approach to locating and gathering evidence are the objectives of the scene recognition stage. The CSI is currently only using his nose, ears, eyes, paper, and pen (Figure 2.1).

Figure 2.1. *Des Moines police officers secure a crime scene related to a double homicide on Nov. 2, 2016, in Des Moines, Iowa.*

Source. https://media.hswstatic.com/eyJidWNrZXQiOiJjb250ZW50Lmhzd-3N0YXRpYy5jb20iLCJrZXkiOiJnaWZcL2NzaS11cGRhdGUtc2VjdXJlLXNjZ-W5lLmpwZyIsImVkaXRzIjp7InJlc2l6ZSI6eyJ3aWR0aCI6ODI4fSwidG9Gb3JtYX-QiOiJhdmlmIn19.

Determining the size of the crime scene is the first step. The house and the immediate area outside could be the crime scene if it is a homicide and there is only one vio was killed there. If there'sthere is a blood trail down the street and any cars in the driveway, the entire neighborhood could be the crime scene. It is essential to secure the crime scene as well as any additional locations that may turn out to be related to the crimehe future. There is really onlyonly one chance for a CSI to conduct a comprehensive, untainted search; in subsequent searches, detectives will touch items, rain will wash away evidence, and furniture will be moved, corrupting the evidence.

The core area, or the most visible ime scene where the majority ofmost of the evidence is concentrated, is typically secured by the first police officers on the scene. Because it is easier to reduce the size of a crime scene than to increase it, the CSI will block off an area when he arrives that is larger than the core crime scene. This is because press vans and bystanders may be crunching through the area that the CSI later determines is part of the crime scene. The process of securing the scene entails erecting a physical barrier out of crime scene tape or other barriers like police cars, sawhorses, or officers, as well as clearing the area of any extra people. Just outside the crime scene, a CSI may set up a "safe area" where detectives can take a break and talk things through without fear of damaging any evidence.

The district attorney must be involved once the CSI has established the crime scene and ensured its security. This is because the CSI requires search warrants in case anyone may have an expectation of privacy in any area of the crime scene. If the evidence a CSI finds is not allowed to be used in court, it is not very valuable. A competent detective rarely searches a scene without a warrant, preferring to err on the side of caution.

The CSI starts a walkthrough of the crime scene after obtaining a search warrant. He proceeds aloed route that is probably goinggoing to have the least amount of evidence that walking through it would obliterate. He notes immediately, during this first walk-through, detait will change over time: what'swhat is the weather like, what time of day is it? He describes any noteworthy sounds (water dripping, smoke alarm beeping, etc.), smells (gas, decomposition, etc.), and anything that seems missing or out of place. This is also the time to check for any potential hazards, such as a gas leak or an irate dog guarding the body and take immediate action to address them. Are there any chairs pushed up against doors? Are there any pillows missing from the bed?

During the recognition stage, the CSI contacts any specialist or additional equipmeves he will require in light ofconsidering specific types of evidence he finds. It might be necessary to send a scissor lvictim's front yard in order toto retrieve a t-shirt that has become lodged in a tree. Experts must examine eviden scene, such as blood splatter spatter on the ceiling or maggot activity on the corpse. Delivering a portion of the ceiling to the lab for blood spatter analysis is challenging, and the activity of the maggots varies minute by minute. In addition to his work as a crime scene investigator, Mr. Clayton would complete this task since he is an eood spatter analysis.

In order toTo find out if the first responders touched anything and to acquire any more information that could be useful in formulating an attack strategy, the CSI speaks with them during this time. When witness interviews are initiated by detectives on the scene, they might provide information that leads the CSI to a specific room ind of evidence. In the event thatIf the victim was yelling at someone over the phone 30 minutes prior to the police arriving, the Caller ID unit is a valuable piece of evidence. A clean-up attempt could be indicated if an upstairs neighbor heard a struggle followed by the sound of water running, and the CSI is aware to search the kitchen and bathroom for blood stains. Mr. Clayton and most other CSIs avoid speaking with witnesses. Mr. Dot Clayton is a forensic scientist and a crime scene investigator; he is not trained in conducting effective interviews. Mr. Clayton only handles the tangible evidence, consulting the on-site detectives for any insightful witness statements.

The CSI builds a rational strategy for this specific crime scene using the data he obtains from scene recognition. The process of investigating a crime scene is not standardized. As Mr. Dot Clayton clarifies, the method used to arrive at a crime scene at a high school wpeople ied is a different (Mr. The methods used to investigate a crime scene involving a person who was raped in a car. These are very different methods from those used at Columbine High School (where Clayton was one of the CSIs who processed the scene after the shootings there). The next step is to thoroughly document every aspect of the sce way that allows people who weren'twere not there to reconstruct it once the CSI has developed a plan of attack to gather all of the evidence that could be relevant to this specific crime. This phase involves documenting the scene.

At a crime scene, police officers are usually the first to arrive. If the offender is still there, they arrest him and, if reqan ambulance. They are in charge ofoversee securing the area to prevent the destruction of any evidence. The CSI team gathers any tangible evidence and meticulously records the crime scene. The district attorney is frequently present to assist in determining whether the inveeed any search warrants in order toto move forward and to help them get those warrants from a judge. To establish a preliminary cause of death, the medical examiner (in the event of a homicide) may or may not be present. If a specialist analysis of the evidence is needed, specialists such as forensic scientists, forensic psychologists, or entomologists may be contacted. Detectives speak with the CSI unit and question witnesses. They follow leads from witnesses and tangible evidence to investigate the crime.

2.1.2. Crime Scene Documentation

The purpose of crime-scene documentation is to produce a visual record that will make it simple for the prosecutor's office and the forensics lab to reconstruct an exact picture of the scene. At this point in the investigation, the CSI uses both film and digital cameras, as well as a variety of lenses, flashes, filters, tripods, sketchpads, graph paper, pens, pencils, measuring tapes, rulers, and notepads. He might also make use of a camera boom and a recorder.

A second walkthrough of the scene is conducted while documenting the scene (staying on the same path as the first walkthrough). If multiple CSIs are present at the scene (Mr. Clayton has both been the only and numerous CSIs present at a scene. Depending on the situation, one CSI may take pictures, another may draw, another may take thorough notes, and still another may conduct a video walkthrough. All of these jobs belong to him if there is only one CSI.

2.1.2.1. Notes

Taking notes at a crime scene is not as simple as it might appear. One of the skills taught to a CSI is scientific observation. A CSI would note "large, brownish-red fluid spreading outward from underside of corpse," as opposed to a layperson who might observe a large, brownish-red stain on the carpet that is spreading outward from the body and write down "blood spreading outward from underside of corpse." This fluid may be blood or, at a certain point, decomposition fluid, which has characteristics similar to blood. Mr. Clayton clarifies that presumptions are dangerous, and opinions are irrelevant in crime scene investigation. A CSI reports factual details from a crime scene without making any assumptions.

2.1.2.2. Photographs

Before handling or relocating any evidence, CSIs take pictures of everything. The corpse and its surroundings will be photographed by the CSI before the medical examiner attends to it. A CSI will take three different kinds of photos to record the crime scene: close-ups, mid-views, and overviews.

Overview shots are the widest possible views of the entire scene. If the scene is indoors, this includes:

- views of all rooms (not just the room where the crime seems to have occurred), with photos taken from each corner and, if a boom is present, overhead
- views of the outside of the building where the crime happened, including photos of all entrances and exits
- views of the building showing its relation to surrounding structures
- photos of any spectators at the scene

A potential witness or even a suspect may be identified by these final images. It is not uncommon for criminals to truly go back to the scene of their crimes (arson cases especially).

The mid-range pictures are next. These images present important pieces of evidence in their contextual setting, encompassing not only the evidence itself but also its placement within a room and its separation from other pieces of evidence.

At last, the CSI takes close-ups of specific pieces of evidence to reveal any serial numbers or other distinguishing features. In order to get the greatest detail and clarity for these images, the CSI used a tripod and expert lighting techniques; these particular shots will give the forensics lab views to help with evidence analysis. A second series of close-up photos is also taken by the CSI, this time with a ruler for scale.

All of the images that the CSI takes are included in the photo log. Every photograph's specifics are recorded in this log, including the image number, the object or scene's description, its location, the time and date of the photo's capture, and any other pertinent descriptive information. The value of the scene's photos is greatly diminished in the absence of a strong photo log. Within the framework of John F. Kennedy's murder, the FBI photographers present at the autopsy neglected to annotate the images they were shooting, and subsequently, investigators were unable to discern between entrance and exit wounds in the images.

2.1.2.3. Sketches

CSIs not only take pictures of the scene, but they also draw sketches to show specific areas of the scene that need precise measurements, as well as the entire scene, which is easier to draw than in a photograph because a sketch can span multiple rooms. The objective is to illustrate the locations of the evidence and how each piece of evidence fits into the overall picture. The dimensions of the room, the height of a door frame, the separation between the window and the door, and the diameter of the hole in the wall above the victim's body are a few examples of the details the sketch artist might include.

2.1.2.4. Video

A video walk-through may also be included in scene documentation, particularly in high-profile cases involving multiple homicides or serial killers. A video recording can provide a clearer sense of the crime scene's layout, including how long it takes to get from one room to another and how many turns are necessary. Additionally, as the investigation progresses, it might turn up something that the investigators missed at the scene because they were unaware of where to look. The CSI records the entire crime scene and its environs from all angles during a video walk-through and offers a continuous audio narrative.

It's time to gather the evidence after the CSI has thoroughly documented the crime scene as it was when he arrived. He now begins to touch objects.

No one involved in the investigation, not even police officers, detectives, or crime scene investigators, cleans up the scene after themselves. Relatives of the victim are frequently left to clean up a graphic crime scene.

But over the past 10 years, some have realized how important it is to hire crime-scene cleaners to handle the dirty work so that landlords and family members don't have to, and some of these individuals have started businesthat specialize in this kind of work. It'sIt is an extremely lucrative, sometimes dangerous, and filthy job. In addition to flat fees (which can reach the thousands) and equipment costs, crime-scene cleanup can cost up to $200 per hour. Because of the danger to anyone entering the scene and the amount of work required to restore the area to a livable state, cleaning up a meth lab can be particularly costly.

2.1.3. Finding Crime Evidence

Finding, gathering, and preserving any physical evidence that could be used to reconstruct the crime and identify the offender in a way that will hold up in court is the aim of the evidence-collection stage. There are various forms of evidence (Figure 2.2).

Some typical kinds of evidence a CSI might find at a crime scene include:

- Trace evidence (gunshot residue, paint residue, broken glass, unknown chemicals, drugs)
- Impressions (fingerprints, footwear, tool marks)
- Body fluids (blood, semen, saliva, vomit)
- Hair and fibers
- Weapons and firearms evidence (knives, guns, bullet holes, cartridge casings)
- Questioned documents (diaries, suicide note, phone books; also includes electronic documents like answering machines and caller ID units)

CSIs start their methodical search for incriminating evidence with preconceived notions about the crime in mind, taking careful notes as they go. The search most likely begins at the scene if there is a dead body there.

Figure 2.2. *Forensic specialists of the German police secure the crime scene after a deadly knife attack on May 10, 2016, in Grafing.*

Source. https://encrypted-tbn0.gstatic.com/images?q=tbn:ANd9GcSeO-6MGzQzn a45XQG58zjDLOSLPbam0Od2bA&s.

2.1.3.1. Examining the Body

A CSI may cho to wait until the body as been emoved where it will be is delivered to the morgue oand thenr gather evidence from the body at the scene of the crime. Either way, the CSI takes pictures and thorough notes while at least visually inspecting the body and its surroundings at the scene.

Before moving the body, the CSI makes note of details including:

- Are there any stains or marks on the clothing?
- Is the clothing bunched up in particular direction? If so, this could indicate dragging.
- Are there any bruises, cuts or marks on body? Any defense wounds? Any injuries indicating, consistent with or inconsistent with the preliminary cause of death?
- Is there anything obviously missing? Is there a tan mark where a watch or ring should be?
- If blood is present in large amounts, does the direction of flow follow the laws of gravity? If not, the body may have been moved.
- If no blood is present in the area surrounding the body, is this consistent with the preliminary cause of death? If not, the body may have been moved.

- Are there any bodily fluids present beside blood?
- Is there any insect activity on the body? If so, the CSI may call in a forensic entomologist to analyze the activity for clues as to how long the person has been dead.

He examines the victim's other side in the same manner after moving the body. In order to help determine an estimated time of death, he may now also take the body temperature and the ambient room temperature. However, the majority of forensic scientists argue that time of death determinations are incredibly unreliable because there are too many variables, and the human body is unpredictable. Additionally, he will obtain the deceased's fingerprints at the scene or in the ME's office. After the CSI has finished recording the body's conditions and those of the immediate vicinity, technicians cover the hands and feet of the deceased with paper bags and wrap the body in a white cloth in preparation for the body being taken to the morgue for an autopsy. The goal of these safety measures is to protect any remaining evidence about the victim. Typically, a CSI will be present at the autopsy to take further photos or videos and gather more evidence, particularly tissue samples from important organs for examination in the crime lab.

2.1.3.2. Examining the Scene

A CSI can select from a variety of search patterns to ensure thorough coverage and optimal resource utilization.

- **The Inward Spiral Search:** Working their way toward the center of the scene, the CSI begins at the edges. When there is only one CSI present at the scene, spiral patterns are a useful technique to employ (Figure 2.3).

Figure 2.3. *The inward spiral search.*

Source. https://media.hswstatic.com/eyJidWNrZXQiOiJjb250ZW50Lm-hzd3N0YXRpYy5jb20iLCJrZXkiOiJnaWZcL2NzaS0xMi5qcGciLCJlZGl-0cyI6eyJyZXNpemUiOnsid2lkdGgiOjQwMH0sInRvRm9ybWF0IjoiYXZpZiJ9f-Q==.

- **The Outward Spiral Search:** The CSI starts at the center of scene (or at the body) and works outward (Figure 2.4).

Figure 2.4. *The outward spiral search.*

Source. https://media.hswstatic.com/eyJidWNrZXQiOiJjb250ZW50Lm-hzd3N0YXRpYy5jb20iLCJrZXkiOiJnaWZcL2NzaS0xMS5qcGciLCJlZGl-0cyI6eyJyZXNpemUiOnsid2lkdGgiOjQwMH0sInRvRm9ybWF0IjoiYXZpZiJ9f-Q==.

- **The Parallel Search:** All of the members of the CSI team form a line. They walk in a straight line, at the same speed, from one end of crime scene to the other (Figure 2.5).

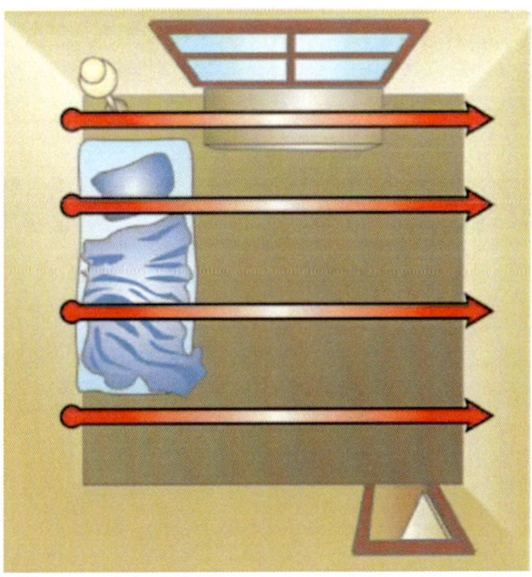

Figure 2.5. *The parallel search.*

Source. https://media.hswstatic.com/eyJidWNrZXQiOiJjb250ZW50Lmhzd-3N0YXRpYy5jb20iLCJrZXkiOiJnaWZcL2NzaS05LmpwZyIsImVkaXRzIjp7InJlc2l-6ZSI6eyJ3aWR0aCI6NDAwfSwidG9Gb3JtYXQiOiJhdmlmIn19.

- **The Grid Search:** A grid search is simply two parallel searches, offset by 90°, performed one after the other (Figure 2.6).

Figure 2.6. *The grid search.*

Source. https://media.hswstatic.com/eyJidWNrZXQiOiJjb250ZW50Lm-hzd3N0YXRpYy5jb20iLCJrZXkiOiJnaWZcL2NzaS0xMy5qcGciLCJlZGl-0cyI6eyJyZXNpemUiOnsid2lkdGgiOjQwMH0sInRvRm9ybWF0IjoiYXZpZiJ9f-Q==.

- **The Zone Search:** In a zone search, the CSI in charge divides the crime scene into sectors, and each team member takes one sector. Team members may then switch sectors and search again to ensure complete coverage (Figure 2.7).

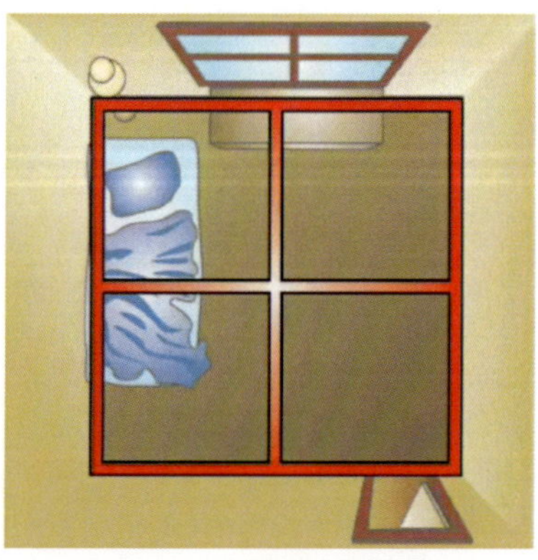

Figure 2.7. *The zone search.*

Source. https://media.hswstatic.com/eyJidWNrZXQiOiJjb250ZW50Lm-hzd3N0YXRpYy5jb20iLCJrZXkiOiJnaWZcL2NzaS0xMC5qcGciLCJlZGl-0cyI6eyJyZXNpemUiOnsid2lkdGgiOjQwMH0sInRvRm9ybWF0IjoiYXZpZiJ9f-Q==.

While searching the scene, a CSI is looking for details including:

- Are the doors and windows locked or unlocked? Open or shut? Are there signs of forced entry, such as tool marks or broken locks?
- Is the house in good order? If not, does it look like there was a struggle or was the victim just messy?
- Is there mail lying around? Has it been opened?
- Is the kitchen in good order? Is there any partially eaten food? Is the table set? If so, for how many people?
- Are there signs of a party, such as empty glasses or bottles or full ashtrays?
- If there are full ashtrays, what brands of cigarettes are present? Are there any lipstick or teeth marks on the butts?
- Is there anything that seems out of place? A glass with lipstick marks in a man's apartment, or the toilet seat up in a woman's apartment? Is there a couch blocking a doorway?
- Is there trash in the trash cans? Is there anything out of the ordinary in the trash? Is the trash in the right chronological order according to dates on mail and other papers? If not, someone might have been looking for something in the victim's trash.
- Do the clocks show the right time?
- Are the bathroom towels wet? Are the bathroom towels missing? Are there any signs of a cleanup?
- If the crime is a shooting, how many shots were fired? The CSI will try to locate the gun, each bullet, each shell casing and each bullet hole.
- If the crime is a stabbing, is a knife obviously missing from victim's kitchen? If so, the crime may not have been premeditated.
- Are there any shoe prints on tile, wood or linoleum floors or in the area immediately outside the building?
- Are there any tire marks in te driveway or in the area around the building?
- Is there any blood splatter on floors, walls, or ceilings?

Physical evidence collection is a laborious process. Every item that the CSI gathers has to be preserved right away, tagged, and recorded for the crime scene file. Depending on the circumstances and available resources, various forms of evidence may be gathered at the scene or in a laboratory. For example, Mr. Clayton never leaves the scene with latent fingerprints. He consistently sends fingerprints to the lab for analysis in a regulated setting. We will discuss how to collect certain kinds of evidence in the next section.

1. Crime scenes are three-dimensional. CSIs should remember to look up.a CSI shines a flashlight on the ground at various angles, even when there'sthere is ty of lighting, he'll create new shadows that could reveal evidence.
2. It'sIt is easy to recover DNA from cigarette butts.

2.1.4. Evidence Collection

The CSI has multiple objectives when gathering evidence from a crime scene: reconstructing the crime, identifying the perpetrator, preserving the evidence for examination, and gathering it in a manner that will be admissible in court.

2.1.4.1. Trace Evidence

Gunshot residue (GSR), paint residue, chemicals, glass, and illegal drugs are a few examples of trace evidence. A CSI may use tweezers, knife, filtered vacuum device, and plastic containers with lids to gather trace evidence. In addition, a biohazard kit with a face mask, gown, disposable latex gloves, booties, and a biohazard waste bag will be available for him.

In cases where a gun is used in the crime, the CSI will gather clothing from the victim and any witnesses so that the lab can perform a GSR test. A close shot may be indicated by GSR on the victim, and a suspect may be indicated by GSR on anybody else. All clothing is placed in sealed paper bags by the CSI before being brought to the lab. He can use a knife to gather any illegal drugs or unidentified powders that he finds at the scene, and he can then seal each sample in a different, sterile container. The substance can be identified, its purity can be assessed, and trace amounts of other substances can be seen in the sample. These tests could identify drug use, drug tampering, or whether the substance could have rendered a victim incapable of life or fatal.

When technicians shake out bedding, clothes, towels, couch cushions, and other items found at the scene, they find a lot of the trace evidence for a crime in the lab. In a sterile room at the CBI Denver Crime Lab, technicians shake out the items onto a sizable white slab that is covered in paper.

Any trace evidence that the technicians find is then forwarded to the relevant department. Items such as dirt, glass, and paint are kept in the trace-evidence lab at the Denver Crime Lab; illegal drugs and other unidentified substances are sent to the chemistry lab; hair is sent to the DNA lab.

2.1.4.2. Body Fluids

Blood, urine, semen, and vomit are examples of bodily fluids that may be discovered at a crime scene. A CSI may utilize smear slides, a scalpel, tweezers, scissors, sterile cloth squares, a UV light, safety goggles, and luminol to locate and gather these pieces of evidence. In order to obtain samples for comparison, he will also utilize a blood collection kit to obtain blood from any suspects or from a live victim.

The CSI takes a blood sample from a deceased victim if there is blood on the body. They can do this by submitting a piece of clothing or by removing some blood from the body with a sterile cloth square and a small amount of distilled water. The lab will do DNA analysis on the blood or saliva taken from the body because it might belong to someone else. This will allow the sample to be compared to blood or saliva taken from a suspect in the future. In order to obtain skin samples, the CSI will also scrape the victim's nails. If there was a struggle, the victim's nails may have contained the suspect's skin, and thus, DNA. The CSI will attempt to send the entire piece of furniture to the lab if there is dried blood on it at the 's not unusual to gather evidence in the form of couches. If the blood is on an object that shouldn'tshould not be taken to the lab, like a wall or bathtub, the CSI can gather it by using a scalpel to scrape the blood into a sterile container. A portable UV light and luminol may also be used by thc CSI to dctcct blood that has bccn washcd off a surfacc.

There might be patterns of blood spatter if there is blood at the scene. These patterns can identify the kind of weapon that was used. For example, when a baseball bat hits a blood source and then swings back, it leaves behind a "cast-off pattern." The droplets are big and frequently have a teardrop shape. This kind of pattern can show that a blunt object was used more than once because the first blow usually does not make contact with any blood. In contrast, a "high-energy pattern" consisting of numerous small droplets could potentially signify a gunshot. An analysis of blood spatter can reveal the direction of the blood flow as well as the number of individual incidents that contributed to the pattern. Examining the stain's size and shape, the blood droplets' size and shape, and their concentration within the pattern are all important aspects of blood pattern analysis. The pattern is photographed by the CSI, who may then bring in a blood-spatter expert to examine it.

2.1.4.3. Hair and Fibers

A CSI can gather any hair or fibers at the scene using combs, tweezers, containers, and a filtered vacuum device. When a live victim of rape is involved, the victim's family is escorted to the hospital by the CSI in order to collect any hairs or fibers discovered during the victim's physical examination. Any hair or fiber evidence is sealed by the CSI and sent to a different container for analysis.

Carpet fibers may be found in a suspect's shoes by a CSI. These fibers can be compared to carpet fibers from the victim's house by the lab. By comparison, analysts can use hair DNA to identify or rule out suspects. A tool or weapon can be recognized as the one used in the crime if it has hair on it. The crime lab can identify the kind of animal (human, dog, cow, etc.) from which the hair originated; if the hair originates from a human, analysts can identify the race of the individual, the area of the body from which it was removed or fell out, and whether or not it was dyed.

2.1.4.4. Fingerprints

Super Glue, brushes, powders, tape, chemicals, lift cards, and magnifying glasses are some of the tools used to recover fingerprints. Fingerprints can be used by a crime lab to identify the victim, identify a suspect, or rule them out. There are several types of prints a CSI might find at a crime scene:

- **Visible**: Left by the transfer of blood, paint or another fluid or powder onto a surface that is smooth enough to hold the print; evident to the naked eye
- **Molded**: Left in a soft medium like soap, putty or candle wax, forming an impression
- **Latent**: Left by the transfer of sweat and natural oils from the fingers onto a surface that is smooth enough to hold the print; not visible to the naked eye

Prints from the offender may appear on porous or nonporous surfaces. Glass, plastic, and metal are nonporous surfaces, whereas paper, unfinished wood, and cardboard are porous surfaces that can accommodate an imprint.

Figure 2.8. *Powders and brushes at the CBI latent-fingerprint lab.*

Source. https://media.hswstatic.com/eyJidWNrZXQiOiJjb250ZW50Lmhzd3N0YXRpYy5jb20iLCJrZXkiOiJnaWZcL2NzaS1wb3dkZXIuanBnIiwiZWRpdHMiOnsicmVzaXplIjp7IndpZHRoIjoyODV9LCJ0b0Zvcm1hdCI6ImF2aWYifX0=.

Usually, a CSI will check surfaces that the offender is likely to have touched for latent prints. For example, it makes sense to search for prints on the outside doorknob and door surface if the front door exhibits indications of forced entry. A latent print may become momentarily visible on a surface if one breathes on it or shines an intense amount of light on it. A latent print is most likely destroyed when a TV detective uses a handkerchief to turn a doorknob. On a nonporous surface, the only way to prevent tampering with a latent print is to avoid touching it. Proper methods for recovering latent prints include (Figure 2.8):

2.1.4.5. Powder (for Nonporous Surfaces)

A CSI uses the powder that contrasts the most with the color of the material holding the print, be it velvet black powder or metallic silver powder. When a print appears, he lightly applies powder to the surface in a circular motion. He then begins brushing in the direction of the ridges in the print. He takes a picture of the print and then lifts it with tape so that it will be more durable in court. He attaches clear tape to the powdered print, smoothly pulls it back, and then attaches it to a fingerprint card that is colored differently from the powder.

Chemicals (for porous surfaces): Iodine, ninhydrin, silver nitrate The CSI sprays the chemical onto the surface of the material or dips the material into a chemical solution to reveal the latent print.

Figure 2.9. *This cast is a student sample. According to Mr. Clayton, footprints found at a crime scene seldom produce such perfect specimens.*

Source. https://media.hswstatic.com/eyJidWNrZXQiOiJjb250ZW50Lmhzd-3N0YXRpYy5jb20iLCJrZXkiOiJnaWZcL2NzaS1mb290d2Vhci5qcGciLCJlZGl-0cyI6eyJyZXNpemUiOnsid2lkdGgiOjI4NX0sInRvRm9ybWF0IjoiYXZpZiJ9fQ==.

Cyanoacrylate (Super Glue) fuming (for porous or nonporous surfaces) In a metal plate, the CSI pours Super Glue and heats it to around 120°F. After that, he puts the object holding the latent print, the plate, and the heat source in an airtight container. The Super Glue fumes reveal the latent print without causing any damage to the material it is on (Figure 2.9).

2.1.4.6. Footwear Impressions and Tool Marks

One example of a two-dimensional impression is a latent fingerprint. Three-dimensional impressions include tool marks on windowsills and footprints left in mud. A CSI makes a casting at the scene if it is not possible to send the entire object containing the impression to the crime lab. A casting kit may contain a bowl, a spatula, several casting compounds (silicone rubber, dental gypsum), snow wax (to make a cast in the snow), and cardboard boxes to store the casts.

A CSI will take a picture of any footprints left in the mud by shoes and then cast the impression. She uses a Ziploc-style bag to combine a casting material and water, and she kneads the mixture for about two minutes, until it has the consistency of pancake batter. After that, she pours the mixture into the track's edge, ensuring that no air bubbles form as it flows into the impression. She lets the material settle for at least half an hour after it fills the impression completely, and then she gently removes the cast from the mud. She places the cast in a paper bag or cardboard box to be transported to the lab without cleaning it or brushing anything off of it because doing so would destroy any traces of evidence.

It is far more difficult to use a cast for comparison with toolmark impressions than it is with footwear. If moving the complete object with the tool mark is not practical, a CSI can create a silicone-rubber cast and cross their fingers. There are two types of tool marks a CSI might find at a crime scene:

- **Impressed**: A hard object contacts a softer object withomoving back and forth (for example, a hammer mark on a door frame). The tool mark is an impression of the tool's shape. It is's difficult to make a definite match with an impressed tool mark.
- **Striated**: A hard object contacts a softer object and moves back and forth (for example, pry marks on a window frame). The tool mark is a series of parallel lines. It's easier to make a definite match with a striated tool mark.

The lab may ascertain whether a tool in evidence is the tool that made the mark and what kind of tool made the mark through toolmark analysis. In order to ascertain whether the marks were created by the same tool, it can also compare the tool mark found in the evidence to another toolmark.

2.1.4.7. Firearms

A CSI puts on gloves, picks up the gun by the barrel (not the grip), and bags everything separately for the lab if she finds any firearms, bullets, or casings at the scene. In addition to matching bullets and casings from the weapon from which they were fired, forensic scientists are also able to recover serial numbers and match bullets and casings from other crime scenes around the state (the majority of ballistics databases are statewide). Using a laser trajectory kit, experts can ascertain the location and height of the bullet's discharge, along with the victim's position at the time of impact, when there are bullet holes in the victim or other objects at the scene. The CSI removes the section of a wall or door frame that has a bullet embedded in it because digging the bullet out could damage the material and render it unfit for comparison.

2.1.4.8. Documents

Any diaries, planners, phone books, or suicide notes discovered at a crime scene are gathered and preserved by a CSI. Along with any other written, typed, or photocopied evidence that may be connected to the crime, he also brings any signed contracts, receipts, and a torn-up letter found in the trash to the lab. A document lab can frequently identify whether a document has been altered or destroyed, including ones that have been burned. Technicians examine documents for signs of forgery, ascertain whether the victim's and the suspects' handwriting matches, and pinpoint the kind of machine that produced the document. They can determine whether a machine found in a suspect's possession is compatible or incompatible with a printer or photocopier that was ruled out at the scene.

When a CSI finds evidence at a scene, she records it with photos, logs it, recovers it, and tags it. An evidence tag can simply display a serial number that matches to an entry in the evidence log that contains this information, or it can include identification information like the time, date, and precise location of the recovery as well as who recovered the item. The photo log, evidence recovery log, written report detailing the crime scene investigation, and all other evidence recovered from the scene are all documented in the crime scene report.

2.2. CRIME SCENE MANAGEMENT

Proficiency in crime scene management is crucial to the investigation process, as evidence gathered there will paint a picture of the events that the court will review during its proceedings. This image will be made up of witness accounts, photos taken at the crime scene, tangible exhibits, and an examination of each of those items in addition to an examination of the crime scene itself. You will discover the procedures and guidelines for handling various significant matters related to crime scene management by reading this chapter. These include:

1. Note taking
2. Securing a crime scene
3. Evidence management
4. Scaling the investigation to the event

2.2.1. Note Taking

The notebook will be the most important document to the investigator, even though they will create other documents to manage the crime scene. The investigator uses the notebook as a personal record of the investigation.

Many variations of police notebooks have emerged over the years. The court will sometimes even accept police notes that have been made on a scrap of paper if that was the only paper available at the time. However, beyond extreme circumstances, in nvestigations, the accepted parameters of a police notes and notebooks are:

- A book with a cover page that shows the investigatorsinvestigator's name, the date the notebook was started, and the date the notebook was concluded
- Sequential page numbers
- A bound booklet from which pages cannot be torn without detection
- Lined pages that allow for neat scripting of notes
- Each entry into the notebook should start with a time, date, and case reference
- Blank spaces on pages should not be left between entries and, if a blank space is left, it should be filled with a single line drawn through the space or a diagonal line drawn across a page or partial page space
- Any errors made in the notebook should only be crossed out with a single line drawn through the error, and this should not be done in a manner that makes the error illegible

The investigator's notebook serr most useful source material in court. The court will permit an investigator to review notes taken during the incident in order toto refresh their memory of what happened and what was done. Upon reviewing an investigator's notebook, the court can be given a circumstantial assurance that the evidence is truthful and accurate if the notes align with the investigator's testimony (McRory, 2014). Alternatively, the defense will examine the evidence more closely if important parts of the investigation are not properly documented or are absent from the notebook. In determining proof beyond a reasonable doubt, the court may give those unrecorded facts less weight in its final considerations.

Good notes provide an investigator with a summary of what they have seen, heard, and done. An order of events from the notes shows the investigator's mental map of the information that was used to establish probable cause for an arrest and charges. Court cases are frequently drawn out by appeals, adjournments, or suspects eluding immediate capture. This may result in a several-year delay between the investigation and the trial. It becomes essential for the investigator to have thorough notes that accurately reflect their investigation in these drawn-out cases in order to jog their memory of the facts.

Even though notepads are essential, cop training frequently places too little emphasis on note-taking techniques. The majority of police investigators learn their note-taking techniques and interpersonal skills via on-the-job training and the "trial by fire" of cross-examination in court. The wide range of situations in which note-taking is required and the impossibility of foreseeing which facts will become crucial in every scenario are probably the causes of this gap in note-taking instruction. So, in order for investigators to become skilled at knowing what to write in their notebook, a mix of education, experience, and common sense will be needed.

It is necessary to provide some clarification on the definition of "notes made at the time of an event," as it is somewhat misleading. In a perfect world, an investigator could work through an investigation with an open notebook, noting down every fact and observation as it happened. It goes without saying that events have a dynamic and unpredictable course. In many cases, an investigator must devote all of their attention to controlling a situation while preserving people's lives and well-being. An open notebook has no place in these situations, and it is evident that the investigator is not taking any notes at that moment. However, notes will be taken as soon as it is practical and after the incident is under control. Though notes taken at the time are usually cited in court, in reality, the notes are those taken as soon as it is practical given the particulars of the incident.

The operational dynamics that exist for investigators are accepted by the courts, and occasionally the question of when the notes were actually composed comes up during the trial. An investigator should therefore be ready to respond to this query at all times. A note in the notebook indicating the start and end times of the note-taking serves as a point of reference to show that the issue is being acknowledged and attended to.

The problem of facts missed and then remembered after the initial notes are finished is another problem associated with the notes taken at the time. There are defects and limitations in human memory. Occasionally, after finishing the first draft of their notes, an investigator will realize at a later date that they overlooked something important. It is inappropriate to go back to the pages of notes taken at the time and try to insert the remembered details on such occasions. The correct procedure for documenting these subsequent fact recalls is to initiate a new note page right away, utilizing the current date and time, citing the prior case notes, prior time, date, and page number, and recording the newly remembered fact or facts. Defense counsel will scrutinize these types of recalled facts and late entries closely, and in some cases, it can be useful if the investigator notes the fact or circumstances that precipitated the recollection of the additional information. After the situation has been brought under control, investigators are often seen carefully recording their memories of what happened. Anyone who has ever been involved in a critical incident—where life and safety have taken precedence—will attest to this.

The following strategies are recommended as a general guide to note taking:

1. Start notes by creating a big picture perspective and then move from the general to the more specific observations. In this big picture, you are creating a perspective of the facts that you have been made aware of to begin an investigation. These big picture facts become the starting point of your mental map of events, and these facts will be the framework to begin thinking about offense recognition and forming reasonable grounds to believe and take action.
2. In more specific terms, and to the extent it is possible, begin recording all dates, times, and descriptions of persons, places, and vehicles as they emerge. You may, in fact, have already started a page in your notebook where some exact times, addresses, license plate numbers, names or persons, and perhaps even blurted statements from a suspect have been jotted down. It is acceptable to use these key pieces of jotted information already recorded to enlarge your detailed notes at the end of the event in a more complete fashion.
3. Record the identities of persons encountered and how the identity of each person was verified. For example: Witness Jane Doe (DOB: 8 May 64) 34345–8 St Anywhere BC Photo drivers license ID
4. Record all statements made by witnesses and victims to reflect an accurate account of the information being conveyed. It is often not possible to record every statement made verbatim in notes, and, in most cases, it is not necessary. Today, technology makes it possible to digitally record the verbatim account being provided by a witness

or a victim. But, merely digitally recording a statement is not sufficient, since statements will frequently form considerations in establishing reasonable grounds for belief to take action. Recording the critical details being conveyed will provide a written record of the facts considered to form reasonable grounds for belief.

5. If a person is a suspect or is a person who may become a suspect, make every effort to record any statements made by that person verbatim. Suspects will often be found at the scene of a crime posing as a witness or even as a victim. Accurately recording the initial statements made by such a person can produce evidence of guilt in the form of statements that are provably false or even incriminating.

It is each investigator's individual duty to record their own interpretation and memory of the event they are seeing as it happens. When investigators work together to produce a version of events that is agreed upon and then write their notes to reflect that version of events, the notes are no longer the individual investigator's personal memory and may be examined as a group version of events intended to produce evidence that does not accurately reflect the facts as each investigator saw them.

Collaborating and taking group notes is sometimes referred to as "boxing of notes," and defense teams may find evidence of this practice if the format and content of each investigator's notebook are nearly or exactly the same. One of the investigative practices' flaws that has been linked to injustices is the boxing of notes practice (Salhany, 2008). Therefore, it is best to avoid having investigators collaborate while taking notes. Any time there is a cooperative effort to revisit a problem and reexamine tangible evidence to make the point more clear for each investigator, it should be documented as part of each investigator's notes.

Even with this warning against group note-taking, there are situations in which it is appropriate to use a group note-taking process. This happens during extensive operations with a large number of participants, occasionally under the direction of an EOC. In these situations, the participants in the command center must devote all of their attention to managing the event, which may take hours or days. It would be inefficient and possibly erroneous for each participant to wait until the lengthy event is over before taking their own notes. As a replacement for taking individual notes in these situations, it is now standard operating procedure to designate one person in the command center to serve as the collective note-maker. In these cases, the person taking notes is referred to as "The Scribe." The Scribe does not take notes in a standard notebook so that those in the command center are aware of what is being noted. In these situations, the notes are written on sizable flipchart paper sheets, which are then posted onto the command center's wall so that each participant can review the information and confirm that it is accurate. The scribe saves the note pages as an exhibit and photographs the entire set of notes at the conclusion of the procedure. The participants usually initial each page. Each command center participant may accept these notes as a legal reference document under this procedure.

2.2.2. Integrity of the Crime Scene

As part of crime scene management, protecting the integrity of the crime scene involves several specific processes that fall under the Tasks category of the STAIR Tool. These are tasks that must be performed by the investigator to identify, collect, preserve, and protect evidence to ensure that it will be accepted by the court. These tasks include:

a. Locking down the crime scene
b. Setting up crime scene perimeters
c. Establishing a path of contamination
d. Establishing crime scene security

When a criminal event is found to have become inactive and the investigator has shifted to a strategic investigative response, the need to protect the crime scene becomes necessary when the investigator arrives at the scene. As you may remember from the Response Transition Matrix, investigators occasionally enter tactical investigative response mode when they arrive at an ongoing incident. Protecting people's lives and safety in these situations comes first; keeping the crime scene and any relevant evidence safe comes second. That is not to say that investigators working in tactical investigative response mode should be careless with evidence or completely disregard it if it can be protected; rather, the court will accept the situation if evidence cannot be protected during tactical investigative response mode.

The court's expectations regarding the preservation of the crime scene and the evidence will alter as soon as the event turns into an inactive incident with a calculated investigative response. Because of this modification, the investigator must take charge of the crime scene and lock it down right away.

2.2.2.1. Locking Down the Crime Scene

At the end of the active event, first responders, witnesses, victims, or the arrested suspect are frequently still inside the crime scene when the shift to a strategic investigative response is identified. Up until now, all of these individuals have been involved in activities at the crime scene that may have contaminated it in different ways. Locking down a crime scene entails stopping any ongoing activity there and requiring everyone to leave and find a place to escape the area surrounding the crime scene. Following the evacuation of all individuals from the scene, the perimeter of the crime scene is physically sealed off with police tape. Creating a crime scene perimeter is the process of marking the boundaries of the scene with tape. Locking down the crime scene is the process of enclosing the scene within a defined perimeter.

2.2.2.2. Crime Scene Perimeter

The investigator determines how large the crime scene must be; the crime scene perimeter establishes the scene's dimensions. The area where the criminal acts have occurred typically determines the size of a crime scene. This covers every location in the scene where the suspect has interacted or engaged in activity, including entry and exit points. Areas where the suspect and victim interacted are anothefine the perimeter. The investigator may need to designate one sizable crime scene or multiple smaller crime scene areas in order toto establish crime scene perimeters in situations where there has been prolonged interapect and a victim over time, whether that interaction took place over a distance or in multiple locations. After taking into accountconsidering the three phases of originating evidence, an investigator might discover that additional crime scenes need to be taken into account, or that pre-crime or post-crime activity necessitates the crime scene perimeter to encircle a larger area.

Creating a crime scene perimeter that defines access is simple for certain crime scenes that have natural barriers, like buildings with doorways. This gets more difficult in outdoor or large indoor public venues where perimeters may need to be defined with tape markers, fencing, and barricades.

Ensuring that no unauthorized individuals cross the crime scene perimeter after it has been established and locked down is imperative. Usually, and ideally, the entry point for the path of contamination will be the onlyaccess to the crime scene.

2.2.2.3. Path of Contamination

A crime scene's potential for contamination cannot be completely eliminatedeliminated. The only thing we can do is try to prevent further contamination from compromising the forensic integrity of the exhibits and the crime scene. After all victims, witnesses, suspects, first responders, and investigators have been removed from the crime scene, it is vital to document in notes or statements the contamination each individual brought to the scene. Documentation of the evidence being gathered will show what has been moved, how it has been handled, and by whom. The investigator can determine the baseline or current contamination status at the crime scene using this informatioht still be able to obtain a valid analysis of an item if it was handled or moved in a way that contaminated it prior to the lock downlockdown, prthat the contamination can be identified and measured. For instance, paramedics have occasionally been on the scene tending to injuredinjure people in cases of severe assaults or even murders. Non-suspect-related DNA transfer between individuals and exhibits mayhile this treatment is underway. One of the first steps in determining the level of contamination that existed at the time of lock downlockdown is to ascertain those possibilities. The next step is to create a desied pathway so that authorized personnel can re-enter the crime scene to carry out their investigative duties now that everyone has leftleft, and the perimeter has been secured. Once the crime scene has been secured, the first investigator to reenter it creates what is known as a "path of contamination." Before reentering, the first investigator will take a picture of the area where the contamination path is expected to extend. Then, the investigator will enter the area while wearing sterile crime scene gear and mark the floor with tape to indicate the path that other investigators must follow. When designing this pathway, the primary investigator will take care to avoid putting it in the way of evidently already-existing evidence and will only place it where it is necessary to obtain a physical view of the entire crime scene. Other investigators and forensic specialists will remain within the path of contamination as they enter the crime scene to carry out their duties. When they leave the path to carry out a specific duty of investigation or examination, they will document their departure from the path and be ready to explain any new contamination they may have caused, such as dusting for fingerprints or removing exhibits.

2.2.2.4. Crime Scene Security

In addition to delineating the crime scene with perimeter tape, a security system must be put in place to guarantee that no unauthorized person or people enter and contaminate the area. A crime scene security officer is tasked with controlling who enters and exits the crime scene in order to achieve this goal. It becomes the assigned security officer's responsibility to guard the crime scene and grant access to only those who are authorized to conduct investigations there. These persons might include:

- Forensic specialists
- Search team members
- Assigned investigators, and/or
- The coroner in the case of a sudden death investigation

Every authorized person entering and leaving the crime scene signs in and out with a brief note explaining their reason for entry, and a document called a "Crime Scene Security Log" is created to keep track of who is coming and going. The crime scene security officer should confront anyone entering or attempting to enter without authorization. If the person is unwilling to leave, they may be taken into custody, removed from the area, and charged with obstructing a police officer.

The Crime Security Log, which can take many forms, must be created and kept up to date by the designated security officer. One page in the security officer's notepad may be all that is needed for a short-term, small-scale investigation; but, for a long-term, large-scale investigation, the log may contain several pages that are handled by multiple assigned security officers who work in shifts. The security log, regardless of its size or format, keeps track of who was present, when they were there, why they were there, and when they left. The example below shows a sample of a crime scene security log (Figure 2.10).

CRIME SCENE SECURITY LOG

ASSIGNED SCENE
SECURITY OFFICER________________ DATE________________

POLICE DEPT________________ FILE NUMBER________________

CRIME SCENE LOCATION ________________________________

Name & Rank	Initials	Date/Time In	Date/Time Out	Duties on Crime Scene	Contamination Caused

Figure 2.10. *Crime scene security log.*

Source. https://pressbooks.bccampus.ca/criminalinvestigation/wp-content/uploads/sites/162/2017/05/CRIME-SCENE-SECURITY-LOG.jpg.

2.2.3. Evidence Management

Analysis is the process that must take place in order to establish links between the victims, witnesses, and suspects in relation to the criminal event, as we have already learned in the STAIR tool. Since the crime scene is frequently the hub of those events, gathering evidence there must be done methodically to ensure that it will be accepted in court. Through evidence transfers, exhibit hair, fiber, fingerprints, and other items requiring forensic analysis can show spatial relationships. Additional physical evidence kindsevidence could provide chronologies and oblique hints about intent, availability, or means. Every piece of evidence found in the actual surroundings of the crime scene is vital to the investigation. The two biggest obstacles to physical evidence at any crime scene are loss of continuity and contamination.

2.2.3.1. Contamination of Evidence

Unauthorized evidence alteration that compromises the original exhibit's integrity or compromises the crime scene's integrity is known as contamination. Unintentional evidence alteration has the potential to remove original evidence transfers, dilute samples, or add deceptive new materials to exhibits. Contamination can undermine the analysis of the initial evidence transfer to the point where the court may reject the analysis and any inference that the analysis might have otherwise demonstrated, much as evidence transfer between a suspect and the crime scene or the suspect and the victim can establish a circumstantial connection.

Contamination can take place in any number of ways including:

- Police or other first responders interfering with evidence during a tactical investigative response
- Suspects interfering with the crime scene to cover up or remove evidence
- Victims or witnesses handling evidence
- Animals, including pets, causing unwanted transfer of evidence or even removal of evidence through contact or consumption
- Weather-related contamination due to rain, wind, or snow diluting or washing away evidence, or
- Crime scene investigators failing to follow proper crime scene management procedures and causing contamination of exhibits or cross-contamination between exhibits during their investigation

For investigators, contamination is an inevitable part of the job; prior to the scene becoming inactive and the authorities being able to lock it down, there will always be some level of contamination. While issues of life and safety are at risk, the court will accept that some contamination is outside the control of the investigator. Once the crime scene is contained and under control, that tolerance for managing contamination shifts dramatically. Crime scene management protocols need to be implemented after the scene has been secured. Crime scene contamination presents three challenges for investigators, namely:

1. Preventing contamination when possible;
2. Controlling ongoing contamination; and

3. Recording the known contamination that has taken place

The word "control" is used in the phrase "control ongoing contamination" because investigators can only try to control ongoing contamination—they cannot completely eradicate it. It is imperative to identify and document any known contamination. In the event that contamination has occurred, it may still be possible to salvage the analysis of contaminated exhibits by identifying and explaining the contamination.

Investigators must take into account the potential for continuous contamination during the crucial time between the crime scene's lockdown and getting a warrant to search it. Under emergency circumstances, the investigator may re-enter the crime scene without a warrant in order to take the necessary precautions to stop or prevent contamination and protect the evidence, provided that there are reasonable grounds to believe that the evidence will be destroyed or damaged by some threat of contamination.

Contamination occurs during the entire process of gathering evidence, including the actual act of going into the crime scene. Preserving the forensic integrity of the crime scene and related exhibits is the aim of managing continuous contamination. Crime scene management protocols are crucial to the investigative process because of this objective.

2.2.3.2. Loss of Continuity

Similar to limiting contamination, protocols for establishing and preserving evidence continuity safeguard its integrity. The judge must be convinced that the exhibit being shown is the same item that was removed from the crime scene in order for any evidence to be accepted by the court. In order to establish "the chain of continuity," which follows each exhibit from the crime scene to the courtroom, evidence must be provided.

The investigator's testimony verifying that the exhibit being shown is the same one that was taken from the crime scene will serve as the proof of continuity. The investigator's demonstration of their markings on the exhibit or its container to the court substantiates this testimony. In addition to the investigator's initials and the time, date, and location of the item's transportation and lockup in the main exhibit holding locker, these markings will also include a notebook entry. An exhibit log that documents the exhibit's location at the crime scene, the person who found it there, and the supporting initials of any other individuals who handled the exhibit while it was being transported from the crime scene to the main exhibit locker serves as additional evidence in support of this claim. The signatures, time, and date of any additional handlers of the item must be recorded along with the exhibit's removal from the main exhibit locker for inspection or analysis. Any individual who has worked with the exhibit must be qualified to testify and offer testimony that upholds the exhibit's continuity. These are basic but essential procedures. Exhibits that are excluded due to lost continuity may be the consequence of not adhering to them strictly.

2.2.3.3. Attention to Originating Stages of Evidence

Determining the location of the criminal event or the extent of the event is one of the major chales in crime scene management. The investigator is given the locations of potential crime scene evidence by making these determinations. It'sIt is frequently not as easy as simply going to one place or reflecting on the criminal incident for a short period of time. There are three time periods during the investigation process where evidence may come from. The stages in question are the pre-crime, criminal event, and post-crime phases.

These three phases of criminal activity may also indicate that there may be additional areas outside of the immediate crime scene where criminal activity and evidence may have also occurred. The important thing to keep in mind regarding the evidence's initial stages is that they all present opportunities to gather information that might link the suspect to the crime. All these phases of the criminal event should be taken into account when developing a theory or designing an investigation strategy.

1. **The Pre-Crime Stage** occurs when evidence of preparation or planning can be found during the investigation. It can include notes, research, drawings, crime supplies or pre-crime contact with the victim or accomplices. Sometimes items of pre-crime origin, such as hair and fiber, will be later discovered at the crime scene creating an opportunity to link the suspect back to the crime.
2. **The Criminal Event Stage** is when the most interaction takes place between the criminal and the victim, or the criminal and the crime scene. During these interactions, the best possibilities for evidence transfer occur. Even the most careful criminals have been known to leave behind some trace of their identity in the form of fingerprints, shoe prints, glove prints, tire marks, tool impressions, shell casings, hair or fiber, or DNA.
3. **The Post-Crime Stage** occurs when the suspect is departing the crime scene. When leaving the crime scene, suspects have been known to cast off items of evidence that can be recovered and examined to establish their identity. This post-crime period is also the stage where the suspect becomes concerned with cleaning up the scene. As much as a suspect may attempt to clean up, evidence

transfers from the crime scene are often overlooked. These can range from hair and fiber on clothing to shards of glass on shoes. Frequently found post-crime are proceeds of the crime. These are often identifiable articles of stolen property with unique marks, victim DNA, serial numbers, or sometimes even trophies that the criminal takes as a keepsake (Figure 2.11).

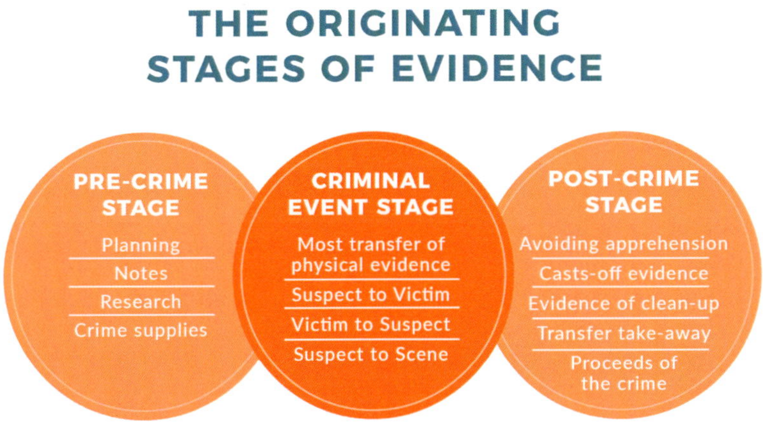

Figure 2.11. *Stages of the criminal event.*

Source. https://pressbooks.bccampus.ca/criminalinvestigation/wp-content/uploads/sites/162/2017/05/Img-07–1024x636.png.

Not every piece of information that seems to be complete and ready to link or imply the guilt of a suspect is evidence. Timelines, spatial relationships, and evidence transfers between the initial stages of the evidence are frequently how it all comes together to form circumstantial pictures that show the identity of the suspect, the crime's fact pattern, opportunity, means, motive, and intent.

2.2.3.4. Enhancing the Value of Evidence Recovered

Physical evidence, sometimes called exhibits, has two distinct levels of investigative value for investigators. Each physical exhibit has a face value at the first level, which is defined by its characteristics and the location within the crime scene. For instance, a bloody shoeprint discovered on the ground at a crime scene indicates that someone entered the arin a specific direction, and transferred blood from a source onto their shoe. These are basic interpretations of the evidence that we are able tocan piece together from our own observations. This same bloody shoeprint might be the subject of forensic analyzes at a later stage, which might yield more details. For instance, a positive match to a suspect's shoe may be made through analysis of the shoeprint pattern, size, and accidental characteristics; similarly, blood samples may be antermine whether the samples match the DNA of a victim or another original source. These initial and secondary level values can both be very helpfulextremely helpful in reconstructing and interpreting the events that occurred at the crime scene.

The physical evidence that must be inspected, taken, and recorded at every crime scene is one of the investigators' top priorities. Finding and recording all of the information and evidence that is available to investigators is one of their biggest challenges, as was previously mentioned. This begs the crucial questions of what will be significant and what will eventually become evidence.

There are some general practices that can be followed, but most seasoned investigators follow the guiding principle of evidence collection to err on the side of caution when determining which items within the crime scene need to be considered and taken as possible evidence when the suspect and the fact-pattern are not immediately apparent. Always prefer more than less. To assist in deciding what could possibly become relevant, investigators need to consider:

- Items that the suspect may have touched or interacted with
- Items that a victim may have touched or interacted with
- Items that the suspect may have brought to the crime scene
- Items that may have passed between the suspect and the victim
- Items that the suspect may have taken from the crime scene
- Items that the suspect may have discarded while departing the crime scene

It is frequently impossible to go back and retrieve lost evidence after the crime scene has been cleared out and left in an open area following the crime scene examination. It is preferable to gather all information that may be relevant at some point in the future.

After the crime scene has been cordoned off and secured, it should be viewed as the first major exhibit in the evidence search process. It must be subjected to documentation using photos, videos, measurements, and diagrams because it is the first large exhibit. There may be other, smaller, and potentially related exhibits hidden within this first, larger exhibit. The items located and their locations can reveal spatial relationships of interaction, providing evidence in favor of a series of events. Investigators will be able to confirm witness and victim accounts, as well as a potential suspect's alibi, using this tangible evidence as the standard of known facts. Level One and Level Two physical evidence establishes the known facts that allow for the development and testing of theories about what happened. Any object that shows a spatial relationship to the location, the people, or the times related to the criminal event may be deemed evidence (Figure 2.12).

Figure 2.12. *Physical evidence of crime.*

Source. https://pressbooks.bccampus.ca/criminalinvestigation/wp-content/uploads/sites/162/2017/05/Img-08–1024x924.png.

At this point, protecting and recording the crime scene is the first thing to do. Investigators will find it useful to understand that a crime scene is more than just a place where items are discovered; rather, it should be viewed as one large exhibit in and of itself. The spatial relationships between the exhibits in the crime scene may serve as circumstantial evidence for the overall event, in addition to the value of each exhibit individually as evidence.

Investigators will carry out a thorough walk-through on the path of contamination, taking pictures and video of the entire crime scene in order to secure it as the first major exhibit. When demonstrating the precise condition of the crime scene before items are moved for forensic analysis, this initial procedure is highly beneficial. This ought to occur right away following the lockdown, and it will serve as a snapshot illustrating the spatial relationships that were in place at the time.

2.2.3.5. Creating a Field Sketch and Crime Scene Diagram

The next stage is to record the crime scene using a crime scene diagram or a field sketch. It is possible to depict the physical dimensions and salient features of the crime scene using either of these methods. The Field Sketch differs from the Crime Scene Diagram in that it is a brief, rough representation of the incident, as suggested by its name. Similar to notes in an investigator's notebook, the field sketch functions as a memory aid. The crime scene diagram is a more formal depiction of the same data that is scaled with the help of measurements and the field sketch. Both of these sketches of the crime scene will depict the same essential details.

- If it is a building, it will show the address of the location, entries, exits, windows, the position of rooms, the position of furniture, and the location of all exhibits relative to the crime.
- In an outdoor crime scene, establishing and documenting the location of the scene becomes more complex. The geographic location of an outdoor scene needs to be established relative to some known geographic location, such as a roadway intersection, a mile-marker, or even by way of fixing of GPS coordinates of latitude and longitude to a permanent fixed object at the crime scene. In some cases, such as a large open field, where no permanent fixed objects are available, it may become necessary to place a fixed object like a steel survey pin to mark a fixed point at the crime scene.
- After the initial diagram features are completed and evidence is collected within the crime scene, each of those exhibits will be shown on the diagram with an exhibit number. That number will be cross referenced to the exhibit log that will be completed by an assigned exhibit custodian as part of the crime scene management team. This process of showing each exhibit as a number eliminates the need to clutter the diagram with written description of each exhibit found. In some cases, where there are many exhibits, writing the description of each exhibit onto the diagram would make it unreadable, cluttered, and confusing.
- In addition to existing features and evidence at the crime scene, the diagram will also show the location of the path of contamination that has been established and the external perimeter of the crime scene.
- As part of accepted protocols, these diagrams are always drawn with an orientation to North at the top of the diagram, and all writing on the diagram is oriented in one direction, namely east to west.

2.2.3.6. The Exhibit Log

The crime scene is secured and assigned exhibit custodian records of the exhibits that have been identified at the scene are created as part of the evidence management process, thereby creating the first link in the chain of continuity. An "Exhibit Log" or "Exhibit Ledger" is the document in which these items are listed. Every exhibit that is located and taken into custody is identified and given a number in this exhibit log or ledger. It indicates the location of the exhibit at the scene and its number, which is placed in the appropriate spot on the crime scene diagram.

The exhibit log documents who took possession of the exhibit and when the exhibit custodian received it. The time and date that the exhibit was put into the primary secure exhibit storage locker are also displayed in the exhibit log. The court will only accept the exhibits if it can be demonstrated that the secured chain of continuity is safe and uninterrupted. The exhibit custodian would disrupt the chain of continuity if they stopped and left the exhibits unattended in a car or in the office while taking care of another issue. An illustration of a typical exhibit log document is the one that follows (Figure 2.13).

EXHIBIT LOG

Assigned
Exhibit Custodian____________________ **Date**________________

File Number________________________

Location____

Exhibit Number	Description	Seized By	Date/Time	Location	Turned Over	Date /Time Secured

Figure 2.13. *Exhibit log document.*

Source. https://pressbooks.bccampus.ca/criminalinvestigation/wp-content/uploads/sites/162/2017/05/EXHIBIT-LOG.jpg.

There are typically two types of evidence found at a crime scene. One is the testimony of witnesses who can attest to what they saw during the illegal event. The other type of evidence consists of tangible objects that can be investigated, deciphered, and used to support claims regarding the criminal incident. To find, gather, and preserve the information that already exists, investigators must take into account certain factors for each of these types of evidence, which raise some similar concerns.

2.2.3.7. Searching for Witness Evidence

It can be as easy as asking people who have stayed at the crime scene to make statements to identify and interview the witnesses to a criminal event. On the other hand, it may be more challenging to locate and identify someone who may have heard or seen something that was related to the illegal incident, even if they do not believe that what they heard or saw was significant or if they do not want to assist the police. The crime scene is where the process of looking for witnesses begins. In addition to locating and speaking with those who are directly present, this search will also try to find out who else may have been there before, during, or after the crime.

- Often, witnesses remaining at the crime scene can assist in identifying other witnesses who were present and have since departed.
- CCTV security cameras can sometimes assist in identifying other witnesses who were present.
- Identifying the vehicles parked in proximity to the crimes scene or returning to the crime scene on subsequent days around the time of the crime can assist in identifying a witness whose normal course of activities may have previously put them in the area at the time of the crime.

Canvassing witnesses is an additional process that can be used in addition to these witness search strategies. Canvassing is a tactic whereby people go door-to-door in the immediate vicinity of the crime to ask neighbors if they have heard or seen anything. Formal media releases are another way that people who have knowledge of a criminal incident can be canvassed to come forward. Time is of the essence, regardless of the witness identification techniques employed. Under normal circumstances, people only remember everyday, unremarkable events for a short period of time because memories fade. The chapter on witness management will cover how to locate and speak with witnesses as well as get their best account of what happened. But, witness evidence is critical to the success of the investigation and needs to be gathered efficiently, accurately, and quickly.

2.2.3.8. Searching for and Identifying Physical Evidence

Physical evidence, as we have discussed earlier in this book, is the investigator's hidden treasure and is essential to confirming or refuting conflicting accounts of events in court. When establishing proof beyond a reasonable doubt, the court can make connections and evaluate tangible evidence. This is known as physical evidence. On the other hand, the court cannot see the physical characteristics of witness testimony. As a result, the court is unable to assess witness testimony with the same level of confidence in verification that it applies to physical evidence since it must accept the perspective and interpretation of events as given by the witness.

In the section below on Originating Stages of Evidence, we examined the periods and potential locations for crime scene evidence. We will now discuss the physical evidence that investigators ought to take into account when determining what could be considered a piece of physical evidence. We will talk about how to look for evidence, when to gather it, how to preserve it, and how to gather it.

These processes present several challenges:

1. **Physical Evidence Can be Transient or Time Sensitive:** As part of the big picture search in the first instance, the investigator must be conscious of physical evidence that needs to be immediately recorded and documented.
2. **Physical Evidence Can be Concealed and May Not be Easily Visible"** Walking onto a crime scene in the first instance, it would be unrealistic for an investigator to believe they will immediately see all the physical evidence that needs to be collected. Items of physical evidence can exist in many forms and discovering their existence is a matter of careful examination of the entire scene. The idea of conducting a big picture search first allows the investigator to not only discover the immediately apparent items, but also for a survey of the crime scene to determine areas where the small scale and more detailed search might be productive.

- **Doors and Windows:** open, locked, or unlock can be relevant to time and means of entry or exit from the scene
- **Condition of Room Lighting:** turned on or off can suggest the lighting conditions at the time of the crime
- Status of appliances in use at the scene can indicate certain activities
  - Last activation of electronic devices can narrow timelines of activity

- Ambient crime scene temperature and body temperature can be relevant in relation to time of death and the progress *rigor mortis* or decomposition

3. **The Immediate Value of an Item May Not be Visible at First Glance:** Moving from the big picture search to identify items in the smaller scale search, investigators can conduct a detailed grid search of the crime scene to locate items that may be very small or are concealed by other objects. These grid searches can be useful in breaking down the crime scene into smaller search areas to make sure that no area goes unexamined. Along with this detailed search for small or concealed items, the investigator needs to consider enlisting the assistance of forensic specialists to search for items that may require enhanced examination and analysis beyond the bounds of regular human senses and perception. For example, the use of black light can reveal body fluid or stains, and latent fingerprints can become visible after fuming or the application of special powder. In most major criminal cases, forensic specialists will be available to assist in conducting the detailed crime scene search. Every investigator must be proficient in recognizing when to utilize of these forensic tools.

4. **The Size or Nature of an Item of Evidence May Make it Impossible to Seize or Preserve:** Among the challenges of gathering evidence at a crime scene are:
   - Some exhibits are too big to be physically seized and brought to court. As previously noted, the entire crime scene and the inherent spatial relationships of objects within that scene could be considered as one big exhibit that needs to be shown to the court. This big crime scene exhibit is captured and can be presented to the court by way of video recording, photographs, crime scene diagram, or using a sample of smaller exhibits within the scene itself.
   - Some exhibits are perishable and impractical to seize and preserve for court. A good example would be the evidence of the dead body in a murder case. The body itself would be impractical to bring to court. It is considered adequate to have photographic evidence and certificates of analysis on pathology samples.
   - Some exhibits are transient in nature and cannot be permanently seized and preserved for court. For example, ambient room

temperature or lighting status at the crime scene needs to be preserved by photographs and measurements in that moment of time and subsequently presented to the court as photographs and readings by the attending investigator.

5. **The Collection of Certain Evidence Can Cause Cross-Contamination to Other Exhibits:** A major consideration in the collection of any evidence at a crime scene is to ensure that evidence with any potential for cross-contamination is handled in a manner that takes precautions against this occurring. In most cases, at major crime scenes, physical evidence is collected by forensic experts. However, this does not preclude the need for investigators to understand the dangers of cross-contamination and the precautions required to prevent it. This is particularly true when it comes to the collection of bodily substances where DNA might be collected. DNA analysis is now so advanced that even a small trace of DNA material can be transferred by the careless or inadvertent handling of one exhibit to the next. This cross-contamination can be avoided or prevented by the practice of handling only one exhibit at a time, marking that exhibit, placing into a secure container, and decontaminating the investigator by changing gloves and discarding any item could have come into contact with the previous exhibit. Despite the assurance that forensic specialists will normally attend a crime scene for evidence collection, it is possible that an investigator at the scene will be forced to handle a number of exhibits to protect that evidence from some type of environmental damage or other security threat.

2.2.4. Scaling the Investigation to the Event

Not every crime scene is significant enough for an investigator to mobilize a team and carry out the evidence management and crime scene procedures covered in this book. Frequently, in cases of minor offenses, a lone detective will be present at the crime scene and perform all of the functions mentioned, albeit on a much smaller scale. The diagram, security log, and exhibit log problems might only apply to information and drawings in the investigator's notebook when this procedure is carried out on a smaller scale by one investigator.

It is crucial to emphasize that, regardless of size, every crime scene investigation must take into account and complete each of the tasks listed below.

Specifically:

- The crime scene must be secured, preserved, and recorded until evidence is collected

- Existing contamination must be considered and recorded
- Cross-contamination must be prevented
- Exhibits must be identified, preserved, collected, and secured to preserve the chain of continuity.

Large scale or small scale, all these issues must be considered, addressed, and recorded to satisfy the court that the crime scene and the evidence were handled correctly.

.REFERENCES

1. Gardner, R. M. (2012). *Practical Crime Scene Processing and Investigation* (2nd ed.). Taylor & Francis.
2. Gardner, R. M., & Krouskup, D. R. (2018). *Practical Crime Scene Processing and Investigation* (3rd ed.). CRC Press. http://dx.doi.org/10.4324/9781315170596.
3. Geller, B. (2017). Current methods used by the Forensic Science Service of the Israel Police for processing human prints at the scenes of serious crime. *Theory and Practice of Forensic Science, 12*(3), 119–121. http://dx.doi.org/10.30764/1819-2785-2017-12-3-119-121.
4. Hill, J., & Trummel, M. (2005). Review of: Practical crime scene processing and investigation review of: Crime scene processing laboratory manual and workbook. *Journal of Forensic Sciences, 50*(4), 1. http://dx.doi.org/10.1520/jfs2005080.
5. Jobela, N. K. (2019). The significance of efficient murder crime scene processing (Master's thesis). http://hdl.handle.net/10500/25739 (accessed on 30 July 2024).
6. Jones, P. (2009). *Crime Scene Processing and Laboratory Workbook*. CRC Press.
7. Kgamanyane, K. I. (2018). The significance of video evidence analysis in the investigation of murder cases against the police (Master's thesis). http://hdl.handle.net/10500/25219 (accessed on 30 July 2024).
8. Ndara, V. (2014). Computer seizure as technique in forensic investigation (Master's thesis). http://hdl.handle.net/10500/13277 (accessed on 30 July 2024).
9. Osman, K., Gabriel, G. F., & Hamzah, N. H. (2021). Crime scene investigation issues: Present issues and future recommendations. *Jurnal Undang-undang dan Masyarakat, 28*(1), 3–10. http://dx.doi.org/10.17576/juum-2021-28-01.
10. Parish, C. L., & Parish-Fisher, C. L. (2012). *Crime Scene Processing and Investigation Workbook*. Taylor & Francis.
11. Pillay, P. D. (2008). The processing of firearms during investigation of a crime scene (Master's thesis). http://hdl.handle.net/10500/2076 (accessed on 30 July 2024).
12. Ribaux, O., Baylon, A., Roux, C., Delémont, O., Lock, E., Zingg, C., & Margot, P. (2010). Intelligence-led crime scene processing. Part I: Forensic intelligence. *Forensic Science International, 195*(1–3), 10–16. http://dx.doi.org/10.1016/j.forsciint.2009.10.027.

13. Wright, D., & You, M. (2012). Can we use crime scene investigation methods in plant pathology? *Microbiology Australia, 33*(1), 40. http://dx.doi.org/10.1071/ma12040.

CHAPTER 3

FORENSIC BIOLOGY AND DNA ANALYSIS

Contents

Introduction 88

3.1. Forensic Biology 90

3.2. A Brief History of Development of Forensic Biology 95

3.3. Overview and History of DNA Typing 97

References 108

INTRODUCTION

The use of biological concepts and methods in the examination of civil and criminal cases is known as forensic biology (Houck Max & Siegal Jay, 2006).

The main focus of forensic biology is the analysis of biological and serological evidence to create a DNA profile that helps law enforcement identify possible suspects or unidentified remains. There are several sub-disciplines within this field, such as forensic pathology, forensic toxicology, forensic entomology, and forensic odontology (Figure 3.1).

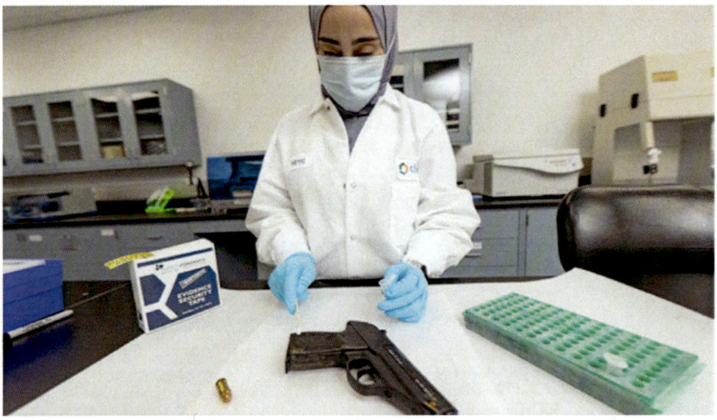

Figure 3.1. *Forensic biology.*

Source: https://www.cfsre.org/images/Forensic_Biology_resize.jpg.

Deoxyribonucleic acid, or DNA, is one of the most often recovered types of evidence from crime scenes. DNA-containing evidence is typically considered biological evidence. In forensic science, biological evidence is acknowledged as the gold standard, despite significant advancements in DNA research.

Biological evidence needs to be initially identified at the scene. This isn't always feasible, in which case an Advanced Light Source (ALS), also known as an alternative light source, is needed. Presumptive tests are carried out to determine the likelihood of the specified biological presence (semen, saliva, blood, urine, etc.) after the source has been identified as a possible source.). If the results are positive, samples are gathered and brought to the lab for examination, where additional and confirmatory testing is carried out.

Paternity testing, identifying missing human remains, cracking cold cases, and linking suspects and/or victims to a piece (or pieces) of evidence, a scene, or another individual (victim or suspect) are just a few of the many uses for DNA analysis. Blood, semen, saliva, epithelial cells, and hair can all yield nuclear DNA evidence if the root is still intact. Furthermore, bone, teeth roots, and hair shafts can all yield mitochondrial DNA (mtDNA).

STR analysis of autosomal short tandem repeats (STR) is carried out for the majority of forensic DNA samples in an effort to highly statistically confidently individualize the sample to one person. Here, autosomal STR markers are employed in forensic DNA typing to find the missing, confirm familial ties, and possibly link suspects to crime scenes.

DNA evidence is analyzed in a lab by extracting, quantifying, amplifying, and visualizing the sample DNA. DNA can be extracted using a variety of techniques, such as differential extraction, Chelex extraction, and organic (phenol-chloroform) extraction.

Quantitative polymerase chain reaction (qPCR), also referred to as real-time PCR, is a popular method for conducting quantitative analyzes. Since qPCR is so accurate, human-specific, qualitative, and quantitative, it is the method of choice for quantifying DNA in forensic cases. This method allows you to analyze changes in amplified DNA fragment fluorescence signals between PCR cycles without stopping the reaction or opening the temperature-sensitive PCR tubes. Fluorescence dye-labeled probes that complement and anneal to the target DNA sequence located between the two primers are used in qPCR reactions in addition to the standard PCR reaction's required ingredients (i.e., template DNA, carefully crafted forward and reverse primers, DNA polymerase, dNTPs, and a buffer solution containing Mg2+). The fluorescent probe has a reporter (R) dye attached at the 5' end and a quencher (Q) dye attached at the 3' end. The reporter and quencher are sufficiently close in space before the DNA strands are extended by the polymerase for the instrument to detect no fluorescence from the reporter because the quencher totally absorbs or masks the reporter's fluorescence. The polymerase's exonuclease activity causes it to degrade the probe's 5' end as it starts to extend the strand. The 5' end releases the reporter dye. The fact that it is no longer quenched makes fluorescence detection possible. A graph is created for the DNA sample, where the y-axis represents the fluorescence and the x-axis represents the number of cycles in the qPCR process. After that, a standard curve plotting the log of known DNA concentrations (x-axis) against the cycle fluorescence threshold (y-axis) is used to compare this. The DNA concentration in the sample can be inferred by comparing the sample data to the ste. This is necessary in order toto proceed with PCR amplification and capillary electrophoresis in order to obtain a DNA profile. Electropherograms are used to create DNA profiles. To find a potential suspect, the obtained profile can be compared to known samples in CODIS. A stistical measure of confidence onin DNA match can be assigned by the DNA analyst based on known frequencies of the genotype present in the DNA profile (Butler John, 2015).

3.1. FORENSIC BIOLOGY

The application of biological science principles and techniques, usually in a medico-legal setting, is known as forensic biology. Forensic biologists examine physiological fluids, tissue samples, and cellular samples that are pertinent to a legal investigation.

To identify and personalize medical samples, the field of forensic biology analyzes bodily fluids using DNA and serological techniques. Blood, semen, and saliva taken from physical evidence or crime scenes are among the materials that are commonly analyzed. These bodily fluids are often produced during violent crimes like murders, sexual assaults, assaults, and hit-and-run accidents. The ultimate objective is to determine the kind of material that is present and then utilize DNA analysis to connect that material to a particular individual.

A forensic biologist starts by assessing the available evidence and investigative data in order to determine the nature of the case and the forensic question or questions that need to be addressed. The first step is to check physical evidence for the presence of blood, semen, or saliva. The submitting agency's requests, the case's specifics, the size and condition of the sample, and the available technology all serve as guidelines for further analysis.

Biological evidence is no longer classified using traditional serology techniques (ABO and polymorphic enzyme groupings). When working on forensic cases, biological evidence is individualized through the use of DNA technology. While biological evidence can be linked to a specific person, the sample's age cannot be ascertained.

The creation of a Georgia DNA database of convicted felons and felony probationers, as permitted by O.C.G.A. 35, is another service provided by Forensic Biology. DNA profiles from casework samples can be compared to the offenders in the Georgia file using this database. Periodically, profiles are also uploaded to a national database. This database makes use of the CODIS (Combined DNA Index System) FBI program. Both the Georgia database and the national database are routinely searched.

The evidence submissions and services offered by forensic biology scientists in the analysis and testing of evidence are summarized below. Blood testing, saliva analysis, semen identification, and DNA typing are among the services offered.

3.1.1. Evidence Submissions

All forensic biology evidence needs to be delivered to the lab in a labeled and sealed container, or in some other way that prevents sample loss or contamination. Paper or cardboard are examples of proper packaging. Evidence shouldn't be preserved in plastic, glass, or metal containers since doing so can encourage the growth of bacteria and mold, which deteriorate biological evidence. In rooms with room temperature and environmental control, dried biological fluids are stable. Heat, moisture, and direct sunlight can all be detrimental to evidence. Only recently harvested bone or tissue, fetal samples, or liquid blood samples ought to be kept in a refrigerator for a brief period of time.

3.1.1.1. Collection and Submission of Known DNA Samples

DNA reference samples from known individuals are the only way to perform a comparison of DNA obtained from evidence. Liquid blood or buccal swabs (preferred) are two possible forms for the DNA reference samples. When appropriate, samples of other people who are suspected of being involved in a crime should be submitted. If recent consensual sex (within 72 hours) is indicated in cases of sexual assault, a known sample from the consenting partner is also required. It is not possible to use samples of convicted offenders that were obtained while they were incarcerated for the CODIS or DNA database.

3.1.1.2. Buccal Swabs (Preferred)

The recommended technique for supplying a reference sample of DNA for DNA comparison is using buccal swabs. By rubbing swabs against a person's inner cheek, buccal swabs are obtained. The swabs can be put in a paper bag or swab box. Private vendors can purchase commercial kits if they so choose. These kits include instructions on how to collect buccal swabs; no specialized medical personnel are needed. NOTE: Avoid gathering liquid samples of semen, urine, or saliva for use as a DNA reference sample. It is also not recommended to gather gum, cigarette butts, or drink containers as recognized reference items.

3.1.1.3. Liquid Blood Samples

When drawing blood (about 5 milliliters) to be used as a DNA reference sample, it should be placed in a purple stopper tube filled with EDTA. Before being delivered to the DOFS laboratory, the blood tube(s) must be properly labeled with the complete name of the donor, the time and date of the blood collection, the donor's name (or initials), the donor's name (or initials), and, if relevant, the name (or initials) of the investigator who was watching the blood collection. Each tube should be sealed separately, and it should be placed inside another sealed container. In the DOFS laboratory, correct routing will be ensured by marking the outer package as "Knowns for DNA." Note: A subject's blood obtained as part of a blood alcohol collection kit cannot be used as a reference sample for DNA analysis.

The laboratory should receive the blood samples as soon as possible after they are collected. Blood should not be frozen, but it can be kept chilled before being transferred if necessary. The blood tubes shouldn't be submitted in a cooler due to their size, but they can be carried to the lab in a cooler. Blood can be mailed or shipped via priority delivery, although it is best to have it delivered in person during business hours. Sending the samples early in the week will prevent a weekend from delaying their arrival. It is not permitted to package liquid blood samples with other tangible evidence.

Written records that come with the sample should inform the analyst of any blood transfusions that have occurred before a known blood sample is collected. Make contact with the designated analyst before a known sample is collected if the individual has had several blood transfusions. In this case, waiting 90–120 days before obtaining the known blood may be required.

It is not appropriate to use bandages or other wound-related samples as a known. Following death, tissue or other suitable samples ought to be taken during the autopsy described in the following section.

3.1.1.4. Tissue and other Biological Samples from Autopsy

Samples taken during an autopsy that are used as knowns depend on how the deceased was feeling. The submission of tissues (including pulled fingernails or toenails), bone with marrow, or other biological samples is acceptable in the event that blood or bloodstain cards are not appropriate or available. It is advised to speak with the manager of forensic biology regarding the most reliable source of samples for analysis, as some tissues are not appropriate for analysis. These submissions need to have sufficient labeling that includes the sample type and additional identifying information. DNA cannot be preserved in formaldehyde (formalin) samples. To ensure the best preservation of sample quality, tissues must be promptly frozen or refrigerated. They should also be shipped on dry ice or placed on ice for priority delivery to the DOFS laboratory.

3.1.1.5. Crime Scene Evidence

It is best to submit the entire object—including any suspected stains—to the laboratory when gathering evidence from crime scenes. If an item cannot be removed or transported, the stain(s) may be removed by cutting them out or, if required, swabbing the item. Prior to packaging, small stains should be gathered on a cotton-tipped applicator that has been dampened with water and allowed to air dry. Because DNA testing is so sensitive, the person taking the sample needs to take extra precautions to avoid contaminating it. This entails donning masks and gloves as well as holding off on sneezing or coughing on the sample.

Clothing from both the victim and the suspect, as well as any items suspected of containing stains from various donors, should always be packaged separately. Before being packaged for delivery, all evidence items need to be thoroughly dried out without the use of heat or sunlight. Wet stains should be spread out on clear paper to dry, as folding wet items can cause multiple stains from the same stain. It is important to carry out air drying in a way that minimizes the loss of other types of evidence, such as hair, fibers, or other trace evidence, and the potential for stain cross-contamination. Drying correctly is especially crucial to reducing DNA deterioration.

3.1.1.6. Sexual Assault Evidence Collection Kits

A commercial version of the GBI Sexual Assault Evidence Collection Kit is available. These kits have been modified to meet the most recent GBI Crime Laboratory protocols as well as suggested national guidelines. The kit is sufficient to obtain enough bodily samples from the victim for a salivary, DNA, or semen analysis. Each kit comes with a comprehensive and detailed instruction sheet for gathering evidence correctly. Suspect identification may not be possible if these samples are not collected, preserved, or handled properly. During the medical examination, no tubes are given to take a known blood sample from the victim. If blood samples are drawn, they ought to be packaged separately and not put inside the sexual assault kit itself.

3.1.2. Testing Times

The completion time for serological testing is highly variable and dependent on number and types of evidence items. The examination time for a single item is estimated below:

- Human blood – several hours to overnight
- Semen – several hours to overnight
- Spermatozoa (sperm) – several hours to overnight
- Saliva – hours

When initial tests are negative and more extensive testing is required, a longer period of time is typically required. These times will also rise dramatically when more and larger items need to be examined.

DNA analysis is a multi-step procedure with multiple quality control stages and established procedures. Its success depends on the documentation and care that the procedures demand. An analysis of DNA can normally take up to 30 days. To find out how long it will take to complete any priority cases, get in touch with Forensic Biology.

3.1.3. Blood Examination

When reasonable justification accompanies the service request, evidence will be examined to:

- Locate bloodstain(s)
- Identify blood by chemical testing
- Determine if of human origin (this analysis is not routinely performed. If blood is suspected to be of animal origin, provide that information upon submission.)

When there is no doubt as to the source of the blood, a blood examination from under the victim's skin or on their clothing will not be conducted. DNA testing on multiple bloodstains taken from a crime scene won't be done for the same reason unless there is a reasonable suspicion that more than one subject is bleeding. To address the issues at hand, the fewumber of samples feasible will be investigated. Weapons taken from a wound by medical or autopsy staff won'twill not always be checked for blood.

3.1.4. Saliva Analysis

When dried stains or questioned samples are submitted, the evidence items will be examined to:

- Locate stain(s) using alternate light source
- Identify amylase (a chemical component of saliva)
- Evaluate suitability of evidence for DNA analysis

The investigator should verify the location's most recent cleaning time and identify the brand(s) that the victim, suspect, or other participants smoked when cigarette butts are submitted for saliva testing.

3.1.5. Semen Identification

When evidence is submitted in a sexual assault case with a suspect identified, the evidence will be examined as appropriate to:

- Locate the semen stain(s) visually or by alternate light source
- Perform chemical tests for seminal fluid
- Examine microscopically for spermatozoa (sperm)
- Test for other semen components when negative for sperm

If requested, the evidence kit from a male victim of sexual assault will have its semen checked. In cases where sperm testing is positive, DNA analysis will be done. Since modern technology enables screening through the detection of male DNA, kits for sexual assault from a female victim with a male subject will be sent straight to DNA analysis.

Collection kits for evidence of sexual assault are usually examined first. Following the completion of the sexual assault kit examination, the victim's clothes, bedding, and other personal belongings can be assessed for examination. However, proper collection of the victim's clothing is still important because in some cases, it may be required for DNA analysis. Clothing or bed linens worn by the suspect are not used for semen identification.

3.2. A BRIEF HISTORY OF DEVELOPMENT OF FORENSIC BIOLOGY

Three phases comprise the evolution of contemporary forensic biology: (1) DNA polymorphism, (2) protein polymorphism, and (3) antigen polymorphism. This history is illustrated in Figure 3.2.

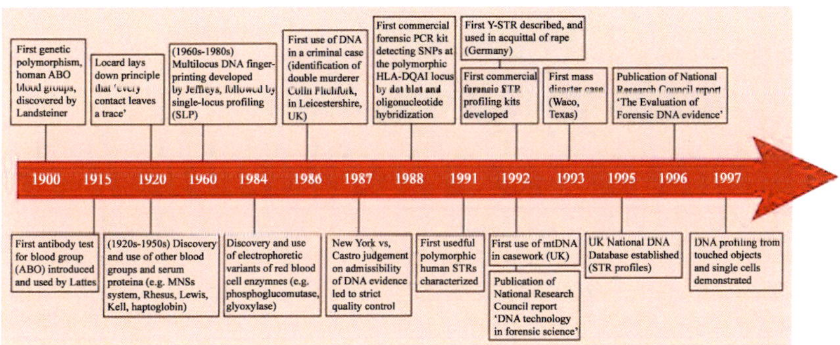

Figure 3.2. *Brief history of development of forensic biology.*

Source: Richard Li. Forensic Biology. CRC Press. ISBN: 978–1-4200–4344–0.

3.2.1. Antigen Polymorphism

Karl Landsteiner made the discovery of the human ABO blood groups in 1900 while researching the reasons behind blood transfusion reactions. Landsteiner won the Nobel Prize in 1930 for his discovery, which allowed blood transfusions to become possible. He also identified the four types of human blood cells: A, B, AB, and O. The blood types were found to be inherited, and different human populations had different frequencies at which the four types appeared. The first antigen polymorphic marker for use in human identification was found as a result of this.

There are now 29 blood group systems known, of which twelve had been identified by the 1960s. Blood group systems are used in forensic laboratories for forensic serology. Although blood group typing can be used to rule out a suspect, the likelihood of a coincidental match between two unrelated individuals makes the case for including a suspect weak.

3.2.2. Protein Polymorphism

Forensic identification uses protein polymorphism in place of antigen polymorphism due to its limitations. At first, a small number of erythrocyte enzyme and serum protein polymorphisms were reported. However, by the 1980s, about a 100 protein polymorphisms had been identified. A few systems, such as the polymorphisms of hemoglobin, serum proteins, and erythrocyte enzymes, were frequently employed in forensic labs. In criminal investigations, the combination of blood groups and protein polymorphism analysis proved more effective in reducing the likelihood of a match between two unrelated individuals. More potent techniques were still being looked for, though.

3.2.3. DNA Polymorphism

Sir Alec Jeffreys created a DNA profiling method in 1984 that involved multi-locus profiling and single-locus profiling subsequently using a variable number tandem repeat (VNTR) technique. A double homicide that was committed in Leicestershire, UK, in the 1980s was solved thanks to this method. It was the first case where DNA evidence was used in a criminal investigation. DNA profiling proved useful during the investigation in identifying the real offender and ruling out an innocent suspect. This instance illustrated DNA profiling's enormous potential for use in forensic investigations.

When compared to previous systems, DNA polymorphism offered several advantages. The most significant is that the method can identify much more individual variability in DNA than antigen and protein polymorphic markers can. The likelihood of two unrelated people sharing the same DNA profile is extremely low. Strong evidence has been provided to support the conclusion that DNA from a crime scene and a suspect originated from the same source due to the high variability of DNA polymorphisms. Later on, forensic labs all over the world began using this technique.

Kary Mullis and associates created the polymerase chain reaction (PCR) method in the middle of the 1980s, which amplifies a very small amount of DNA. Mullis was awarded a Nobel Prize in 1993 for his invention, which had a significant influence on molecular biology. Additional methods have been developed for forensic DNA testing since the introduction of PCR.

Forensic DNA analysis is made feasible by the use of PCR-based assays in situations where minute amounts of DNA, such as hairs and cigarette butts, can be recovered from a crime scene. The forensic DNA testing's sensitivity has significantly increased thanks to these assays. Single nucleotide polymorphisms (SNPs) at the HLA-DQA1 locus (previously known as DQα) were used in a PCR-based assay for the first time in forensic applications in 1986. The high likelihood (roughly 1 in 4,000) of a match between two unrelated individuals was a significant drawback of the assay. In forensic labs, amplified fragment length polymorphism (AFLP) at the D1S80 locus has also been used. PCR can be used to amplify the small size VNTR marker D1S80 locus. Before the advent of short tandem repeat (STR) assays, the HLA-DQA1 and AFLP assays were employed for a few years.

STR loci were first used by forensic laboratories in the late 1990s. When compared to VNTRs, STRs have a number of advantages. For instance, because of their smaller size, STRs can be amplified by PCR, significantly increasing the assay's sensitivity. STR markers also exhibit a great deal of variability. The likelihood of a match between two unrelated people is incredibly low when multiple STR loci are used. DNA testing has led to the identification of the offenders and the exoneration of innocent people who were wrongfully convicted.

The UK created its first national DNA database for criminal investigations in 1995. The United States and a number of other nations had established their own national DNA databases by the end of 1998. For the Combined DNA Index System (CODIS), 13 STR loci have been chosen by the US. The national DNA databases are valuable tools for resolving legal disputes.

Forensic testing has also made use of a different method called mitochondrial DNA (mtDNA) profiling. Since maternal DNA is inherited genetic material, it is especially helpful in identifying humans. Multiple copies of mtDNA are present in every cell. Because nuclear DNA is either severely degraded or present in very small amounts, as in the case of shed hairs, mtDNA typing can be helpful for analysis in these situations.

As an alternative, Y chromosome polymorphic markers have also been used in forensic DNA testing. Since Y chromosomal markers are inherited from fathers, they can be utilized in paternity tests. In cases of sexual assault, these markers are also very helpful when analyzing DNA from multiple contributors.

3.3. OVERVIEW AND HISTORY OF DNA TYPING

A young University of Virginia student awoke in the early morning hours of August 26, 1999, to find a gun aimed at her head. She and her male companion for the night were made to roll over on their stomachs by the attacker. Fearful, they submitted to their assailant. The thief took some money from the man, covered his head with a pillow, and then sexually assaulted the woman. After that, the intruder blindfolded her and led her around the house while looking for more things to steal. She was wearing her own shirt.

The male student was sexually assaulted while the intruder held his gun to the back of his head, threatening to blow his head off if he looked at him. In an attempt to remove any traces of the crime, the attacker made the young woman take a shower. The assailant took the money, the victims' confidence, and their sense of security with him when he left before dawn after helping himself to a can of beer. But despite his best efforts to be cautious and clean up after the sexual assault, the attacker had left behind enough bodily fluids for investigators to connect him to this violent crime.

Saliva from the beer can was taken by the police investigating the crime. Furthermore, minute amounts of semen that were invisible to the unaided eye were discovered by evidence technicians on the bed linens. These samples, along with control samples from other residents of the house where the crime took place, were sent to the Virginia Department of Forensic Sciences in Richmond. Although the bed linens and the beer can had identical DNA profiles, no suspect had yet been identified. The victims' only description, given to police due to the extreme darkness and blindfold, was that the suspect was black, medium in height, and had a heavy set.

The names of over 40 people, some from the sex offender registry and some with lengthy criminal histories, who were stopped late at night in the vicinity of the home invasion were compiled into a suspect list by the Charlottesville Police Department. Sadly, there were no more leads to follow, which left the victims, other University of Virginia students, and their parents afraid and suspicious. Nearing their limit, the police thought of approaching a large number of the individuals on the suspect list to offer their voluntary blood samples so that a DNA comparison could be made. The police were frustrated as DNA evidence systematically ruled out the top suspects.

The lead detective on the case, Lieutenant J.E. "Chippy" Harding of the Charlottesville Police Department, then got what he calls "one of the most exciting phone calls in my 22 years of law enforcement" on October 5, six long weeks after the crime had been committed. Samples from the crime scene were compared to a sample of a convicted offender that was submitted to the Virginia DNA Database several years prior, and a match was found. At the beginning of October 1999, the Virginia DNA Database received 8,000 new samples, including the DNA sample belonging to Montaret D. Davis of Norfolk, Virginia. All felons and juveniles convicted of serious crimes who are 14 years of age or older have been required by Virginia state law since 1989 to submit blood samples for DNA testing.).

After a fast search for Mr. Davis, it was discovered that he was being held at the Albemarle Charlottesville Regional Jail. Paradoxically, he had been ordered by the court to report to jail on the day of the rape due to a parole violation, which happened to be weeks earlier. It's incredible that he turned himself in at 6 p.m., 14 hours after the sexual assault! Without the power of DNA testing and an ever-expanding database, it's unlikely that Mr. Davis would have ever been placed on the suspect list, unless he had boasted about his crime. Mr. Davis was given a 90-year prison sentence after a jury found him guilty of rape, forced sodomy, and kidnapping in April 2000, among other offenses (Lee et al., 1994).

Since its introduction in the middle of the 1980s, DNA typing has completely changed forensic science and law enforcement's capacity to match criminals to crime scenes. The power of a silent biological witness at the crime scene has resulted in thousands of cases being closed, innocent people being freed, and guilty suspects being punished.

3.3.1. Overview of the Criminal Justice System

The three main components of the criminal justice system are (1) law enforcement, (2) scientific analysis, and (3) legal proceedings, as shown in Figure 3.3. Police detectives and investigators provide forensic laboratories with evidence they have gathered from crime scenes.

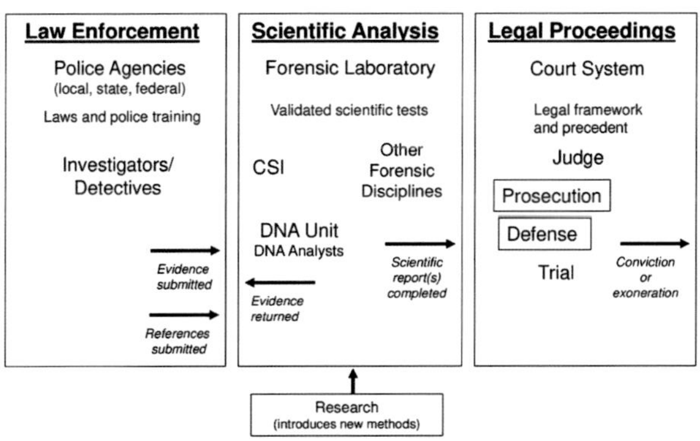

Figure 3.3. *Illustration of the interactions between the three components of the criminal justice system.*

Source: John M. Butler. Fundamentals of Forensic DNA Typing. ISBN: 978–0-12–374999–4.

Next, as in the case of the recently discussed Virginia case, this evidence is cross-referenced with suspect reference samples (if available) or, in the case of DNA or fingerprints, it is searched against a database of prior offenders. After the evidence has been analyzed and compared to reference samples, a scientific report is generated. Law enforcement and the legal community (prosecutors or defense attorneys) use this report to inform their decisions, which could lead to the presentation of the evidence in court (Figure 3.3).

The scientific report and testimony from the forensic expert conducting the analysis are normally admitted to support one side in the court proceedings against the defendant, assuming the defendant does not enter a guilty plea. Legal proceedings are normally pursued in a court of law. A determination of guilt or innocence, manifested as acquittal, conviction (with fine or imprisonment or both), or some combination of the two, will follow an examination of the evidence presented against the defendant.

3.3.2. A Brief History and Overview of Forensic DNA Analysis

The term "DNA fingerprinting," also known as DNA typing (profiling), was initially used in 1985 by Alec Jeffreys, an English geneticist. Dr. Jeffreys discovered that repetitive DNA sequences were found in specific DNA regions that were next to each other repeatedly. Additionally, he found that the quantity of repeated sections in a sample might vary from person to person. Dr. Jeffreys invented the method for analyzing the length variation of these DNA repeat sequences, which allowed for the creation of the capacity to conduct tests for human identity.

The term "variable number of tandem repeats," or VNTRs, was coined to describe these DNA repeat regions. Because Dr. Jeffreys' method involved cutting the DNA regions surrounding the VNTRs with a restriction enzyme, it was named restriction fragment length polymorphism (RFLP). After helping with an English immigration case, this RFLP technique was soon applied to the resolution of a double homicide case. DNA typing techniques have been widely used for human identity testing ever since.

In the last 25 years, there has been a significant increase in the use of DNA evidence in paternity and genetic genealogy testing, as well as crime scene investigations. Hundreds of thousands of DNA tests are performed annually in North America by about 200 forensic laboratories, both public and private, as well as a few dozen paternity testing facilities. Additionally, there are forensic DNA programs in the majority of Europe, South America, and Asia, as well as in Australia, New Zealand, and a few African nations. The popularity of DNA testing among law enforcement will lead to an increase in the number of laboratories performing the test worldwide.

Law enforcement has been able to link offenders to their crimes since the mid-1990s thanks to computer databases that contain DNA profiles from crime scene samples, convicted offenders, and in some cases, people who have just been arrested for a crime. The global application of this technology has resulted in the resolution of tens of thousands of crimes, including heinous serial crimes committed by repeat offenders.

It is unlikely that other classes of genetic markers will have a significant influence on the forensic community for the foreseeable future due to the expansion and efficacy of national DNA databases of convicted offenders, which currently contain millions of DNA profiles with a particular set of core STR loci. Rather than replacing the core STR loci that serve as the standard for data interchange in today's national DNA databases, single nucleotide polymorphisms (SNPs) and other potential forensic DNA typing systems will likely be used in addition to them.

3.3.2.1. Some Basic Principles

It is important to remember a few fundamentals of DNA analysis before we get started on our review of forensic DNA typing principles. First off, every person has a unique genome (i.e., entire genetic composition) inherited from their parents, with half coming from the mothother half from the father, with the exception of identical twins. However, forensic DNA analysis only looks at a small portion of the human genome's genetic variation to distinguish between individuals in order toto reduce testing time and cost. Genes are not examined in the current STR-based DNA tests. Little to no information can be obtained about ethnicity, disease susceptibility, or other phenotypic traits like eye color, height, or hair color using the STR markers that are currently in use. Less than 4,000 nucleotides, or 0.0006% of the material, are analyzed from highly variable and nondescript regions out of the more than 6 billion nucleotides found in the diploid human genome. For comparison, the nuclear DNA in a single cell would be more than 100,000 miles (160,000 km) long if each nucleotide were 1 inch (2.5 cm) in length; however, forensic DNA tests only look at roughly 300 feet (90 m) of this data. Based on measured frequencies of specific genetic attributes among unrelated individuals, statistical calculations are conducted to estimate the occurrence of a random match, since only a fraction of the available DNA information is examined.

Utilizing STR markers in DNA analysis, human identity testing has several applications: (1) parentage analysis to determine paternity; (2) disaster victim identification to reconstruct lives following significant natural or man-made disasters; (3) genetic genealogy and ancestry testing to try to better understand one's ancestry; and (4) historical and missing persons investigations to help connect recovered bones from unknown individuals to their relatives. In the event that a soldier is killed in action and needs to have their remains identified, the US military has been gathering direct reference blood stains from active duty members since the early 1990s. These blood stains are preserved for later analysis. The military can achieve its objective of having no more unknown soldiers in this way.

It is crucial to remember that meticulous execution is necessary for accurate results from forensic DNA testing. Forensic DNA laboratories adhere to strict guidelines and detailed procedures to ensure that the data they collect is of the highest caliber. The data generated during a forensic investigation needs to be trustworthy and able to withstand close examination in court. The next section goes over the procedures for processing a forensic DNA sample.

3.3.3. Steps in DNA Sample Processing

Dr. Jeffreys originally described VNTR sequences, which are smaller versions of STRs. Certain procedures involving biology, technology, and genetics are applied to samples taken from crime scenes or utilized in other types of human identity testing (Figure 3.4).

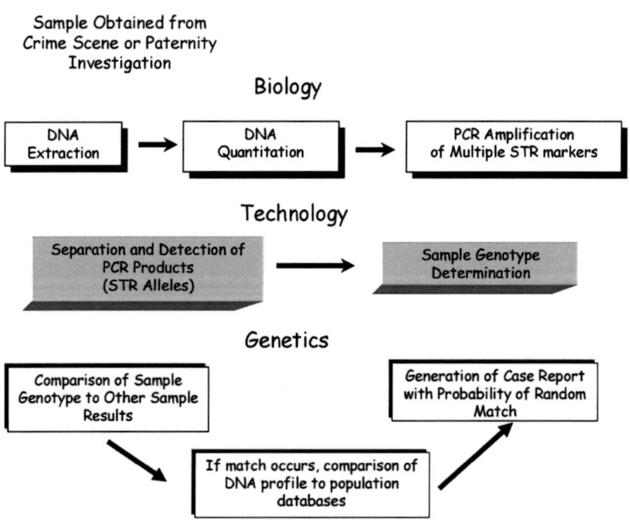

Figure 3.4. *Overview of biology, technology, and genetic components of DNA typing using short tandem repeat (STR) markers.*

Source: John M. Butler. Fundamentals of Forensic DNA Typing. ISBN: 978–0-12–374999–4.

3.3.3.1. Biology

DNA is first extracted from its biological source material after biological material from a crime scene or paternity investigation has been collected. The amount of DNA recovered is then measured. Following the separation of DNA from its cells, certain sections are replicated using a method called polymerase chain reaction, or PCR. Very small amounts of DNA can be examined because PCR creates millions of copies of each DNA segment of interest. In order to maximize the amount of information gleaned from each DNA test and reduce the quantity of DNA used, multiple STR regions can be analyzed concurrently.

3.3.3.2. Technology

The resulting PCR products are then detected and size-separated to provide a characterization of the STR region under investigation. Nowadays, the most common separation technique is capillary electrophoresis (CE). Compared to previous techniques, fluorescence detection methods have significantly improved the sensitivity and ease of measuring PCR-amplified STR alleles. The ABI Prism 310 and 3,130xl Genetic Analyzers are currently the main instrument platforms used in the United States and other countries for fluorescence detection of STR alleles. Sample genotyping is the process of determining the number of repeats in a DNA sequence after the STR alleles have been found.

3.3.3.3. Genetics

A sample's combined individual STR genotypes yield its final DNA profile, which is compared to those of other samples. In the case of a forensic investigation, these other samples would include known reference samples such as those taken from the victim or suspects, which are compared to the crime scene evidence. A child's genotype would be compared to that of his or her mother and the suspected father(s) during a paternity investigation. The samples may be regarded as having come from different sources if there is no match between the forensic sample under question and the known sample. The claimed father is ruled out as the child's biological father if there is no evidence of a biological relationship between the child's DNA profile and that of the claimed father. "Exclusion" is the word used to describe when two DNA profiles do not match (Butler John, 2005).

If there is a match, or "inclusion," a population database—a collection of DNA profiles from unrelated members of a specific ethnic group—is consulted to estimate the uniqueness of the obtained DNA profile. For instance, African Americans and Caucasians have different population databases for comparative analysis because of slight genetic differences between the two groups. Ultimately, a paternity test result or case report is produced. Usually, this report contains the random match probability (i.e., a determination of the observed DNA profile's rarity) for the relevant match. The likelihood that a randomly chosen person from a population will have the same genotype combination or STR profile at the tested DNA markers is known as the random match probability.

3.3.4. DNA Typing

DNA typing can be used as an investigative or trial tool to:

- Identify the donor(s) of biological evidence
- Exclude a falsely accused suspect
- Associate serial rapes or other series of similar crimes
- Determine victim identity when other identification is not available
- Determine parentage in criminal cases only (it is recommended to call the forensic biology manager to discuss this service prior to submission of samples.)

Court challenges to the use of DNA technology have evolved over time from arguing that the technology is in some way improper from a scientific standpoint to criticizing the statistical analysis used in the case. The GBI Crime Lab has interpreted the data responsibly and conservatively, and it will do so going forward.

3.3.4.1. STR Typing

Forensic biology creates DNA profiles for comparison to known individuals and entry into the DNA database (CODIS) using commercially available STR (short tandem repeat) chemistries. The current chemistry includes the 20 CODIS Core Loci as required by the FBI for NDIS participating laboratories. For DNA identification, STR analysis is frequently employed. A statistic known as a frequency is typically reported when a DNA comparison is carried out and the evidence corresponds to a known individual.

3.3.4.2. Y-STR Typing

Special challenges with DNA evidence are presented by sexual assault kits. Any male contribution may be "masked," or concealed, by an excess of female DNA. Short tandem repeats (STRs) on the male-specific Y chromosome are used in Y-STR typing. Since females lack the Y chromosome, Y-STR typing ignores the female DNA. In cases other than sexual assault, mixtures of DNA with low levels of male-specific DNA and high levels of DNA collected from evidence can also be used for Y-STR typing. Identifying the paternal lineage of male perpetrators and excluding or including male suspects are examples of additional uses. Under certain conditions, Y-STR typing can be carried out.

3.3.4.3. TrueAllele Casework Operations – Complex DNA Mixtures

In scenarios where intricate STR mixes are derived from evidence and appropriate DNA reference samples are provided, the collected DNA data can be scrutinized utilizing probabilistic genotyping software, specifically TrueAllele®, offered by Cybergenetics. Cybergenetics' TrueAllele® technology, which was developed utilizing MATLAB®, employs sophisticated statistical techniques to glean identification details from the DNA data. TrueAllele® functions as an autonomous computer system and software application designed for decoding DNA data. Under certain conditions, TrueAllele® may be utilized to analyze previously uninterpreted data.

3.3.4.4. Parentage Testing

When there are unidentified remains or in criminal cases, forensic parentage determination will be carried out. DNA reference samples from a "true trio"—the mother, the putative father, the child, or the offspring—are needed for criminal cases. DNA reference samples from a first degree relative—that is, the biological father, mother, or child, excluding siblings—must be submitted in order to identify the remains.

3.3.4.5. Hair

Hairs with visible roots can be subjected to DNA testing. The GBI Trace division will inspect the hairs and cut the hair roots for DNA analysis if appropriate hair roots are found. Because there is very little DNA in hair roots, hair will not be subjected to DNA analysis if additional probative forensic results are available.

3.3.4.6. Fingernails

The possibility of biological material being present must be supported by investigative data (victim or subject injured via scratching of nails, etc.).

3.3.4.7. Contact DNA

Touch DNA, low template DNA, trace DNA, and skin cell DNA are other names for contact DNA. In this category, DNA is transferred from a person to an object through contact with the latter. A certain amount of DNA is still needed to get a dependable, repeatable result, even with today's more sensitive

DNA chemistries that require fewer samples. Things that a person handles on a regular basis are favored over items that are handled sparingly. Hats and shirts that have been worn are regarded as contact DNA. Complex mixtures produced by contact DNA analysis are frequently incomprehensible using conventional mixture deconvolution techniques.

Without prior management approval, GBI will frequently conduct contact DNA analysis on violent crimes (such as sexual assaults, homicides, armed robberies, etc.) and certain burglaries (such as those involving a serial nature or extremely high dollar or value amount). In all other situations, laboratory personnel will assess the samples provided and the case history to decide whether DNA analysis is the best testing method or if other strategies, like latent prints or trace evidence, would be more appropriate.

3.3.4.8. M-Vac Material Collection

When more conventional techniques like swabbing and cutting proved ineffective, the M-Vac used a wet vacuum to gather biological material. It can be used to process harder-to-swab areas as well as larger areas within a single sample. When certain requirements are satisfied, M-Vac testing might be carried out.

3.3.4.9. Genetic Genealogy

The DNA data generated by the GBI differs from that used in genetic genealogy databases, and the GBI does not conduct genetic genealogy analysis. Samples that produced CODIS profiles but did not reveal the identity of the subject could be appropriate for genetic genealogy research.

3.3.5. Combined DNA Index System (CODIS)

The FBI maintains the CODIS database of DNA profiles. Convicted offenders and casework are included in these DNA profiles. Every state that provides information to CODIS defines a convicted offender differently. “Forensic unknowns” comprise the casework database. These comprise blood profiles from assault, burglary, and homicide cases as well as foreign DNA profiles from cases involving sexual assault. The software is provided by the FBI. States that have been given approval can upload their profiles toNational Database so that they can be compared to those of other states.

Users cannot upload profiles of suspects, victims, or elimination blood samples (e.g., consensual partners’ DNA profiles in sexual assault cases). Any DNA recovered from evidence turned in tointo the GBI that doesn’t come from the victim or person(s) eliminated and satisfies eligibility requirements is uploaded into CODIS and searched. The agency representatives involved will be notified and informed of any necessary action on their part if there is a potential match (hit) between cases. The officer will be notified to submit a fresh sample of the convicted felon for confirmation if a hit is made with a felon with a criminal record. There is no need to request a routine search in CODIS because all DNA profiles are continuously compared to all newly added profiles.

REFERENCES

1. Bond, J. W. (2007). Value of DNA evidence in detecting crime. *Journal of Forensic Sciences, 52*(1), 128.
2. Brettell, T. A., Inman, K., Rudin, N., & Saferstein, R. (1999). Forensic science. *Analytical Chemistry, 71*(12), 235R.
3. Butler, J. (2005). *Forensic DNA Typing: Biology, Technology, and Genetics of STR Markers* (2nd ed.). Elsevier. ISBN 978-0-12-147952-7.
4. Butler, J. (2015). *Advanced Topics in Forensic DNA Typing: Interpretation*. Academic Press. ISBN 978-0-12-405213-0.
5. Carey, L., & Mitnik, L. (2002). Trends in DNA forensic analysis. *Electrophoresis, 23*(10), 1386.
6. DeForest, P., Gaensslen, R., & Lee, H. C. (1983). *Forensic Science: An Introduction to Criminalistics*. McGraw-Hill.
7. Deng, Y. J., et al. (2005). Preliminary DNA identification for the tsunami victims in Thailand. *Genomics, Proteomics & Bioinformatics, 3*(3), 143.
8. Fisher, B. A. J., & Fisher, D. R. (2012). *Techniques of Crime Scene Investigation*. CRC Press. ISBN 978-1-4398-1005-7.
9. Gill, P. (2002). Role of short tandem repeat DNA in forensic casework in the U.K.: Past, present, and future perspectives. *Biotechniques, 32*(2), 366.
10. Gill, P., et al. (1991). Databases, quality control and interpretation of DNA profiling in the Home Office Forensic Science Service. *Electrophoresis, 12*(2–3), 204.
11. Gill, P., et al. (1994). Identification of the remains of the Romanov family by DNA analysis. *Nature Genetics, 6*(2), 130.
12. Gill, P., Jeffreys, A. J., & Werrett, D. J. (1985). Forensic application of DNA 'fingerprints.' *Nature, 318*(6046), 577.
13. Holland, M. M., et al. (1993). Mitochondrial DNA sequence analysis of human skeletal remains: Identification of remains from the Vietnam War. *Journal of Forensic Sciences, 38*(3), 542.
14. Houck, M., & Siegal, J. (2006). *Fundamentals of Forensic Science*. Academic Press. ISBN 978-0-12-356762-8.
15. Lee, H. C., et al. (1994). DNA typing in forensic science. I. Theory and background. *American Journal of Forensic Medicine and Pathology, 15*(4), 269.
16. Primorac, D., & Schanfield, M. S. (2000). Application of forensic DNA testing in the legal system. *Croatian Medical Journal, 41*(1), 32.

17. Varsha, S. (2006). DNA fingerprinting in the criminal justice system: An overview. *DNA and Cell Biology, 25*(3), 181.
18. Williamson, R., & Duncan, R. (2002). DNA testing for all. *Nature, 418*(6898), 585.

CHAPTER 4

FORENSIC CHEMISTRY AND TOXICOLOGY

Contents

Introduction 112

4.1. Concept of Forensic Chemistry 112

4.2. Role of Vibrational Spectroscopy in Forensic Chemistry 117

4.3. Alcohol 128

4.4. Toxicology 132

4.5. Action of Poisons 140

References 150

INTRODUCTION

Forensic Chemistry and Toxicology are crucial branches of forensic science that play an essential role in the criminal justice system by analyzing physical evidence from crime scenes to identify substances and their effects on the human body. Forensic Chemistry involves the application of chemical principles and techniques to identify and characterize chemical substances. This can include the detection of drugs, explosives, poisons, and other hazardous materials. Forensic chemists use various methods such as chromatography, spectroscopy, and mass spectrometry to analyze samples from crime scenes, suspects, and victims. They work to determine the composition, concentration, and origin of chemical evidence, which can provide critical information about the circumstances of a crime. On the other hand, Forensic Toxicology focuses on the study of the effects of chemicals, including drugs and toxins, on biological systems. This field combines principles of toxicology, pharmacology, and pathology to understand how substances can cause harm and contribute to death or injury. Forensic toxicologists analyze biological samples like blood, urine, hair, and tissues to detect and quantify the presence of toxic substances. They play a vital role in postmortem investigations, DUI cases, and poisoning incidents by determining whether and how substances contributed to an individual's condition or demise. Both fields require a high level of expertise and accuracy, as the results of their analyzes can be pivotal in legal cases. Forensic chemists and toxicologists must meticulously document their processes and findings, and their work often culminates in providing expert testimony in court. They must also stay current with advancements in technology and methodology to ensure their techniques remain reliable and admissible in court. The collaboration between forensic chemists and toxicologists with other forensic scientists, law enforcement, and legal professionals is essential for the successful resolution of cases. Their combined efforts help to establish a clear understanding of how chemical evidence fits into the broader context of an investigation, thereby supporting the pursuit of justice. In summary, Forensic Chemistry and Toxicology are indispensable for detecting and interpreting chemical evidence in criminal investigations. Their meticulous analyzes provide critical insights into the presence and impact of substances in various contexts, from drug-related offenses to poisoning cases, significantly contributing to the accuracy and fairness of the criminal justice system.

4.1. CONCEPT OF FORENSIC CHEMISTRY

The use of chemistry and its subfield, forensic toxicology, in a legal context is known as forensic chemistry. The identification of unknown materials discovered at a crime scene can be aided by a forensic chemist. Experts in this domain possess an extensive range of techniques and tools to assist in the identification of unidentified compounds. These consist of thin layer chromatography, atomic absorption spectroscopy, gas chromatography-mass spectrometry, high-performance liquid chromatography, and Fourier transform infrared spectroscopy. The variety of techniques is crucial because of the potential for unknown substances to be present at a scene, as well as the destructiv certain instruments. In order toTo preserve evidence and ascertain which destructive techniques will yield the best outcomes, forensic chemists prefer to start with nondestructive methods. Forensic chemists frequently provide expert witness testimony in court regarding their findings, along with other forensic specialists. The Scientific Working Group on the Analysis of Seized Drugs is one of the agencies and regulatory bodies that have proposed a set of standards that forensic chemists adhere to. Apart from the group's suggested standard operating procedures, individual agencies have their own guidelines for the quality assurance and control of their instruments and results. Forensic chemists regularly check and confirm that their instruments are operating correctly and are still able to detect and measure various qu different substances in order toto guarantee the accuracy of what they are reporting.

4.1.1. Role of a Forensic Chemistry

The role of a Forensic Chemist is integral to the criminal justice system, involving the application of chemical principles and techniques to analyze physical evidence from crime scenes. A forensic chemist is responsible for identifying and characterizing chemical substances, which can include drugs, explosives, poisons, and other hazardous materials. Their work often begins with the collection and preservation of samples from crime scenes, ensuring that evidence is not contaminated or degraded.

Forensic chemists utilize a variety of analytical methods such as chromatography, spectroscopy, and mass spectrometry to analyze these samples. Chromatography helps separate mixtures into individual components, spectroscopy provides information about the molecular structure, and mass spectrometry identifies the chemical composition of substances. Through these techniques, forensic chemists can determine the identity, concentration, and origin of chemical compounds.

One of the key roles of a forensic chemist is in drug analysis. They identify and quantify controlled substances in seized materials, which is crucial for law enforcement agencies to charge individuals with drug-related offenses. Forensic chemists also play a vital role in toxicology by analyzing biological samples to detect the presence of drugs, alcohol, and poisons, aiding in investigations of overdose deaths, impaired driving, and poisoning cases. In addition to identifying substances, forensic chemists may be involved in reconstructing events at a crime scene. For example, in cases involving explosions or fires, they analyze residues to determine the type of explosive or accelerant used, helping to establish whether a fire was accidental or intentional. They also analyze trace evidence like paint, glass, and fibers to link suspects to crime scenes.

Forensic chemists must meticulously document their procedures and findings, as their analyzes often serve as critical evidence in legal proceedings. They are required to produce detailed reports and may be called upon to provide expert testimony in court, explaining their methods and results to judges and juries. This role demands not only technical expertise but also the ability to communicate complex scientific information clearly and accurately.

Furthermore, forensic chemists must stay current with advancements in analytical techniques and technology to ensure their methods are reliable and legally admissible. They often collaborate with other forensic specialists, law enforcement personnel, and legal professionals to provide a comprehensive understanding of the evidence in a case.

4.1.2. Role in Investigations

Investigators can get leads from forensic chemists' analysis, and they can use it to support or contradict their suspicions. Investigators can learn what to search for during their search by identifying the different substances that were discovered at the scene. Forensic chemists can identify whether an accelerant, like gasoline or kerosene, was used during the fire investigation; if so, this indicates that the fire was started on purpose (Walter Stern, November 1995). Additionally, forensic chemists can reduce the pool of potential suspects to those who would be in possession of the drug used in the crime. For instance, the identification of RDX or C-4 in explosive investigations would point to a military connection because those mateis utilized by both the military and demolition companiesboth the military and demolition companies utilize TNT, its identification would expand the pool of potential suspects. Certain poisons can be found during poisoning investigations, which can help detectives know what to look for when questioning possible suspects (Halford, Bethany, February 6, 2012). For instance, ricin-related inquiries would direct investigators to seek out the castor oil plant's seeds, which are ricin's precursors.

In drug and alcohol cases, forensic chemists also assist in verifying or disproving the suspicions of investigators. Because there are precise blood alcohol content cutoffs where penalties start or escalate, forensic chemists' instruments, which can detect minute quantities, can be crucial in cases like driving while intoxicated. The amount of drug detected in a person's system can either confirm or rule out overdose as the cause of death in cases where overdose is suspected.

4.1.3. Methods of Forensic Chemistry

Forensic chemists utilize an array of tools to identify unidentified materials discovered at a crime scene (Gaensslen, Kubic Thomas, Desio Peter, & Lee Henry, 1985). A substance can be identified using a variety of techniques, and the examiner must decide which approach will yield the most accurate results. When conducting an examination, forensic chemists may take into account factors such as the instrument's destructive naturmount of time it will take to examine a substance. In order toTo preserve the evidence for additional analysis, they prefer to start with nondestructive methods. When a destructive method is employed, nondestructive techniques can also be used to reduce the number of options, increasing the likelihood that the right approach will be taken the first time.

4.1.3.1. Spectroscopy

Forensic chemistry uses two primary stand-alone spectroscopy methods: FTIR and AA spectroscopy. FTIR is a nondestructive method for identifying substances by using infrared light. According to Sanford Angelos and Mike Garry (August 5, 2011), the attenuated total reflectance sampling technique does away with the requirement that materials be prepared prior to analysis. ATR FTIR analysis is a quick and simple initial step in the analysis of unknown substances because it requires no preparation and is nondestructive. FTIR instruments are equipped with databases that can be used to search for known spectra that match the unknown's spectrum, making it easier to positively identify the substance. Although it is not impossible, the cumulative nature of the response poses unique challenges for FTIR analysis of mixtures. FTIR is an unacceptable method of identification for novel mixtures because they can be difficult to resolve, while common mixtures have known spectra on file. When analyzing an unknown that contains multiple substances, the resulting spectra will be a combination of the individual spectra of each component (Izzia Federico, Nunn Simon, & Bradley Michael, August 1, 2008). But forensic chemists can use the device to identify the general chemical structures that are present, which helps them choose the most appropriate technique for further analysis using different instruments. A methoxy group, for instance, will produce a peak in the range of 3,030 and 2,950 wavenumbers (cm^{-1}).

Destructive methods such as atomic absorption spectroscopy (AAntify the constituent elements of the sample under study. In order toTo conduct this analysis, AAS heat-treats the sample to an extremely high temperature, which breaks the substance's atomic bonds and releases free atoms. The sample is then exposed to radiation in the form of light, which causes the atoms to leap to a higher energy state. In order to test for each element, forensic chemists can use a matching light wavelength that elevates the atoms' energy states while the element is being analyzed. Because of this and the fact that it is a destructive method, AAS is typically used as a confirmatory technique following preliminary testing that has shown the presence of a particular element in the sample. When compared to a blank sample, the concentration of the element in the sample is directly proportional to the amount of light absorbed. When heavy metal poisoning, including that caused by arsenic, lead, mercury, or cadmium, is suspected, AAS can be helpful. The amount of the material in the sample can show whether or not heavy metals caused the death.

4.1.3.2. Chromatography

Methods of spectroscopy come in handy when the material under examination is either a common mixture or pure. An unknown mixture needs to be dissected into its component parts in order to be analyzed. Chromatography techniques facilitate the separation of mixtures into their constituent parts, enabling the independent analysis of each component. A speedier substitute for more involved chromatography techniques is thin layer chromatography (TLC). TLC can be used to separate the constituent parts of inks and dyes for analysis. Examining notes or fibers left at the scene can be done with this because each company's product varies slightly and can be observed with TLC. The requirement that the components be soluble in the solution used to transfer them up the analysis plate is the only constraint on TLC analysis. The mobile phase is the term for this resolution. The forensic chemist can use the distance that each component traveled to compare unknowns with known standards. For every extracted component, this distance is referred to as the retention factor (R_f) in relation to the starting point. An indication of the identity of the unknown can be found if every R_f value corresponds with a known sample.

It is possible to separate different ingredients from a mixture that has been dissolved in a solution using high-performance liquid chromatography (HPLC). For nonvolatile mixtures that are unsuitable for gas chromatography, HPLC is utilized. This is helpful in drug analysis when the pharmaceutical is a combination drug because each component can be verified because the components would separate, or elute, at different times. The HPLC column's eluates are then fed into a variety of detectors, which cause the eluates to elute off the column and produce a peak on a graph corresponding to their concentration. Since pharmaceuticals are the most frequently tested item of interest with HPLC and have UV absorbance, the most common type of detector is an ultraviolet-visible spectrometer. Similar to liquid chromatography, gas chromatography (GC) is employed for volatile mixtures. The most popular GC instruments in forensic chemistry use mass spectrometry as their detector. To ascertain precisely what was used in explosions, poisoning, and arson investigations, GC-MS can be employed. GC-MS instruments have the potential to identify substances with concentrations within the femtogram (10^{-15}) range. However, in actual use, the practical detection limit for GC-MS is in the picogram (10^{-12}) range because of signal-to-noise ratios and other limiting factors, like the age of the individual parts of the instrument. Chemists can utilize the quantitative data that GC-MS provides to ascertain the potential effects of the substances it finds on a particular person. To quantify the amount of a substance, GC-MS instruments require approximately 1,000 times more than what they require for simple detection; the limit of quantification is usually in the nanogram (10^{-9}) range.

4.2. ROLE OF VIBRATIONAL SPECTROSCOPY IN FORENSIC CHEMISTRY

The study of electromagnetic radiation's interaction with matter to clarify details about molecular dynamics and structure, the sample molecules' environment and state of association, interactions with solvents, and numerous other subjects is known as molecular spectroscopy (Graybeal, 1988; Colthup et al., 1990; Schrader, 1995). This interaction is contingent upon the inherent characteristics of the material, which are categorized according to the energy and frequency range of the electromagnetic radiation used for probing, e.g., ultraviolet-visible (UV-Vis), infrared (Kocak et al., 2006).

A material's complex refractive index describes the intrinsic properties that control how it interacts with electromagnetic radiation (Kocak et al., 2006) typically shown as having two parts: the absorption index, which is imaginary, and the refractive index, which is real. A material's complex refractive index is a function that expresses how the material reacts to applied electromagnetic radiation. The frequency of the applied electromagnetic radiation determines both the refractive and absorption indices (Kocak et al., 2006). Various spectroscopic probes are employed to monitor and quantify the interactions between the material and the applied radiation. The type and nature of the spectroscopic technique chosen will depend on these measured observables (such as transmittance, reflectance, and emittance), which can be expressed in terms of the material's intrinsic properties, its molecular makeup, and the wavelength of the illuminating radiation. Numerous spectroscopic techniques are required because of the broad range of samples being studied. The amount of time required for analysis and investigation will be reduced by choosing the right technique (Diem, 1993; Schrader, 1995; Mirabella, 1998). Atoms with a specific mass are joined by elastic covalent bonds to form molecules. They are therefore able to move in periodic motions and vibrate continuously in relation to one another. These vibrations' associated energies are quantized, meaning that only particular vibrational energy levels are permitted within a molecule (Colthup et al., 1990; Levine, 1991). The frequency of the electromagnetic radiation that illuminates a molecule must coincide with the vibrational frequency of a bond for the molecule to absorb radiation (Colthup et al., 1990). The example of a child on a swing can be used to illustrate this phenomenon: energy can only be transferred to the swing if its frequency and phase coincide with the swing's movement.

This field of spectroscopy in which the vibration of molecules is involved is called vibrational spectroscopy (Colthup et al., 1990; Diem, 1993; Schrader, 1995). Vibrational spectroscopy involves different methods, the most important of which in observing the vibration of molecules are infrared and Raman spectroscopy. Depending on the nature of the vibration, which is determined by the symmetry of the molecule (Cotton, 1990); vibrations may be active or forbidden in the infrared or Raman spectrum (Cotton, 1990; Levine, 1991; Diem, 1993).

Depending on whether two molecules have distinct environments, isotopic distributions, configurations or conformations, or other factors, their infrared and Raman spectra will differ (Diem, 1993; Schrader, 1995). The distinctive vibrational frequencies of molecules are identified by vibrational spectroscopy, which offers comprehensive details on chemical bonding and, consequently, molecular structure. As a result, the analysis and identification of small particles is its most popular application. As a result, the method is well suited to the examination of forensic materials, including papers, textile fibers, inorganic compounds, adhesives, explosives, paint chips from automobiles, inks, and pieces of polymer.

4.2.1. Infrared Spectroscopy

Infrared spectroscopy, like all other spectroscopy, operates on the same basic principles: a sample is exposed to a radiation source, like a globar or another infrared emitting source (Kocak, 1998; Griffiths & de Haseth, 2007). This mid-infrared region range (roughly 400–4000 cm^{-1}) of infrared radiation interacts with a molecule and its chemical bonds. The mid-infrared spectrum is where the majority of organic functional groups have their rotational and vibrational frequencies. Following interaction with the sample, the infrared radiation is collected by an infrared-sensitive detector, such as a focal-plane array (FPA) detector in infrared imaging, or a deuterated triglycine sulfate (DTGS) or mercury cadmium telluride (MCT) detector (Kocak, 1998; Griffiths & de Haseth, 2007).

In classical dispersive infrared instrumentation, a Czerny Turner monochrometer (Ingle & Crouch, 1988; Strobel & Heineman, 1989; Skoog et al., 2007) is used to disperse the infrared light into a single wavelength to plot the spectrum of intensity versus wavelength or wavenumber (Ingle & Crouch, 1988). In modern Fourier transform instrumentation, a Michelson interferometer is used. Based on the development of interferometry, Michelson developed the interferometer in 1880 to study the speed of light (Kocak, 1992; Griffiths & de Haseth, 2007). Using the Michelson interferometer, an interferogram is created by the interference of two or more radiation beams (Ingle & Crouch, 1988; Kocak, 1998; Griffiths & de Haseth, 2007). As a result, all frequencies are detected at once in the time or distance domain. The two domains of time or distance and frequency contain the same essential information, and they are interconvertable by fast Fourier transformation (Kocak, 1998; Griffiths & de Haseth, 2007). The spectrum is then plotted as intensity versus wavelength or wavenumber.

An essential method for identifying a class of compound groups or a single compound contained in a specimen is infrared spectroscopy. It can be used, for instance, to distinguish between paints such as alkyds, acrylics, nitrocellulose, and so forth, and fibers such as acrylics, nylons, or polyesters (Kirkbride, 2000). It can elicit structural information that may be challenging to elicit with other techniques, which gives it a significant advantage over them. In order to provide a molecular "fingerprint" and a quick and sensitive method of determining the composition of a sample, spectral data, which represent absorption at specific wavelengths of infrared light, are used to characterize chemical and structural groups within the sample. This makes it possible to characterize stereoisomers using the technique. For instance, it can be a very effective method of differentiating between other stereoisomers, such as the isomeric group of cocaine, or the group butyl nitrate, isobutyl nitrate, or isoheroin and heroin, or between positional isomers of aromatic substances, such as different isomers of dimethoxyamphetamine or trimethyl benzene (Kirkbride, 2,000). Because salts and free organics have different spectral characteristics, infrared spectroscopy can be a useful tool in drug determination. While the N—H stretch in its free base is above 3,000 cm^{-1}, the N—H stretch in an amine salt is found between 2,500 and 3,000 cm^{-1}. Consequently, within the frequency range of the N—H stretch, the spectral characteristics of drug-free bases and their salts are significantly different.

This method's detection limit is typically in the microgram range, but it can be reduced by employing infrared microscope techniques. The method is inexpensive and time-efficient because it works fairly quickly and needs little sample preparation.

4.2.2. Infrared Sampling Techniques

4.2.2.1. Transmission Spectroscopy

The qualitative and quantitative measurement of a material's transmittance or absorbance as a function of wavelength or wavenumber is referred to as transmission spectroscopy. The method entails measuring the transmittance of the radiation by passing an infrared parallel beam through a sample that is positioned within the spectrometer's light beam. This relationship between the incident electromagnetic beam and the path length and the concentration of absorbing media is described by Lambert–Beer's law:

$$A = -\log \frac{I}{I_0} = abc$$

where A represents absorbance, I stands for light intensity, a for absorptivity or extinction coefficient, b for beam length in the absorbing medium, and c for absorbing species concentration. The path length or sample thickness, the sample's absorption coefficient, reflectivity, angle of incidence, polarization of the incident radiation, and, in the case of particulate matter, the size and orientation of the particles all affect the resulting spectrum. Up until the early 1960s, transmission spectroscopy was the only technique that was widely used. As a result, there are vast libraries of transmission spectra easily accessible. Even though the frequency response varies between techniques based on factors outlined below, these are often used for comparison of spectra obtained by other methods. It is possible to sample gases, liquids, and solids using this method. However, the analyst frequently needs to perform a thorough and occasionally time-consuming sample preparation in order to generate useful spectra. Selecting the right sample compartment, or cell, is frequently crucial. Peak forms and intensities may change as a result; for instance, a tiny bubble in a liquid cell will skew intensity ratios.

4.2.2.2. External Reflection Spectroscopy

The use of infrared spectroscopy to characterize light reflected from smooth surfaces, like metals, semiconductors, and liquids, is known as external reflection spectroscopy. Two classes of samples can be analyzed with this method. The first is made up of a highly reflective substrate (often metal) that has been coated with contaminants, films, etc). The metal reflects the sample beam, which then interacts with the film. As the metal is mostly noninteracting, the outcome is really the film's absorption spectrum. This application is also known as double transmission or reflection-absorption. Specular reflection, or the front-surface reflection from a material's exterior surface, is a second kind of external reflection study. The angle of incidence and reflection in specular reflection are equal. The normal is used to measure these angles, and then the reflecting surface. In actuality, the majority of external reflection experiments combine the sample's specular and reflection-absorption components. When interpreting external reflection spectra, it is important to take these possibilities into account because the two will have different spectral features.

The polarization, angle of incidence, and optical characteristics of the substrate all affect the external reflection spectra. Because the phase shift of the reflected light varies with angle of incidence and the sensitivity of the reflected light increases with p-polarized incident light, an optimal sensitivity is achieved at large angles of incidence with p-polarized light. Less sensitivity occurs for s-polarized light because the electric field at the interface has very small values at all angles of incidence. To convert reflectance spectra into absorption-like proportional spectra a Kramers–Kronig transformation (Kocak et al., 2006) should be employed, which is easy to accomplish nowadays, owing to readily available software and computerized spectrometers. Reflection methods are just as common as traditional methods because they need little to no sample preparation. It is a nondestructive technique that requires no sample preparation for measuring coatings and surfaces. It is helpful in forensic science to examine and differentiate illegal substances like cocaine. Koulis et al. (2001) collected and compared the external reflection spectra of cocaine salt and cocaine base.

4.2.2.3. Attenuated Total Reflectance

Fahrenfort and Harrick separately proposed the use of internal reflection in 1959 for the first time in infrared (IR) spectroscopy. When using the internal reflection mode, the sample is in contact with an infrared transmissive material that has a higher index of refraction than the sample. The internal reflection element (IRE) designates the higher-refractive-index material. ZnSe, Ge, and diamond are typical IREs. Diamond internal reflection elements are used in the majority of forensic applications due to their increased durability. The IRE's interface with the sample receives radiation from the spectrometer's source at an angle that causes all of the radiation to be internally reflected. This process results in the production of an evanescent wave a few micrometers above the IRE's surface. An attenuated total reflectance (ATR) spectrum is created when the sample absorbs and attenuates the evanescent wave at a characteristic wavelength that corresponds to an IR absorption band. ATR is a surface analytical technique that is especially helpful for strongly absorbing or thick samples because the magnitude (the depth of penetration) of the evanescent wave is tiny, only a few micrometers. A number of variables, including the wavelength of the radiation, the angle at which it enters the crystal, and the refractive indices of the sample and the crystal, can influence the depth of penetration. The data from transmission measurements and the data from ATR measurements are not the same. As a result, only broad qualitative comparisons should be made between them. It is noteworthy, nevertheless, that optical distinctions rather than compositional ones account for these variations between the two methods.

An internal reflection element can be intimately contacted by any surface when using ATR spectroscopy, unlike external reflection spectroscopy, which demands smooth surface characteristics. The method has found many uses in the analysis of various sample types across a broad spectral range. Pressure-sensitive adhesive tapes can be analyzed using ATR for forensic purposes. While some tapes are used to package drugs and other illicit materials, duct tapes are used to bind victims of violent crimes. The primary chemical components of these can be identified using ATR spectroscopy, which enables the characterization of tapes that are submitted as proof to establish whether two samples are comparable or distinct. On occasion, it is also possible to identify the brand and place of origin of these tapes. One important thing to remember is that ATR is a nondestructive method. The pressure used to create a good contact between the sample and the crystal, however, may crush the sample, making it semi-destructive in certain situations.

4.2.2.4. Diffuse Reflectance Spectroscopy

The radiation that enters a specimen at a shallow depth and then reemerges after scattering off within the sample is known as diffuse reflectance. It is predicated on diffraction in addition to reflection and refraction. Using an infrared detector, these emerging photons from the sample will be gathered and examined. The diffuse reflectance method works well with inhomogeneous materials that are powdered or can be powdered because one of its key components is the scattering of radiation within the sample. Using this method, a solid that has been appropriately reduced in size can be sampled neat or combined (to a maximum of 10%) with nonabsorbing powder, like KCl or KBr. To guarantee deeper penetration of the incident light into the sample, the process calls for grinding and diluting the sample with KBr or KCl. The diffuse reflectance technique has the benefit of having a wide solid sampling range; this is especially helpful when a very wide range of solid samples need to be analyzed, as in forensic laboratories. A thorough investigation into the application of the diffuse reflectance technique in forensic analysis was presented by Suzuki and Gresham. They obtained the spectral results at two extreme concentrations with a lower limit of 20 μg by analyzing the antidepressant drug Alprazolam. Generally speaking, there are a number of benefits to the diffuse reflectance technique, including low sample preparation requirements, high sensitivity (less than 100ng in certain situations), and suitability for extremely weakly absorbing samples the way pigment particles or other scattering inclusions affect paint layers. The well-known Kubilka–Munk equation, which is used to translate the measured reflectance spectrum into a proportional representation resembling absorption, can be obtained from this model. This conversion program is now included in almost all contemporary Fourier transfer (FT)–IR instrument software packages.

4.2.2.5. Infrared Microspectroscopy

Forensic scientists usually use the conventional light microscope, which is a useful analytical tool, and they are experienced with its operation. It is employed in the examination of criminal evidence, such as paints, bullets, documents, hair and textile fibers, and crystals used in illicit drug sales. Even non-technical people may be able to understand the interpretation of these microscopic images, which are powerful pieces of evidence in court. When, for instance, two colored fibers appear similar under microscopic analysis but are actually stained with two different dyes, or when two textile fibers appear similar under visual microscopical analysis but differ in their molecular composition, there may be difficulty in differentiating the data obtained from a visual microscope. Even though a polymer's cross section may exhibit a uniform microstructure, photooxidative degradation may have occurred.

An analyst can get an infrared spectrum, or "molecular fingerprint," of a sample by combining a traditional light microscope with infrared spectroscopy techniques. This helps the analyst get around the challenges of differentiating the aforementioned molecular differences. It is simple to obtain high-quality infrared spectra for the chemical composition of an unknown substance as small as a few micrometers in area using infrared microspectroscopy. This allows the analyst to locate the area within the specimen and obtain its spectral mapping. Spectral mapping is the process of gathering spectra inside a sample while preserving the infrared microscopy-derived spatial resolution. Within the sample, spectra that were gathered at various locations can be found spatially. These data can be mapped to a specific infrared light band to determine the spatial distribution of the different chemical components in the sample.

The presence and distribution of a nonhomogeneous specimen's constituent parts can be easily identified through the use of IR spectral mapping (e.g, distribution of drugs in human hair). There has been a lot of research done in this field, and many intriguing findings have been made. Individual hairs may disclose a substance's hydrophobic or hydrophilic properties through microscopic probing of small areas within longitudinally microtomed hair sections, which provides a profile of drug deposition along a growth line. Beyond traditional transmission techniques, infrared microspectroscopy can record ATR, diffuse, internal, or specular spectra. Only the sample itself influences the type of analysis technique that is selected. When examining tiny paint samples from auto accidents, for instance, infrared microscopy can be used to analyze them. For instance, in hit-and-run incidents, the victim's clothing may contain tiny paint chips. A paint chip is embedded, and a thin section is cut and examined using a microtome. Using the car paint chip library search function, this paint chip analysis can help determine the make, model, and year of production of the vehicle. Additional forensic examples might include concentrated extracts of low-dosage drugs and single textile fibers as proof of contact.

4.2.3. Raman Spectroscopy

Raman spectroscopy investigates the vibrational states of complex molecules, just like infrared spectroscopy does. Nonetheless, the excitation mechanism used in Raman spectroscopy differs from that of infrared spectroscopy. Raman is more interested in the radiation that the sample scatters than in the radiation that it absorbs. The material in a Raman spectrometer iosed to a monochromatic (laser beam) light source that is much more powerful than what is needed to induce a transition between vibrational energy states. There won'twill not be an absorption transition because the energy of the illuminating radiation doesn't match a molecular energy level. Scattering is the name given to this kind of interaction—where there is no absorption—between the molecule and the illuminating light. Rayleigh scattering is the name given to this kind of scattered light that results in photons that have the same energy or color as the stimulating radiation.

The incident photon and the molecule will collide elastically in Rayleigh scattering. The energy and, thus, the frequency of the scattered photon are the same as thoscident photon because this kind of collision leaves the molecule's rotational and vibrational energy unaltered. The scattered radiation's strongest component seems to beis this. 1928 saw C. V. The Raman effect is the name given to the other kind of scattering that Raman described. However, when a molecule ends up in an excited state rather than returning to its initial energy level, Raman scattering happens. The scattered photon's energy and frequency arealtered from those of the exciting photon. The Raman effect can be described as an inelastic collision between the incident photon and the molecule where, as a result ofbecause of the collision, the vibrational and rotational energy of the molecule is changed by an amount ΔE, where ΔE is the difference between incident and scattered radiation. This change will cause a small fraction of the scattered radiation to exhibit shifted frequencies that correspond to the sample's vibrational transitions.

Ground-state molecules produce lines shifted to energies lower than the source, whereas excited vibrational states of molecules produce lines at higher frequencies. These lines are known as Stokes and anti-Stokes bands, respectively, and are the outcome of the light's inelastic collision with the sample. Since the sample's molecules are in the ground state, the Stokes band is more intense and less energy from the source radiation is preferable than energy gain at room temperature. The fourth power of the incident radiation's wavelength determines the inverse relationship between the weak Raman signal and its strength. For this reason, it is preferable to use relatively short wavelength radiation in the visible spectrum when using Raman. This could cause the specimen to glow. Fluorescence is highly undesirable because it is likely to block the weak Raman signal. To partially mitigate this issue and suppress the fluorescence effect, three laser wavelengths can be used: a red He–Ne laser (at 632 nm), a near-infrared (NIR) diode laser (at roughly 785 nm), and an Nd: YAG laser (at 1,064 nm).

Although both Raman and IR spectroscopy techniques probe the vibrational states of a specimen and are utilized for qualitative analysis and the elucidation of molecular structures, their mechanisms of origin are entirely different, and their spectra are not identical. If a molecule experiences a change in its dipole moment during its regular vibration, infrared absorption can be observed. The dipole moment's change during this vibration determines the strength of an infrared absorption band.

On the other hand, if a molecule's polarizibility changes during its regular vibration, a Raman active vibration can be found. How easily the electrons in a molecule are moved by the incident light's electric field is known as its polarizibility. A Raman band's intensity is determined by how its polarizibility changes during vibration. Therefore, for molecules containing functional groups like C—O, C—N, N—H, and O—H, infrared spectroscopy is a very helpful probe. For nonpolar bonds like C—C, C—C, and N—N, infrared spectroscopy offers minimal information. Conversely, Raman spectroscopy can offer valuable insights regarding the bond's polarizability. Strong Raman bands are produced by nonpolar bonds, especially double and triple bonds. Since the majority of fibers are made up of lengthy chains of aromatic rings or C–C bonds, Raman is therefore thought to be more helpful in the identification and comparison of fibers. Raman methods are also helpful for a variety of pigments and dyes, including azo linkage and aromatic rings.

When analyzing samples of forensic evidence, where the possibility of losing or destroying the sample is crucial, Raman spectroscopy offers a number of advantages over IR spectroscopy. This is especially crucial when examining fiber samples that have been placed on a glass slide for examination under a microscope. Samples for light microscopy analysis must be embedded on glass slides. Before doing an infrared analysis, the fiber must be taken off the slide and cleaned because glass absorbs infrared light very strongly. There could be a significant chance of losing an evidence sample in this case. However, the sample does not need to be removed from the slide in order to be analyzed directly in Raman spectroscopy. Forensic research labs have long employed Raman spectroscopy. But thanks to recent, highly developed instrumentation advancements, it can now be used in forensic labs. When compared to 20 to 30 years ago, the instrumentation has come a long way in the last 10 years. Rapid spectrum acquisition is now possible, and the method is now more user-friendly and sensitive. One of the most well-liked spectroscopy topics in recent years has been Raman spectroscopic imaging.

4.2.4. Applications of Vibrational Spectroscopy in Forensic Analysis

Forensic science research and applications have long relied heavily on vibrational spectroscopy. In fact, the method has emerged as a crucial resource in a number of forensic science domains. Applications for physical evidence in criminal investigations have grown significantly; these include the examination of documents, fibers, explosives, polymers, paints, drugs, and inks. Additionally useful for examining materials taken from crime scenes, such as blood, clothing, and soil particles, are vibrational spectra. Using Raman spectroscopy to analyze automotive paints allows one to ascertain the paint's origin and, consequently, the kind of vehicle. Finding the paint's source is crucial forensic evidence in many auto accidents, especially those involving hit-and-run incidents.

Other paint kinds, such as white household paints, which are regarded as significant forensic evidence, have been examined by a number of researchers using vibrational spectroscopy techniques. But unlike automotive paints, which can be identified by type or color, many household paints are white, making color identification impossible. Raman spectroscopy is a helpful technique for differentiating the paint's composition, which is why it's necessary. Bell et al. (2005) have shown that there is a lot of promise for using Raman spectroscopy to analyze white paints.

Numerous vibrational spectroscopy techniques have been employed for this purpose. Vibrational spectroscopy is an effective tool for analyzing evidence samples for the presence of explosive materials. Bartick and Mount (2001) provided an example of how to analyze suspicious explosive components that were submitted as case evidence using Raman and infrared spectroscopy. Evidence samples were taken from the residence of a suspect who was suspected of making bombs. All the ingredients required to make hexamethylenetriperoxideamine (HMTD), an extremely unstable explosive material, were included in the evidence. One of the most important items discovered was a bottle of liquid stabilizer developer called Welloxide. Hydrogen peroxide is an ingredient in the hair coloring developer Welloxide. One ingredient in the creation of HMTD is hydrogen peroxide. Batrick in the El. examined Welloxide using Raman and IR spectroscopy techniques to see if there was enough H_2O_2 present to create HMTD. They consequently came to the conclusion that the suspect had enough H_2O_2 in his possession to make a bomb. Their preferred technique, however, was Raman spectroscopy, which clearly displayed the presence of the O—O stretching peak of hydrogen peroxide at 876 cm−1document. However, the peak of interest in the infrared spectrum remained weak and could not be observed until the water spectrum was subtracted.

In order to track down the source of a package, forensic evidence such as the characteristics of plastic bags used to pack drugs is crucial in court. Causin et al. (2006) have employed the ATR infrared spectroscopy method to distinguish and isolate seemingly identical plastic shopping bags used for packaging individual doses. Their research demonstrated that ATR spectroscopy, when used in conjunction with other methods, can be a valuable technique for differentiating mass-produced plastic bags and for tracing the origin of illicit drug doses with noteworthy outcomes.

Another crucial method for analyzing pressure-sensitive tapes is ATR. Merrill (2000) examined four distinct kinds of pressure-sensitive adhesive tapes: duct tapes, electric tapes, packing tapes, and office tapes. She did this by using the ATR technique with single-reflection diamond IRE.

Maynard et al. (2001) used the diffuse reflectance IR spectroscopy technique to study personal lubricants found in sexual assault cases. Using extracts from the lubricant specimen, they were able to define classes and subclasses of these lubricants. The samples used were categorized in groups of three bases: siloxane-, poly(ethylene glycol)-, and glycerin-based lubricants. The infrared results indicated that the base component of each lubricant does not change over the course of three months, and it is possible to identify lubricant traces at least three months after preparing a sample for analysis.

Kimberley et al. (2004) demonstrated the possible use of Raman microspectroscopy to determine the presence of drugs on U.S. dollar bills, which requires minimum sample handling and preserves the sample for further analysis. They were able to measure Raman spectra and identify individual crystals on the currency in a heterogeneous mixture of three compounds:

benzocaine, isoxsuprine, and norephedrine. Forensic investigators have been particularly concerned about documents pertaining to fraud and threatening letters that are generated on printers and copy machines. For crime scene investigators, tracking down the printer or copy machine's model and place of origin is crucial information. Merrill along with others. (2003) used an address label mailed to the victim's residence to trace the origin of a packaged bomb. Investigators believed that a worker at a company with 400 copiers of 61 different models may have mailed the bomb. Out of the 61 models that were available, they requested copies of 61 documents. To prepare the sample, they heated the paper's back and placed it on aluminum foil that was fastened to a glass microscope slide. Using microscopic reflection–absorption infrared spectroscopy, which reflects light from aluminum foil back to the detector, spectra were obtained. The investigators were able to identify the model of the copier and the suspect by examining the documents and comparing the spectra with the ink taken from the address label.

4.3. ALCOHOL

A beverage that contains ethanol is called an alcohol. Fermentation of grains, fruits, and some sugar resources produces ethanol. Chemically speaking, it is a class of compounds with a "-OH" group on their saturated carbon chain. Alcohol is another depressant. At low doses, it can ease anxiety, produce euphoria, and enhance sociability; at high doses, however, it can lead to stupor, inebriation, and even death. Frequent alcohol use can lead to addiction, cancer, and other problems. 33% of people worldwide are alcohol consumers. Alcohol-containing beverages are generally divided into three classes, i.e., wines, spirits, and beer, with alcohol percentages ranging from 3 to 50%. Alcohol has almost a sweet taste when diluted, but it burns when concentrated. The liver breaks down 90% of the alcohol that is absorbed into less harmful metabolites. Alcohol depresses the cerebral cortex's cells in the central nervous system (CNS). Its negative effects, such as a decline in psychomotivation and cognitive abilities, are widely known. Different brands have different alcohol percentages (ABVs). For instance, beers have 5 percent ABV, wines have 13–22% ABV, fortified wines have 15–22% ABV, spirits have 30–40% ABV, fruit juice has less than 0–1 percent ABV, and cider/wine coolers have 4–8 percent ABV.

4.3.1. Blood Alcohol Test

The purpose of a blood alcohol test is to measure the body's alcohol content. Blood alcohol concentration (BAC), which represents the percentage of alcohol in the blood, is the name given to this test result. It is directly correlated with the amount of alcohol in the body, and alcohol impairs people's ability to make decisions, exercise self-control, and exhibit other traits. For 12 hours, this test can detect the presence of alcohol in the blood. Within minutes of ingesting an alcoholic beverage, blood is measured because alcohol is absorbed so quickly. The maximum blood alcohol content (BAC) can be attained an hour after alcohol consumption. Food consumption can affect the outcome. Nearly 90% of alcohol is broken down by the liver; the remaining 10% is released through urine and exhalation.

4.3.2. Sample Collection

When alcohol-related intoxication results in death, the viscera are removed and preserved in saturated saline. The preservation of the sample is crucial because improper preservation can completely destroy the examination. Samples are typically drawn from the urine and blood. Before poking a sterile needle into the suspect's skin, it must be cleaned with a swab of a nonalcoholic disinfectant such as aqueous mercuric chloride or aqueous benzalkonium chloride (Zephiran). Using an alcoholic disinfectant may cause false-positive test results or contribute to blood alcohol content readings that are not accurate. A test tube is filled with 5–10 ml of the sample (blood); an anticoagulant, like potassium oxide and EDTA, and a preservative, like NaF, are then added; the test tube is then refrigerated at 40°C. The preservative will hinder the growth of microorganisms, and the anticoagulant will stop blood from clotting. Along with being collected in the customary way, the urine sample is preserved by adding 30 mg of phenyl mercuric nitrate for every 10 milliliters of urine.

4.3.3. Extraction of Ethyl Alcohol From Biological Materials

Acid distillation is used to separate ethyl alcohol from biological materials. It is best to analyze the viscera, vomit, stomach contents, and other materials individually. After taking about 50–100 g of the viscera, it is finally minced by thinned gruel with three–five additions of water and sulfuric acid. It is then transferred to steam distillation, where it is typically heated in a water bath. During the summer, it is especially important to keep the condenser and receiving flask well-chilled with ice. The condenser's outlet should be dipped in a small amount of water or NaOH solution. To prevent bumping, a small amount of pumice stone is kept inside the flask. Collecting the distillate in 4–5 fractions is preferable; the first fraction should not be more than 20 ml, and the remaining fractions should each be 50 ml. Alcohol and other volatile acids, etc., are present in the distillate.

4.3.4. Chemis of Ethyl Alcohol

There are some tests which show the presence of ethyl alcohol in the exhibits.

4.3.4.1. Iodoform Test

It is also referred to as the triiodomethane reaction and is used to identify the presence of CH_3CH (OH) in alcohol. In this reaction, primarily, two different types of mostly chemically equivalent mixtures are used. A positive result is indicated by a pale-yellow precipitate. "R" in the structure above can represent any hydrocarbon group, including an alkyl or hydrogen group. If R stands for hydrogen, then primary alcohol ethanol is the compound that we might be able to locate. The only alcohol that causes an iodoform reaction is ethanol. It produces secondary alcohol groups if R is any hydrocarbon group. Because tertiary alcohols lack hydrogen atoms, they are unable to contain R groups.

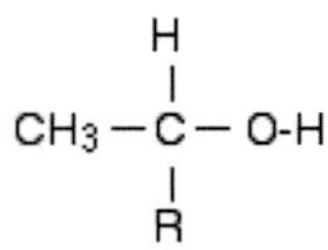

A few drops of 10% NaOH are added drop wise to 1 milliliter of distillate until the solution turns brown and warms for a few minutes. To turn the color yellow, add a few drops of iodoform solution.

The mixture needs to be heated once more over a low flame or in a water bath; as it stands, a precipitate turns yellow. It is necessary to examine the precipitate under a microscope. Iodoform's distinctive hexagon-shaped crystals are observed, typically indicating the presence of ethanol, acetaldehyde, and isopropanol, which upon prolonged exposure transform into a structure resembling a flower. In this test, oxidation is done first, then substitution and hydrolysis.

4.3.5. Sulphomolybdic Acid Test

In 25 milliliters of concentrated sulfuric acid containing the reagent, add one gram of molybdic acid. After it's hot, combine 2 ml of this reagent with 2 ml of distillate. A deep blue ring will form at the point where the two liquids converge. Because of the ethyl alcohol, the mixture will turn a deep blue color when shaken. This highly sensitive test yields a negative result when used with acetone, acetaldehyde, and a diluted methyl alcohol solution. After several minutes, only the strong methyl alcohol solution exhibits a light blue color.

- **Ethyl Benzoate Test:** 2 ml of the distillate should be combined with 2 drops of benzoyl chloride. Gradually add 10% sodium hydroxide to the mixture until it turns alkaline. The pleasant, fruity scent of ethyl benzoate will take the place of the unpleasant smell of benzoyl chloride when heat is applied. In contrast to the iodoform test, methyl alcohol also passes this test.

4.3.6. Determination of Ethyl Alcohol in Blood/Urine

Alcohol detection in the body is crucial in cases of intoxication. The best course of action is to watch for behavioral abnormalities in the suspect; however, the only way to confirm this is to examine the suspect's breath, blood, and urine. With the aid of breath-analyzer devices such as Alco-Sensor, Breathalyzer, etc., an immediate analysis of breath alcohol can be carried out. However, a modified version of the Kozelka and Hine/Cavett method could be used to determine the blood's alcohol content. Many techniques for figuring out how much alcohol is in bodily fluids have been published in recent years. The findings of an analysis comparing the advantages of the Kozelka and Hine and the micro Cavett methods were published by Kent-Jones and Taylor. The Kozelka and Hine method is less precise and requires more time, but it produces good reproducibility. The micro Cavett method is more accurate, but it has significant reproducibility issues. The micro Cavett method was modified by Nickolls, and the results seem to be more accurate than they were with the original method. This procedure is more frequently used for routine laboratory work due to its simplicity.

- **Cavett Method/Kozelka and Hine Method:** This method's basic idea is the easy oxidation of alcohol by acetic acid in the presence of oxidizing agents like potassium dichromate and sulfuric acid. Each milliliter of N/20 potassium dichromate solution undergoes reduction, which is equal to 0.575 milligrams of alcohol.
- **Widmark's Formula:** This formula is used to estimate the amount in which alcohol is present in the body.

a. For blood analysis

$a=cpr.a=cpr.$

Here, a = Total amount of alcohol absorbed in the body; p = Weight of the person; c = Concentration of alcohol in the blood; r = Constant which is 0.5 in women and 0.68 in men

b. In urine analysis.

$a=3/4qpr.a=3/4qpr.$

Here, a = Total alcohol content present in the body; p = Total weight of the person; q = Alcohol concentration in the urine; r = Constant, namely, 0.68 for men and 0.5 in women.

4.3.7. Instrumental Technique of Analysis of Ethyl Alcohol

4.3.7.1. Gas Chromatography

The amount of ethanol in the blood, urine, and serum can be measured using a variety of techniques. Gas chromatography is one of the most significant techniques (GC). After the sample is injected into a heating chamber, its high temperature causes the alcohol to evaporate. The vapors are then transported through a column filled with an adsorbent material by an inert carrier gas, such as nitrogen. The way various component types are separated depends on how differently they bind together, i.e., partition coefficient in the direction of the stationary adsorbent phase, which is subsequently detected. Such a chromatogram is useful for both qualitative and quantitative analysis.

Various components of gas chromatography are:

- Carrier gas
- Flow regulator
- Injector
- Column
- Stationary phase
- Oven
- Detectors
- Display device

4.4. TOXICOLOGY

The Greek word "Toxicon," which was used to refer to a poisonous substance in arrowheads, is where the word "toxicology" originates. The science that describes the characteristics, source, knowledge, lethal dose, fatal effect, analysis, and treatment options of poisons is known as toxicology. Toxicology is more accurately defined as the study of the harmful effects that physical or chemical agents have on living things. A "toxicologist" is qualified to investigate and assess the effects on the health of people, animals, and the environment. In toxicological research, the possibility of functional effects like neurobehavioral and immunological effects is evaluated along with the cellular, biochemical, and molecular mechanisms of action.

Toxicology is a broad field of study that frequently necessitates specialization due to the variety of chemicals and the potential harm they may cause to the environment. Toxicologists play a crucial role in decision-making processes due to our society's reliance on chemicals and the need to evaluate potential risks. When it comes to the investigation and examination of the physical and chemical characteristics of poisons, the current description would be slightly changed but not necessarily inaccurate. In this case, "physical properties" refers to appearance, for example color, state, boiling point, melting point, and so forth. One crucial aspect of chemical properties is the study of the body's action, including metabolism, as well as the lethal dose and toxicity. Finding any poison inside the body, estimating it quantitatively and qualitatively, and interpreting the findings of the corresponding toxicological analysis are additional tasks in the field of toxicology. Any substance that can result in illness or death when consumed in large enough quantities is considered poisonous. The maxim "sufficient quantity" is used in this definition.

4.4.1. History of Toxicology

There are numerous plant poisons that are listed in the older Indian text Rig Veda (12th century BC). But the study of toxicology goes all the way back to when people first used plant and animal venoms for assassination, hunting, and warfare. Toxicology is still working to understand the mechanisms behind venom toxicity. There must be a long and thorough history prior to the discovery of these poisons. It is assumed that early humans classified certain plants as dangerous and others as harmless. Perhaps the same can be said for how snakes and other animals are categorized.

Information about numerous well-known poisons, such as hemlock, aconite, opium, and metals like arsenic, lead, copper, and an can be found in the ancient book Ebers Papyrus. Lead was one of the first elements to be identified as a mineral poison, having been found as early as 3,500 BC. Lead was widely used in plumbing, but it was also used to make vessels and containers, which resulted in widespread, long-term health issues. There'sThere is also a suggestion that they were familiar with plants that contained compounds resembling digitalis and belladonna alkaloids. While the Book of Job talks about poison arrows, Hippocrates kept track of different poisons and clinical toxicology principles pertaining to bioavailability in remedy and over dosage. Ancient Greek literature is replete with references to poisons and their applications. According to some Homeric interpretations, Odysseus obtained poisons for his arrows.

Aristotle's pupil Theophrastus included numerous allusions to toxic plants in his work De Historia Plantarum. The first attempt at a classification of poisons was made by the Greek physician Dioscorides, who worked in the Roman emperor Nero's court. His classification was enhanced by descriptions and diagrams. Not only did his division of poisons into plant, animal, and mineral categories last for 16 centuries, but it is still a useful classification today. In his experiments with remedies, Dioscorides discovered the application of emetics in cases of poisoning and the use of caustic substances and cupping glasses in cases of snakebite. Animal and plant poisoning was a common occurrence. Socrates (470–399 BC) is arguably the most famous victim of poisoning utilized as a state method of execution. It is estimated that a cup of hemlock extract was the appropriate dosage for him.

While organic chemistry was still in its infancy until 1800, by 1825 successful synthetics of war gases such as phosgene ($COCl_2$) and mustard gas (bis [β-chloroethyl] sulfide) had been achieved. The German forces employed these two substances as chemical warfare agents in World War I, along with chlorine gas. Throughout World War II, they were kept in storage, and in the 1980s, Iraq utilized them during the Iran-Iraq War (Marine Corps History). More than 10,000 organic compounds, such as carbon tetrachloride, diethyl ether, carbonic acid, and chloroform, had been produced by 1880, and byproducts of coal and petroleum gasification were traded. During the 19th century, experimental toxicology expanded quickly in tandem with the development of organic chemistry.

4.4.2. Classification of Toxicology

The field of toxicology can be further divided into the following sub-disciplines:

4.4.2.1. Environmental Toxicology

The study of chemicals that contaminate food, water, soil, or the atmosphere is the focus of environmental toxicology. It also addresses harmful materials that find their way into bodies of water like lakes, rivers, streams, and the ocean. The effects of toxic substance exposure on living things, including humans, animals, and plants, are covered in this area of toxicology.

4.4.2.2. Occupational Toxicology

The field of industrial or occupational toxicology studies the consequences of chemical exposure on workers' health. The need to safeguard employees from hazardous materials and create a secure work environment gave rise to this field. According to estimates, industrial chemical-related occupational diseases result in between 50,000 and 70,000 fatalities as well as 350,000 new cases of illness annually in the US. The World Health Organization estimates that 100 million occupational injuries worldwide result in 0.1 million fatalities. Additionally, it's estimated that India accounts for 17 million non-fatal occupational injuries (17% of global totals) and 45,000 fatal injuries (45% of global totals due to occupational injuries) annually. India is responsible for 1.9 million cases (17%) of occupational diseases worldwide and 0.12 deaths globally (17%) of all deaths resulting from these diseases.

4.4.2.3. Regulatory Toxicology

The goal of regulatory toxicology is to create concentration-based guidelines for "safe" exposure by collecting and assessing available toxicological data. The goals and methods used in science and regulatory policy diverge significantly. Science is methodical, incremental, and evidence-based in its pursuit of identifying natural phenomena. It does this without bias.

4.4.2.4. Food Toxicology

The field of food toxicology deals with providing consumers with a safe and palatable food supply. In order to improve the food's flavor, aroma, or appearance, several ingredients may be added during processing. You can alter the texture and flavor of food by adding fats, oils, sugars, starches, and other ingredients. To determine whether and to what extent these additives may have negative effects, research is done on each of them. Food allergies are a second area that interests me. One common example is lactose intolerance, which affects a large number of people. A food crop may also be exposed to harmful substances like pesticides, and plants may absorb lead, arsenic, and cadmium from the naturally occurring materials in the soil and water. Finding the acceptable daily intake threshold for those substances is the responsibility of toxicologists.

4.4.2.5. Clinical Toxicology

The study of diseases and illnesses brought on by either short-term or long-term exposure to hazardous chemicals is known as clinical toxicology. ER doctors are among the clinical toxicologists who need to understand the symptoms of exposure to a wide range of toxic substances in order to treat patients appropriately.

4.4.2.6. Descriptive Toxicology

It is the goal of descriptive toxicology to compile toxicological data from animal testing. These kinds of studies determine the concentration of a chemical at which disease or even death is likely to occur. Toxicology testing, which yields data for safety assessments and legal obligations, is the primary focus of a descriptive toxicologist. Appropriate toxicity tests in animal experimentation or cell culture systems are intended to produce data to evaluate the risks that particular chemical exposure poses to humans and the environment. As with drugs and food additives, the concern might only extend to effects on humans. However, the risks posed by chemicals such as herbicides, insecticides, solvents, etc., are not the only things that toxicologists in the chemical industry need to worry about. with possible consequences not only for humans but also for fish, birds, plants, and other elements that could upset the ecosystem's delicate balance. Naturally, descriptive toxicology and mechanistic studies go hand in hand because the former helps to generate hypotheses for mechanistic toxicology while the latter offers valuable insights into the mechanism of action of chemicals. Regulatory toxicologists also use these studies as a crucial part of their risk calculations.

4.4.2.7. Analytical Toxicology

Analytical toxicology analyzes bodily fluids, stomach contents, excrement, or skin to determine the toxin. It also includes using analytical chemistry tools to evaluate chemicals that could have an impact on living things in a qualitative or quantitative way.

The substance that needs to be measured is typically a xenobiotic that the organism's metabolism may have changed or transformed. The specimen that needs to be examined often consists of a matrix made of solid tissues or bodily fluids that have been extracted from the organism. Analytical toxicologists can face challenges related to the analyte's identity as well as the matrix's complexity.

4.4.2.8. Mechanistic Toxicology

Mechanistic toxicology observes the mechanisms by which harmful substances produce their effects. When attempting to determine how a toxic substance causes harm, it is important to consider various factors such as the size of the molecule, the specific tissue type or cellular components affected, whether the substance dissolves easily in water or fatty tissues, and whether effects observed in animals can be predicted in humans.

4.4.2.9. Forensic Toxicology

The study of forensic toxicology aids in the establishment of causal links between drug or chemical exposure and the harmful or fatal consequences that follow. In order to support legal administration, forensic toxicology discusses the use of traditional toxicology in criminal investigations.

It can be compared to a cross between advanced forensic medicine and analytical chemistry or fundamental toxicology. The main focus of forensic toxicology is also on the medical-legal aspects of the harmful effects of chemicals on humans and animals. In post-mortem investigations, the knowledge of forensic toxicologists is mainly applied in determining the cause of death and analyzing its circumstances.

4.4.3. Forensic Toxicology and its Significance

The mechanism of toxicity frequently gives a forensic toxicologist insight into how a chemical or physical agent can result in death or incapacitation. Descriptive toxicology can be used to predict the toxic effects of related chemicals if the mechanism of toxicity is understood. The basic ability of a chemical agent to negatively impact an organism is known as toxicity. These substances are better known as xenobiotics. e. foreign material. Drugs, industrial chemicals, naturally occurring poisons, and pollutants found in the environment are examples of xenobiotics. Risk is the likelihood that a particular negative outcome will materialize. It is frequently expressed as the proportion of cases within a particular population over a given time frame. A risk estimate may be derived from actual cases or, alternatively, from projections of cases in the future using speculative calculations. For regulatory purposes, toxicity rating and toxicity classification are applicable. An arbitrary grading of doses or exposure levels that result in toxic effects is called a toxicity rating. These classifications could be "extremely toxic," "very toxic," "moderately toxic," and so forth. The most frequent ratings are related to acute toxicity. The process of classifying chemicals into general groups based on the most significant toxic effect is known as toxicity classification. These classifications may encompass allergenic, neurotoxic, and carcinogenic, among others. This classification may serve as information and a warning with administrative value.

Experience- and research-based knowledge from the toxicological sciences is increasingly impacting human and environmental health worldwide, as well as our personal lives. A compound's toxicological effects have an impact on a variety of products and services, pharmaceuticals, manufacturing procedures, waste remediation, legal actions, and general policy decisions. As toxicology's impact on social issues grows, so does our need to become more aware of the moral, legal, and societal ramifications of toxicological testing and research. Due to the widespread use of thousands of pharmaceutical and chemical agents and their annual increase, poisoning has emerged as one of the most frequent medical emergencies worldwide. Over the past few decades, poisoning and drug abuse cases have steadily increased in India. Precise identification of poisoning is necessary for medicinal and medicolegal purposes in both the living and the deceased. During life, poisons are typically found in bodily fluids like blood, urine, or gastric lavage; however, after death, they are found in the contents of the stomach, bowel, and viscera in addition to urine and vomitus. Vitreous humor is one of the best samples to add to blood in a cadaver because it doesn't break down as quickly and is fairly simple to remove during an autopsy. In the past, forensic toxicological analysis has concentrated on the use of bodily fluids, such as blood and specific organs, in the investigation of intoxication-related deaths. However, in certain situations—like exhumation cases—putrefaction and contamination make appropriate tissue sampling challenging. Given its potential as a drug depot, bone marrow could be a useful substitute specimen in certain situations. The foundation of the science of toxicology as it is applied today was established by determining the toxicological potential of these recently developed compounds. The field of toxicology has grown to encompass a wide range of topics, such as occupational poisoning, exposure to environmental pollution, radiation effects, and, sadly, biological and chemical warfare. It has also expanded to include studies of the risks associated with the use of pharmaceuticals, pesticides, and food additives. However, the person who has held the title of toxicologist for the longest is the forensic toxicologist. The primary focus of a forensic toxicologist is the identification and quantification of toxins found in bodily fluids and tissues taken during an autopsy. Occasionally, they may also examine blood, urine, or stomach contents taken from a living individual. Following the completion of the analysis, the forensic toxicologist interprets the findings regarding the effects of the poison on the victim's physiology and/or behavior. Any substance has the potential to be poisonous if used improperly. The dosage, appearance, and mode of administration may all be done improperly. For instance, taking too much of the regular sugar we eat on a daily basis can cause a diabetic attack. In a similar vein, breathing regular oxygen can be fatal if even a single intravenous bubble is injected. The toxicity of smoke and soot was also noted by the Italian physician Ramazzini and the Swiss alchemist and physician Paracelsus.

4.4.4. Development and Advances of Forensic Toxicology

Forensic Toxicology has evolved significantly since its inception, driven by advancements in science and technology, which have enhanced its capabilities and applications in the criminal justice system. The development of forensic toxicology can be traced back to the early 19th century when scientists first began to systematically study the effects of poisons on the human body. One of the landmark cases in forensic toxicology history was the trial of Marie Lafarge in 1840, where chemist Mathieu Orfila's work in identifying arsenic poisoning played a crucial role, establishing the importance of toxicological analysis in legal investigations. The advent of analytical chemistry techniques in the late 19th and early 20th centuries marked a significant milestone in forensic toxicology. Methods such as colorimetry, spectrophotometry, and later gas chromatography (GC) and high-performance liquid chromatography (HPLC) allowed for more accurate and sensitive detection of drugs and poisons in biological samples. The introduction of mass spectrometry (MS) further revolutionized the field by providing precise identification and quantification of chemical substances, even at trace levels.

In recent decades, forensic toxicology has benefited immensely from the integration of advanced technologies and interdisciplinary approaches. The development of liquid chromatography-tandem mass spectrometry (LC-MS/MS) has set new standards for sensitivity and specificity, enabling the detection of a wider range of substances, including new synthetic drugs and emerging contaminants. Additionally, the use of immunoassays and enzyme-linked immunosorbent assays (ELISA) has enhanced the ability to screen large numbers of samples quickly and efficiently.

Advances in molecular biology and genetics have also influenced forensic toxicology. Techniques such as polymerase chain reaction (PCR) and DNA profiling have expanded the scope of toxicological investigations to include genetic susceptibility to certain toxins and the metabolism of drugs, which can provide insights into individual variations in response to substances. This has led to the field of pharmacogenomics, which studies how genetic differences affect drug metabolism and toxicity, aiding in personalized medicine and toxicological assessments.

Digital forensics and data analytics have further augmented forensic toxicology. The development of comprehensive toxicology databases and bioinformatics tools allows for rapid comparison of analytical data with known substances, improving the accuracy and speed of toxicological analyzes. Machine learning algorithms and artificial intelligence are increasingly being applied to predict toxicological outcomes and identify patterns in complex datasets, enhancing the interpretive capabilities of forensic toxicologists.

The ongoing research and development in the field continue to address emerging challenges. The rise of novel psychoactive substances (NPS) and the opioid crisis have spurred efforts to develop new detection methods and analytical standards. Forensic toxicologists are also exploring non-invasive sampling techniques, such as hair, salivaand breath analysis, to complement traditional blood and urine tests, offering less invasive and more accessible means of monitoring drug use and exposure.

In summary, the development and advances in forensic toxicology have transformed it into a sophisticated and integral part of forensic science. Continuous innovations in analytical techniques, molecular biology, and digital technologies have expanded itstheir capabilities, enabling more accurate, sensitive, and comprehensive toxicological analyzes. These advancements have not only improved the detection and interpretation of toxic substances in various forensic contexts but also enhanced the overall effectiveness of the criminal justice system in addressing drug-related and poisoning cases.

4.5. ACTION OF POISONS

Every poison affects a victim's body in a nearly identical way. Frequently, they either obstruct the flow of oxygen into the tissues or obstruct the respiratory system by inhibiting process-related enzymes. The sites of action in this are the ganglions, synapses, and the myoneural junction. Death may result from the hyperexcitation of both voluntary and involuntary muscles in certain insecticidal poisoning cases.

- **Local Action**: Local action refers to taking direct action on the body part that is impacted. Examples include the effect on motor and sensory nerves, congestion and inflammation caused by irritants, irritation and inflammation in strong mineral acids and alkalis, etc.
- **Remote Action:** Because the poison is absorbed into the person's system, remote action has an impact on them. For instance, once alcohol enters the system, it has an impact on the individual.
- **Local and Remote Actions:** Both distant and local organs may be impacted by certain poisons. As a result, they have a toxic effect after being absorbed into the body, such as oxalic acid, and not only harm the area in contact with the poison.
- **General Action**: When a poison, such as mercury or arsenic, is absorbed, it affects multiple bodily systems. This is known as general action.

4.5.1. Factors Modifying the Action of Poisons

A poison's intrinsic qualities, such as its physiochemical and pharmacological makeup, determine how toxic it is.

The action of poisons mainly depends upon the following factors discussed below:

1. **Forms of Poison:** There are three forms of poison:

i. **Physical Form:** Gaseous/volatile/vaporous forms of poisons act faster than liquid poisons as they are quickly absorbed. Similarly, liquid poisons act faster than solid poisons.

Gaseous or volatile > liquid > solid.

For solid poisons, powdered poisons act quickly than the lumps. For example, there are certain seeds that escape the gastrointestinal tract as they are solid, but when crushed, they can be fatal.

For solids: powdered > lumps

ii. **Chemical Form:** Few substances like mercury or arsenic are not poisonous as they are insoluble and cannot be absorbed when they are in combination with other substances like mercuric chloride, arsenic oxide, etc.

In other cases, the action is vice versa. For example, there are some substances that become inert in combination with silver nitrate and hydrochloric acid and are deadly and poisonous when present in pure forms.

iii. **Mechanical Combination:** The effect of poisons is significantly altered when they are combined with inert substances.

2. **Quantity:** Large doses of toxin cause much lethal effect. But this statement is not always true. For example, sometimes when a toxin is taken in very large amount, the body produces a mechanism against it such as vomiting, and thus the intensity of the toxin is reduced.

3. **Concentration:** The absorption speed of poison is dependent on concentration; thus poison of higher concentration is fatal. However, there are still some exceptions. For example, a dilute oxalic acid is less corrosive, but the absorption rate is high and so it is more dangerous.

4. **Methods of Administration:** It has a unique role in the process of absorption. It is fastest through inhalation and then through injection as compared to the oral mode.

5. **Condition of the Body:** Different persons react differently when exposed to a poison. It is because the condition of our body is also responsible for the increase or decrease of the effect of a poison on the body:

i. **Age:** Children and older people are more affected than an adult by the same quantity of toxin.

ii. **Sleep:** The body functions are slower during sleep; thus toxin circulation in the body is also slower.

iii. **Health:** Healthy persons can tolerate a toxin better than a weak or ill person.

6. **Dosage:** The poison's effect is contingent upon its dosage. It is claimed that a substance's potency determines whether it is a poison

or a cure. Generally speaking, a material is deemed poisonous at a predetermined threshold. This amount is taken into account based on the average impact on the population, even though it is not set for every individual. Poisoning a person has two major effects on their body: the immediate death and the subtle chronic toxicity over time.

In small doses, certain poisons can be fatal, but in larger amounts, others can have an impact. One way to understand the importance of a dose is to use the example of a metal that is necessary for food, such as iron, copper, manganese, zinc, etc., it can be fatal if the dosage is greater than what the body needs.

i. Effective Dose (ED): The effective dose is the quantity of a substance at which it shows its effect in the population. In most cases, ED50 is measured as a dose which induces a response in half of the targeted population.

ii. Lethal Dose: The lethal dose (LD) 50 is the amount of drug which is expected to cause death of 50% population.

7. Hypersensitivity: In essence, it is the kind of reaction the body starts when it comes into contact with any other material. It may occasionally be connected to an allergy. It is assumed that hypersensitivity is not influenced by incorrect dosages. There is a dose associated with each substance that determines the amount needed to make a person hypersensitive to that particular substance. In actuality, the allergic reaction is toxic and occasionally lethal.

8. Idiosyncrasy: It is described as a genetically mediated response that the body produces to a chemical. This particular type of person only affects those who are genetically susceptible to that specific chemical or substance; they have no effect on other people. In these situations, the patient may feel uncomfortable for a few hours or, if the dosage is high, may even die. For instance, certain people have a peanut allergy.

9. Tolerance: It is the ability of a person to react normally to a chemical without producing any negative effects. It's a state in which there is little to no reaction to a chemical. Tolerance is induced through essentially two different kinds of mechanisms. Initially, there is very little toxin left at the effective site. We refer to this as dispositional tolerance. The second reason is that the tissues' reaction to the toxin is diminished. Regularly taking a small amount of a medication can also help build tolerance. We can explain this by using alcohol as an example. When a person drinks alcohol for the first time, they will experience some effects even at small amounts. However, over time, these effects will lessen and they will also be able to tolerate large amounts.

10. **Individual Susceptibility:** It is described as the various reactions that various people have to a specific toxic substance. It might be brought on by exposures to environmental or occupational factors. It is influenced by intricate genetic variables. The degree of exposure determines its impact. Due to the fact that each person's genes are unique, the same level of exposure can have no effect on one person, cause illness in another, and even be fatal in another.

4.5.2. Route of Administration of Poison

The route of administration, which can be identified by the place where a drug is applied, is the means by which a drug, toxin, or poison is ingested or administered into a person's body. It is mostly classified on the basis of its target:

- Topical—which has a local effect
- Enteral—which has a wide effect, i.e., affect the whole system
- Parental—which follows a systemic action

Poisons are given or taken so that death can occur at once by shock due to stoppage of body's vital systems. Drug addicts take drugs through inhalation or injection. Route of administration plays a very important role in determination of death by poison as time in which death occurs are fastest in inhaled poisons, relatively slow in injected and lastly when ingested orally.

Some important features that are considered during the administration of poisons and can make a poison fatal are:

- Rate of dissolution of the poison that depends upon the physical form of the poison, i.e., gaseous, vapors, liquid, solid, etc.
- The surface area affected at the site of administration of the poison
- The circulation rate of blood in that route
- The solubility of the poison, i.e., lipid soluble or water soluble
- The concentration of the poison
- The time required by the poison to be absorbed completely from the site of administration

Routes of administration can be classified into two categories:

1. Enteral routes/gastrointestinal routes.
2. Parenteral routes.

1. **Enteral Routes:** When the drug is administered through the gastrointestinal tract, it is defined as an enteral route. It has both oral and rectal routes. It also includes sublingual and sublabial routes. It is comparatively a slower mode of action for absorption of drugs:

- **Oral Route:** Generally absorption takes place in the tongue and the gums of the oral passage. The pH of the buccal cavity and mouth ranges from 4 to 5. Sublingual and supralingual routes have a significant role in absorption. The sublingual absorption is faster as the toxin is transformed directly to the heart, but it takes more time.
- **Rectal Route:** Administration of drugs can be done through anus which directly absorbed in bloodstream through membrane of mucous. This administration can cause the burning of tissues or bleeding in rectum as the area is very sensitive.
- **Parental Route:** It includes all the other routes that does not involve the gastrointestinal tract. It has a systemic effect on the body. It has the following categories of administration:
  - **Intradermal:** Here, the administration of drugs takes place from surface of skin. This type of poisoning is mostly found in chronic poisoning cases.
  - **Intravenous:** It is one of the fastest modes of drug administration as the injection is directly taken and the drug is transferred directly into the veins and thus is directly circulated into the blood quickly. Immediate death might be caused by this type of drug.
  - **Intraosseous:** It involves an administration of a drug directly into the bone marrow. This mode is actually used for administration of drugs for medical purposes.
  - **Intra-Arterial:** It involves an administration of a drug into the artery directly through injection. It is a fast mode of administration.
  - **Intramuscular:** In this mode, the drug or poison is administered into the muscle of the thigh, upper arm, or buttock. The time required in this mode is greater than other parental modes.
  - **Subcutaneous:** In this mode, the drug is injected into the layer beneath the skin, i.e., the subcutaneous layer. The drug then goes to the small blood vessels and then to the bloodstream. This mode is used for mostly those protein drugs that would be destroyed if administered through the gastrointestinal tract.

– **Inhalation:** In this mode, the nose is the primary path. Because of the presence of mucous membrane, the nasal aperture is very absorptive. The microparticles of poisons are easily absorbed and transported quickly to the lungs. From the lungs, they are circulated into the blood.

4.5.3. Classification of Poison

Poisons can be classified in various categories depending upon their as follow (Figure 4.1):

1. **On the Basis of Mode of Action**: On the basis of mode of action poison can be categorized into (i) Corrosive Poisons (ii) Irritant poisons, (iii) Neurotic Poisons, (iv) Cardiac Poisons and (v) Asphyxiants.

i. **Corrosive Poisons:** Corrosive poisons are the poisons which cause inflammation at the site of contact. Both strong acids and alkalis are comes under this category.

- **Strong Acids:** Concentrated sulfuric acid, nitric acid and hydrochloric acid
- **Strong Bases:** Sodium hydroxide, potassium hydroxide and ammonium hydroxide.

ii. **Irritant Poisons:** Irritants are those substances which cause irritation, pain, excessive vomiting. These are further divided into (a) inorganic poisons, (b) organic poisons and (c) mechanical poisons.

a. **Inorganic Poisons:** Inorganic poisons are consisted of:

- **Metallic**: Lead, arsenic, mercury, antimony, copper and zinc etc.
- **Non-Metallic**: Chlorine, bromine and iodine etc.

b. **Organic Poisons:** Organic poisons consist of poisons of both vegetable origin and animal origin.

- **Animal Poisons:** Snakes venom, scorpion venom, spiders etc.
- **Vegetable Poisons**: Croton oil, castor oil etc.

c. **Mechanical Poisons:** Mechanical poisons are the poisons which cause irritation, perforation obstruction in the gastrointestinal tract. For example, powder glass, diamond dust etc.

iii. **Neurotic Poisons:** Neurotic poisons are the poisons which affects the different part of central nervous system such as cerebral poisons, spinal poison, peripheral poisons etc., and these constitute of following poisons:

- **Cerebral Poisons:** Alcohol, opium, barbiturates, benzodiazepines etc.
- **Spinal Poison:** Strychnine.
- **Peripheral:** Curare

iv. **Cardiac Poisons** – Digitalis, tobacco.

v. **Asphyxiants** – CO, CO_2 etc.

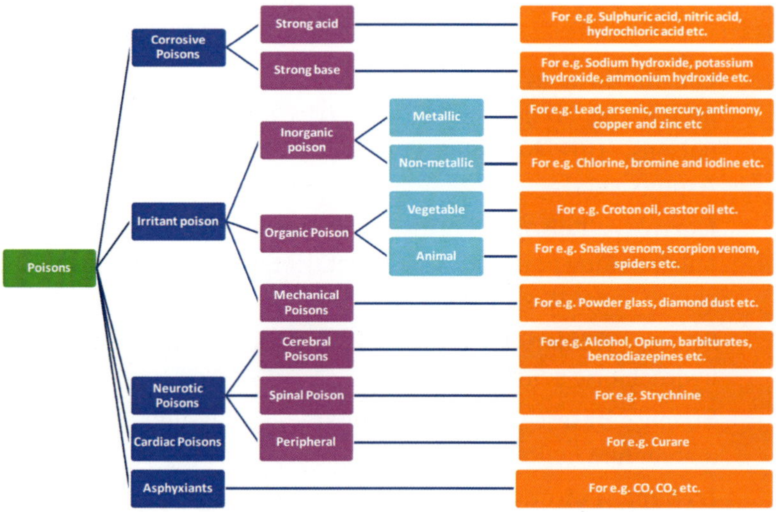

Figure 4.1. *Classification of poison.*

Source: https://epgp.inflibnet.ac.in/epgpdata/uploads/epgp_content/S001608/P001743/M022130/ET/1504246953Module9.pdf.

1. **On the Basis of Their Physical State**: Based on physical state, poisons can be grouped into (i) solid poisons, (ii) liquid poisons and (iii) gaseous poisons (Figure 4.2).

i. **Solid Poisons:** Solid poisons don not get absorbed easily into the blood. These should be dissolved properly in liquid to get absorbed. For example, lead, arsenic, mercury etc.

ii. **Liquid Poisons:** Liquid poisons contain both organic and inorganic liquid. Organic liquids are more volatile than inorganic liquids. Liquid poison can be absorbed when administered orally or by inhalation or through skin. As organic liquids are vaporizes and organic vapors are absorbed by lungs such as chloroform, acetone etc., and the organic vapors which are soluble in lipids get easily absorbed through skin for e.g., furfural.

iii. **Gaseous Poisons:** Gaseous poisons are absorbed by inhalation such as carbon dioxide, carbon monoxide etc. In atmosphere, there are aerosols particles in air and these are either inhaled or deposited on the skin. They causes marked effect on lungs when inhaled during breathing and causes obstruction into the lungs (asbestos) in comparison to those absorbed through skin. Fibers and dust are also the examples of aerosols.

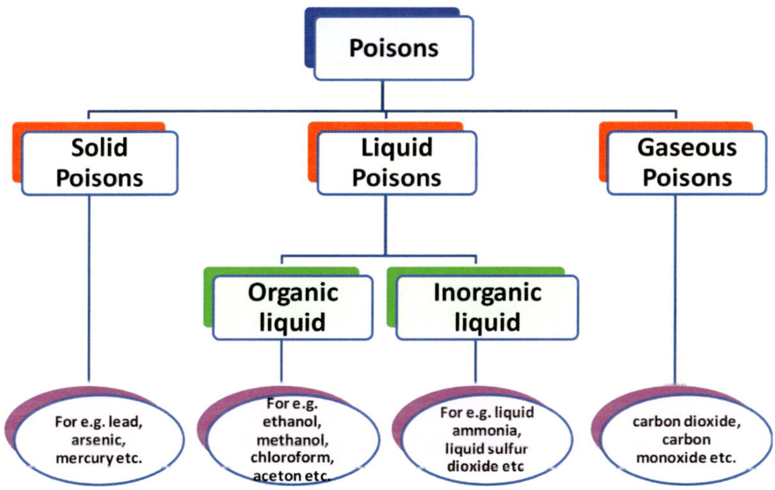

Figure 4.2. *Physical state of poisons.*

Source: https://epgp.inflibnet.ac.in/epgpdata/uploads/epgp_content/S001608/P001743/M022130/ET/1504246953Module9.pdf.

2. **Medicolegal Classification of Poison**: Based on intention behind the crime, poisons are classified into (i): Homicidal poisons, (ii) Suicidal poisons, (iii) Accidental poisons, (iv) Abortifacient poisons, (v) Stupefying agent/poisons, (vi) Agents used to cause bodily injury (vii) Cattle Poison (viii) Used for malingering (Figure 4.3).

i. **Homicidal Poisons:** The poisons which are used to kill the other person are known as homicidal poisons such as aconite, *Abrus precatorius*, *Strychnos nux-vomica* etc.

ii. **Suicidal Poisons:** Suicidal poisons are those poisons which are used for self killing such as opium, barbiturate, organophosphorus, organochloro compounds.

iii. **Accidental Poisons:** Accidental poisons are those poisons which cause toxicity by accidents or used in mistaken of others: Snakes bite, CO, and child takes dhatura's seeds in mistaken of capsicum seeds as it resemble to capsicum seed.

iv. **Abortifacient Poisons:** The poisons winch are used to procure abortion are know as abortifacient poisons for examples Quinine (alkaloid), Calotropis etc.

v. **Stupefying Agent/Poisons:** Stupefying agents are those poisons which are used to stupefy or fool the person for example Dhatura and chloral hydrate are used to rob the stranger or for the commitment of other crimes.

vi. **Agents Used to Cause Bodily Injury:** Usually corrosive acids are used to cause injury on faces and known as vitriol throwing.

vii. **Cattle Poison:** Agents which are used to kill livestocks are known as cattle poisons. *Abrus precatorius*, *Calotropis* are used to kill cattle.

viii. **Used for Malingering:** Some times *Semicarpus anacardium* is used by malinger to escape from duties as these produces to produce an artificial bruise.

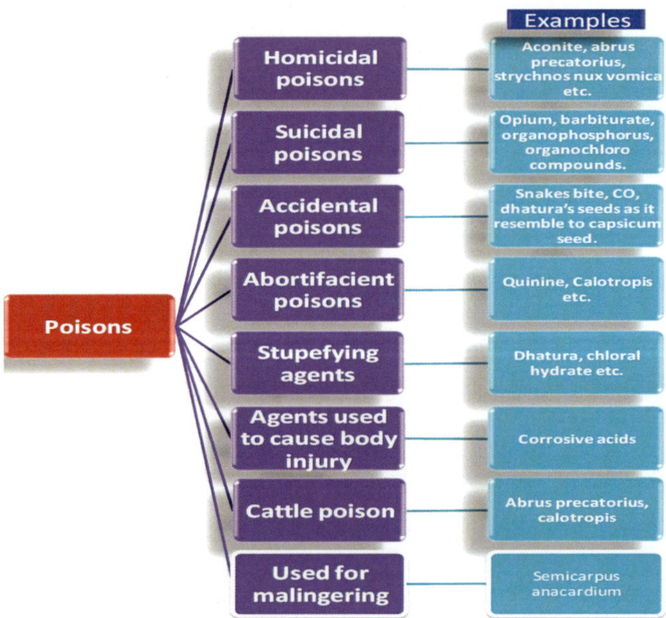

Figure 4.3. *Medicolegal classification of poison.*

Source: https://epgp.inflibnet.ac.in/epgpdata/uploads/epgp_content/S001608/P001743/M022130/ET/1504246953Module9.pdf.

3. **Toxico-analytical Classification**: Poisons can also be classified on the bases of method used for extraction or analysis into (i) Gaseous and volatile substances, (ii) Organic non-volatile substances, (iii) Metallic poisons and (iv) Anion. Therefore, this classification is known as toxico-analytical classification.

i. **Gaseous and Volatile Substances:** Poisons which are isolated by distillation or by headspace are categorized into this group. Volatile substances (methanol, ethanol, benzene, toluene, acetone etc.) can be separated from gaseous (ethane, butane etc.) poisons because they can be extracted with alternate methods.

ii. **Organic Non-Volatile Substances:** Compounds which are isolated by solvent extraction methods include in this group. For example, drugs such as opiates and synthetic narcotics, sedatives and hypnotics, stimulants, antidepressants etc., and pesticides which include insecticides, fungicides, herbicides, rodenticides, nematocides etc. In this group pesticides can be separated from drugs, though both are organic non-volatile substances which are isolated by solvent extraction method.

iii. **Metallic Poisons:** The substance which are isolated by dry ash method or by wet digestion method constituting this group. The commonest poisons are arsenic, lead, mercury, etc.

iv. **Anions Poisons:** Anions are isolated by dialysis. Most commonly encountered anions in poisoning cases are bromide, cyanide, fluoride, hypochlorite, nitrate, nitrite, phosphate, sulfide, sulfate etc.

REFERENCES

1. Alzate, L. F., et al. (2006). The vibrational spectroscopic signature of TNT in clay minerals. *Vibrational Spectroscopy, 42*, 357–368.
2. Angelos, S., & Garry, M. (2011). Seized drug analysis using FT-IR and mixture searching for more effective identification. *Forensic Magazine*. Advantage Business Media.
3. Bajgar, J. (2004). Organophosphates/nerve agent poisoning: Mechanism of action, diagnosis, prophylaxis, and treatment. *Advances in Clinical Chemistry, 38*(1), 151–216.
4. Bartick, E. G. (2002). Application of vibrational spectroscopy in criminal forensic analysis. In *Handbook of Vibrational Spectroscopy*. Wiley.
5. Bartick, E. G., & Mount, K. H. (2001). Analysis of a suspect explosive component: Hydrogen peroxide in hair coloring developer. *Forensic Science Communications, 3*(4).
6. Bell, S. E. J., et al. (2005). Forensic analysis of architectural finishes using Fourier transform infrared and Raman spectroscopy: II. White paint. *Applied Spectroscopy, 59*(11), 1340–1346.
7. Campion, A., & Kambhampati, P. (1998). Surface-enhanced Raman scattering. *Chemical Society Reviews, 27*, 241–250.
8. Causin, V., et al. (2006). A quantitative differentiation method for plastic bags by infrared spectroscopy, thickness measurement and differential scanning calorimetry for tracing the source of illegal drugs. *Forensic Science International, 164*, 148–154.
9. Choi, W. Y., Kim, H. J., Na, J. Y., Lee, S. J., Lee, Y. J., & Park, J. T., et al. (2016). Analysis of death due to poisoning in Gwangju and Jeollanam-do areas. *Korean Journal of Legal Medicine, 40*(3), 72–77.
10. Colthup, N. B., Daly, L. H., & Wiberley, S. E. (1990). *Introduction to Infrared and Raman Spectroscopy*. Academic Press.
11. Cotton, F. A. (1990). *Chemical Applications of Group Theory*. Wiley.
12. De Boer, A. G., Moolenaar, F., De Leede, L. G. J., & Breimer, D. D. (1982). Rectal drug administration. *Clinical Pharmacokinetics, 7*(4), 285–311.
13. De Gelder, J., et al. (2005). Forensic analysis of automotive paints by Raman spectroscopy. *Journal of Raman Spectroscopy, 36*, 1059–1067.
14. Dedrick, R. L., Myers, C. E., Bungay, P. M., & DeVita, V. T. (1978). Pharmacokinetic rationale for peritoneal drug administration. *Cancer Treatment Reports, 62*, 1–13.
15. Diem, M. (1993). *Introduction to Vibrational Spectroscopy*. Wiley.

16. Donaldson, A. E., Larsen, G. Y., Fullerton-Gleason, L., & Olson, L. M. (2006). Classifying undetermined poisoning deaths. *Injury Prevention, 12*(5), 338–343.
17. Everall, N. (2004a). Depth profiling with confocal Raman microscopy: I. *Spectroscopy, 19*(10), 22–27.
18. Everall, N. (2004b). Depth profiling with confocal Raman microscopy: II. *Spectroscopy, 19*(11), 16–27.
19. Fredrick, K. A., et al. (2004). Identification of individual drug crystals on paper currency using Raman micro spectroscopy. *Spectroscopy Letters, 37*(3), 301–310.
20. Gaensslen, R. E., Kubic, T. A., Desio, P. J., & Lee, H. C. (1985). Instrumentation and analytical methodology in forensic science. *Journal of Chemical Education, 62*(12), 1058–1060.
21. Gerrard, D. L. (1994). Raman spectroscopy. *Analytical Chemistry, 66*(12), 547–557.
22. Graybeal, J. D. (1988). *Molecular Spectroscopy*. McGraw-Hill.
23. Griffiths, P. R., & de Haseth, J. A. (2007). *Fourier Transform Infrared Spectroscopy*. Wiley.
24. Halford, B. (2012). Tracing a threat. *Chemical & Engineering News, 90*(6), 10–15.
25. Harrick Scientific Corp. (1987). *Optical Spectroscopy: Sampling Techniques Manual*. Harrick.
26. Harrick, N. J. (1987). *Internal Reflection Spectroscopy*. Harrick Scientific Corporation.
27. Herzberg, G. (1945). *Infrared and Raman Spectra of Polyatomic Molecules*. D. Van Nostrand.
28. Humecki, H. J. (1995). *Practical Guide to Infrared Microscopy* (Vol. 19). Marcel Dekker.
29. Ingle, J. D., Jr., & Crouch, S. R. (1988). *Spectrochemical Analysis*. Prentice Hall.
30. Izzia, F., Nunn, S., & Bradley, M. (2008). Analysis of mixtures by FT-IR: Spatial and spectral separation of complex samples. *Spectroscopy Online*.
31. Kalasinsky, K. S. (1993). Hair analysis by infrared microscopy for drugs of abuse. *Forensic Science International, 63*, 253–260.
32. Katon, J. E., & Sommer, A. J. (1992). IR micro spectroscopy. *Analytical Chemistry, 64*(19), 931–940.

33. Kirkbride, K. P. (2000). *Analytical Techniques/Spectroscopic Techniques*. Academic Press.
34. Kocak, A. (1998). *Design and Construction of the Step-Scan Fourier Transform Vibrational Circular Dichroism, Part I*. City University of New York.
35. Kocak, A., et al. (2006). Using the Kramers–Kronig method to determine optical constants and evaluating its suitability as a linear transform for near-normal front-surface reflectance spectra. *Applied Spectroscopy, 60*(9), 1004–1007.
36. Kortum, G. (1969). *Reflectance Spectroscopy*. Springer-Verlag.
37. Koulis, C. V., et al. (2001). Comparison of transmission and internal reflection infrared spectra of cocaine. *Journal of Forensic Sciences, 46*(4), 822–829.
38. Krishnan, K., & Hill, S. L. (1990). FT-IR micro sampling techniques: Practical Fourier transform infrared spectroscopy. Academic Press.
39. Levine, I. N. (1991). *Quantum Mechanics*. Prentice Hall.
40. Lewis, E. N., & Levin, I. W. (1995). Fourier transform spectroscopic imaging using an infrared focal-plane array detector. *Applied Spectroscopy, 49*(5), 672–678.
41. Macht, D. I. (1938). A drug or poison? *The Scientific Monthly, 47*(1), 34–40.
42. Maynard, P., et al. (2001). A protocol for the forensic analysis of condom and personal lubricant found in sexual assault cases. *Forensic Science International, 124*, 140–156.
43. Merrill, R. A. (2000). Analysis of pressure sensitive adhesive tape: I. Evaluation of infrared ATR accessory advances. *Journal of Forensic Sciences, 45*(1), 93–98.
44. Merrill, R. A., et al. (2003). Forensic discrimination of photocopy and printer toners: I. The development of an infrared spectral library. *Analytical and Bioanalytical Chemistry, 376*, 1272–1278.
45. Mirabella, F. M. (1998). *Modern Techniques in Applied Molecular Spectroscopy*. Wiley.
46. Peter, J. V., Sudarsan, T. I., & Moran, J. L. (2014). Clinical features of organophosphate poisoning: A review of different classification systems and approaches. *Indian Journal of Critical Care Medicine, 18*(11), 735.
47. Prinzmetal, M., Sommer, H., & Leake, C. D. (1932). The pharmacological action of "mussel poison". *Journal of Pharmacology and Experimental Therapeutics, 46*(1), 63–73.

48. Schrader, B. (1995). *Infrared and Raman Spectroscopy*. VCH.
49. Skoog, D. A., et al. (2007). *Principles of Instrumental Analysis*. Thomson Brooks/Cole.
50. Strobel, H. A., & Heineman, W. R. (1989). *Chemical Instrumentation: A Systematic Approach*. Wiley.
51. Wasserman, D., & Dawson, C. R. (1943). The toxic principle of poison ivy and other related plants. *Journal of Chemical Education, 20*(9), 448.
52. Yip, L., Dart, R. C., & Hurlbut, K. M. (1998). Intravenous administration of oral N-acetylcysteine. *Critical Care Medicine, 26*(1), 40–43.

CHAPTER 5

FORENSIC ANTHROPOLOGY AND ODONTOLOGY

Contents

Introduction 156

5.1. Definition, AIM and Scope of Forensic Anthropology 157

5.2. Biological Profiling of Skeletal Remains 163

5.3. Evolution of Forensic Anthropological Methods of Identification 171

5.4. Forensic Odontology: Bite Mark Analysis 180

5.5. Importance of Dental Records in Forensic Odontology 192

References 199

INTRODUCTION

The application of anthropology's anatomical science and its many subfields—such as forensic taphonomy and archaeology—in a legal context is known as forensic anthropology. When a person dies in a plane crash and their remains are burned, mutilated, decomposed, or otherwise unidentifiable, a forensic anthropologist can help identify the deceased. Mass grave and genocide investigations and documentation are also greatly aided by forensic anthropologists. Forensic anthropologists frequently appear in court as expert witnesses alongside forensic pathologists, forensic dentists, and homicide investigators. It is possible for a forensic anthropologist to ascertain an individual's age, sex, stature, and race by utilizing physical markers found on a skeleton. Forensic anthropologists can utilize skeletal abnormalities in addition to physical characteristics to determine a person's cause of death, past trauma (e.g., broken bones, medical procedures), and diseases (e.g., bone cancer).

The study of human skeletal variations and the historical contributions of different anthropologists are key components of the techniques used to identify a person from a skeleton. Based on physical traits, estimates can be made by gathering thousands of specimens and analyzing variations within a population. With these, it might be possible to identify a set of remains. Over the course of the 20th century, forensic anthropology developed into a fully recognized forensic specialty that involves the collection of data on decomposition and its effects on skeletons by a number of research institutions and trained anthropologists.

In the context of criminal justice, the handling, inspection, and assessment of dental evidence is the practice of forensic dentistry, also known as forensic odontology. It is possible to use forensic dentistry in both criminal and civil law. When identifying information is otherwise hard to come by or nonexistent, such as when identifying burn victims by looking up their dental records, forensic dentists help investigating agencies identify human remains. In order to ascertain the age, race, occupation, prior dental history, and socioeconomic status of individuals who are unknown, forensic dentists may also be asked to help.

Photographs taken both before and after the death, radiographs, and DNA analysis can all be used by forensic dentists to reach their conclusions. Bite marks, whether they were made by the attacker, the victim, or an object discovered at the crime scene, are another kind of evidence that can be examined. This latter use of forensic dentistry, however, has proven to be very contentious because there are no empirical studies or other supporting data that bite marks can exhibit enough detail for a positive identification, and there are multiple cases where experts' assessments of the same bite mark evidence differ significantly.

5.1. DEFINITION, AIM AND SCOPE OF FORENSIC ANTHROPOLOGY

People have always been interested in their surroundings, other living things, the universe, and even their own existence. Man's insatiable curiosity leads him into the depths of history, the complexities of political systems, biology, and many other academic disciplines. But anthropology is, to put it beautifully, a patchwork of many different scientific and humanities disciplines combined. Anthropology provides answers to questions about the past and present of humanity, and these answers are based on facts rather than the wild speculations of human imagination. Building a knowledge base with multiple dimensions that covers a wide range of topics and streams is what anthropology does. In addition to its theoretical components, it applies its knowledge base to solve societal issues. Simply put, it is study of human being with time and space. Anthropology is a subject divided into following branches:

- Physical / Biological anthropology
- Social / cultural anthropology
- Archaeology
- Linguistic Anthropology

The study of biological and physical anthropology examines how humans evolve physically. Physical and biological anthropology examines the various ways that humans have interacted with their surroundings since the beginning of life. It delves deeply into the ways that social milieu and the external environment impact human lives. It examines the stages of human evolution, the variables influencing those stages, and the drawbacks. e. Physical anthropology also includes the study of illness and other conditions, as well as, very practically, their causes and remedies. Physical anthropology therefore offers more innovative viewpoints and practical applications in daily life.

Numerous elements make up society, including people, culture, resources, etc. Humans are social animals that undergo a process of fusion. It implies that people have an impact on society and are impacted by it in turn. Political society, such as a nation or state, and natural society, such as a family, exist. These societies are entwined as well.

Archaeology is a manifestation of human creativity and building ability. It's creativity, and it happens through a process at a certain moment. It operates on a temporal scale at a specific moment. It also has a temporal component. Using a population-oriented methodology, bio-archaeology usually entails the analysis of artifacts and human remains from a whole historic or prehistoric cemetery. Finding the victim and determining the cause and manner of death are the main goals of an investigation when a human body is found. These objectives are typically fulfilled by the law enforcement organization and the forensic pathologist conducting the autopsy if the remains are discovered not too long after the death. However, the services of a forensic anthropologist are frequently required when the remains are not found until after death. The forensic anthropologist is the most qualified to determine an individual's age, ancestry, sex, stature, and level of trauma in cases involving skeletal remains.

Therefore, the subfield of biological anthropology known as "forensic anthropology" applies anthropological knowledge to medico-legal procedures. The field recovery of partially or fully skeletonized remains, as well as their laboratory management and analysis, are all included in forensic anthropology. It entails identifying the individual's unique characteristics, estimating the time since death and the manner and cause of death, determining whether the skeletal remains are of animal or human origin, counting the number of individuals represented, determining the race, sex, age, and stature of the individuals concerned, identifying any pathology, injuries, and anomalies, and investigating the identity of the individual by comparing post-mortem skeletal evidence with ante-mortem records or portraits. An investigative team's forensic anthropology department is a crucial part of the field, lab, and courtroom. Forensic anthropologists, for instance, might collaborate with radiologists, forensic pathologists, odontologists (dentists), police investigators, crime scene technicians, molecular geneticists, and fingerprint specialists during the identification process. If a case proceeds to trial, the team is augmented with additional forensic specialists, such as ballistics experts, trace evidence examiners, and document examiners, all of whom provide testimony regarding their respective scientific or technical findings.

Forensic Anthropologist is helpful for the Court of Law as follows:

- Human or not
- Race
- Individual Identification
- Minimum number of individuals
- Age Determination
- Sex Determination
- Number of Individuals
- Disease Processes

5.1.1. Historical Development of Forensic Anthropology

Thompson, in his work from 1982, outlined three stages in the evolution of forensic anthropology: prior to 1939, 1939 to 1972, and post-1972. The foundations of forensic anthropology can primarily be traced back to the realm of anatomical sciences. In the era preceding 1939, anatomy departments were the primary drivers of the methodology surrounding human skeletal variation, employing cadaver collections that were classified by age, ancestry, sex, and health conditions.

It was undoubtedly during this time that physical anthropologists and anatomists were frequently consulted by law enforcement agencies regarding human skeletal remains. Prominent figures in this field during this period included Thomas Dwight from Harvard University, H.H. Wilder of Smith College in Massachusetts, and the Field Columbian Museum in Chicago, among others. Ernest Hooton from Harvard University and Ales Hrdlicka also showed interest in this field during this era. Hrdlicka, in particular, played a significant role in the establishment of the American Association of Physical Anth ropologists in 1930 and the launch of the American Journal of Physical Anthropology in 1918. Hrdlicka also consulted with law enforcement agencies, including the FBI, on a number of skeletal cases.

Hooton later publish "Medico-legal Aspects of Physical Anthropology" in Clinics, in which he described the dim prospect of new methods in the field of physical anthropology in a forensic context, undoubtedly because of the lack of attention given to the field. In 1939, W.M. Krogman published "A Guide to the Identification of Human Skeletal Material" in the FBI Law Enforcement Bulletin, marking the beginning of the second period of forensic anthropology development. This publication represented the first major contribution by a trained anthropologist on the topic of human skeletal identification for medico-legal purposes. Krogman's publication allowed the forensic community, as well as other physical anthropologists, to view physical anthropology in a forensic context. At the close of World War II, several physical anthropologists were consulted in the identification of war casualties. Among the anthropologists who contributed their expertise were H.L. Shapiro of the American Museum of Natural History in New York, F.E. Randall of the U.S. Army's Office of the Quartermaster General, and Charles Snow of the University of Kentucky. Krogman's "Guide" became a manual used by the anthropologists in the identification process. A central laboratory was established for this purpose in 1947 in Hawaii and was headed by Charles Snow. Not long before, in the early 1940s, T.D. Stewart began his routine consultation with the FBI for forensic skeletal cases. This relationship, initiated by Hrdlicka, represented an early phase of a long history of collaboration between the FBI and the Smithsonian.

The first forensic anthropology textbook, "The Human Skeleton in Forensic Medicine," was written by Krogman in 1962. It was revised and updated in 1986 by Krogman and Iscan and contains a collection of methods and case studies related to the identification of human remains. Krogman provided techniques in the text for determining age, ancestry, sex, and stature in addition to individualizing traits and restoring facial features on the skull. The establishment of the Physical Anthropology section by the American Academy of Forensic Sciences (AAFS) in 1972 marked a watershed in the field of forensic anthropology. The section discussed the rise in forensic anthropology textbooks. Stewart released Essentials of Forensic Anthropology in 1979. The courtroom procedures related to expert testimony were covered in a chapter for the first time in this textbook. Writings by anthropologists for other anthropologists as well as, crucially, for other scientists and law enforcement officials began to appear after 1972. The field of forensic anthropology currently publishes works on a broad spectrum of subjects. As was common during the field's early development, anthropologists are no longer restricted to studies involving the estimation of age, ancestry, sex, and stature. While much work remains to be done in refining and testing these methods, the reach of the anthropologist extends well beyond them. Hrdlicka was a trailblazer in the field of American physical anthropology, having been instrumental in the establishment of both the American Journal of Physical Anthropology and the American Association of Physical Anthropologists. While Hrdlicka is primarily recognized for his research on anthropometry and the population of the New World, he had a wide range of interests and pursuits, including forensic subjects. Hrdlicka studied legal medicine as part of his training, and his early research was on forensic problems pertaining to the biology of aberrant behavior. He became involved in legal matters pertaining to American Indian ancestry and skeletal analysis while working at the Smithsonian's Department of Anthropology. The FBI was aware of Hrdlicka's expertise as early as 1918, and by 1936 at the latest, the FBI was sending specimens to Hrdlicka for identification.

Through the work of Jean-Joseph Sue, a French art anatomy instructor at the Louvre in Paris, the seeds of what would become forensic anthropology were sown in France. He published measurements of cadavers ranging in age from young adult to fetus in 1755. While the work's primary goal was to give artists accurate information about body proportions and how they changed with age, it also sparked significant interest in France and led to studies on stature calculation. Sue's measurements became more widely known when Mathieu-Joseph-Bonaventure Orfila published them in two medico-legal textbooks at the beginning of the 1800s. For many years, the two databases comprised the sources used by the medico-legal community to assess stature from incomplete remains. Orfila (1831) added his own measurements to Sue's.

5.1.2. Definition of Forensic Anthropology

The field recovery of partially or fully skeletonized remains, as well as their laboratory management and analysis, are all included in forensic anthropology. It entails identifying the individual's unique characteristics, estimating the time since death and the manner and cause of death, determining whether the skeletal remains are of animal or human origin, counting the number of individuals represented, determining the race, sex, age, and stature of the individuals concerned, identifying any Y, injuries, and anomalies, and investigating the identity of the individual by comparing post-mortem skeletal evidence with ante-mortem records or portraits.

A Guide to the 'Identification of Human Skeletal Material' and The 'Human Skeleton in Forensic Medicine- (1962) were published by WM Krogman in 1939. Other anthropologists used this published work to develop forensic anthropological techniques.

The Essentials of Forensic Anthropology: Especially as Developed in the United States by TD Stewart was published in 1979, and Krogman and M.Y followed in 1986. Age, sex, race, and stature are the "big four" that Iscan defined in forensic anthropology for the identification of skeletal remains in criminal investigations. This served as the basis for the development of forensic anthropology; since then, a large number of books and articles have been published, and research has been done all over the world.

Snow (1973) offered a somewhat broader definition of forensic anthropology to include applications to "problems of medical jurisprudence."

In 1976, T. D. Stewart defined forensic anthropology as "that branch of physical anthropology, which, for forensic purposes, deals with the identification of more or less skeletonized remains known to be, or suspected of being, human." (Sigler-Eisenberg, 1985)

The application of physical anthropology's knowledge and methods to issues with medical and legal implications is known as forensic anthropology. Typically, the objectives are to help identify human remains and ascertain the circumstances surrounding the remains, particularly in relation to any indications of foul play. Skeletal evidence that has been extracted from fleshed remains or mostly or entirely skeletonized remains make up the majority of the material that is examined. In addition to providing a global comparative population perspective, forensic anthropology offers techniques and experience in the interpretation of skeletal remains to a case.

The application of anthropological and skeletal biological principles to medico-legal issues is known as forensic anthropology. The phrase "medico-legal" describes how medical science can provide information on legating details are supplied by the American Board of Forensic AnthropologyThe American Board of Forensic Anthropology supplies the definition of forensic anthropology and further elucidating details: The application of physical or biological anthropology to the legal system is known as forensic anthropology. Forensic anthropologists who specialize in physical or biological anthropology mainly study human skeletons.

5.1.3. Scope of Forensic Anthropology

- In both legal and humanitarian contexts, forensic anthropologists analyze skeletal, badly decomposed, or otherwise unidentified human remains.
- In order to analyze human remains and assist in the investigation of crimes, forensic anthropologists employ standard scientific methods originally developed in physical anthropology.
- Forensic anthropologists not only help locate and retrieve human skeletal remains, but they also analyze skeletons to determine a deceased person's age, sex, ancestry, stature, and distinctive characteristics.
- Originate in the skeleton. Forensic anthropologists often collaborate with odontologists, forensic pathologists, and homicide investigators to determine the identity of a deceased person, record skeletal trauma, and/or calculate the post-mortem period.

A forensic anthropologist's training in biological, taphonomic, archaeology, and cultural anthropology makes them valuable for investigating crimes and crime scenes. They can recognize cultural markers that distinguish ethnic, religious, or national groups thanks to their training in cultural anthropology. They are qualified to excavate crime scenes and secret graves because of their training in anthropology, archaeology, and taphonomy. The most significant contribution made by anthropologists is specifically taphonomy, or "the interpretation of all events affecting the remains between death and discovery." Their background in biological anthropology equips them with the knowledge and abilities to examine skeletal remains and related evidence in order to establish genocide.

When examining the surreptitious graves and remains of murder victims, the forensic anthropologist help in solving the problem as follows:

- First, determine various demographic attributes of the victim such as ancestry or ethnic group, sex, age, and stature of the individual.
- Second, collect evidence of traumatic injury to determine the nature and cause of the trauma to assist in the determination of the manner of death.

- Third, based on knowledge of decomposition and deterioration of human remains after death, estimate the time that passed since the individual died, or the post-mortem interval (PMI).
- Fourth, assist in the location of remains buried or left on the surface of the ground in a way that allows the collection of all relevant evidence needed for the forensic investigation.
- Fifth, using knowledge of skeletal features, forensic anthropologists can provide information unique to each individual to obtain a positive identification.
- Furthermore, because forensic anthropology uses both clinical and actuarial judgment, it can be considered a clinical practice. The practitioner's ability to make clinical decisions depends on their ability to integrate knowledge gained from both academic coursework and practical, clinical examination of human remains. Actuarial judgment, on the other hand, necessitates interpretations based on computations made with the aid of empirically proven formulas.

5.2. BIOLOGICAL PROFILING OF SKELETAL REMAINS

5.2.1. Demography

The "big four" of Krogman's skeletal examinations are age, sex, ethnic group, and stature. Every characteristic significantly reduces the number of potential "matches"—sex alone halves the pool. A skeleton that is complete and undamaged allows for extremely accurate assessment of these factors. With the latest systems, it is possible to determine sex with certainty, estimate age to within five years, and approximate stature with a typical deviation of roughly 1.5 inches (3.5 cm). But since incomplete and fragmented specimens are more common, forensic anthropologists need to be prepared to extract as much information as possible from each bone. The categories of ethnicity, age, sex, stature, and build are examples of demographic traits.

5.2.2. Ethnic Group

An ethnic group can be thought of as the coarse classification apparatus for biological traits. Primitive Negro, Mongoloid, and Caucasoid are the three main ethnic groups. But because of admixture, there will always be cases that are unclear. Furthermore, there is a great deal of variation within each group, and one factor in racial classification is skin color. The best indicator of racial phenotype in the skeleton is cranio-facial morphology. Negroids are usually characterized by an extended, low, slender skull with alveolar prognathism and a broad, flat nose with gentle sills. There are racial variations in other bodily areas. Negroids have a straight femur bone, while Caucasoids have a forward-curving femur. Although measurements are more accurate, negroids have narrow pelvises. Disparities in overall body proportions are replicated by size differentials. Comparatively speaking, limb lengths are longer in negroids than in Caucasoids; for mongoloids, the opposite is true (Figure 5.1).

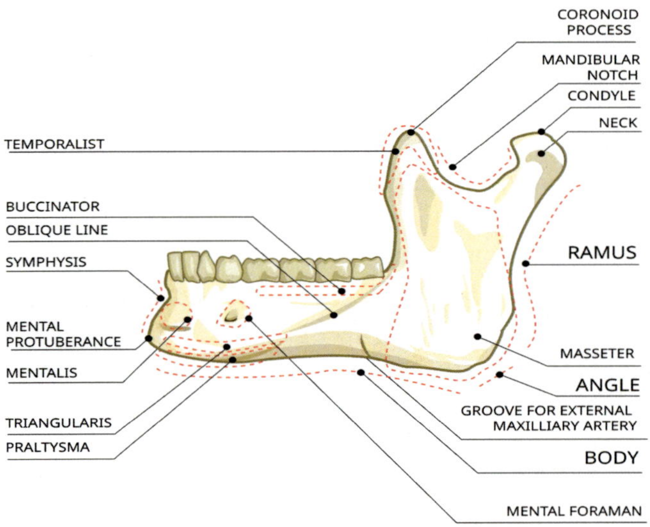

Figure 5.1. *Mandible.*

Source: https://www.intechopen.com/chapters/73372.

Table 5.1. *Differentiating Features and Points Between Ethnic Groups*

Characteristics	Europeans Origin	Asian Origin	African Origin
Protrusion of jaws	Orthognathic	Prognathic	Prognathic
Nasal spine	Prominent, large, or long	Medium, tilted	Little or no nasal spine
Nasal aperture	Narrow	Medium	Wide
Nasal sill	Single and sharp	Single and sharp	Double or guttered

Zygoma	Single	Forward projecting (extra bone present)	Single
Dentition	More crowded	Less crowded	Less crowded
Palate	Narrow	Wide	Intermediate palate width
Dental row	Parabolic curve	Simple elliptical (rounded)	Hyperbolic curve (U-shape)
Incisors	Blade shape	Shovel shape	Blade shape
Palatal suture	Arched or jagged	Straight	Not straight
Maxillary molars	Carabelli's cusps	Four cusps	Four cusps
Cranial suture	Simple	Complex and/ or with sutural bones	Simple
Chin	Square and projecting	Blunt	Retreating
Cranium	High	Low and sloping	Low and with post-bregmatic depression
Anterior curvature of femur Bone	More curved	Straighter	Straighter

https://www.intechopen.com/chapters/73372.

5.2.3. Sex

Assuming that the adult skeleton is complete or at least exhibits an intact pelvis, determining the sex is typically possible with 100% precision. But as was already mentioned, incomplete forensic skeletons are rare, and the bones that are present might not be visibly dimorphic. There isn't a distinguishing marker for the main sexual features. Gender differences in immature skeletons have been measured, but they are not as noticeable until secondary sex characteristics start to emerge in adolescence. Measurements of growth-based differences between males and females have been used in an attempt to sex prepubescent bones, but the results are far from realistic. An assessment of the pelvis can be used to determine an adult's sex. With systematic data on cranial morphology, experts can arrive at conclusions with up to 90–95% accuracy. However, since sex-linked distinctiveness differs amongst groups, the observer needs to be well-versed in population-specific variants. While females retain the straight, juvenile arrangement, adult males have been observed to have a distinct angulation or flexure at the level of the occlusal surface of the molars in the posterior ramus.

5.2.4. Age

The structure and growth of the centers of ossification serve as a starting point for the bony skeleton arrangement, which is not absolute at first. At both ends of long bones, there are diaphyses (shafts) and epiphyses until the start of adolescence.

These are connected by emergent areas known as cartilaginous metaphysis, which are replaced by bone at the point of complete development. Because each bony joint develops at a different age and in a specific order, age estimation from roughly 13 to 18 years old can be done within a year by following the sequence of epiphyseal union. Adolescents between the ages of 13 and 18 exhibit the humerus bone's proximal epiphysis opening and lower epiphysis merging. The body's fusion of joints then determines age.

Age estimation becomes much more challenging once development is inclusive because post-maturity age changes are often subtle, uneven, and highly variable between individuals due to remodeling rates and patterns being sensitive to numerous internal and external factors. The most accurate method of estimating age is now found to be the sterna end of the rib. A comparison of similar people's pubic symphysis and ribs revealed that the rib could replicate age two times more precisely (Figure 5.2, Table 5.2).

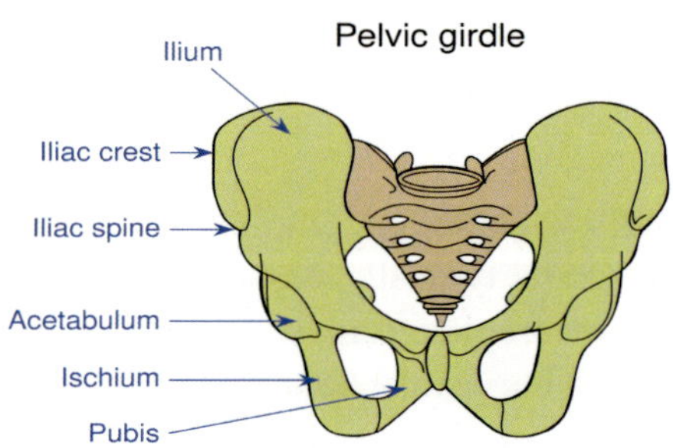

Figure 5.2. *The pelvic girdle.*

Source: https://www.intechopen.com/chapters/73372.

Table 5.2. *Differentiating Features Between Male and Female for Sex Determination*

Characteristics	**Male**	**Female**
Occipital protuberance	More prominent	Less prominent
Mastoid process	Larger	Smaller
Supraorbital ridges	Prominent	Absent
Upper orbital margin	Rounded	Sharper
Ramus of mandible	Wide, sharply angled, flared	Narrow, chin less angled
Chin	Squared, protuberant	Rounded or pointed
Ossification of ribs	Marginal	Central
Ribs' ends' appearance	Crab claw-like	Rough planar end
Pelvis	Larger and more robust	Wider and larger pelvic inlet
Pubic bone	Triangular	Rectangular
Subpubic angle	Narrow	Wide
Subpubic concavity	Absent	Developed
Parturition pits	Absent	Developed
Characteristics	**Male**	**Female**
Ilium	Narrow	Wide
Sciatic notch	Narrow and deep	Wide and shallow
Sacrum	More curved, longer, and narrower	Flatter, broader, and smaller
Muscle attachment in pelvis	More	Less
Humerus head diameter	>47 mm	<43 mm
Radius head diameter	≥24 mm	≤21 mm

Femur head diameter	47.5 mm	42.5 mm
Q-angle in femur bone	Smaller (11.2 ± 3)	Larger (15.8 ± 4.5)
Knee	Larger	Smaller
Zygomatic arch	Broader	Narrower
Sternum	Body is more than twice as large the manubrium length	Body is less than twice the manubrium length

Source: https://www.intechopen.com/chapters/73372.

There are numerous techniques for estimating age, each with pros and cons. There isn't a single aging technique that is 100% accurate.

There are two areas of concern: (1) individual variation as indicated by the method's standard deviation; and (2) disparities between the sample and the original population. Unless there is absolutely no other option, no aging process should be used alone. Naturally, there are less options for methods when the only material that can be accessed is partial or fragmentary remains. When approximating age, always provide a range. Giving a 3- to 5-year range and completely missing the recognition is far worse than including a 10- to 12-year age range, especially for large individuals, and successfully matching the lost person by other uniqueness (Table 5.3).

Table 5.3. *Age Determination in Male and Female*

Characteristic	**Age Estimation**
Metopic suture fusion	Closure by 1–2 years, fusion by 7–8 years
Lateral portion of occipital bone fusion with squamous bone	1–3 years
Basioccipital fusion with occipital	5–7 years
Fusion of occipital with sphenoid	11–16 years (in females), 13–18 years (in males)
Mandibular symphysis fusion	6–8 months

Medial clavicular epiphysis	Mid-twenties or 15–35 years
Coracoid Process in scapula	15–17 years
Glenoid epiphysis	17–18 years
Acromial epiphysis	~20 years
Ribs' head epiphysis	17–25 years
Segment 3 and 4 of sternum	4–10 years
Segment 2 with 3–4 of sternum	11–16 years
Segment 1 with 2–3–4 of sternum	15–20 years
Xiphoid to body	40+ years
Xiphoid appearance	3–6 years
Transverse lines (S1 and S2) in sacrum	Mid-twenties or later
Humerus distal epiphysis	11–15 years female, 12–17 years male
Humerus proximal epiphysis	13–17 years female, 16–20 years males
Radial distal epiphysis	11–13 years female, 14–17 years male
Radial proximal epiphysis	14–17 years female, 16–20 years male
Ischiopubic ramus	5–8 years
Acetabulum	11–17 years
Ischial tuberosity	16–20 years
Femoral distal epiphysis	14–18 years female, 16–20 years male
Femoral head fusion	12–16 years female, 14–19 years male
Tibial distal epiphysis	14–16 years female, 15–18 years male
Tibial proximal epiphysis	13–17 years female, 15–19 years male

Source: https://www.intechopen.com/chapters/73372.

5.2.5. Stature

The femur and tibia are typically the two most important primary components of height. As a result, the best estimate of height is obtained using regression formulas derived from tibial and femoral lengths. These formulas apply to all long bones, which provide greater precision than arm bones. In fact, they might be the only parts where attempts have been made to increase accuracy by utilizing the combined support of multiple bones. Body proportions vary depending on the sex and ethnic group.

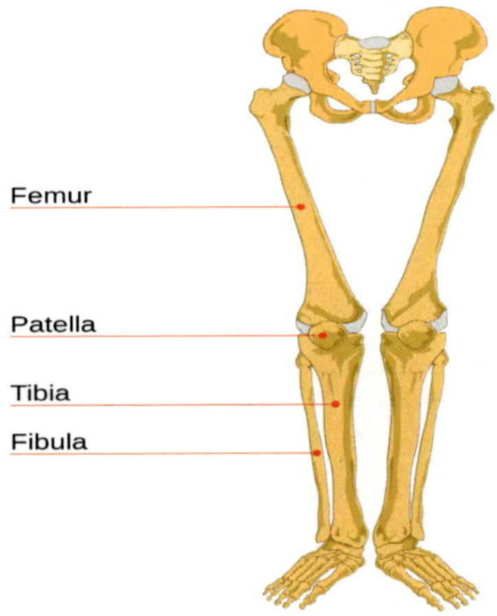

Figure 5.3. *Lower limb bones.*

Source: https://www.intechopen.com/chapters/73372.

For example, compared tocCaucasoids, negroids have longer limb bones relative to stature. Therefore, it is crucial to use the appropriate regression formulae for the evaluation of statur toto determine sex and ethnic group in sort. Trotter standards apply to both negroids and Caucasoids. Fine muscle fibers and smooth bone surfaces are characteristics of a sedentary or graceful person. It's important to remember that while men naturally have more muscle than women, their attachment sites are not as developed in men as they are in female body builders.

Not everyone who is small has a thin build, and not everyone who is very tall is necessarily massive. It is possible to estimate standard weight for a given height, but it is not possible to determine obesity from skeleton measurements. It is important to determine the focus's sex and ethnic group before beginning any stature analysis because the formulas for estimating stature vary depending on these factors. On an osteometric board, long bones are frequently measured. Large sliding calipers are also very useful for measuring tree diameters. Most measurements of long bones are simple maximum lengths. This involves taking measurements of the ulna, fibula, femur, radius, and humerus. The tibia has some additional complexity. Next, with both condyles in contact with the osteometric board, the femur is measured.

This length, also known as the oblique length or bicondylar length, is especially useful because it aligns the femur with its anatomical position. In addition to stature, bicondylar length reveals information about sex. Measure each bone in accordance with the instructions, then enter the measurement into the appropriate formulas (Table 5.4, Figure 5.3).

Table 5.4. *Stature Estimation Using Gleser Formula*

Ethnic Group	Bone	Male	Female
European	Humerus	2.89 * L + 78.10 ± 4.75	3.36 * L + 57.97 ± 4.45
	Radius	3.79 * L + 79.42 ± 4.66	4.74 * L + 54.93 ± 4.24
	Ulna	3.76 * L + 75.55 ± 4.72	4.27 * L + 57.76 ± 4.30
	Femur	2.32 * L + 65.53 ± 3.94	2.47 * L + 54.10 ± 3.72
	Tibia	2.42 * L + 81.93 ± 4.00	2.90 * L + 61.53 ± 3.66
	Fibula	2.60 * L + 75.50 ± 3.86	2.93 * L + 59.61 ± 3.57

Source: https://www.intechopen.com/chapters/73372.

5.3. EVOLUTION OF FORENSIC ANTHROPOLOGICAL METHODS OF IDENTIFICATION

In a medicolegal investigation into death, forensic identification of the deceased is crucial. This holds true for both the routine inquiries into sudden individual deaths and the mass fatality investigations involving a large number of human remains or fragments of human remains.

5.3.1. Anthropological Methods for Identification

Depending on whether the forensic anthropologist is a full-time employee of the medicolegal jurisdiction as opposed to a contractor, the anthropologist's contribution to the identification process differs by jurisdiction. Compared to those who consult, those who are embedded in a medical examiner/coroner operation usually participate in a wider range of identification process components, such as the use of anthropological methods and administrative duties. We concentrate on the fundamental role that forensic anthropologists play in identification: they compare postmortem radiographic images that the medicolegal agency obtains from the deceased directly to antemortem radiographs that can be linked to suspected deceased individuals. By removing biological markers of age, sex, ancestry, and stature from unexplained human remains, anthropologists can further influence the identification process by creating a biological profile that restricts the range of individuals that a deceased person can be identified with. Some anthropologists use techniques called facial approximation and superimposition, which are generally helpful in removing candidates for identification or in narrowing candidate pools, but not in identification itself (Crowder, Wiersema, Adams, et al., 2016).

In order to determine whether the similarity between two images of the same skeletal feature constitutes identification, forensic anthropologists use their in-depth knowledge of the skeleton and its variability. The general morphology and contour of the bones, the patterns of the trabecular bones, the morphology of the sinuses, and the existence and form of orthopedic or surgical devices are all taken into account in this comparison. Generally speaking, a bony feature's likelihood of having discriminatory value increases with its morphological complexity. Therefore, the majority of the body's bones may aid in identification; however, due to their intricate morphology, some skeletal features—such as the frontal sinuses, petrous temporal bone, and dentition—are preferred over others. Certain anatomically complex elements have diminished utility due to their anatomical location within the body and how they appear on antemortem imaging. For example, the vertebral column has extremely complex morphology, especially in older people with degenerative changes. However, the anthropologist typically views the vertebral column through the anterior ribs, sternum, and thoraco-abdominal organs on anterior-posterior chest radiographs. The frequency of imaging in the antemortem record is another factor to take into account. For instance, chest radiographs are frequently used for identification despite being challenging to use for the previously mentioned reason. This is due to their high availability. According to the author's observations, there also appear to be differences in the prevalence of antemortem records between the deceased medicolegal population and the lay population (e.g., higher incidence of interaction with the criminal justice system and/or healthcare system), which can be useful for anthropologists looking for antemortem records.

In the third decade of the previous century, the first report of radiograph comparison for the purpose of forensic identification of the deceased was published. To verify the identity of a severely decomposed individual, we looked at the morphology of the mastoid processes and nasal accessory sinuses. A plethora of published attempts to compare antemortem and postmortem radiographs in order to directly extract diagnostic information from skeletal remains have been documented in the literature that followed, especially between 1995 and 2008. Numerous publications describe individual identifications made using radiographic imaging of the cranium, including the mastoid sinuses, nasal sinuses, cranial suture patterns, frontal sinuses, and orthopedic/surgical devices from various parts of the body, as well as features of the postcranial skeleton, including the leg and foot, chest, clavicles, pelvis, vertebral column, and the hand and wrist (Ubelaker & Jacobs, 1995).

The frontal sinuses are a highly variable and individualistic feature of the human skull that have drawn a lot of attention. They also summarize the development of identification methods from anecdotal accounts of comparisons to the development of methods for image comparison that include statistical measures of likelihood. This article is not intended to be an exhaustive review of the literature on identification techniques based on every part of the skeleton. The frontal sinus is used in the next paragraph to illustrate the evolution of radiograph identification techniques, as well as issues and factors to be taken into account.

Numerous articles have been published on the subject of radiographic evaluation of the frontal sinuses in personal identification. The bulk of the early publications, however, are case reports that do not address the limitations mentioned in the NAS report, nor do they present techniques for future application or meet the requirements of the Daubert guidelines.

Quatrehomme and Fronty, for instance, propose a workable method for personal identification from the frontal sinus: the simple superimposition of ante- and postmortem conventional radiograph images. The authors do not address the method's subjectivity, but they do acknowledge the significant challenge of orienting the skull correctly for postmortem imaging.

Kirk et al. published the results of a survey of 39 cases in which identifications were made in Ontario, Canada, based on nonmetric comparison of frontal sinus configuration. Only three of the 39 cases were considered unidentifiable using the frontal sinus because of poor film quality and the remaining 36 produced "conclusive postmortem to antemortem pattern matches." The identifications were made based on uniqueness, as perceived by the viewer, between superimposed ante- and postmortem anteroposterior radiographs of the skull. They also refer to the "quantitative" association of 16 cases. This quantification involved measurement of the maximum vertical and horizontal dimensions of the sinuses. "Any discrepancy between antemortem and postmortem values greater than 5 mm was classified as a metric nonmatch." Although less subjective than the identifications made solely on the basis of simple superimposition of ante- and postmortem imaging, this technique does not provide either a statistical measure of the strength of the associations or error rates associated with its use. More comprehensive systems for classifying and/or identifying crania according to variability of the frontal sinuses have been presented by Yoshino et al., Yoshino et al., Schuller, Reichs, and Reichs and Dorion. Yoshino et al. developed a potentially repeatable methodology for personal identification from conventional radiographs of the frontal sinuses. The method involved the development of a code number from the classification of six independent characteristics of the frontal sinuses. The code was a series of numbers that was statistically unlikely to be derived from more than a single individual by virtue of its length and the number of possible combinations represented by all of its possible variations. Yoshino used the skulls of 35 Japanese adults (21 males and 14 females) to develop the technique. They tested the technique on a single forensic case and concluded that the technique is of "considerable value in cases in which dental remains are not available." Reichs and Dorion and Reichs modified this technique for use with axial computed tomography (CT) scans of the skull. Their argument is essentially that future use of CT imaging will far outweigh the use of fronto-occipital radiographs, and that identification techniques based on radiographs will someday become obsolete. Thus instead of conventional radiography, they developed a method similar to that of Yoshino et al. using axial CT imaging. They evaluated a slightly different series of characteristics than Yoshino et al. that were more effectively imaged on CT scans, including bilateral dimension, bilateral asymmetry, superiority of side, distribution of partial bony septations, number of partial bony septations, distribution of complete bony cells, and number of complete bony cells. They suggested that scoring these attributes on several consecutive CT slices added to the length of the code derived, and therefore, to its statistical uniqueness.

5.3.2. Development of Quantitative Methods for Identification

In the past 10 years, especially since the release of the NAS report, there has been a noticeable increase in the number of publications that confirm the validity of every facet of forensic anthropological analysis. Numerous forensic anthropologists perform analyzes, such as estimating sex and age, which require statistical validation of established anthropological techniques like pubic symphysis or sternal rib end aging. However, historically, the process of identifying deceased individuals through radiograph comparison has been subjective. Subjective comparison of skeletal radiographs has a valuable discriminatory value, and forensic anthropologists will probably continue to use these methods as identification tools in the future. This is partly because radiograph identification techniques for each bone in the body cannot be validated by anthropologists, and we are unable to predict which bone or bones may be available for comparison in a particular case. Nonetheless, it is widely acknowledged that the creation of verified identification techniques is crucial. "Forensic anthropologists prioritize estimation problems over evidentiary problems because they are trained primarily as physical anthropologists." Steadman and associates describe how Bayesian statistics—specifically, likelihood ratios—are used to validate identification techniques used in anthropology. They clarify the conceptual and practical distinctions between the general population and suitable reference samples. In addition to new data that can be used to determine the frequency of particular identifiers within the population at large, the authors identify a number of databases that can be used as references for population at large estimates.

The main issue with radiograph comparisons used historically has been their apparent or actual lack of repeatability. Repeatability depends on the objectivity of the methodology used, and it is challenging to establish objectivity when employing methods that rely on the subjective assessment of the investigator regarding specific features, like a specific shape, degree of symmetry, or side dominance. As an illustration, the characteristics of the frontal sinuses assessed in the works of Yoshino et al. and Dorion and Reichs are capricious. More readily repeatable character assessments are required. Through a variety of techniques, some writers have attempted to improve the objectivity of radiography techniques. As was already mentioned, Kirk et al. recorded the maximum width and length of the sinuses in a sample of 39 crania in an effort to provide quantitative robusticity to the radiographic analysis of frontal sinuses, in addition to the more subjective variables used in previous studies. Reipert and associates. concluded a study using a computer program called FoXSIS to lessen subjectivity in the analysis of the frontal sinuses in order to "improve the objectivity of X-ray comparison for the identification of unknown individuals." 30 skulls' worth of computed tomography data were gathered, and the data were transformed into virtual X-ray representations. The main benefit of the program, according to the authors, was that it quantified the "probability of identity" without relying on more arbitrary and variable identity measures like side dominance, shape, and symmetry levels. This was made possible by the program's use of digital measurements of the skull's features (Riepert, Ulmcke,

Schweden, & Nafe, 2001). Techniques that rely on the premise that a large number of possible combinations make it statistically unlikely for two people to have the same or similar codes also have a problem.

This is problematic because there is no attempt to balance the different characters in relation to one another, at least not with the methods mentioned above. For instance, an individual's probability of having one or a few frontal sinus septations is significantly higher than that of having six or seven, which increases the statistical probability that two people may actually share the same code for that specific trait.

There is an issue with many of the traits that Reichs and Yoshino et al. took into cby ChristensenChristensen published the most impartial and statistically sound examination of the frontal sinuses. She quantified the superior border of the frontal sinuses using elliptical Fourier analysis (EFA), a geometric morphometric method that imposes a set of coordinate data points to a closed curve.

The outlines were then quantified using the coordinate data by creating a set of coefficients that serve as a numerical representation of the curve. She drew a line through the inferior-most extensions of the curves on the left and right sides to close it inferiorly.

She then traced the superior border of the frontal sinuses of 808 different people. To see how well the EFA-generated outlines could be used to associate the right images, the Euclidean distances between them were compared. Compared to the distances between individuals, the Euclidean distances between repeat images from the same subject were substantially shorter. She assessed the statistical strength of the associations with positive outcomes using typicality statistics.

he comes to the conclusion that "there is a quantifiable and significant difference between the shapes of individual frontal sinus outlines" because there is very little chance of using her method to make an incorrect association between two outlines.

A technique for comparing ante- and postmortem axial CT images of the temporal bone's petrous region was created by Wiersema. The axial head CT images of 115 different people provided the data for the study, and the Euclidean distance between images of the same person and images from different people was compared.

To create the data used in the statistical analyzes, two-dimensional coordinate data from 36 landmarks on each CT image were computed and the distances between each coordinate point were recorded. Measurement subsets were created based on two different models: the study author's anatomical criteria were used in the first model, and principal components factor analysis was used in the second model to determine which subset had the highest statistical significance (Figures 5.4–5.6).

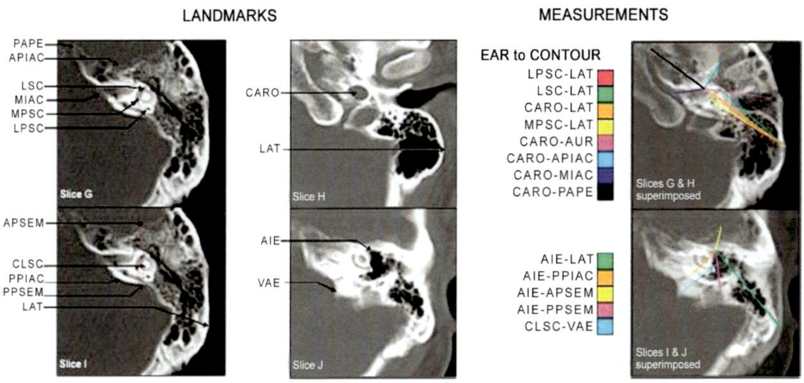

Figure 5.4. *The first two columns illustrate the landmark locations in the inner and middle ear segments of the petrous part of the temporal bone used in this research. The third column illustrates the measurements between the landmarks in the inner and middle ear segments. The measurements are color-coded according to the legend located between columns 2 and 3.*

Source: https://www.ncbi.nlm.nih.gov/pmc/articles/PMC6474555/.

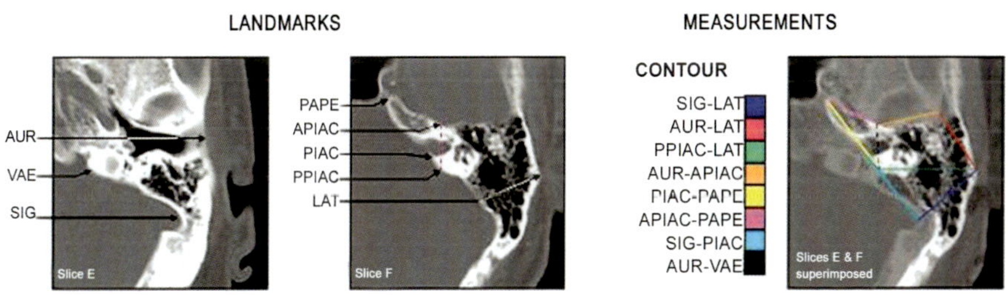

Figure 5.5. *The first two images (labelled slices E&F) illustrate the locations of the landmarks around the contour of the petrous part of the temporal bone. The third image illustrates the measurements between the landmarks around the contour of the petrous part of the temporal bone. The measurements are color-coded according to the legend located between the second and third images.*

Source: https://www.ncbi.nlm.nih.gov/pmc/articles/PMC6474555/.

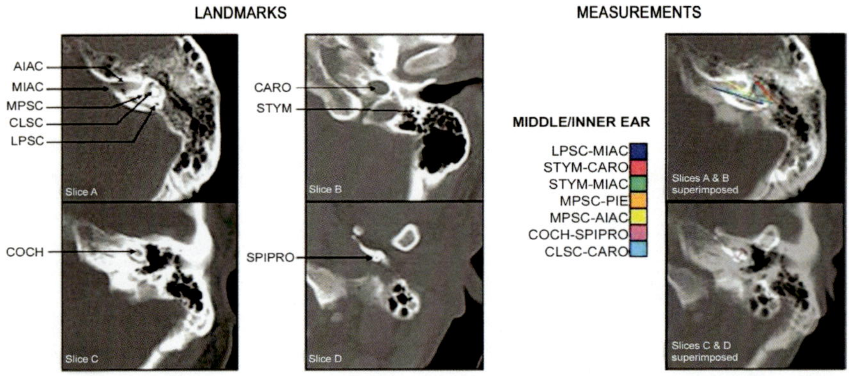

Figure 5.6. *The first two columns illustrate the remaining landmark locations in both the inner and middle ear, and the contour segments of the petrous part of the temporal bone. The third column illustrates the measurements between the measurements that extend between the landmarks of the inner and middle ear, and the contour of the petrous part of the temporal bone. The measurements are color coded according to the legend located between columns 2 and 3.*

Source: https://www.ncbi.nlm.nih.gov/pmc/articles/PMC6474555/.

Next, in order to assess the relative effectiveness of both models in matching replicate images to one another, the measurement sets of the two models were compared using nearest neighbor analysis. Both models produced very accurate results. The biological model produced three false nearest neighbor matches, while the principal components factor analysis model produced five. The discrepancies between the first and second scans' axial planes seem to have caused the errors. We next computed likelihood ratios and posterior probabilities to examine the outcomes of the nearest neighbor comparisons in light of Bayes' Theorem. Indicating that 1) there is significant individual variability in the measurements of the petrous portion used in this research and 2) this variation represents a high level of potential accuracy in the application of this method in the identification of forensic remains, the likelihood ratios and posterior probabilities were very high for both models.

Derrick along with others provide a mathematically validated automated method for comparing cervical spine lateral images that can be used by coroner's and medical examiner's offices. The program calculates the probability that any two radiographs in a collection of images of the cervical spine have similar vertebral body morphology. To assess the method's sensitivity, repeatability, and reliability, six validations were carried out. The success rate in matching the test image to the right image in the array is 92–100%, according to the authors. The success rate is higher for cervical vertebrae than for lumbar vertebral bodies, which are more likely to be partially obstructed by intermediate objects and have a less distinct morphology (Figure 5.7).

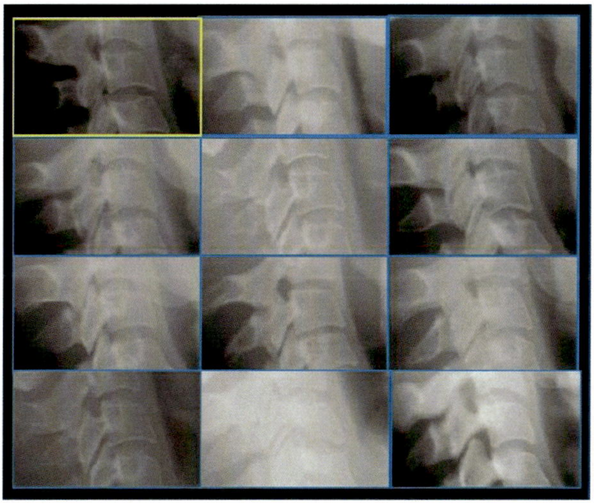

Figure 5.7. *Sample test array.*

Source: https://www.ncbi.nlm.nih.gov/pmc/articles/PMC6474555/.

The limited availability of antemortem lateral cervical spine radiographs is the method's drawback. Assuming that antemortem lateral CT scout images of the head and neck are suitable for comparison would greatly increase the method's usefulness.

5.3.3. Forensic Anthropological Identification in the Mass Fatality Context

There is a thorough discussion of the anthropologist's role in the context of mass fatalities elsewhere. That article, however, does not address the methodological problems pertaining to the identification of common, unidentifiable tissue that occasionally remains after a mass fatality incident, or of fragmentary remains. For post-disaster fragmentary remains, many radiography techniques used for daily cases are not appropriate. The frontal sinus, one of the skeleton's more diagnostic regions, is seriously vulnerable to damage. The petrous portion of the temporal bone and other skeleton segments that are resistant to taphonomic destruction should be the main focus of current and future methods used in the context of mass fatalities. The availability of antemortem radiographs may make it more challenging to use radiographic techniques because the victims of mass fatality incidents are frequently laypeople rather than deceased medicolegal individuals.

5.4. FORENSIC ODONTOLOGY: BITE MARK ANALYSIS

A subspecialty of dentistry known as forensic odontology is concerned with the appropriate management, examination, and presentation of dental findings in the interest of justice.

Identification of people whose bodies have been disfigured in fire accidents, major natural disasters, sexual assaults, and other incidents has been made possible in large part by forensic odontology. Bite marks, saliva, teeth, rugoscopy, tooth prints, cheiloscopy, photographic analysis, dental casts, molecular techniques, and radiographs are some of the methods used in forensic dentistry. For the purpose of identifying specific individuals in criminal cases, dental evidence preservation is extremely important.

5.4.1. History

In the past, bite marks were used to identify an individual. At Reverend George Burroughs' trial in Salem, Massachusetts in 1692, testimony was given regarding a bite mark that Reverend Burroughs had left on one of the witches. One of the women who was charged with witchcraft provided evidence of his biting. He died by hanging.

In 1954, Texas became the first appellate court to accept bite marks as proof. Instead of a dentist, a firearms expert examined a bite mark on a piece of cheese that was left at the scene of a crime.

The Ted Bundy case is arguably the most well-known criminal case to result in a conviction based on bite mark analysis. He killed and sexually assaulted many women, most notably Lisa Levy and Martha Bowman.

Bundy had left an impression on Levy's buttock that forensic experts could utilize. This mark was ultimately what found Bundy guilty in 1979 of killing Levy and the other women he killed. Due to his severely crooked lower teeth, Bundy's bite mark identification was based solely on their impression.

5.4.2. Crimes Involved in Bite Marks

Teeth are often used as a weapon to inflict damage on an attacker in situations involving life-or-death struggles between attackers and victims. For the victim, this may be their only practical defense strategy. However, it is noteworthy that perpetrators of sexual assaults frequently bite their victims as a sign of dominance and rage. Bites marks are associated with a number of crimes, including homicide, self-inflicted injuries, kidnapping, violent crimes, and sporting events (Vartika Chaddha, Aman Chowdhry, et al., 2018).

- **Violent Crimes:** In violent crime cases, victims may sustain bite marks as a result of the attacker biting them or the victim biting the aggressor in self-defense. Petaciae, or central or peripheral suck marks, are visible after sexual bites where the teeth are used to hold during sucking.
- **Child Abuse Cases:** Children who have suffered bites from humans are not uncommon, but when they are, they are either not properly examined or not acknowledged. Older children exhibit bite marks that indicate either sexual abuse or assault.
- **Sporting Events:** In this case, the bite marks are created when the victim bites the attacker while playing sports like boxing, rugby, or soccer. Mike Tyson's bite of Evander Holyfield's ear on June 28, 1997, is the most famous and horrifying biting incident in sports history. A similar incident happened when South African player Eben Etzebeth was bitten on the arm by Argentina's Leonardo Senatore during the 2013 Rugby Championship. In the most recent instance, during the Tokyo Olympics semifinal in 2021, India's Ravi Dahiya suffered a painful bite to his right bicep from opponent Nurislam Sanayev.
- **Self-Inflicted Bite Marks:** There's a chance the bite was self-inflicted if it appears on a portion of the body that the victim can reach with their mouth. Children frequently have them on their forearms. People with mental health disorders and intellectual disabilities may also bite themselves.
- **At the Scene of Crime:** Sometimes the material left at the scene has the traces of the offenders' teeth. These bite marks can appear on the skin, soft tissues, and inanimate items like clothes, fruits, and food.

5.4.3. Steps in Bite Mark Record (ABFO Guidelines 1986)

The American Board of Forensic Odontology (ABFO) has established guidelines for gathering and examining bite marks from suspects and victims. The procedures for recording Bite Marks are displayed in Table 5.5:

Table 5.5. *Steps Involved in Bitemark Recording*

From victim	From suspect
Consent	Consent
History	History
Documentation	Clinical examination
Photography	Photographs
Saliva swab	Impressions
Impression and model	Bite samples
UV illumination	
First aid	

Source: Shebah C, Sheethal A, Harshita BR, Preethi P, & Prasanna RK, A Review on Bite Marks in Forensic Dentistry. doi:10.26420/austinjdent.2022.116.

5.4.3.1. Obtaining Evidence from the Victim

1. **Consent:** The victim's evidence collection process cannot start until the required consent has been granted. The victim has to sign the written consent in front of a witness.
2. **Documentation of History:** It is necessary to compile a thorough medical history of the person, including a history of dental procedures. It should also be ascertained whether the bite mark has been impacted by embalming, decomposition, washing, or other processes.
3. **Photography:** Photography is the primary means of documenting and protecting the bite mark and plays a major role in the preservation of the evidence. Photos provide the most dependable way to save the data because skin marks can change over time. Because victims' appearances can vary, the photos need to be taken at a 90° angle to the injury, ideally every 24 hours for both living and deceased victims. A scale developed by members of the American Board of Forensic Odontology (ABFO) and designated as the ABFO scale no. has become the standard. 2. Obtaining serial photos of bite mark injuries is valuable. One more option to traditional photography is video imaging. In addition to traditional color and monochrome films, ultraviolet photography is advised during the initial interaction and for a few days afterward (Franklin & Curtis, 2001).
4. **Saliva Swab:** It is necessary to swab bite mark injuries in order

to recover trace evidence. Saliva or human cell stains need to be gathered for DNA analysis. Saliva is the secreted "ABO" antigen by humans. The mouth cavity, the control area, and the biting area should all have swabs taken. Because of assaults and rapes, oral swabs should be obtained for semen. It is recommended to analyze the sample materials as soon as possible, failing which frozen storage and cold transportation should be used. The double swab technique and the saline washing technique are the two methods used (Sweet & Bowers, 1998; p. 43).

i. **Saline Washing Technique:** This method involves rinsing the bite mark area with regular saline and collecting the resulting saliva solution in a Petri dish. After high-velocity centrifugation, the filtrate is examined under a microscope, and the supernatant is discarded.

ii. **Double Swab Technique:** The area that came into contact with the tongue and lips is first rinsed with a cotton swab that has been moistened with distilled water. To remove the dried saliva from the surface, apply gentle pressure and rotate the object for a duration of 7 to 10 seconds. The residual saliva that the first swab left on the skin is then collected using a dry swab. For at least 45 minutes, the two swabs are air dried at room temperature. After drying, swabs are packaged and delivered to the lab. The identical procedure is used to prepare a control sample, except saliva is not swabbed.

5. **Impression and Model:** To create stone models, impressions of the bitten area should be taken in order to maintain its three-dimensionality. Rubber-base and silicone-base impression compounds are the materials used to record the bite marks at the location. There are two ways to take impressions:

i. **Method I:** The bite area is covered with the impression material. A wire gauze is placed and additional material is injected over it.

ii. **Method II:** Using cold cure a special tray is constructed pertaining to the shape of bite mark and an impression is taken. Master casts ought to be poured with type-IV stone. Duplicate casts should also be fabricated. Either epoxy resin clear material or visible light cure may be used to make rigid model.

5.4.3.2. First Aid

1. **Stop Bleeding**: If there's bleeding, raise that area of the body and apply firm pressure to the wound, with sterile gauze or clean cloth until bleeding stops.

2. **Clean and Protect:** Sterile medical gloves should be worn to reduce risk of contamination. If the wound is mild and there is no blood, clean it with mild soap and rinse for several minutes under running water. Apply antibiotic ointment and cover the wound with sterile gauze.
3. **Get Medical Help:** Medical practitioners should be consulted about any human bite that has abraded the skin, as there is a high risk of infection. If the infection is untreated, it may lead to lack of mobility, damage to tendons or nerves, stiffness and numbness in the area. Deeper wounds may require stitches and also tetanus shot or booster. Antibiotic therapy maybe prescribed to prevent bacterial infection.

5.4.3.3. Obtaining Evidence from Suspect Consent

The odontologist must ensure that a proper court order, search warrant, or signed informed consent with precise instructions on what and how evidence is to be collected is obtained before collecting proof from suspected biters. The victim has to sign the written consent in front of a witness. Before beginning the procedures, the odontologist must explain them to the patient. As part of the case file, a copy of these reports ought to be kept. Without the suspect's consent, taking a dental impression could be interpreted as an attack on him by the specialist. As a result, the person who takes the impressions may face legal repercussions from such a course of action.

- **History:** A thorough history of the individual, including history of dental treatments before and after the bite marks has to be noted. Medical history to document any medication the suspect has been taking at or before the date of bite.

5.4.3.4. Clinical Examination

- **Extra-Oral Examination:** Both soft and hard tissues are recorded in this process. It is necessary to estimate the maximum opening, account for any variations in opening or closing, TMJ status, occlusal disharmonies, balance and tone of the muscles, and address facial asymmetry. In addition to the presence of facial hair, it is necessary to take notice of any facial scars or evidence of previous medical procedures.
- **Intra-Oral Examination:** Taken salivary swabs are necessary. Teeth that are broken or missing should be noted. The tongue is examined to determine its size, function, and any abnormalities, including lip and tongue piercings, bifid tongue, and ankyloglossia. It is necessary to record the periodontal status while paying close attention to mobility.

5.4.3.5. Photographs

Additional oral photos include views of the entire face and profile. An intraoral picture of the teeth in a normal occlusion, with maximum opening and biting edge-to-edge, should be included, along with frontal views and two lateral views. It is important to take care to eliminate any unwanted shadows. To achieve these outcomes, Digital Single Lens-Reflex (DSLR) cameras are used.

5.4.3.6. Impressions

Two impressions of each arch are taken using materials specified by the American Dental Association (ADA), and master casts are created using type II stone. Documenting the interocclusal relationship is important. The master cast can be used to create duplicate casts.

Two sets of casts are used: one for comparability and the other for direct evidence. Impressions are obtained both with and without the removable prosthesis in place if one is present. Soft tissue records, including teeth, should not be modified in any way, including by cutting, filing, or other means. Sample bites are molded into the proper shape to replicate the kind of bite that is being studied.

5.4.3.7. Bite Samples

Using materials approved by the American Dental Association, such as Aluwax or Copra wax, a sample bite in centric occlusion should be recorded. These samples are instantly photographed and kept for later analysis.

5.4.4. Bite Analysis

Verifying whether the injury is a bite mark is the first step in bite mark analysis, after which a statement regarding its forensic significance is given. An analysis of a bite ark goes like this:

- **Demographics:** includes name of the victim, case number, date of examination, referring agency, person to contact, age, race and, sex of the victim and name of the examiner.
- **Location of Bite Marks:** There are bite marks on different parts of the body. Bite marks can be broadly categorized as either sexual or non-sexual. The arms, legs, fingers, hands, chest, and ears are the areas most frequently affected by non-sexual bite marks. In contrast, genitalia, the breast, neck, thigh, axilla, buttock, upper back, arm, cheek, etc., may all have sexual bite marks. The following body parts are most frequently affected by bite marks: the breast, arm,

genitalia, back, thigh, legs, nipple, hand, buttock, abdomen, waist, face, neck, and so forth.

1. **Shape, Size and Arrangement of Teeth:** Bite marks can have a round, crescent, ovoid, or uneven shape. Whereas the canine incisors produce triangular marks, the human incisors produce rectangular marks when cut crosswise. The bite mark's vertical and horizontal dimensions are recorded, ideally in metric units. Comparable are the primary dental characteristics, such as tooth size and arrangement, and secondary characteristics, such as gaps or broken teeth. For the bite mark to be deemed a match, there must be a match between the prominent and secondary dental features. It is important to record tooth numbers, missing teeth, and where tooth marks are located.
2. **Size of Dental Arch:** The dental arches' definition of the bite-mark size relationship may indicate an adult or child's bite. It is made up of U-shaped arches with an open space between them, which is typically where bruises appear. Adult arches range in diameter from 25 to 40 mm on average from dog to dog.
3. **Suction Marks:** A group of punctate hemorrhages are known as suction marks or hickeys. A "sun-burst"-like central ecchymotic area surrounded by radiating linear abrasions is typically observed following sexually-oriented crimes. These bruises are the result of blood leaking from capillaries as a result of suction or negative pressure.
4. **Type of Injury:** The seven types of injuries seen in bite mark are:

- Petechial Haemorrhage – a small bleeding spot
- Contusion – ruptured blood vessels
- Abrasion – undamaging mark on skin
- Avulsion – skin is torn off
- Laceration – near puncture of skin
- Incision – neat punctured or torn skin
- Artefact – bitten off piece of body

These further can be classified into four degrees of impression clearly defined, obviously defined, quite noticeable and lacerated.

- Clearly defined – marks that are a consequence of application of substantial pressure.
- Obviously defined – due to mild pressure.
- Quite noticeable – due to vigorous pressure
- Lacerated – a deep cut or tear in the skin

5. **Color of the Wound:** The color should be noted e.g., red, purple etc.
6. **Evaluation of the Bite Mark Photographs:** This is a significant step during examination. Images should be of sufficient resolution to permit amplification to life-sized dimension without pixilation.

5.4.5. Methods of Analysis

5.4.5.1. Odontometric Triangle Method

Three points are marked on the tracing of bite marks and tooth models using the objective odontometric triangle method. Three points are connected to form a triangle: two on the canines' outermost convexity and one in the midline between the maxillary central incisors. We compute and compare the three lines and angles. This is carried out for the models of the upper and lower teeth and contrasted with the specimen's markings. After a careful analysis, conclusions are drawn.

5.4.5.2. Comparison Technique

1. **Direct Method/ Cast on Photo Method:** Using this method, models or finger print powder lift models are directly compared to photographs. Using this method, bite mark models from the suspect can be directly overlaid on a life-size picture to show how they work. The finger print powder lift technique entails dusting the bitten skin with the proper powder and brush, then using finger print tape to transfer the marks to an acetate sheet. Investigators should take extra care not to damage the print when developing it.
2. **Indirect Method-Overlay:** To record the suspect's biting edges, an opaque overlay must be prepared using the indirect method. Transparent overlays are created by freehand tracing a dental model's occlusal or incisal surfaces onto an acetate sheet. The sheet is then placed over scaled 1:1 photos, allowing for comparison. Transparent overlays are thought to be arbitrary, easily manipulated, and irreproducible when used. In lieu of free hand tracing, photocopier-generated overlays are thought to be a superior substitute for matching the correct bite mark to the correct set of models. The four methods of bite mark overlay production are:

- Computer based;
- Radiopaque wax method;
- Xerographic; and
- Hand traced.

5.4.6. Factors Influencing Severity of Bite Marks

5.4.6.1. Force- Original Injury Inflicted

The biting teeth and tongue create negative pressure, which causes extra-vascular bleeding and bruises the bite mark injury's center. These bruises exhibit color changes over time as the skin of the living person heals from the injury. Examining the four degrees of impression can assist in determining the type of violence:

a. Significant pressure,
b. First degree pressure
c. Violent pressure
d. Skin violently torn from body

5.4.6.2. Anatomical Location

Because bite marks are influenced by the mechanical characteristics of tissue, they can differ from one site to another. For instance, breast tissues are naturally softer than those of the back. Less fibrous tissue, more subcutaneous fat, and lower muscular tone in body parts with loose skin make them more prone to bruising. The way that the skin contracts and relaxes during movement influences how the bite mark appears on the individual. Children tend to have more bruising because of their delicate, loosely attached skin as well as subcutaneous fat. Less elasticity and subcutaneous fat in the elderly are linked to increased bruising, whereas more subcutaneous fat and delicate skin are linked to increased bruising in women.

5.4.6.3. Time of Examination

The amount of force used and how long the victim has been bitten determine how long the bite mark will last. After a bite, bruises may develop four hours later and go away in 36 hours. The morphology of the abrasions within the mark is preserved, making them important features for identification. As swelling goes down and tissue repair begins, the bite mark will become more noticeable over time.

5.4.7. Bite Marks Characteristics

A unique attribute, feature, or pattern within the mark is called a characteristic. Class characteristics and individual characteristics are the two categories of characteristics.

5.4.7.1. Class Characteristics

The Manual of the American Board of Forensic Odontology (ABFO) states that a characteristic that sets apart a bite mark from other wounds is called a class characteristic. The first step in evaluating the indentations is to confirm that class attributes are present. Depending on what caused the injury—primary or permanent teeth, maxillary or mandibular teeth—the dimensions vary. Furthermore, the perpetrator's arch dimension will determine how big the injury is overall. The class characteristics designate whether it comes from a human, animal, or other group. "Tooth class characteristics" and "bite mark characteristics" are the two categories of class characteristics.

According to tooth class characteristics, the anterior teeth are the primary biting teeth. Each sort of tooth in the human dentition has class attributes (tooth class qualities) that separate one tooth type from the others.

- **Incisors:** Rectangular shaped mark
- **Canines:** Triangular markings with variations
- **Premolars:** Single or dual triangle, appearing as diamond shaped
- **Molars:** Rarely leave marks, but when present appear quadrilateral in shape.

5.7.7.2. Individual Characteristics

A feature that deviates from the expected result in a particular group is called an individual characteristic. There are two categories: dental characteristics and arch characteristics.

- **Arch Characteristics:** By separating one person's arch from another, the arch characteristics serve as a type of individual characteristic that aids in individual differentiation. It is predicated on the idea that some people may exhibit certain patterns, traits, or features while others may not. Rotated teeth, alterations in the size and shape of the arch, diastema, displaced or drifting teeth, etc are some of the symptoms.
- **Dental Characteristics:** They specifically refer to a single tooth, which distinguishes one tooth from the other. Different people have different teeth in terms of where they are in the dental arch, as well as differences in size and shape. Dental traits that aid in identification include retained deciduous teeth, crowding, attrition, spacing, and fractured, rotated, or supernumerary teeth.

5.4.8. Range of Conclusions for Bite Marks

A range of conclusions can be reached when reporting a dental identification. The American Board of Forensic Odontology recommends that these be limited to the following four conclusions:

- **Excluded:** The inconsistency between the bite mark and the suspect's dentition suggests that the mark was not caused by the suspect's teeth. The bite mark cannot have been caused by the suspect because the antemortem and postmortem data are obviously untrustworthy.
- **Inconclusive:** To make any conclusions, there is not enough forensic information to link the suspects' dentition and the bite mark injury.
- **Possible Biter:** The suspect's teeth may resemble the bite mark, but other dentition may also resemble it. The bite mark and the suspect's dentition are consistent, but there aren't any traits that match for us to be positive that the suspect's teeth could have left the bite mark. The postmortem and antemortem records are trustworthy, but the quality of the evidence makes it impossible to determine a person's identity with certainty.
- **Probable Biter:** The suspect's teeth exhibit certain individual characteristics that correspond with the bite mark. There aren't any confusing variations. The evidence strongly points to the suspect as the source, though it could also have been caused by other people.
- **Reasonable Medical Certainty:** Without a doubt, the suspect's teeth match the bite mark pattern. There are no differences between the antemortem and postmortem data; they match exactly.

5.4.9. Controversies Regarding Bite Mark Evidence

Bite marks should be used with caution when presented as evidence in a crime scene because they are not as precise as DNA. The evidence may change depending on a number of factors, including the bite mark's collection, recording, comparison, interpretation, preservation, and reporting. Bite marks are hardly useful for a conclusive conviction; they are only useful for including or excluding the biter from the group of suspects. As a result, there has always been disagreement over bite marks' admissibility as proof.

The most well-known exoneration involving bite mark evidence is the Ray Krone case, in which the man was wrongfully charged with homicide and given the death penalty. The victim's remarkable bite mark served as the sole piece of evidence. Krone's teeth matched the victim's bite mark, according to a forensic odontologist. Further investigation and DNA evidence proved Krone's integrity, and in 2002 he was let out of jail.

After serving 15 years in prison on charges of assaulting Sabina Kulakowski, Roy Brown was released on the basis of bite mark evidence. According to Dr. Edward Mofson, bite marks discovered on Kulakowski's body matched Brown's teeth. DNA testing on the culprit's saliva stains was done 15 years after the conviction, eliminating Brown and coordinating with another suspect, Barry Bench. Brown was eventually cleared after the lead prosecutor acknowledged his innocence.

Levon Brooks served 16 years in prison for the unintentional assault and killing of a 3-year-old girl. Dr. Michael West, a forensic odontologist, determined that the marks on the victim's body corresponded with Brooks' dentition after comparing the dentitions of 13 suspects. Brooks was charged with capital homicide and sentenced to prison as a result. It was discovered through additional DNA testing and confession that Justin Albert Johnson was the murderer. Dr. West had looked over and ruled out the dental impressions of 12 suspects, including Johnson. On February 15, 2008, Brooks was freed after Johnson's admission.

Even forensic odontologists admit that in the past, they have made mistakes in identifying the suspect. Investigation of the cases' facts and circumstances, however, reveals that a number of other factors were also having an impact. It is necessary to grasp the causes and make an effort to clarify the how, why, and where of the erroneous convictions in order to be able to take steps to reduce the likelihood that such failures will happen in the future.

5.4.10. Recent Advances – Digital Methods

- **Image Perception Software Procedure:** Using a bite mark photo, the image perception software selects an area of interest. The forensic odontologist can choose areas with comparable gray values by assigning distinct colors to different levels of gray values. By deleting some pixel intensity regions, it is possible to isolate the area of the image that displays the bite mark. A complete copy of the bite mark is generated. Using Photoshop®, the colored bite mark image is then superimposed over the original bite mark photo.
- **Automated Dental Identification System (ADIS):** This computerized program examines victims after death by using their oral characteristics as a basis. It is more accurate and efficient in terms of time than traditional methods. In addition to shortlisting several digital dental records that are exact duplicates of the subject's, it provides computerized examination and analysis of digital radiographs and dental images, which are challenging to evaluate only by visual inspection.

- **3D Reconstruction of Bite Marks:** Using 3D-CBCT instead of the traditional method has the advantage of requiring less sample handling, which results in fewer alterations to the original bite mark discovered at the crime scene. It also minimizes angular distortions, improves bite mark reproduction, makes information easier to store and retrieve, and ensures that records are permanent.
- **Odontosearch:** It offers a methodical way to evaluate how frequently a dental code occurs. The dentist's clinical experience determines how closely a post-mortem and ante-mortem dental code match. It contrasts criminal and missing person databases. It facilitates the odontologist's assessment of the individuality of a patient's potential filling arrangement.

5.5. IMPORTANCE OF DENTAL RECORDS IN FORENSIC ODONTOLOGY

Teeth preserve information that is retained for the duration of life and beyond due to their physiological variations, pathologies, and therapeutic effects. In certain situations, the teeth may reveal information about the identity of the biter and be used as weapons.

5.5.1. Determining Identity Through Dental Forensics

Due to their ability to withstand even the most extreme environmental conditions and trauma, teeth and jaw structures play a crucial role in the process of identifying a person. This is especially true for the teeth because of the cementum and tooth enamel's natural durability. The identification of dental remains is crucial in cases where a deceased person has been burned, dismembered, skeletonized, or decomposed. The main benefit of dental evidence is that, similar to other hard tissues, it is frequently preserved following demise. Even a person's dental health varies over the course of their life, and the proportion of teeth that are filled, missing, and decayed can be measured and compared at any given time.

When postmortem alterations, traumatic tissue damage, or the absence of a fingerprint record render the use of visual or fingerprint methods invalid, dental identification takes on a major role in the identification of remains. The concepts of exclusion and comparison are the cornerstones of dental identification. When ante mortem records of the presumed deceased are available and circumstantial evidence points to the decedent's identity, for instance, or when ante mortem records of other questionable, unidentified individuals are available and need to be ruled out, dental identification is used. A list of potential participants is necessary for identification in order to locate the relevant ante mortem records. The success of identification depends on these records' accuracy and availability. Regretfully, inadequate record-keeping by dentists frequently leads to confusion that prevents dental identification.

5.5.2. Structure and Development of Teeth

With five surfaces on each of the 32 teeth that make up the average adult human dentition, there are 160 possible combinations for surface anatomy and dental restorations in terms of configuration, size, shape, material, and wear patterns. This doesn't even consider—and isn't limited to—things like decay, extra or missing teeth, dental arch alignment, individual tooth positioning, and prosthetic appliances. Other distinguishing features for antemortem and postmortem comparisons are orbital outlines, bone trabecular patterns, and maxillary sinus patterns. The number of points of concordance required to make a decision on a dental identification is a question that comes up frequently. This is not as important, though, as the uniqueness or exclusivity of the relevant points of comparison. In addition, the investigator should be able to indicate whether the identification is "positive within reasonable scientific certainty" when all of the concordance points in a given case are taken into account as a set of aggregate data."

The following categories and terminology for body identification are suggested for use in communicating the results of forensic odontology identification investigation:

- **Positive Identification:** The antemortem and postmortem data match in sufficient detail to establish that they are from the same individual. In addition, there are no irreconcilable discrepancies.
- **Possible Identification:** Commonalities exist among the comparable items in the ante mortem and postmortem databases, but enough information is missing from either source to prevent the establishment of a positive identification.
- **Insufficient Identification:** The available information is insufficient to form the basis for a conclusion.
- **Exclusion:** Unexplainable discrepancies exist among comparable items in the ante mortem and postmortem databases. The antemortem and postmortem data are clearly inconsistent.

5.5.3. Forensic Dentists Area of Practice

1. **Identification of Found Human Remains and Dental Profiling:** A "Picture" of the individual's general features can frequently be produced by the forensic dentist. Post-mortem Dental Profiling is the name given to this procedure.

2. **Sex and Race:** A person's race, age, and sex can be ascertained using the bones and teeth of the craniofacial complex, which are essential identification tools for forensic odontologists. These features also effectively distinguish one person from another and one population from another. When the reconstruction of facial soft tissues is based on the skull and facial bones, this anatomic material can be utilized for identification. Soft-tissue thickness points can be connected with sculpting clay using standard anthropologic thickness measurements at specific facial points, and the reconstructed features can occasionally be digitally represented on a computer screen. Computers have been helpful for facial superimposition techniques because they allow components to be added directly to cranial features. As a result, it is possible to see the skeletal structures underneath the soft tissue, which allows for accuracy verification. These methods produce a reconstruction of the soft-tissue features' contours, enabling visual identification. Then, different versions can be replicated and stored for comparative analysis.

3. **Age Estimation of Both the Living and Deceased:** Age determination using dental data Age estimation is a branch of the forensic sciences and ought to play a significant role in the identification process, particularly in cases where there is no access to the deceased's personal records. Due to minor differences in tooth emergence and formation, the primary method of determining an individual's age for younger people is dental estimation based on chronological age. Techniques involving the observation of the morphologically distinct stages of mineralization are typified by the use of radiographs. These decisions also take into account the stage of eruption, the degree of root and crown structure formation, and the degree to which primary and adult dentitions are mixed together.

4. **Recognition and Analysis of Bite Marks Found on Victims:** Bite mark analysis is another field that makes use of tooth characteristics, albeit on a more practical level. In violent incidents where the victim bites the attacker or the attacker bites the victim in self-defense, bites on human tissue may be seen. Although the comparison of bite marks to crime scenes is relatively new, police investigators have long observed that, in certain cases, perpetrators leave their bite marks on food items, chewing gum, or—more frequently—the skin of their victims in homicide, rape, and child abuse cases.

   The comparison of bite marks serves as a crucial example of dentistry's contribution to forensic science. A suspect's dentition's dental features are compared to the bite-mark pattern. A bite-mark pattern can appear on food, other objects, or the victim of an attack or murder, depending on the situation. An attacker who is still alive may also have bite marks left on them from a deceased victim. Other than situations involving physical or sexual abuse or domestic violence, biting can be a child's way of expressing themselves when verbal communication breaks down. Sports competitions and playground altercations can lead to biting injuries.

The forensic odontologist must first ascertain from the evidence whether the pattern is actually the consequence of biting. The pattern can be compared to the suspect's dentition for inclusionary or exclusionary purposes once it has been established that it is related to the teeth, was not created by a tool, instrument, or article of clothing, and does not represent any type of cutaneous lesion, infection, or injury. A pattern mark's qualities must be identifiable and distinguishable in order for it to be evaluated. Anatomical features, tooth form, and dentition shape can all combine to form a representative pattern. There are several techniques available to the forensic odontologist to achieve these objectives. The specific method used would depend on the facts of each case as well as the analyst's skill and preference because there is no one right way to analyze bite-mark evidence.

5. **Assessment of Cases of Abuse / Analysis of Dental Malpractice Claim:** Identification of abuse in people of all ages is greatly aided by forensic odontology. The forensic odontologist is also increasingly being consulted in cases of suspected human abuse, particularly involving minors. When it comes to bite marks and patterned injuries associated with child abuse, family members, friends of the family, siblings, paramours, and caregivers are frequently at the top of the suspect list. When faced with unusual oral injuries, the dentist should be on the lookout for signs of abuse of children, the elderly, or spouses. This is especially true when there are accompanying head or body injuries. While the dentist may not often be concerned about child abuse or abuse against individuals of any other age, it is their legal duty as primary health care providers to report such cases to the appropriate authorities. Regrettably, reports from dentists are not common.

   The main barriers that keep dentists from becoming involved in abuse cases are their ignorance of abuse, their ignorance of the legal requirements to report it, their fear of having to deal with an irate parent, their skepticism about the possibility that parents or other caregivers could be abusive or neglectful, and their fear of losing their patience and, consequently, their income. When a dentist steps in to stop violence of any kind, their main responsibility is to stop the violence, not to try to work out personal issues or give abuse victims counseling. When a dentist encounters violence, simply identifying the telltale signs of abuse, having a private conversation with the patient about these concerns, and knowing whom to refer abuse victims to are appropriate objectives.

6. **Genetics / Source of DNA:** Tooth an important source of DNA in Forensic odontology. DNA is a genetic blue print that makes living being.

i. **Importance of Dental DNA Testing**

- Crime solving – matching suspect with evidence
- Accidents Victims – after Airplane crash
- Soldiers in war – who is the Unknown Soldier
- Paternity testing – who is the father
- Immigration testing – are two people related
- Missing person investigation – whose remains
- Convicted felons databases cases solved

It is the duty of every practitioner to comprehend the forensic ramifications of practicing their particular profession. A greater incentive to keep clear, legally compliant records and help law enforcement identify victims and suspects should come from a dentist's appreciation of the forensic industry.

5.5.4. Mass Causality Incidents

The bulk of cases requiring dental identifications are mass disaster identification transport accidents, especially aircraft accidents where trauma and fire are frequently severe. An additional cause of numerous identification issues is fires inside and the collapse of densely populated buildings. The investigative team's makeup varies based on the type of disaster, and the forensic odontologist is typically one of its members. In addition to the forensic odontologist, the team typically consists of a pathologist, several specialists with experience in the type of disaster in question, and a coordinator or head of the team. When there is a fire or other serious trauma, physical characteristics are frequently lost. Teeth are resistant to most traumas and fire because of their high calcification. When soot and smoke are deposited on teeth and heat and flames have broken down tooth enamel, dental examinations become considerably more difficult.

Unless they are in direct contact with flames, teeth and restorations are typically resistant to heat. Most of the time, preservation is feasible.

5.5.5. Radiographic Examination

The most precise and trustworthy way to identify remains is to compare antemortem and postmortem radiographs. Only radiograph analysis can identify observations such as unique restoration shapes, root canal treatment, buried root tips, bases under restorations, tooth and root morphology, and patterns of the sinuses and jawbone. Sometimes there may be only one tooth left, in which case a positive identification can be made by comparing the radiographs. It is crucial that all routine radiographs exposed during a dental practice be properly fixed and cleaned so that they remain viewable years later. Original ante mortem dental radiographs are extremely valuable for comparison. When the film's angulat ions match those of the original films, the best results are produced in the x-ray tube. When there are few restorations available for antemortem–postmortem comparison, identification becomes problematic.

Due to the effectiveness of preventative measures, fewer individuals now require dental restorations today. Nevertheless, during certain stages of human tooth growth, digital dental X-ray overlays can be utilized for identification purposes. This technique enables the analysis of the spatial alignments of a tooth's root and underlying structures in both pre-death (antemortem) and post-death (postmortem) records. In situations where an antemortem record is absent, the deceased's postmortem chart may serve as a reference for determining identity differences through comparison with other available antemortem records.

5.5.6. Developmental Applications

As a scientific discipline, forensic odontology is still developing. The use of computers is expanding across a wide range of applications, including bite mark evidence photos, x-ray film enhancement, and identification matching support. Bite mark evidence is being examined in greater detail by using a scanning electron microscope to magnify individual components. Alternative light sources include infrared, ultraviolet, and so forth. is very beneficial in visualizing alleged healed skin injuries. To better capture bite or patterned skin mark evidence on camera, these light sources, which come in a variety of wavelengths, can either penetrate the skin's surface or filter out any debris that may be covering it.

5.5.7. Dental Record as a Legal Document

By analyzing dental evidence in various circumstances, the forensic odontologist supports law enforcement authorities. The dentist is the legal owner of the dental record, which includes both objective and subjective patient data. It is necessary to document the findings of the physical assessment of the dentition, surrounding structures, and supporting oral health. The outcomes of clinical laboratory tests, study casts, pictures, and radiographs are also added to the record and ought to be preserved for a period of 7 to 10 years. Recording staff members should initial or sign each entry. Instead of erasing changes from the record, make the necessary corrections by simply drawing a single line through any incorrect information. This technique eliminates any doubts regarding fraudulent intent to change recorded information while preserving the original entry's readability. Dental records created by computers are becoming more prevalent. The obvious benefit of an electronic record is its ease of networking and transfer for regular professional consultations or forensic cases where identification of the patient is required through dental records. Nonetheless, maintaining patient privacy raises ethical concerns when using electronically managed dental records. The computer enhancement of dental lesions or restorations on electronically generated dental radiographs also carries the risk of insurance fraud. Whether dental records are kept on paper or in a computer database, adhering to record management guidelines guarantees that all dental data that might be needed to address a forensic issue is kept up to date and easily accessible.

5.5.8. Presenting Evidence in Court as an Expert Witness

Police investigators or medical examiners will call forensic dentists. In many jurisdictions, there is a push to establish an emergency call-out protocol. An expert who provides this knowledge and experience to a court or other judicial or quasi-judicial body is known as an expert witness. In most jurisdictions, it is required to report any incident of human abuse to the appropriate authorities. The dentist also needs to be aware that future legal proceedings might require their testimony. In the event that there is an oral injury, the dentist should keep accurate and thorough records of all findings for review by law enforcement. Radiographic studies that are required ought to be kept on file. To document injuries, photos of the injury or injuries are frequently useful. In the interest of justice, forensic odontology handles the administration, review, assessment, and presentation of dental evidence in criminal or civil proceedings. Expertise in testing techniques, investigative background, and aptitude for making sound decisions are just a few of the factors that make an evidence evaluation and assessment effective.

REFERENCES

1. Al-Talabani, N., Al-Moussawy, N. D., Baker, F. A., & Mohammed, H. A. (2006). Digital analysis of experimental human bitemarks: Application of two new methods. *Journal of Forensic Sciences, 51*, 1372–1375.
2. Chaddha, V., Chowdhry, A., & Popli, D. B. (2018). Bite mark analysis: An Indian perspective - Science of failure or failure of science? *Journal of Indo-Pacific Academy of Forensic Odontology, 7*, 1.
3. Crowder, C. M., Wiersema, J. M., Adams, B. J., et al. (2016). The utility of forensic anthropology in the medical examiner's office. *Academic Forensic Pathology, 6*(3), 349–360.
4. David, M. P., & Saxena, R. (2010). Use of frontal sinus and nasal septum patterns as an aid in personal identification: A digital radiographic pilot study. *Journal of Forensic Dental Sciences, 2*(2), 77–80.
5. Franklin, D. W., & Curtis, D. J. (2001). Bitemark overlay technique: Photocopy technique. In *The Dental Clinics of North America, Forensic Odontology* (pp. 395–397). Philadelphia, PA: W.B. Saunders Company.
6. Krauss, T. C. (1993). Forensic evidence documentation using reflective ultraviolet photography. *Photo Electronic Imaging, 11*, 300–308.
7. Moser, R. P. Jr., & Wagner, G. N. (1990). Nutrient groove of the ilium, a subtle but important forensic radiographic marker in the identification of victims of severe trauma. *Skeletal Radiology, 19*(1), 15–19.
8. Riepert, T., Ulmcke, D., Schweden, F., & Nafe, B. (2001). Identification of unknown dead bodies by X-ray image comparison of the skull using the X-ray simulation program FoXSIS. *Forensic Science International, 117*(1–2), 89–98.
9. Sigler-Eisenberg. (1985). Forensic research: Expanding the concept of applied archaeology. *American Antiquity, 50*(3), 650–655. https://doi.org/10.1017/S0002731600086467.
10. Steadman, D. W., Adams, B. J., & Konigsberg, L. W. (2006). Statistical basis for positive identification in forensic anthropology. *American Journal of Physical Anthropology, 131*(1), 15–26.
11. Steele, C. (2008). Archaeology and the forensic investigation of recent mass graves: Ethical issues for a new practice of archaeology. *Archaeologies, 4*(3), 414–428.
12. Stephan, C. N., & Guyomarc'h, P. (2014). Quantification of perspective-induced shape change of clavicles at radiography and 3D scanning to assist human identification. *Journal of Forensic Sciences, 59*(2), 447–453.

13. Stephan, C. N., Amidan, B., Trease, H., et al. (2014). Morphometric comparison of clavicle outlines from 3D bone scans and 2D chest radiographs: A shortlisting tool to assist radiographic identification of human skeletons. *Journal of Forensic Sciences, 59*(2), 306–313.
14. Sweet, D., & Bowers, C. M. (1998). Accuracy of bite mark overlays: A comparison of five common methods to produce exemplars from a suspect's dentition. *Journal of Forensic Sciences, 43*, 362–367.
15. Ubelaker, D. H., & Jacobs, C. H. (1995). Identification of orthopedic device manufacturer. *Journal of Forensic Sciences, 40*(2), 168–170. https://doi.org/10.1520/jfs15335j.
16. Wilson, R. J., Bethard, J. D., & DiGangi, E. A. (2011). The use of orthopedic surgical devices for forensic identification. *Journal of Forensic Sciences, 56*(2), 460–469.

CHAPTER 6

FORENSIC PATHOLOGY

Contents

Introduction 202

6.1. Overview of Forensic Pathology 202

6.2. Cause and Manner of Death 209

6.3. Autopsy 210

6.4. Death Investigation 250

References 264

INTRODUCTION

An apathologist is a physician who specializes in studying and diagnosing human disease. A forensic pathologist is a medical professional who specializes in studying trauma, or injuries and damage that result in death, in addition to diseases. The term "seeing with one's own eyes" (Oxford English Dictionary, 2005) refers to the Greek autopsia, which is where the modern autopsy got its start. It involves standardizing the dissection of a corpse to ascertain the cause and manner of death. Regrettably, the number of autopsies has steadily declined in the past 50 years; less than 5 percent of hospital deaths are routinely autopsied, compared to 50% in the years after World War II'sIt is unfortunate, as autopsies serve as a valuable quality assurance instrument for physicians, offering a "reality check" on their diagnoses and feedback on the efficacy of their treatments. However, autopsies performed in an attempt to solve a murder differ greatly in a number of ways, including who performs them, when and how they are performed, and the social function they fulfill.

6.1. OVERVIEW OF FORENSIC PATHOLOGY

The subspecialty of pathology that focuses exclusively on the investigation of unexpected, violent, or sudden deaths is called forensic pathology. Forensic pathology, then, is the application of pathological and forensic scientific methods to the study of fatal incidents. More broadly, forensic pathology can be seen as a subfield of forensic medicine, which is a somewhat broader field that uses forensic sciences to address medical problems (Dix & Calaluce, 1998).

Performing medicolegal autopsies is the primary responsibility of most forensic pathologists, though the specifics of each case vary greatly. Only in certain nations, like Australia, will forensic pathologists conduct autopsies at the State Coroner's (a lawyer and judicial officer) request. A person other than a forensic pathologist is also designated as the official, legally mandated person responsible for the investigation of sudden deaths in some jurisdictions in the United States, such as most coroner systems and some county-based medical examiner systems (such as the local medical examiner or coroner). In these situations, the primary role of the forensic pathologist is to conduct autopsies upon request from the coroner or medical examiner (ME) in the area. The forensic pathologist is responsible for carrying out the official investigation of such deaths, including death certification, in other jurisdictions, such as different state, regional, and metropolitan medical examiner systems. Forensic pathologists conduct autopsies in both natural and unnatural death situations in some nations, but they are only involved in suspicious or violent death cases in other jurisdictions.

Three components make up a forensic death investigation: (1) the preliminary investigation, which involves assessing the scene; (2) the examination of the body, which might or might not entail performing an autopsy; and (3) the follow-up investigation that comes after. Initial and follow-up investigation responsibilities are largely determined by the legally-mandated standards for a given state or jurisdiction, and they frequently involve death investigators who are not pathologists. It is crucial to understand that the forensic pathologist's conclusions and opinions may be significantly influenced by the results of both the initial death investigation and the follow-up investigations conducted after the autopsy. For this reason, before conducting the autopsy, forensic pathologists typically try to learn as much as they can about a specific death investigation.

The external examination, the internal examination, and the ancillary procedures comprise the three components of the autopsy. Examining and recording a body's outward characteristics is part of the external examination. Height, weight, estimated age, race, gender, eye and hair color, dentition, tattoos, and scars (surgical or otherwise) are examples of routine information. When determining the identity of the decedent, or deceased person, the external examination might be very important.

The internal examination entails opening each body cavity surgically, removing the organs, and dissecting them to determine whether illness or injury is present. A "complete" autopsy typically entails the removal and examination of the brain, neck structures, and trunk organs (chest, abdomen, and pelvis). A "limited" autopsy, in which only a few designated organs are examined, may be carried out in specific cases. Other times, highly specialized dissections may be performed in great detail to pinpoint specific injuries, like a strangulation injury to the neck, or underlying diseases, like inherited heart disease. An extensive range of ancillary procedures, which offer information not available from routine dissection, may also be performed as part of a forensic autopsy. These procedures include toxicology, microbiology, chemistry, microscopic examination, and CT scanning/x-rays.

The precise and thorough documentation of findings is an essential component of the practice of forensic pathology. The documentation process includes things like autopsy reports, photos, tissue samples, autopsy notes, and evidence gathering. It is necessary that every person examined in a death investigation office be positively identified, even though not every death that is referred to one will necessitate an autopsy.

The process of filling out an official "death certificate" with multiple pieces of personal information, including name, birthdate, and social security number (if applicable), is known as "death certification." Furthermore, the "cause" and "manner" of death are officially documented. The illness, injury, or combination of these that resulted in death is referred to as the cause of death. The means or conditions by which the cause of death transpired are referred to as the manner of death. Natural and unnatural deaths are the two most common options; the latter category includes homicide, suicide, accident, and undetermined.

In the legal system, forensic pathologists are frequently obliged to give formal testimony about the deaths they have looked into. Although testimony in criminal cases predominates, it is also frequently heard in civil cases. In other cases, forensic pathologists advise police and lawyers on matters pertaining to injuries, illnesses, or fatalities (Graham & Hanzlick, 1997).

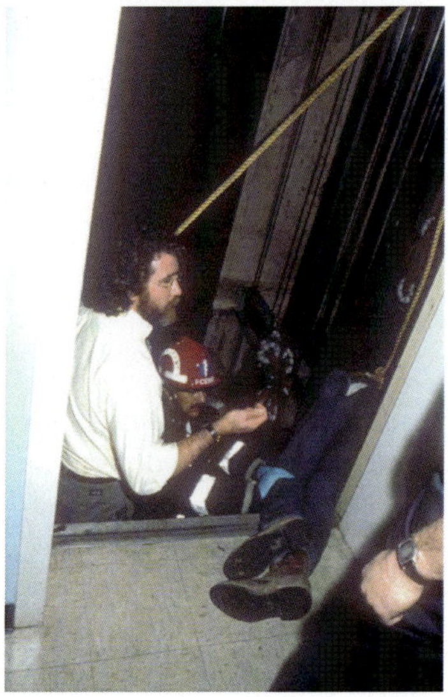

Figure 6.1. *Scene investigation is one of the most important aspects of a death investigation. Depending on the jurisdiction, forensic pathologists may or may not participate in this aspect of the investigation, although most will visit at least an occasional scene, particularly if asked to do so by police or investigators. In this case, a forensic pathologist supervises as an elevator shaft accident victim is extricated by fire department personnel.*

Source: Joseph A. Prahlow and Roger W. Byard. Atlas of Forensic Pathology. Springer. doi: 10.1007/978–1-61779–058–4.

Presently, in order to become a forensic pathologist in the United States, one must first successfully complete medical school (MD or DO degree), then anatomic pathology residency program, forensic pathology fellowship program, and finally both. An individual must first earn certification in anatomic pathology and then in forensic pathology from the American Board of Pathology (ABP) in order to work as a forensic pathologist. In other nations, institutional evaluation takes place during forensic pathology residency, and board certification is not mandatory. An important portion of anatomical pathology is covered in a series of exams offered by the Royal College of Pathologists of Australasia in Australia, which is dedicated to forensic pathology education (Figure 6.1–6.10).

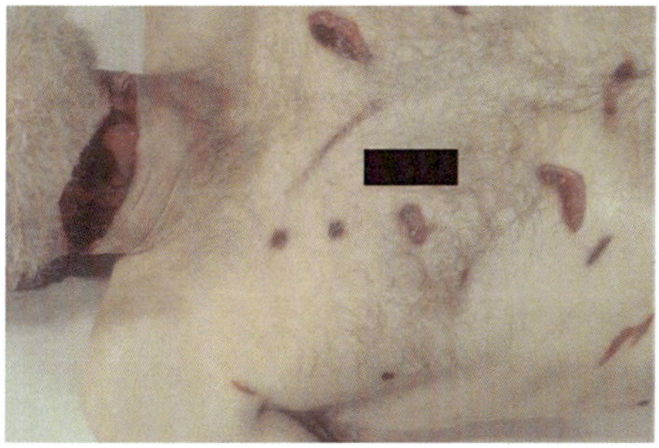

Figure 6.2. *The external examination is a very important part of a forensic autopsy. In some cases, particularly in homicide cases with multiple injuries, the external examination requires much more time than the internal examination. In the example shown, a case with multiple injuries, including blunt force, sharp force, and gunshot wounds, the external examination took several hours to complete.*

Source: Joseph A. Prahlow and Roger W. Byard. Atlas of Forensic Pathology. Springer. doi: 10.1007/978–1-61779–058–4.

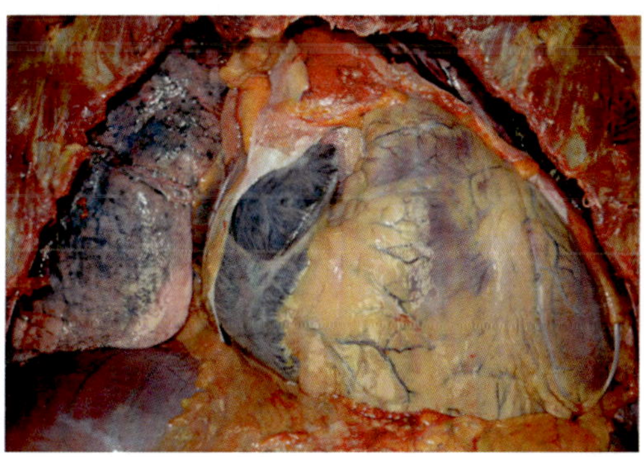

Figure 6.3. *The internal examination allows the forensic pathologist to identify diseases and injuries at autopsy, and to collect tissue samples and certain types of evidence. In this case, showing the internal appearance of the chest, after removal of the chest plate and the anterior (front) part of the pericardial sac, a markedly enlarged heart is evident. The structure to the left of the heart in the photograph is the right lung. Immediately below the lung is the right side of the diaphragm.*

Source: Joseph A. Prahlow and Roger W. Byard. Atlas of Forensic Pathology. Springer. doi: 10.1007/978–1-61779–058–4.

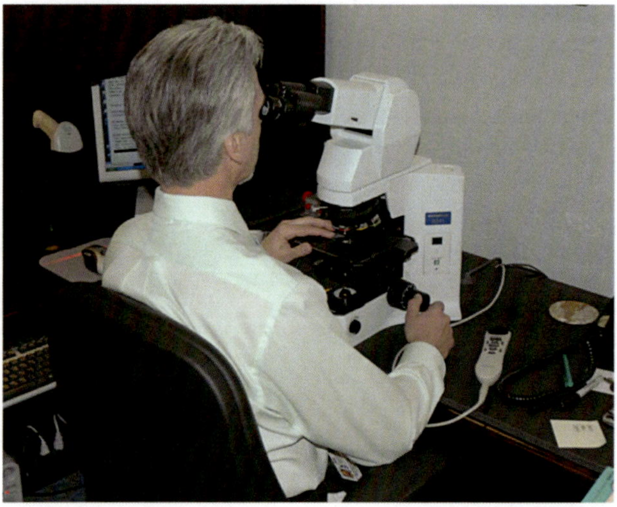

Figure 6.4. *Microscopic examination may be a very important part of a forensic autopsy, particularly in cases where the cause of death is a natural disease process. In this photograph, a forensic pathologist is viewing slides under a light microscope.*

Source: Joseph A. Prahlow and Roger W. Byard. Atlas of Forensic Pathology. Springer. doi: 10.1007/978–1-61779–058–4.

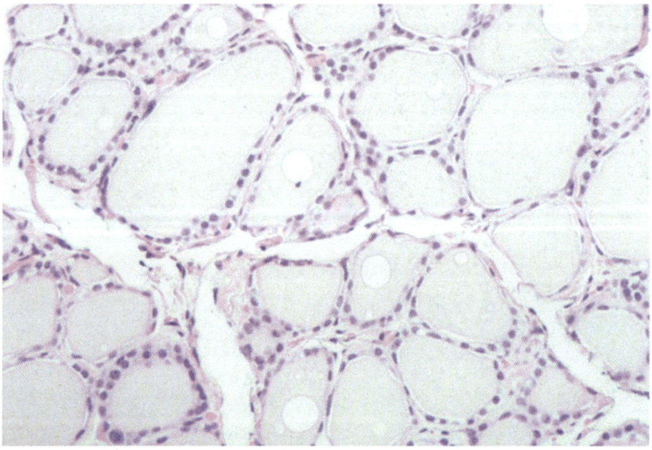

Figure 6.5. *Microscopic section of normal thyroid gland.*

Source: Joseph A. Prahlow and Roger W. Byard. Atlas of Forensic Pathology. Springer. doi: 10.1007/978–1-61779–058–4.

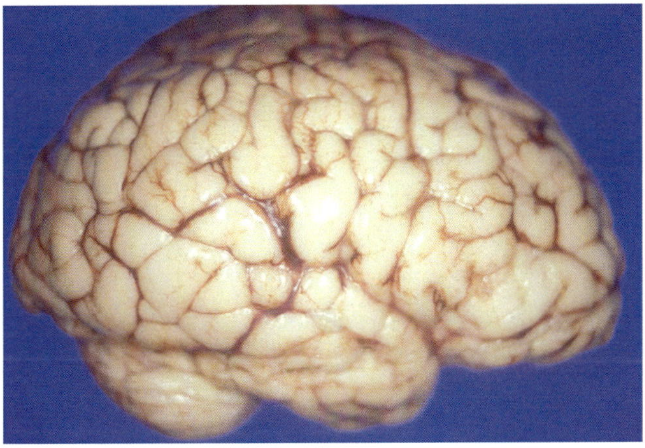

Figure 6.6. *An infant brain that has been "fixed" in formalin for several weeks following autopsy. The brain shows signs of swelling or "edema."*

Source: Joseph A. Prahlow and Roger W. Byard. Atlas of Forensic Pathology. Springer. doi: 10.1007/978–1-61779–058–4.

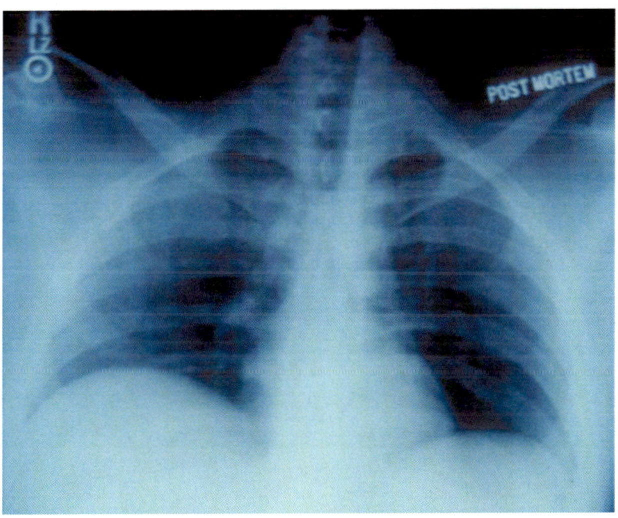

Figure 6.7. *The ability to perform and evaluate x-rays is a necessary part of the forensic autopsy. X-rays are primarily utilized to locate projectiles (bullets), to evaluate injury, and to aid in identification. This is an example of a normal postmortem chest x-ray.*

Source: Joseph A. Prahlow and Roger W. Byard. Atlas of Forensic Pathology. Springer. doi: 10.1007/978–1-61779–058–4.

Figure 6.8. *A forensic pathologist participating in a videotaped deposition. A court reporter documents the proceedings.*

Source: Joseph A. Prahlow and Roger W. Byard. Atlas of Forensic Pathology. Springer. doi: 10.1007/978–1-61779–058–4.

Figure 6.9. *Testifying in court proceedings, including criminal and civil trials, is an important part of the role of a forensic pathologist.*

Source: Joseph A. Prahlow and Roger W. Byard. Atlas of Forensic Pathology. Springer. doi: 10.1007/978–1-61779–058–4.

Figure 6.10. *A forensic pathologist participating in a deposition along with attorneys from both sides of the case.*

Source: Joseph A. Prahlow and Roger W. Byard. Atlas of Forensic Pathology. Springer. doi: 10.1007/978–1-61779–058–4.

6.2. CAUSE AND MANNER OF DEATH

There are two categories for the cause of death: primary and secondary. The three-link causal chain known as the primary cause of death, or immediate cause of death, explains why life ends by beginning with the most recent condition and working backward in time. For example:

1. Most recent condition (coronary bypass surgery, for example) due to or as a consequence of;
2. Next oldest condition (a rupture of the heart's lining due to tissue death from lack of oxygen, for example) due to or as a consequence of; and
3. Oldest (original, initiating) condition (coronary artery disease, for example)

Every condition follows from the one that came before it. It is not necessary to always use all three causes; at least one must be listed. Usually listed is the secondary cause of death, which includes circumstances like intense heat or extremely cold temperatures that are unrelated to the primary cause of death but significantly contribute to the person's demise.

A medicolegal autopsy differs significantly from a typical hospital autopsy. With the family's consent and the doctor's request, the hospital performs the autopsy. Thc autopsy is not carried out if the family objects for religious or personal reasons. On the other hand, a medicolegal autopsy is carried out as part of a legal medical examination of a deceased person.

A body examination to ascertain the cause of death may be ordered by the coroner or medical examiner in cases where a person passes away suddenly, abnormally, or under suspicious circumstances. The process by which the causes of death emerged is known as the manner of death. Generally speaking, only four causes of death are recognized: natural, accidental, suicide, and homicide. The cause and manner of death need to be determined because the deceased might have ended their life in a way that raises red flags with the authorities. A medicolegal autopsy may also be performed to identify the deceased, determine the exact time of death, or gather information about the circumstances of the death. While the cause of death is frequently known, the manner and mechanism of death—which are vital to the objectives of a medicolegal autopsy—may not be immediately apparent. Consider a body discovered at the foot of a cliff: The pathologist may never know from the autopsy results alone whether the victim was pushed, jumped, or slipped. The cause of death may be the obvious one (a fractured skull). It is crucial to remember that if an unnatural event initiates a series of direct consequences, the final mode of death is determined by the nature of the initial event. An example of an accidental death would be an elderly person who falls, breaks their hip, and then passes away in the hospital from a pulmonary embolus, or blood clot in the lung. A case that may be more challenging to evaluate is the one of a young person who is assaulted, sustains a severe closed head injury, and passes away in a chronic care facility three years later without ever regaining consciousness. In this case, homicide is the cause of death.

A pathologist is qualified to perform a hospital autopsy, but to interpret fatal trauma and morbid anatomy, they need more training than a regular medical student. In as many as half of the fatal gunshot wounds, trauma surgeons misinterpreted the number and locations of the entrance and exit wounds, according to a study by Collins and Lantz (1994).

6.3. AUTOPSY

The term "autopsy" refers to a surgical procedure known as "post-mortem examination," "obduction," "necropsy," or "autopsia cadaverum." It involves a thorough examination of a corpse through dissection to ascertain the cause, manner, and manner of death; alternatively, the exam may be carried out to assess any disease or injury that may be present for research or educational purposes. For non-human animals, the word necropsy is typically used.

A pathologist is a type of medical professional who specializes in performing autopsies. An autopsy is only necessary in certain situations and for a very small percentage of deaths. The cause of death is typically ascertained by a coroner or medical examiner.

6.3.1. Purposes of Performance

Autopsies are performed for either legal or medical purposes. Autopsies can be performed when any of the following information is desired:

- Manner of death must be determined
  - Determine if death was natural or unnatural
  - Injury source and extent on the corpse
- Post mortem interval
- Determining the deceased's identity
- Retain relevant organs
- If it is an infant, determine live birth and viability

Forensic autopsies, for instance, are conducted when the cause of death may be criminal in nature, whereas clinical or academic autopsies are conducted to determine the medical cause of death and are utilized in cases where the cause of death is unknown or uncertain, as well as for research objectives. There are two types of autopsies: those in which an external examination is sufficient and those in which the body is dissected and an internal examination is carried out. In certain instances, authorization from the next of kin may be necessary for an internal autopsy. The body is sewn back together to reassemble it after an internal autopsy is finished.

6.3.2. Etymology

- **Autopsy:** The term "autopsy" derives from the Ancient Greek αὐτοψία *autopsia*, "to see for oneself," derived from αὐτός (*autos*, "oneself") and ὄψις (*opsis*, "sight, view"). The word has been in use since around the 17th century.
- **Post-Mortem:** The term "post-mortem" derives from the Latin *post*, 'after,' and *mortem*, 'death.' It was first recorded in 1734.
- **Necropsy:** The term "necropsy" is derived from the Greek νεκρός 'death' and ὄψις (*opsis*, 'sight, view').

6.3.3. Purpose of Autopsy

The main objectives of an autopsy are to ascertain the cause, manner, and mode of death, as well as the patient's prior health and whether any pre-death medical diagnoses and treatments were appropriate. Since 1955, the number of hospital autopsies in the majority of Western nations has been declining annually. Critics, such as pathologist and former editor of JAMA George D. Lundberg, contend that the decrease in autopsies is having a detrimental effect on hospital care because errors that cause fatalities are frequently not looked into, meaning that lessons are not learned. Autopsies may also be performed for educational or scientific purposes if the subject has given permission for one prior to death. When a patient passes away suddenly, when a doctor is unable to record the death, or when the cause of death is thought to be unnatural, an autopsy is typically conducted. These tests are carried out by a medical examiner, coroner, or procurator fiscal acting under legal authority; the deceased's family members are not required to give permission. The most extreme example is when murder victims are examined by medical examiners, who are specifically searching for evidence of the murder technique or cause of death, such as bullet wounds and exit points, signs of strangulation, or poisoning residue. Certain religions, such as Islam and Judaism, typically forbid conducting autopsies on their followers. Families are usually advised by organizations like Misaskim in the US and ZAKA in Israel on how to make sure that an unnecessary autopsy is not performed. In clinical medicine, autopsies are performed to detect medical errors or previously undetected conditions that could pose a risk to the living, such as exposure to hazardous materials or infectious diseases. A study that focused on myocardial infarction (heart attack) as a cause of death found significant errors of omission and commission, i.e., a sizable number of cases ascribed to myocardial infarctions (MIs) were not MIs and a significant number of non-MIs were MIs.

According to a systematic review of autopsy studies, a significant diagnostic error will be found in approximately 25% of autopsies. This rate has, however, declined over time, and the study predicts that 8–24% of autopsies in a modern US institution will identify significant diagnostic errors.

According to a comprehensive meta-analysis, roughly one-third of death certificates are false, and half of autopsies result in findings that were not suspected before the patient passed away. Furthermore, it's estimated that more than 25% of unexpected findings can only be histologically diagnosed, i.e., by biopsy or autopsy, and that roughly 25% of unanticipated findings—or 5% of all findings—are significant and can only be diagnosed based on tissue.

According to one study, autopsies identified 171 missed diagnoses (out of 694 total diagnoses), including, among other things, 21 malignancies, 12 strokes, 11 myocardial infarctions, 10 pulmonary emboli, and 9 endocarditis.

One study, which concentrated on intubated patients, discovered that abdominal pathologic conditions, such as infarctions, bowel perforations, or abscesses, were just as common as pulmonary emboli in contributing to class I errors. Although abdominal pain was the most common complaint among patients with abdominal pathologic conditions, most of them did not pursue this symptom because the results of their abdominal examinations were deemed unremarkable.

6.3.4. Types of Autopsy

Though medical conventions and legal systems vary considerably from country to country, there are generally two main types of autopsy:

- The clinical or academic autopsy is one in which the medical attendants, with the consent of relatives, seek to learn the extent of the disease for which they were treating the deceased patient. In most jurisdictions this type of autopsy should not be held to determine the nature of the fatal disease because, if this was unknown to the physicians, the death should have been reported for medico-legal investigation.
- The medico-legal or forensic autopsy, which is performed on the instructions of the legal authority responsible for the investigation o suspicious, obscure, unnatural, litigiouslitigious, or criminal

deaths. This legal authority may be a coroner, a medical examiner, a procurator fiscal, a magistrate, a judge, or the police, the systems varying considerably from country to country.

Most systems do not require the consent of the relatives because it would defeat the purpose of the legal investigation if the autopsy could not be performed due to objections from potential guilty parties.

In many jurisdictions the medico-legal autopsy is often further subdivided into:

- Those held on apparently non-criminal deaths, such as accidents, suicides, deaths from sudden natural causes, or associated with medical and surgical treatment, industrial deaths, and so on.
- The truly forensic autopsy held on suspicious or frankly criminal deaths, usually at the instigation of the police. s comprise murder, manslaughter, infanticideinfanticide, and other categories that vary in different jurisdictions.

There is little use in going into detail because the pathologists that handle these categories differ greatly across locations. They also differ in type. What matters most is that the pathologist handling each kind of case must have training and experience specific to that field. Unfortunately, pathologists with little experience in forensic procedures often perform medico-legal autopsies, especially in major criminal cases, due to a lack of staff, inadequate resources, or flaws in the system.

The division of forensic pathologists from those who claim to be university professors is another grave flaw in many nations. Being a credible and convincing teacher requires ongoing practical experience in the subject matter.

The fact that doctors performing medicolegal autopsies lack any training in pathology is even more regrettable. This terrible practice is prevalent and unavoidable in many developing nations due to a lack of resources, but it is also present in some regions of Europe, the Americas, and other regions. This is detrimental to the high caliber of knowledge required to assist law enforcement and carry out the administration of jad opinion is frequently worse than none at allnone since, in the latter scenario, the legal authorities won't be duped by the frequently dogmatic errors of a novice physician and will at least be aware of the weakness in their evidence.

6.3.5. The Procedure for a Forensic Autopsy

Regardless of the cause of death, an autopsy is generally performed in the same way, but there are a number of related issues that change depending on the situation. For instance, dissection in a criminal abortion or fatal rape is different from that of a drowned body, and the procedural precautions needed in a murder are not required in a sudden natural death.

6.3.5.1. The Objectives of an Autopsy

- To make a positive identification of the body and to assess the size, physique and nourishment.
- To determine the cause of death or, in the newborn, whether live birth occurred.
- To determine the mode of dying and time of death, where necessary and possible.
- To demonstrate all external and internal abnormalities, malformations and diseases.
- To detect, describe and measure any external and internal injuries.
- To obtain samples for analysis, microbiological and histological examination, and any other necessary investigations.
- To retain relevant organs and tissues as evidence.
- To obtain photographs and video for evidential and teaching use.
- To provide a full written report of the autopsy findings.
- To offer an expert interpretation of those findings.
- To restore the body to the best possible cosmetic condition before release to the relatives.

6.3.5.2. Preliminaries to an Autopsy

Before the body is even approached, a number of preliminaries are necessary.

6.3.5.2.1. Authorization and Consent

The appropriate authority requests that a medico-legal autopsy be performed. The pathologist is not allowed to start his examination until he is certain that authority has been granted regarding that specific death. Different methods will be used depending on the situation: written agreements, verbal or recorded messages, or implicit standing agreements may all be used to convey such authority.

When two governmental bodies are involved, it needs to be evident which one has the primary authority to request an autopsy. For instance, in England and Wales, the coroner is the only authority with the authority to order an autopsy, but the police may ask a pathologist to examine a body externally at the scene of death. The final say in the matter remains with the coroner, even though in cases of serious incidents he or she should follow the Chief of Police's advice when selecting a pathologist.

The relatives are not asked for permission to autopsy in a medico-legal autopsy because that consent cannot be revoked. Unless the situation is extremely urgent, it is customary to notify them prior to the autopsy as a courtesy. Generally speaking, though, a family member will have arrived to identify the body before the examination starts. When performing autopsies in situations where authorization or consent are unclear, pathologists should exercise caution. Sometimes a "consent document" for a hospital death is obtained, but a medico-legal investigation is later launched because of the case. The coroner or other official should decide whether to order the pathologist's own autopsy (possibly using a different pathologist), and only then can the pathologist proceed under the "consent" authority. The consent document typically reverts to validity if that official chooses not to move forward.

In a medico-legal case, permission to retain autopsy material (from small fluid samples to the entire body, if needed) is typically granted by the original authority for the examination. Nonetheless, there is a great deal of variance in the legal aspects of tissue and organ retention amongst nations, and every pathologist needs to become completely knowledgeable about local laws.

According to the laws governing the English coroner, the pathologist is rcquircd to prcscrvc any tissuc that could hclp with thc ongoing invcstigation into the death. However, under the Human Tissue Act 1961 and the soon-to-be Human Tissue Act 2005, the coroner (or procurator fiscal in Scotland) only has the negative authority to prohibit the use of tissues or organs for purposes other than the investigation of the death. As a result, the coroner cannot give positive consent for the use of these for transplantation, teaching, or research. Instead, the relatives must provide this consent if the coroner does not object.

6.3.5.3. Who May Be Present at an Autopsy

Again, laws and rules governing the conduct of medico-legal examinations vary from country to state. It is important to note that every pathologist needs to be aware of and follow the laws that are relevant to their profession, even though it is useless to attempt to survey these.

The location and time of the autopsy are frequently required to be disclosed to represented by an attorney or medical professionalan attorney or medical professional can represent them. There are certain jurisdictions, such as Britain, where there is no explicit prohibition against relatives attending in person, and the writers have personally experienced this on multiple occasions. If the pathologist feels uncomfortable performing the autopsy, he has the option to decline. A second autopsy is often conducted in homicide cases by a different pathologist who is working for the defense attorneys defending the accused. Usually, this happens later, after the defendant has been charged and given legal counsel, but occasionally, the second pathologist attends the initial autopsy. This is more beneficial and in order than a subsequent examination of heavily dissected and autolyzed tissues.

The coroner, medical examiner, or other appropriate legal authority authorizes such attendance. In the hopes of receiving the same treatment when the roles are reversed, the first pathologist should extend all civility and accommodations to his colleague.

Naturally, other authorized attendees include the officers or representatives of the department presiding over the autopsy, such as a coroner, magistrate, or judge. If the death is suspicious or criminal, the police are also there, along with their technical teams. The decision of the official commissioning the exam will determine whether or not additional physicians and medical students are permitted. Since the doctor has the most up-to-date knowledge of the patient's medical history, it is almost always customary to permit – in fact, encourage – the presence of the physician when the deceased was receiving medical care prior to death. The pathologist should make an effort to keep the number of people present to a minimum in a criminal or suspicious case. In addition to the increased risk of confidentiality breaches, the sheer volume of people—especially large police officers—can result in an overcrowding of the mortuary. This impairs mobility, diverts attention, and increases the risk of infection and contamination—particularly in light of the current concerns regarding the transmissibility of the HIV virus and the various forms of hepatitis (B, C, D, and E). No one, not even senior police officers not directly involved in the investigation, should be there as a casual observer. As forensic and police procedures become more sophisticated and complex, an increasing number of people are packed into the mortuary, which is overflowing with equipment such as cameras, videos, recorders, crime scene kits, and more, leaving little space for the pathologist to move around.

The pathologist should list and identify everyone present at an autopsy on a suspicious or criminal death on the autopsy report.

6.3.6. Examination of the Scene of Death

The pathologist ought to be present at the scene of death prior to the removal of the body in cases involving homicide, suspected homicide, and other dubious or unclear cases. Again, local practices differ, but any physician identifying themselves as forensic pathologists should always offer to go with the police to the scene of the crime. For pathologists who work with the police either full-time or frequently, this responsibility is frequently formalized and included in a contract of service. In many other jurisdictions, including the American medical examiner systems and the European State and University Institutes of Forensic Medicine, there is typically a prearranged duty roster for attendance at death scenes. In England and Wales, "Home Office Pathologists" are always available for these types of visits. When a skilled forensic pathologist arrives at the scene of death, their primary responsibility is to evaluate the surrounding conditions, the body's position, and the surrounding environment. Crime can be quickly ruled out in a significant number of cases in favor of accidents, suicide, or even natural causes. This is a very helpful and economical function, since when the pathologist finds innocent circumstances, a fictitious murder investigation that may have involved numerous police officers, numerous cars, and other pricey public facilities may be quickly terminated.

The pathologist should constantly be prepared with the necessary tools so they can quickly investigate a scene. If it becomes necessary to perform autopsies in areas without adequate mortuary facilities, additional equipment might need to be brought. Most forensic pathologists keep a "murder bag" in their car, and while each specialist has their own set of tools, the following is a suitable assortment:

- waterproof apron and rubber gloves
- thermometer, syringes and needles, sterile swabs
- autopsy dissection set, including handsaw
- cutting needles and twine for body closure
- swabs and containers for blood and body fluids
- formalin jars for histological samples
- plastic bags, envelopes, paper, spare pen and pencil
- printed body charts for recording external injuries
- hand lens, electric torch, mini-tape recorder
- camera, usually 35 mm single-lens reflex with electronic flash. The recent advent of compact digital cameras or digital video cameras with the facility to take still pictures has made instant reviewing possible.

The thermometer comes in two varieties: the traditional long chemical mercury type that measures from 0 to 50°C, or the more recent electronic digital type that has a thermocouple-carrying probe. The equipment varies according to the facilities that are probably going to be available. In developed nations, hospitals and municipal morgues are likely to have excellent mortuary facilities, and law enforcement agencies are likely to have vast expertise with photography, specimen containers, and other aspects of crime scenes. In underdeveloped nations and isolated regions of other states, the pathologist might need to be almost self-sufficient when it comes to both the crime investigation and the ensuing autopsy. The skilled forensic pathologist will always have rain or snow gear and rubber boots on hand for any call, in addition to their medical kit (Figure 6.11).

Figure 6.11. *The scene of a rape-homicide. The attending pathologist must record the posture, state of clothing and general relationship of the victim to the surroundings, but limit the examination at the scene to avoid any interference with the vital process of obtaining trace evidence. Rectal temperatures should not be taken until all swabs are completed, usually in the mortuary. Temperatures can be taken in the ear or deep nostrils, though with severe head injuries (as here) even this must be done with care.*

Source: Pekka Saukko and Bernard Knight. Knight's Forensic Pathology, Third Edition. Hodder Arnold. ISBN: 978 0 340 76044 4.

The pathologist's actions at the scene of death are determined by the specific circumstances. A lot will depend on how readily police and forensic science support is available. For instance, at a crime scene in Britain, a number of teams arrive, including photographers, video operators, and Scene of Crime Officers (SOCOs), whose job it is to track down the evidence. Along with their police liaison officers, fingerprint officers, and, of course, the investigating officers from the Criminal Investigation Depat, scientists from the closest forensic laboratory frequently attend.

If there isn'tis not a backup available, the pathologist needs to attempt gathering evidence on their own, but they should stick to their area of expertise. To the greatest extent feasible, the pathologist should follow the police's instructions regarding how to approach the body in order to preserve the surrounding area. Access outside is usually restricted to a single path denoted by tapes, and within a building, the lead detective will typically indicate a path to the body.

The doctor should not smoke, touch anything needlessly, or leave any of their own belongings or debris lying around. In order to prevent unintentionally bringing fibers, hairs, and other materials from the visitor to the crime scene, disposable overalls and overshoes are being provided to those who attend crime scenes more frequently.

When a forensic physician has to examine live victims or suspects in the capacity of both a pathologist and a clinical medico-legist, or "police surgeon," they have to change into new protective gear or change out of their old clothes to prevent the transfer of trace evidence, like hairs or fibers, from victim to suspect.

The pathologist should be highly perceptive and minimally active. If the person is inside, they should determine the layout of the space and record the body's position in relation to any nearby objects. Sometimes a sketch or his own photo is helpful, and some pathologists record the death scene instantly with a Polaroid, digital, or video camera.

Figure 6.12. *Scene of a homicide-suicide where the locus of bodies should be widely marked off by tape to restrict access, and the actual body protected by a shelter from the weather and unauthorized onlookers.*

Source: Pekka Saukko and Bernard Knight. Knight's Forensic Pathology, Third Edition. Hodder Arnold. ISBN: 978 0 340 76044 4.

Any apparent reason for the death should be investigated, and any blood splashes or pools should be reported in connection with the body's location. It is important to observe the shape of these splashes because blood that lands obliquely takes the form of a pear with its sharp end facing the direction of flight, whereas blood that strikes a surface perpendicularly leaves a circular mark (Figure 6.12).

The pathologist approaches the body after taking pictures of it in its original position and confirms with the investigating officers that it is okay for him to do so. It is possible to examine it closely and feel the skin to determine its temperature. Examining the hands, eyes, and neck is possible, as is carefully moving clothing aside to look at the upper chest or throat when needed. Before there is any more agitation, the police should take pictures of any pertinent discoveries (Figure 6.13).

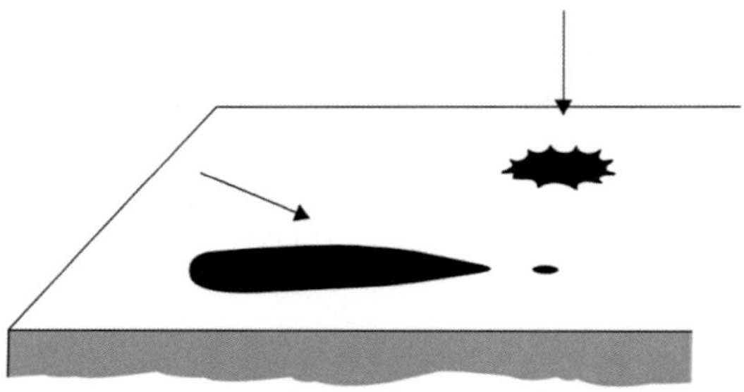

Figure 6.13. *At a scene of crime, the position of the body at the time of an assault can sometimes be clarified by observing the direction of blood splashing that may have been thrown off a weapon or bloodstained hands. Blood striking vertically causes round or crenellated circles, while blood hitting at an angle is lance-shaped with the narrow end facing the direction of travel. There is often a preceding drop of blood in advance of the major splash, forming an 'exclamation mark' stain.*

Source: Pekka Saukko and Bernard Knight. Knight's Forensic Pathology, Third Edition. Hodder Arnold. ISBN: 978 0 340 76044 4.

It is imperative to honor the requests of forensic scientists and scene of crime officers if they still need samples at this point. In order to gather any stray hairs or fibers, they might wish to "tape" the body, which entails running adhesive tape over the skin and garments. After that, the body can be carefully moved to examine the sides and underneath to make sure no weapon, object, or piece of evidence is disturbed. Due to the unique aspects of every case, a predetermined routine cannot be recommended. The main goal is to evaluate the entire scene before the scientific teams have completed their work with the least amount of disruption to the clothing and body.

6.3.6.1. Estimating the Post-Mortem Interval at the Scene

One can evaluate the general temperature of the hands and face by touching them, and one can test the limbs gently to determine the degree of rigor mortis.

As soon as the body is discovered, the ambient (environmental) temperature needs to be recorded. Ideally, this is done by police scene investigators, who typically arrive at the scene before a pathologist. It is best to take the ambient temperature as close to the body as feasible because even inside of buildings or rooms, microenvironments can exist. In order to estimate post-discovery distortions of temperature, information about the extent of potential disturbances to the ambient temperature, such as opening doors and windows, turning on or off fireplaces, and turning on central heating, should be sought. It is debatable whether a thermometer should be inserted into the rectum at this point in the investigation.

This usually entails removing pants or trousers or in any other way disturbing clothing at a crime scene, usually in small, dimly lit spaces or out in the open. By introducing seminal fluid from the anal margin into the rectum, it also runs the risk of contaminating the rectum and perineum, which reduces the value of later examinations in that area and the collection of semen swabs. Rectal temperature taking at the scene should only be done if forensic scientists or police scene of crime officers are satisfied that trace evidence from the clothing, swabs from the vulva, vagina, and anus, etc., is present. This is because many violent crimes nowadays have overtones related to sexuality or homosexuality. can be successfully obtained prior to the performance of rectal thermometry.

Put another way, a cost-benefit analysis needs to be done right there at the scene to determine whether the small potential benefit of an earlier measurement justifies the challenges of taking a rectal temperature. In numerous instances where the corpse has evidently remained in the area long enough for the core temperature to attain room temperature, or where additional circumstantial evidence suggests that the exact time of death is known with more precision than thermometry can provide, there is no harm in delaying the process until the body is brought to the mortuary for autopsy. This typically occurs right after the body is removed from the scene, according to British customs.

Temperature readings are warranted and much more work needs to be done at the scene if transportation issues or a lack of facilities cause the autopsy to be postponed for several hours.

Using a location other than the rectum is an option. Because of their erratic exposure to air temperature, the axilla and mouth produce low readings that are not consistently correlated with the deep temperature. The auditory meatus, or nostril, is more beneficial when the thermometer or thermocouple probe is inserted as deeply as feasible. These locations offer the great advantage of being easily accessible without requiring the removal of clothing and providing accurate, repeatable readings without the need for swabbing in order to look into potential sexual assaults.

The pathologist's next task is to make sure the body is moved to the mortuary for autopsy with the least amount of disturbance and evidence loss possible after performing the best examination possible under the circumstances. He ought to oversee the removal himself or, at the very least, assign the task to someone else he trusts to be cautious and capable. Every hand needs to be contained in a bag and fastened at the wrist with string or adhesive tape. Place a comparable bag over the head. Although the packing method can differ, paper bags are typically advised.

The body needs to be carefully placed in a "body-bag" with a zip closure or transferred to a sizable, brand-new plastic sheet that is at least two meters square. If a sheet is used, the edges need to be wrapped around the body and taped down. Retaining any loose items, hairs, or fibers that might be sticking to the body or the clothing is the goal of the exercise. After the body is removed from the mortuary, the forensic laboratory takes the sheet or bag so they can check it for traces of evidence. The police or another organization, like the coroner or his officer, is in charge of transporting the body. The body should be transported to the selected mortuary by hearse, van, or police transport while still wrapped in plastic. It should then be placed inside a stiff fiberglass "shell" or regular coffin.

Preventing physical harm during the removal process is crucial; however, in challenging or unreachable locations, this may not always be feasible. When there is a fire, the body may sustain significant damage either before or after recovery, sometimes as a result of no one noticing it among the smoke- and frequently wet-filled debris. One such scene that the author (BK) has witnessed involved firefighters walking over two bodies for several hours before realizing that they were buried beneath charred furniture and other debris. Splits in joints that resemble antemortem injuries are easily caused by handling brittle, charred bodies.

In conclusion, a pathologist's duties at a suspicious death scene include assessing the circumstances, protecting any delicate evidence, supervising the body's removal, and, if it is reasonable, providing an expert opinion regarding the cause of death. He is not there to play the role of a modern-day Sherlock Holmes, offering unproven theories about unrelated medical issues or trying to draw erroneous conclusions from the scanniest of evidence. The pathologist can make his greatest contributions as a member of a cohesive, well-coordinated team of specialists, each of whom is an expert in their own field.

6.3.7. Property, Clothing and Identification

The pathologist should observe the clothing and other items on the body that he will be performing an autopsy on, regardless of whether he has visited the scene of the death. This holds true for all suspicious or criminal deaths as well as the excessive number of industrial and traffic accidents, as well as victims of drowning, falls from a height, and other incidents.

The clothing may have been removed before the body was transferred to the mortuary in many cases when the death occurred in a hospital or accident department, making it impossible to examine the clothed body there. The pathologist should permanently request that no clothing be removed from a body brought to the mortuary following a traffic accident or other incident where trauma was the preliminary cause of death. This is unless, of course, the victim was still alive when they arrived at the hospital and undressing was done prior to resuscitation or other treatment being attempted. Second best, the clothing that has been taken off should go to the mortuary with the body so that it can be checked for damage, stains, and other evidence, if needed. Sadly, before it can be seen, such clothing is often destroyed.

Clothes and other personal belongings should be treated as significant pieces of evidence by the mortuary staff, and a system should be put in place to identify, keep, and store them for the protection of valuables as well as for the sake of evidentiary purposes. Identification is aided by the items in the pockets, documents, keys, and other items. The pathologist may occasionally be interested in this aspect, even though it is primarily the responsibility of the police. Identification is aided by the clothing itself, including the style, fabric, color, and labels.

When there is a trauma death, the clothing damage should correspond with the body injuries. In order to account for movement and displacement during life, the location of external lesions on the body must be compared to wounds from slashes, stabs, tears, and, in particular, firearm wounds in clothing. When clothing damage does not match the injuries, it may be a sign that the wounds were self-inflicted.

Although the forensic science laboratory is primarily responsible for detecting the presence of bodily secretions such as blood, seminal, vaginal, and others on clothing, the pathologist may be the first or only person to do so. Gunshot residues on clothing may contain crucial information regarding the ammunition's identity and discharge range in firearm-related fatalities.

When it comes to traffic fatalities, things like ripped clothing, grease marks, dirt on the road, broken lamps or windscreen glass, and even paint or metallic pieces from the vehicle can all help piece together the events and identify the unidentified vehicle in a "hit-and-run" accident. Additional items connected to the body that might be useful are medications, like insulin or amyl nitrite, that could help identify the type of illness the deceased had. Empty drug or poison containers may be found with the body in some suicides. Other useful artifacts are things like inhalers, syringes, external pacemakers, and hearing aids. The pathologist should oversee and support the mortuary technician during the meticulous removal of clothing, particularly in cases involving criminal activity or suspicions. This is because some technicians may not be cognizant of the significance of clothing in the reconstruction of events.

Unless it could impede any injuries or soiling, it is best to remove clothing in the standard manner, pulling over the head and limbs, if the body is not bleeding or otherwise fouled. It might be wise to cut off part or all of the clothing if the rigor is severe or if there is blood on the hands or face. If forensic scientists are present, they should be consulted before proceeding with this so that any cuts are made in a way that minimizes any potential interference with subsequent laboratory testing. Cuts should, in any case, not go through any existing stains or damage to the clothing. To give the clothes a chance to "breathe," each piece should be put into its own paper bag.

6.3.7.1. Identification of the Body

Identification of an unexplained body is a significant forensic task. However, the formal recognition of the subject of an impending autopsy is what matters here. A pathologist must make sure the corpse in front of him is, in fact, the right person before performing any examinations or starting any mutilating dissections.

Every medico-legal case requires that the body be identified by a responsible party. This is typically a close friend or family member of the deceased who examines the face of the body and attests verbally to a police officer, mortuary staff member, or physician that it is, in fact, "John Smith." When a body is severely burned, disfigured, or decomposing, efforts at identification must be made by displaying any family documents or personal belongings like jewelry or clothes.

The name, address, serial number, and other pertinent information are carried on a label or tag that the police officer, nursing staff, or mortuary attendant attaches to the body in non-criminal cases, such as sudden deaths, the majority of accidents, and suicides. This label can be securely fastened to a toe or worn on a sturdy wrist or ankle bracelet. Some mortuaries use permanent markers to write the name on the leg, but these can become smeared or hidden during the autopsy.

The pathologist should always confirm their identity by comparing the toe label or bracelet with the documents allowing the autopsy. If there is a discrepancy, he should call back the police officer or even the relative to confirm the identity. If the details don't match, he shouldn't proceed with the autopsy until the issue is resolved.

Numerous errors have been committed in the past, leading to bad press, awkward inquiries, and even legal repercussions. Lax identification practices frequently result in autopsies on the wrong person, erroneous causes of death, relatives attending the wrong funeral, and even the cremation of the wrong body. The body should always be labeled as soon as it enters the mortuary to prevent confusion. The pathologist and regular mortuary staff may not be aware of other parties moving occupants around, such as night porters, so labels on refrigerator doors and shrouds become detached.

Some sizable mortuaries employ unique identification techniques. One that the writers are aware of has an automated camera installed in the mortuary entrance's ceiling. Each body that is wheeled in is photographed while still on its trolley, and a board with the serial number clearly visible is positioned across the upper chest to ensure that the record number appears on the face in case there is a later discrepancy.

When dealing with grave cases like homicide, the pathologist must not depend on secondary identification evidence like a toe label. He needs verbal confirmation that the body they are both seeing is "John Smith" prior to the autopsy. This individual needs to be a family member or a police officer who has previously received formal identification of the body from a relative.

The date, time, and specifics of the person who identified the body to the pathologist must be noted in the autopsy report by the pathologist in order to ensure "continuity of evidence" for legal purposes, which the defense cannot successfully contest at a later trial.

6.3.8. The Use of the History of the Case

Similar to clinical medicine, the deceased person's history plays a crucial and essential role in the investigation. However, there is more debate regarding how much of an impact it should have on the pathologist's determination of the cause of death, as will be covered in more detail below.

When compared to hospital "clinical" cases, the history in medico-legal autopsies is frequently incomplete, nonexistent, or deceptive. In the event that an individual is discovered deceased and had no prior medical attention, there might be very little information available. When someone is involved in a criminal death, it's possible that they are the ones who know the most about it. As such, they may choose to keep quiet or provide a skewed, deceptive, or entirely false account of what happened. Then, the forensic pathologist frequently faces a limited or inaccurate history.

Due to a lack of knowledge and comprehension, medical facts are frequently misrepresented, even when they are provided by relatives in good faith. It might be transmitted by a police officer or another non-medical individual, further distorting it, so that the pathologist only receives a jumbled history. The latter should make additional requests to the commissioning authority, such as the police or coroner, in an effort to make up for information gaps. The pathologist ought to make every effort to get in touch with the physician who may have recently treated the deceased. However, in the rush of forensic work, often on the weekends or at night, the autopsy may need to proceed without further history.

Though more detail may be obtained afterwards, the course of the autopsy might well have been different if such knowledge was available beforehand. For instance, the author (BK) once conducted an autopsy on a coal miner who had no prior medical history other than his occupation and a persistent chest ailment. The body was released for burial after an autopsy determined that there was enough cardiopulmonary disease to explain the death. The police in the rural area where the man died did not promptly provide information about the discovery of an empty sleeping pill bottle and a suicide note with his body until the next day. Paradoxically, the history is often less important in violent deaths where the wounds are self-evident, though a good description of the circumstances may assist in interpreting the direction of injuries, the nature of the weapon and other aspects.

As in the case mentioned above, the pathologist is usually directed to the proper ancillary investigations by the history in autopsies. In the past, a few pathologists have argued that the autopsy should be conducted "blind," meaning that the pathologist's opinion won't be influenced by the history. This is obviously unfeasible because every autopsy would then have to be extremely thorough, involving techniques like the excision of the spinal cord in every case and any potential ancillary investigations like toxicology, microbiolvirology, radiology, diatoms, histology, and so forth. There would be no way to determine what was relevant and what wasn'twas not. Apart from the intolerable burden of work, the expense of such an approach would tive, if applied to all autopsies.

When a person passes away in a foreign state and then returns home, there are frequentlyfrequent special issues. The degree of pathological and administrative sophistication of the foreign nation has a significant impact on the problems. When these are low, it may be difficult to get a good history—or any history at all—even after attempting to use diplomatic or international law enforcement channels. Sometimes, a 'doctor-to-doctor' approach by telephone or fax may be the best way of obtaining information. Even a foreign country's official cause of death could be unreachable or so nebulous (like "heart failure") that it serves no purpose. Prior autopsies could have been insufficient, subpar, or even fraudulent; for example, they might have discovered a sutured skin incision without any underlying organ dissection. Numerous analyzes of these problematic autopsies have been published, and a call for an international death certificate has been made.

When there are few or no objective autopsy findings, problems can arise. Next, the pathologist must decide whether to declarof death is unknown or to determine the cause of death based on his or her subjective understanding of the purported historyhistory, which may be inaccurate. This issue is by no means unique. For instance, people with epilepsy or asthma have been known to pass away suddenly and unexpectedly; an autopsy in these cases typically reveals no sufficient morphological reason for the death. The sudden infant death syndrome is another excellent example, in which the history is typically virtually blank and there are, by definition, no notable autopsy lesions.

Even though there is a clear clinical history of a rectal temperature of 26°C, there may be nothing to uncover at autopsy in cases of hypothermia where the patient is warmed up in the hospital but passes away in a day or two. Moving on to more forensic scenarios, a body may be pulled from a river following the discovery of clothing and a suicide note on the bank; however, an autopsy may reveal no signs of drowning at all.

In these situations, should the pathologist certify "hypothermia" or "drowning," and then possibly face legal challenges from an attorney arguing that the pathologist relied solely on hearsay and lacked objective evidence, or should he decline to offer a cause of death and risk being accused of obstruction or perversity?

Providing the pathologist determines that the history is strong enough, the best course of action is for him to state the most likely and reasonable cause of death. However, he should make it clear in his autopsy report discussion that this opinion is based on a consideration of the circumstances and is not a dogmatic statement of the kind that could be made if the victim had been shot through the brain. In cases where the autopsy report is preceded by a summary of the patient's medical history, the pathologist must be cautious in identifying what, in his opinion, is "hearsay." He should therefore say, "I was told that the deceased was struck on the head by two men," rather than, "The deceased was struck on the head by two men." The autopsy report should contain a final commentary that includes a "differential diagnosis" in cases where the cause of death is unclear, as well as a justification for the final opinion or an acknowledgement that it is impossible to decide between possible outcomes. It should not be a simple recitation of the anatomical findings.

The real "cause of death" phraseology, which will be recorded in national and legal records in the World Health Organization-mandated format, presents the biggest challenge. This prevents the pathologist from expressing preferences or providing justifications; instead, he or she is limited to entering the pathologist's most reasonable option or, in all honesty, declaring that the cause is "undetermined."

6.3.9. Precautions Regarding Potential Infective Conditions

Drug addicts and people who engage in promiscuous sexual behavior are frequently involved in forensic situations, and their statistical risk of HIV and hepatitis infection is significantly higher than that of the general autopsy population. Those who work with post-autopsy samples in laboratories, morgues, police departments, and pathology departments are at risk because of this. Although there has been much written about these risks, no agreement has been reached. However, the Royal College of Pathologists (1995) published a very good survey.

According to one school, regardless of the case, all autopsies should be performed with the utmost caution to avoid any infectious risks. That being said, this is nearly hard to accomplish in a busy coroner's or medical examiner's office, and it doesn't address the issue of potentially contaminated material being sent to other labs.

Pre-autopsy testing for hepatitis and HIV using blood from a femoral needle puncture is a more popular protocol. When the results are received, decisions about how to proceed with the autopsy or, in cases where the risk-benefit ratio is high, whether to abandon it, can often be made in a matter of hours. If the results are positive, the autopsy will typically be conducted with extra caution, wearing protective gear such as masks, visors, and metal gloves. Access to observers will also be restricted, senior technicians will be chosen, and laboratories handling samples will receive warnings.

Hepatitis poses a greater risk than HIV infection in this regard. However, to date, approximately 100 healthcare professionals have contracted HIV as a result of specific occupational exposure, and one pathologist has been known to contract the virus while performing autopsies. In the USA, three morticians may have become HIV positive due to their line of work.

The duration of a deceased person's potential HIV infection varies. Viral samples from liquid blood kept at room temperature for two months were found to contain infectious virus, which can survive for three weeks in high concentrations. Bankowski et al. (1992) discovered that the virus survived for 51% of the 21 hours after death in the plasma and monocyte fractions of infected cadavers. Other studies discovered that corpses could survive for 18 to 11 days following their demise. A virus was found in the spleen 14 days after the death. It appears that refrigeration has little effect on viability. Douceron et al. (1993) determined that there was no safe maximum period of time at which corpses ceased to be an infectious risk after cultured blood and effusions from chilled bodies and obtained viable virus up to 16 days post-mortem. Offering post-exposure prophylaxis following a significant percutaneous exposure to HIV patient blood or tissues is now standard practice in industrialized nations. Additional infections: TB, hepatitis viruses, anthrax, plague, Marburg, Creutzfeldt-Jakob, Green Monkey diseases, etc., are often governed by particular health and safety laws that differ from nation to nation.

6.3.10. The Autopsy: External Examination

The external examination is far more important in forensic cases than it is in "clinical autopsies," which are used to assess natural disease—especially in cases where the victim died from trauma. In the latter case, the external description may have the greatest medico-legal significance because conclusions regarding the type of weapon, the angle of attack, and other crucial details are frequently drawn from the external evidence. Consequently,ic pathologist needs to take all the time required to carefully examine the body's surface and not be too eager to use the knife in order toto obtain tissue samples for histology, which is better justified in a strictly clinical autopsy (Figure 6.14).

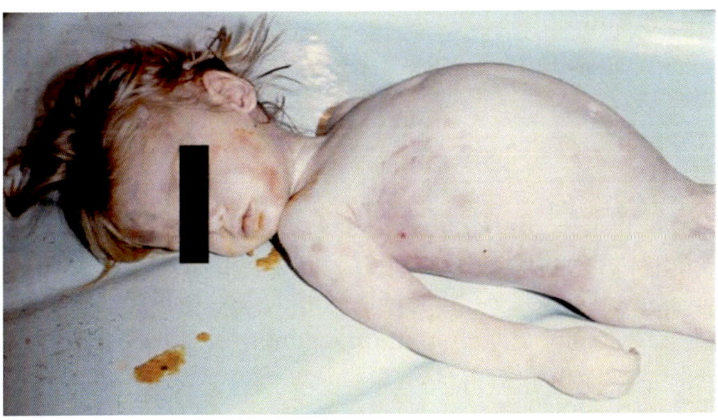

Figure 6.14. *External examination must note every feature; here there is obvious abdominal distension in a battered child with facial bruising. The intestine had been ruptured by a blow, and oxygen administered by the ambulance crew escaped to distend the peritoneal cavity.*

Source: Pekka Saukko and Bernard Knight. Knight's Forensic Pathology, Third Edition. Hodder Arnold. ISBN: 978 0 340 76044 4.

Although the process for an external examination will inevitably change depending on the circumstances, some general guidelines always hold true. The process that follows is a good starting point and can be modified to suit individual preferences. The following section discusses modifications made to criminal cases to satisfy the requirements of the scientific and investigative teams.

- After identification and removal of any clothing, the race and gender are noted. The apparent age is assessed in children by size and in adults by changes in skin and eyes, such as the loss of skin elasticity, senile hyperkeratosis, Campbell de Morgan spots, senile purpura and arcus senilis. Hair color, tooth loss and arthritic changes are also obvious signs of aging. The apparent age should be compared with the alleged age and enquiries made about any obvious discrepancy, in case it is the wrong body, an error which plagues most autopsy rooms from time to time.
- The body length is measured from heel to crown (in infants, more detailed measurements are described later). Ensure that the attendant does not take the 'undertaker's height' from toe to crown, as due to the plantar flexion of rigor, this can be a considerable number of centimeters more than the live standing height.

  It should also be appreciated that the post-mortem height may differ from the known living height by several centimeters. There are several opposing causes of variation, which do not necessarily cancel each other.

  For example, muscle flaccidity allows joints to relax, unless rigor is present, but intervertebral discs appear to shrink, allowing shortening.
- The body weight in kilograms is measured if facilities are available; if not, it should be estimated. The weight of infants must always be measured. The general nutrition and physique is assessed in terms of obesity, leanness, dehydration, edema, emaciation, and so on.
- The state of cleanliness, personal hygiene, hair and beard length, toenail and fingernail state, and urinary and fecal soiling is noted. Any parasitic infestation, such as fleas or lice, is combated before proceeding.
- The general skin color is noted, especially hypostasis. Congestion or cyanosis of the face, hands and feet is sought. Localized discoloration, especially unilateral in a limb, suggests arterial

embolism or incipient gangrene. Pink or brownish pink patches over the large joints may indicate hypothermia. Other abnormal colors include the brownish hue of methemoglobinemia in some poisonings, the bronze speckling of clostridial septicemia and the dark red of cyanide that somewhat resembles the cherry-pink coloration of carboxyhemoglobin. Naturally racial pigmentation will modify the ease with which abnormal skin coloration can be seen.

- Congenital deformities of any type are recorded, from talipes equinovarus to spina bifida, from a naevus to extra toes. Acquired external marks may be important for identification purposes or in relation to past injuries and disease. Tattoos, circumcision, amputations, surgical scars, old fracture deformities and scars of injuries, burns or suicidal attempts on the wrist and throat are noted. Increasingly, artifacts – both external and internal – arise from resuscitation attempts and must be carefully distinguished from original trauma. This emphasizes the importance of the history, to determine whether cardiopulmonary resuscitation was attempted by trained or untrained persons.
- The hands should be carefully examined for such signs as old and new injuries, defense wounds, bruised knuckles and electrical marks. The latter are often insignificant and difficult to see unless the rigor of flexed fingers is overcome, either by force or even cutting the flexor tendons at the wrist.
- Vomit, froth or blood may be present at the mouth and nostrils, and feces and urine may have been voided. This must be correlated with the degree of post-mortem decomposition, which often leads to purging of fluids from orifices; most forensic pathologists have had the experience of being called by the police to the scene of 'a fatal hemorrhage,' to discover only bloody fluid being purged by gases from a decomposing corpse.

Vaginal discharge or bleeding is noted and the ears examined for leakage of blood or cerebrospinal fluid. Post-mortem ejaculation of semen from the external meatus is of no significance and can be seen in any type of death. It was shown by Mant (1984) not to be associated with sexual activity immediately before death. It is not particularly associated with asphyxial deaths, as sometimes stated (Figure 6.15).

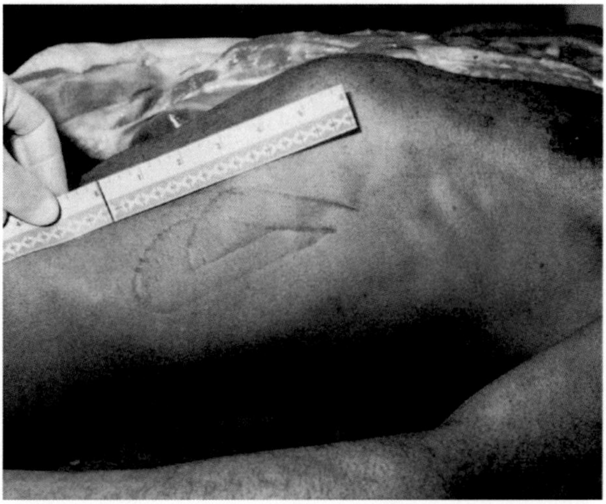

Figure 6.15. *Post-mortem artifacts on the body of a homicide victim. These are due to defibrillator paddles applied in a hospital casualty department.*

Source: Pekka Saukko and Bernard Knight. Knight's Forensic Pathology, Third Edition. Hodder Arnold. ISBN: 978 0 340 76044 4.

- The degree of rigor mortis is assessed by flexing the arms and legs to test the resistance.
- Recent injuries (other than scars already noted) are carefully examined. In fact, this part of the autopsy is often the most significant element of forensic cases. Injuries may be conveniently recorded in the mortuary by marking them on printed body diagrams. The forms can be secured on a clipboard and the data later transcribed into a written description for the autopsy report. The original diagrams should be retained, as their production may be demanded in court if there is controversy about any particular injury.

It is important to distinguish between abrasions, bruises, lacerations, incised wounds, burns, and other types of traumatic lesions. When applicable, a description of the size, form, and state of each injury's margins should be provided. It needs to be measured precisely in terms of its length, width, orientation with respect to the body's axis, and position in relation to surface anatomical landmarks. For instance, a thoracic knife wound could be explained as follows, with any medical jargon explained using everyday language:

On the left upper chest, there was an oblique stab wound with the inner end lower than the upper outer end. The incision measured 20 mm in length, but when the edges were in opposition, it grew to 22 mm. The center's maximum width measured 4 mm. The wound's center was located 6 cm from the midline, 7 cm from the left nipple, and 18 cm below the left clavicle (collar bone), just below the line that joins the nipples. The wound was elliptical in shape, with the inner lower end being slightly more sharply cut than the rather blunt upper end, and measuring 132 cm above heel level. The incision was shelved downward, exposing subcutaneous tissue on the inside of the upper margin.

This account, in conjunction with the police photos, will provide a clear picture of the wound at any time in the future, even during the trial, which might take place months later. The injury's location is connected to prominent anatomical sites, and its elevation above the floor may be significant if the victim's and the attacker's stature and the angle of attack are raised as legal considerations. The occiput, the tip of the ear, the vertex, and the head's center line can all be used as reference points on the scalp. There are several prominent landmarks on the face, including the eyebrows, nose, lips, point of chin, and angle of the jaw. Similar measurements of the lesion size are required when there are large areas of bruising or abrasion, but more general descriptions of the position, like "covering the external aspect of the left thigh" or "extensive bruising 23 cm by 18 cm on the right side of the chest extending from axilla to costal margin," may bc sufficient (Figure 6.16).

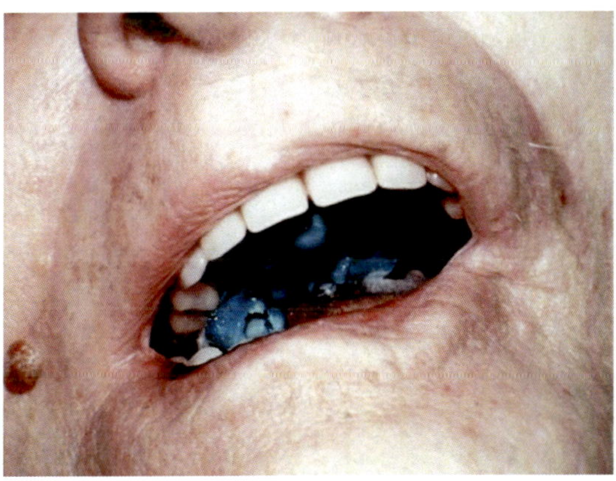

Figure 6.16. *Full external examination is vital, including the interior of the mouth. Here a large number of amylobarbitone capsules offer a presumptive cause of death, though analytical confirmation is still required.*

Source: Pekka Saukko and Bernard Knight. Knight's Forensic Pathology, Third Edition. Hodder Arnold. ISBN: 978 0 340 76044 4.

The same method is used to describe other injuries, such as gunshot wounds, taking care not to remove any powder residues or other traces of evidence before the forensic scientists have gathered their samples.

When a head injury occurs, any traces of evidence are first collected and the scalp is examined in its original state. Then, using a sponge and water, gently remove any clotted blood that often hides the injuries. Following examination of this stage, it is typically necessary to carefully remove hair from the area surrounding the wounds in order to photograph and document the entire extent of the lacerations, paying particular attention to the condition of their margins. The best tool for this kind of shaving is a scalpel with a fresh blade; to prevent inadvertent cuts, the blade should be held nearly parallel to the surface. The pathologist should perform the procedure themselves; a mortuary technician should not be assigned this task. Any artifactual cuts can then be identified as such and not mistakenly assumed to be a part of the original wound.

- A thorough examination of the eyes is necessary, particularly to look for petechial hemorrhages on the sclera, conjunctivae, and outside of the eyelids. Even though they don't always point to an asphyxial process, these petechiae need to be explained. Additionally, look for petechiae in the skin of the face, particularly in the areas around the mouth, chin, and forehead, as well as behind the ears. It is important to distinguish between these fine petechiae and the coarser intradermal blood spots that are frequently observed across the upper chest or shoulders. These latter blood spots are caused by postmortem hypostasis in a body that has significant agonal venous congestion, particularly if that surface of the body has been dependent. There is no diagnostic value to hemorrhages in postural hypostasis because genuine ante-mortem bleedings cannot be distinguished from bleedings that typically occur after death (Figure 6.17).

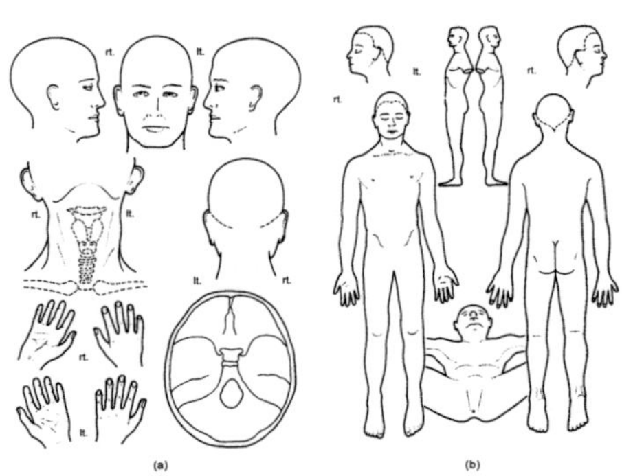

Figure 6.17. *(a, b) Typical examples of the many anatomical diagrams available for the recording of external findings at autopsy.*

Source: Pekka Saukko and Bernard Knight. Knight's Forensic Pathology, Third Edition. Hodder Arnold. ISBN: 978 0 340 76044 4.

The iris musculature's rigor can produce any degree of constriction, which may be uneven on either side, so the size of the pupils is rarely useful. It is important to take note of defects such as lens opacity, false eyes, and contact lenses. The degree of visual acuity during life cannot be determined by any kind of post-mortem examination, although vision loss is undoubtedly likely in cases of significant defects like cataracts or significant vitreous hemorrhages.

- Foreign objects, medications, broken teeth, bruised lips, and gums (particularly the torn frenulum from chi, bitten tongues from epilepsy, and jaw injuries can all be seen in the mouth. Prior to autopsy, dentures should be recognized and taken out. Although they shouldn'tshould not, gastric contents in the mouth should be reported in case of ante-mortem regurgitation. Dried powder on the lips could indicate that you've recently taken medications or toxins; irritating poisons can cause corrosion of the mouth, lips, and chin. Bleeding from the mouth, nose, or ears needs to be noted and then examined internally to determine the source. A foamy, occasionally blood-tinged liquid can emerge from the mouth, nose, or both in cases of drowning and pulmonary edema caused by a number of conditions. Sometimes, froth is pink or, to be honest, has a red tint. This is not particularly important unless it is severe, like in cases of drowning, sudden infant death, and other illnesses with noticeable pulmonary edema; small pulmonary or even pharyngeal vessel rupture may cause some blood to seep into the foam (Figures 6.18–6.20).

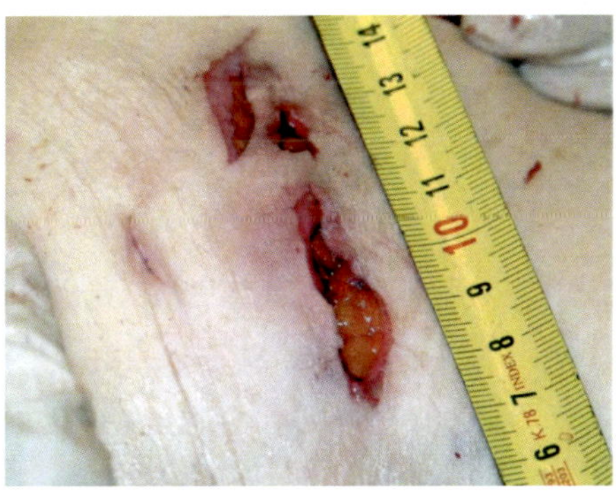

Figure 6.18. *Examination and photography of injuries; after full preliminary examination and forensic sampling, the area is cleaned, shaved if necessary, and photographed with a scale adjacent to the injuries.*

Source: Pekka Saukko and Bernard Knight. Knight's Forensic Pathology, Third Edition. Hodder Arnold. ISBN: 978 0 340 76044 4.

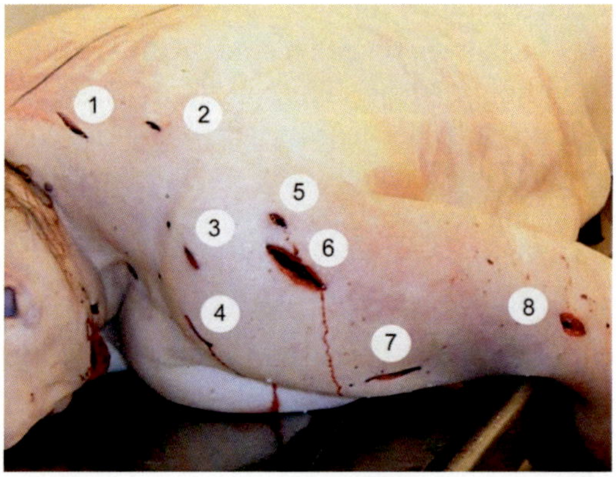

Figure 6.19. *Where there are numerous similar lesions, it assists the clarity of the autopsy report if numbers used during photography match those listed in the autopsy protocol.*

Source: Pekka Saukko and Bernard Knight. Knight's Forensic Pathology, Third Edition. Hodder Arnold. ISBN: 978 0 340 76044 4.

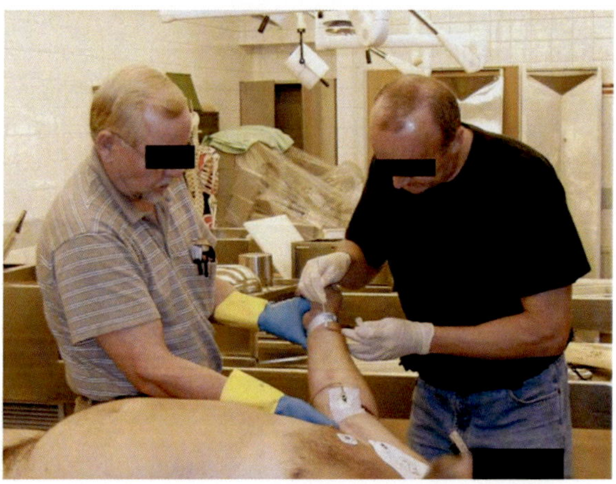

Figure 6.20. *Scene of crime officers recovering trace evidence from hands before a homicide autopsy. The pathologist must offer the rest of the team every facility to complete their work before he begins his dissection.*

Source: Pekka Saukko and Bernard Knight. Knight's Forensic Pathology, Third Edition. Hodder Arnold. ISBN: 978 0 340 76044 4.

- Both the anus and the external genitalia need to be carefully examined. Because of the sphincter's laxity, a broadly open, patulous anus is frequently observed postmortem, so the latter's condition can be deceiving. The orifice frequently allows visibility of the inner mucosa. This also applies to newborns and kids, so a diagnosis of sexual abuse should not be made in the absence of additional supporting data, such as recently shed mucosal tears or semen-positive swabs.

The existence of the "funnel-shaped" anus is questionable due to its extreme rarity. A funnel-shaped body is a typical anatomical variation in which the anus is positioned deep between the buttocks, sometimes with a skin commissure above it to give the impression of being even deeper. The so-called "shiny, silvery hyperkeratinized skin of the habitual pederast" is also not very helpful in terms of diagnosis because the same appearance can be caused by chronic irritation from scratching, which is frequently linked to viral infections, hemorrhoids, or threadworms. The only trustworthy indicators are recent tears, old scars, and mucocutaneous eversion—however even these symptoms can be brought on by extreme, protracted constipation.

Examining the vulva and vagina is done to rule out any obvious disease or injury, unless the case suggests some kind of sexual interference, in which case a more thorough examination and specialized autopsy technique are performed. The penis, glans, and scrotum should all be generally inspected, and the testes should be felt, as part of a routine examination of the male genitalia. Note that circumcision might (rarely) help with identification.

6.3.11. The Autopsy: Internal Examination

With some modifications based on the circumstances of the death and the demands of the specific investigation—be it a criminal case, a civil lawsuit, or an accident investigation—the dissection in a forensic case is essentially the same as any other autopsy. A number of manuals are available for conducting autopsies, and there is also one for mortuary technicians to follow. For those who are not used to examining the deceased and may be forced to undergo autopsies due to unforeseen circumstances, only a summary of the procedure is provided here.

The typical incision, which veers to avoid the umbilicus, is nearly a straight line from the laryngeal prominence to the pubis. Even a high-necked shroud won't be able to conceal the suture line from family members if the upper end of this incision is extended above the larynx.

Another popular technique is to make a "Y-shaped" cut that descends from behind each ear to a point above the manubrium. To prevent deforming the front of the neck, this procedure is frequently used on newborns and other desired locations. The Y-incision or even a deep "U-shape" draped across the upper chest is preferred, especially in the USA.

The Y-incision is recommended in cases of strangulation, hanging, and any other condition where the larynx may be harmed because it allows for a wide approach to the neck structures by separating the skin of the upper neck from the mandible. Here, Prinsloo and Gordon (1951) described congestive artifactual hemorrhages in the neck structures, which can be confused with actual ante-mortem trauma. Therefore, the incision should not be made until the skull-cap and brain have been removed. Gordon et al. (1988) have also recommended that in all autopsies, the brain be removed first to allow for the detection of abnormal odors before the smell from the opened abdominal cavity overpowers the scene.

When facial dissection is required to check for deep bruises or bony damage, the Y-incision is al. If careful dissection is used, it is actually possible to remove the entire face from the skull and replace it with minimal impact on the final cosmetic appearance. In order toTo remove the entire anterior neck and facial skin, the transverse scalp incision and the Y-incision in the neck are joined behind each ear.

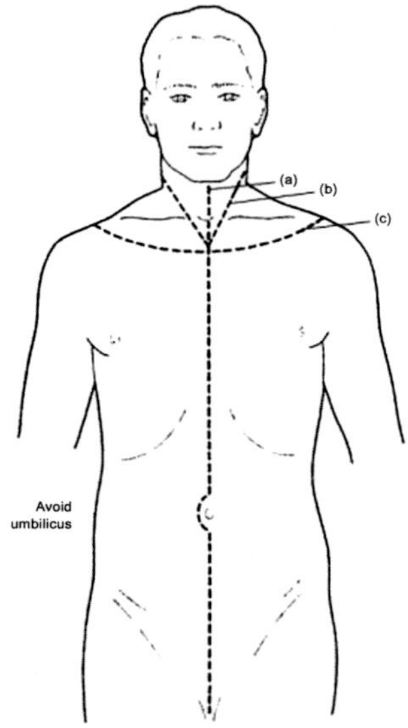

Figure 6.21. *Autopsy incisions: (a) standard midline, (b) 'V-shape' and (c) subclavicular.*

Source: Pekka Saukko and Bernard Knight. Knight's Forensic Pathology, Third Edition. Hodder Arnold. ISBN: 978 0 340 76044 4.

Let's go back to the autopsy in general: to prevent cutting underlying structures, particularly the trachea, the primary incision over the neck should be small. The thorax can be cut all the way down to the sternum, but the abdomen needs to be carefully cut, with just skin and fat being cut. Next, the peritoneum needs to be slightly punctured, and a finger should be inserted to lift it away from the intestines. In order to prevent cutting through the intestines, the knife is then used to make cuts outward along the length of the abdomen. The incision that is made to gain access to the skull begins behind each ear and ends over the head's crown. Keeping this posterior to the actual vertex will help to conceal the stitching, especially in areas where the hair is sparse or nonexistent. When a child has a lot of hair, it is especially important to wet the hair and comb it forward and backward from a transverse parting made in the line of the intended incision. The hair can be combed back later to hide the stitching, so it is not cut at that point (Figure 6.21).

6.3.11.1. Exposing the Body Cavities

The skin, subcutaneous tissues, and fat are peeled off laterally from the primary incision, being cautious not to allow the knife's edge or tip to pierce the skin—particularly around the neck, where the repair may look unsightly. The tissues are removed up to the outer third of the clavicles and the lateral neck edge. The tissues, including the pectoral muscles, flay off over the thorax to the costal margin further posteriorly and to the midaxillary line in the upper part.

The anterior wall of the abdomen is also divided. This can be done in two steps: either all of the skin, fat, and muscle can be reflected together, or the skin and fat can be removed in stages to reveal the muscles. The muscle needs to be severed from the costal margin. If there is thick fat covering the area, transverse relieving incisions can be made on the lower abdominal wall's peritoneal surface, being careful not to pierce the skin.

6.3.11.2. Opening the Thorax

First, disarticulating both sternoclavicular joints opens the thorax. To do this, move the shoulder tip with one hand in order to locate the joint capsules. The joints are then separated by inserting the knife point vertically and cutting it laterally in a half-circle. At the conclusion of the subsequent procedure, the clavicles can be cut through if they are ankylosed, which happens frequently in old age. This involves cutting the ribs, and a handsaw or rib shears can be used to do this. The costal cartilages in children and many adults can be cut through with a knife, although this only exposes a relatively small portion of the chest. A sturdy knife should be kept for this purpose in older bodies to prevent blunting the knife required for organ dissection. In infants, the soft cartilage is easily divided with a scalpel. Even though the other ribs can be cut with a knife, the first one frequently needs to be sawed through.

With a saw, the ribs are cut from a point on the costal margin to the sternoclavicular joints or in the vicinity, lateral to the costochondral junctions. When using a saw, it must be held at a low angle, especially if there are pleural adhesions, to prevent the tip from severing the lung beneath. The section is lifted and dissected away from the mediastinum once the sternum and medial rib segments are free. The knife is kept close to the bone to prevent cutting the pericardium. Before being set aside, the sternal plate is checked for fractures or other lesions; damage from the significant trauma of resuscitatory cardiac massage is frequently discovered at this stage.

It is now possible to examine the entire abdomen and thorax. It is important to evaluate the degree of lung inflation, taking note of any asymmetry in inflation, emphysema, overdistension, and complete or partial collapse. The most reliable confirmation, if a pneumothorax has been suspected beforehand, comes from a post-mortem radiograph. As an alternative, after filling the reflected skin with water, the chest wall can be punctured in the midaxillary line to see if bubbles escape. This test is rarely successful and isn't possible if the pleural cavity and bronchial tree are in patent communication. When the knife tip pierces the intercostal muscles and parietal pleura, a hiss of escaping air may be audible if there is a noticeable tension pneumothorax. The pleural cavities are examined for the presence of gastric contents, adhesions, pus, blood, and fibrin.

6.3.11.3. Examining the Abdomen

When the peritoneal cavity is initially opened, ascites, fecal fluid, pus, and blood may have already leaked out before the abdomen is examined. There could be fat necrosis or inflammation in the omentum.

The bowel loops are examined after being moved aside for any anomalies, particularly infarction, peritonitis, and ileal distension. Take care not to confuse post-mortem hypostasis with either strangulated bowel or mesenteric embolism necrosis. When the gut is stretched out, hypostasis typically has irregular segments, whereas infarction occupies one continuous section. If infarction is well established, the bowel wall will be lusterless and friable. However, the dark color may be similar in both cases. The bowel is gently removed to reveal the posterior region of the abdomen, where an aneurysm or a retroperitoneal hemorrhage from a ruptured aorta may be seen (Figure 6.22).

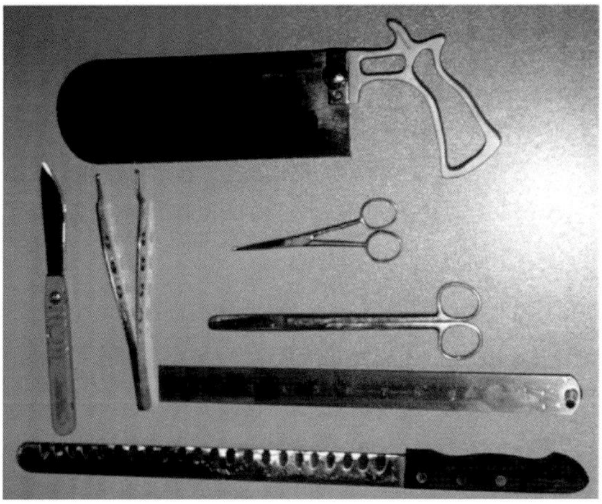

Figure 6.22. *The minimum instruments needed for performing an autopsy. Any further items may be useful but not essential.*

Source: Pekka Saukko and Bernard Knight. Knight's Forensic Pathology, Third Edition. Hodder Arnold. ISBN: 978 0 340 76044 4.

6.3.11.4. The Collection of Body Fluid Samples

Blood and other bodily fluid samples, as well as tissues, are required for laboratory analysis in a significant number of forensic autopsies, almost all of which have criminal overtones. Blood and other bodily fluids are typically taken early in the autopsy process if they are needed for toxicological, biochemical, microbiological, or serological investigations.

The type of test will determine where the data is collected. When sampling is necessary for toxicological analysis, great caution should be taken. Visceral blood should not be used for sample collection, particularly for small molecules such as alcohol and many medications that can readily diffuse after death. Even though heart blood is a convenient source of samples and is recommended in older textbooks, post-mortem diffusion from the stomach and intestine may contaminate it. The cellular barrier made up of serous membranes and mucosa degrades after death, allowing substances from the airways, stomach, and intestine to move to other organs in the main thoracoabdominal cavity and misleadingly raising the true ante-mortem blood level.

Pounder (1985) discovered that while femoral blood remained uncontaminated, blood samples taken from thoracic vessels showed significant concentrations of alcohol and paracetamol due to a slurry placed in the trachea after death to mimic gastric contents. This does not matter for substances like carboxyhemoglobin, but if visceral blood is collected, alcohol is a prime example of a potential source of error. The better choices for collection sites are:

- by needle and syringe puncture of the femoral vein before the autopsy dissection begins. This requires practice but, in adults, 20 ml can usually be aspirated without trouble. This is the method of choice if only an external examination is possible.
- from the subclavian or external iliac veins after the body has been eviscerated. By holding a small container under the cut end of a subclavian vein and raising the arm, blood can be collected directly. If the flow is slow, the arm can be massaged towards the shoulder. Similarly – and preferably if volume is required – by cutting across the iliac veins at the brim of the pelvis, a container can be dropped into the pelvis with its mouth under the vein and blood massaged into it by firm pressure moved up the inner thigh. As all these containers will be soiled externally, the blood should be decanted into a fresh tube for transmission to the laboratory.

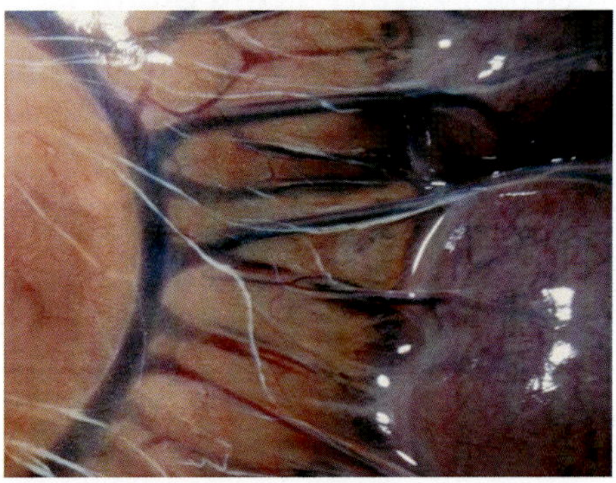

Figure 6.23. *White shining fat droplets (chylomicrons) in mesenterial lymphatic vessels suggesting postprandial state.*

Source: Pekka Saukko and Bernard Knight. Knight's Forensic Pathology, Third Edition. Hodder Arnold. ISBN: 978 0 340 76044 4.

- when the skin is dissected off the neck, the internal jugular vein is exposed, especially if a sternomastoid muscle is divided and pulled aside. When cut, a copious flow of blood is usually obtained, which can be collected directly into a container. The only disadvantage of this method is that if the blood wells up from the thoracic inlet via the superior vena cava, heart blood is likely to be admixed, with the possible errors mentioned earlier. If the blood is collected from the upper segment of the jugular, then blood from the head is collected: this flow can usually be stimulated by raising and lowering the head during collection (Figures 6.23 and 6.24).

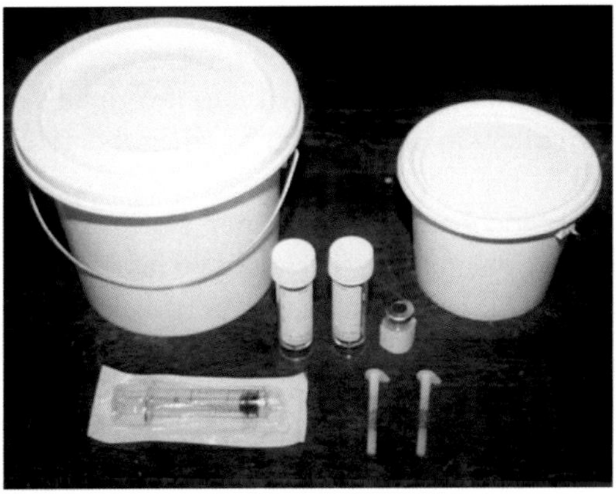

Figure 6.24. *Toxicology kit issued by the home office forensic science laboratories. Contained in a plastic bag are a large liver tub, a smaller stomach tub, two universal (30 ml) containers, one rubber-capped fluoride vial for blood alcohol, and a syringe and two needles.*

Source: Pekka Saukko and Bernard Knight. Knight's Forensic Pathology, Third Edition. Hodder Arnold. ISBN: 978 0 340 76044 4.

Any blood vessel can be used to collect samples for microbiology, serology, and analysis of substances like carboxyhemoglobin, which are not absorbed from the gastrointestinal tract. However, blood should never be extracted from the general body cavity after evisceration because it may be contaminated by fluids that have leaked from other structures, such as mucus, urine, pus, or serous fluids.

Traditionally, heart blood has been used for microbiological culture; however, there is no special benefit to this over peripheral blood. It is best to use a sterile scalpel to open the heart later and remove the vegetations or cusps of the mitral or aortic valves for direct culture if an infectious endocarditis is suspected. In any other case, a peripheral vein is used to draw blood for a culture in cases of suspected septicemia.

Urine can be drawn by suprapubic puncture with a long needle and syringe, or it can be drawn via catheter prior to autopsy. It is typically obtained, nevertheless, following the opening of the abdomen but prior to the removal of the organs. Urine is drawn from the bladder using a syringe or straight into a container if the fundus is punctured. If nearly empty and compressed, the fundus is squeezed upward, gripped, and cut, with the contents extracted using a syringe. Urine must be carefully cleaned to prevent blood contamination.

Cerebrospinal fluid and vitreous humor may need to be removed for toxicological analysis or attempts to calculate the time since death using the potassium content. It is imperative to aspirate vitreous humor carefully in order to obtain dependable results. After removing the eyelid, a 5 ml syringe with a fine hypodermic needle attached is inserted into the globe's outer canthus. The lid will conceal any indication of interference when it is released, covering the tiny puncture mark. To prevent aspirating material close to the retina, which has a noticeably different chemical composition because fragments of detached retina may enter the aspirate, the needle should be inserted into the center of the globe. As much of the fluid as you can should be removed slowly and gently in order to create a mixed fluid; keep in mind that the chemical composition of each eye can vary slightly, so use both. To enhance the eyes' esthetic appeal, the globes can be re-inflated with water after the vitreous has been removed.

The same technique used on living patients can be used to extract cerebrospinal fluid: inserting a needle into the space between the lumbar spines. An adult must be pulled into flexion while lying sideways on the autopsy table; a baby can be held upright by an assistant in a fully flexed position. An alternate method entails puncturing the cisterna through the atlanto-occipital membrane.

Since there is no pressure inside the theca of a cadaver, the fluid must be actively aspirated; occasionally, external punctures are the only way to obtain fluid. The only option left is to attempt to open the skull and puncture the ventricles through the exposed brain surface. After the brain is removed, it is usually pointless to try to extract clear cerebrospinal fluid from the inside of the skull. Blood-stained fluid can be centrifuged until it becomes clear, but the chemical makeup of the fluid is then unpredictable.

6.3.11.5. Removal of the Viscera

An altered Rokitansky technique is used to remove the organs en bloc following an examination of the body cavities. The intestine is removed first, as shown below.

The small intestine's coils are visible when the omentum is raised higher. It is possible to identify the uppermost portion of the jejunum, which joins the duodenum's termination retroperitoneally. Here, the knife is used to pierce the mesentery and cut through the gut. Little contents are lost if this is not done, but two string sutures may be inserted through the hole and tied before cutting the gut between them if it is necessary to keep the small intestinal or duodenal contents. Cutting along the mesentery close to the bowel attachment and stopping when the ileocaecal valve is reached is how the intestine is removed.

In order to prevent puncturing the lumen, the caecum is then mobilized medially using manual traction and as little knife work as possible. The omentum is drawn downward to draw the transverse colon tense against the mesocolon, which is cut through, being careful not to open the nearby stomach, once the hepatic flexure is reached. Subsequently, the splenic flexure is drawn downward and medially, causing the sigmoid colon to separate from the posterior abdominal wall. While some pathologists simply lay the stomach outside the body, leaving the sigmoid and rectum attached, the upper rectum is cut across.

Extraction of the neck structures To facilitate the excision of the neck structures, a block positioned 10–15 cm above the cadaver's shoulders should be positioned beneath it. As a result, the neck is extended and the head can drop back. The well-known "undertaker's fracture," which is a subluxation of the lower cervical spine brought on by tearing of the intervertebral disc at approximately C6–7, should be avoided at all costs by handling the body gently. This may be misconstrued as an antemortem injury, particularly in the presence of the other common artifact, which is hemorrhage over the cervical spine's anterior longitudinal ligament. After that, the neck structures are released by inserting a knife under the upper neck's skin and into the floor of the mouth. The tongue is then released by circling the inside of the jaw with the knife. A cut is made through the tonsillar region and the tissues at the back and sides of the pharynx. The tongue is then drawn down and the remaining tissues behind the larynx are divided to release the neck structures. Fingers are then passed up behind the mandibular symphysis to grasp the tongue. In order to remove the carotids along with the laryngeal structures, this should be done as far lateral as possible. It is now advised to examine the glottis and pharynx prior to any additional disruption in order to check for abnormalities such as bleeding or obstructions in the upper airway.

6.3.11.6. Removal of the Thoracic Contents

By dividing the subclavian bundles of vessels and nerves, the trachea and esophagus are released. The knife is inserted from inside the thorax and passed around the medial ends of the clavicles and first ribs. The thoracic spine attachments are carefully cleared with the knife, being careful to keep it on the bone and not stray anteriorly to injure the esophagus or aorta. The neck structures are held up and pulled caudally with gentle traction. With minimal traction, the hand should move from the neck structures to the area beneath the lungs' upper lobes, lifting both the lungs and the mediastinum as the knife passes through the midline structures and reaches the diaphragm. Using the neck structures as a handle to drag out the thoracic viscera may cause them to be torn off if the strain is applied too intensely. Furthermore, transverse intimal tears from traction may occur in the descending aorta; these tears resemble the real "ladder tears" that are frequently observed in traffic accidents.

Clean lung removal may be impeded by pleural adhesions. It is possible to cut through them if there are just a few. Adhesions that completely obliterate the pleural cavity can be removed by creating a cleavage plane with the hand and removing the adhesions. Adhesions can occasionally be thick, hard, or even calcified, particularly in cases of industrial chest disease and older tuberculosis. The lung can then be removed by creating a cleavage plane by forcing a hand through the slit created by running a knife the entire length of the parietal pleura over the inner anterior aspect of the ribs, and then forcing the parietal pleura off the ribs and intercostal muscles.

6.3.11.7. Removal of the Abdominal Organs

The diaphragm is cut and the chest organs are retracted into the thorax once they are liberated. The left diaphragm leaf should be stretched while the liver and spleen are pulled medially by one hand, and the knife should be used to cut it through laterally, close to the costal margin. The incision goes behind the kidney, which is mobilized forward, and curves posteriorly beneath the organs to the spine, where it must cut through the cruciate ligaments.

After that, the knife cut ends at the pelvic brim and curves up over the psoas muscle. The operator repeats the process on the other side, circling the body as needed. The abdominal viscera are then carried towards the feet by gently pulling the chest organs forward. Any resistance must be transected because it is usually the result of partially severed cruciate ligaments.

The iliac vessels and ureters, which are cut through, will eventually hold the organs inverted across the pubis. The entire viscera will then be removed to the dissecting bench, which needs to have running water and adequate lighting.

6.3.11.8. Removal of the Pelvic Organs

The type of case determines how the pelvic contents are treated. Men's bladders can be opened widely and the mucosa and trigone examined before the prostate is cut for examination if pelvic lesions are not thought to be the cause of death. The inguinal canals are made wider by the knife, allowing the testes to be thrust upward through them. The uterus is cut in the middle, from the fundus to the cervix, after the ovaries are removed and the tubes are inspected from above in female patients. One can enucleate the pelvic contents to examine a person of any gender more thoroughly. After removing the bladder from the pubis, the knife is passed around the pelvic bowl circumferentially. The pelvic organs can be lifted out once the walls are free, which is accomplished by making a cut through the lower rectum and beneath the prostate. The knife was passed around the wall of the pelvic bowl, in front of and below the bladder, and around the ovaries and tubes in women, which are mobilized forward. The rectum and vaginal vaults are transected, releasing their entire contents. When it appears that there may have been an abortion or sexual meddling.

6.3.11.9. Removing the Brain

The head is then the focus of attention. From a point behind the ear to the equivalent location on the opposite side, the scalp is cut across the posterior vertex. If a Y-incision is made on the neck, the limbs of the Y may extend all the way across the scalp, particularly in cases where a dissection of the face is required.

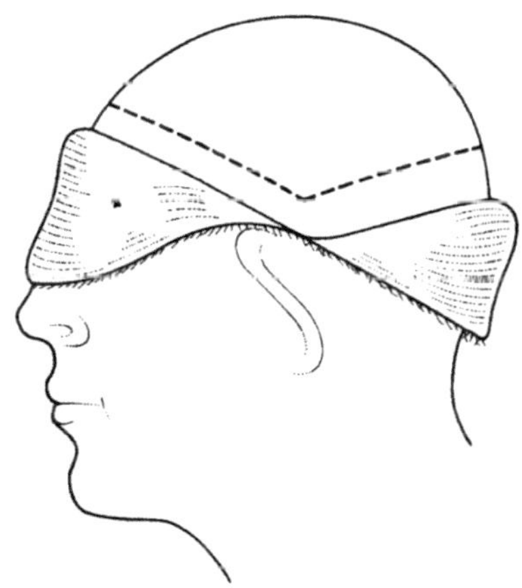

Figure 6.25. *Angled saw-cuts for removal of skull-cap to avoid slippage during reconstruction.*

Source: Pekka Saukko and Bernard Knight. Knight's Forensic Pathology, Third Edition. Hodder Arnold. ISBN: 978 0 340 76044 4.

The lower forehead and the occiput receive reflections of the tissues in both directions. The deep scalp tissues can be separated by traction, but they frequently need to be cut free with a knife. In addition to looking for bruises, the scalp should be reflected back up to the nape of the neck in cases where head injuries are suspected or present. Special attention should be given to the tissue beneath and behind each ear where injuries resulting in vertebrobasilar artery damage occur. In cases of facial injuries, it is possible to peel back the skin from the jaw line and down from the forehead, with excellent results provided that care is taken to avoid puncturing the facial skin during removal (Figure 6.25).

Using power or hand tools, the skull is sawed through. If the incision is made along a circumference, the calvarium will slide unsightly and make it difficult to reconstruct the head. An angled removal is required, with one horizontal cut from the forehead to behind the ears connected by a second that crosses the occipitoparietal region at a shallow angle and travels upward diagonally. It is important to avoid placing this posterior saw-cut on the skull too vertically, or it will force its removal through an aperture that is too small, which could injure the brain.

When all of the cutting has been done, the calvarium is extracted using leverage. Even to make sure that the dura is preserved, forensic autopsies should not be conducted with a mallet and chisel. It is not reasonable to have an unmarked dural membrane because of the increased risk of fractures from excessive hammering. Any skilled pathologist can identify a cut dura with ease. Examining the exposed dura and brain's surface and determining whether edema, bleeding, or inflammatory conditions are present are more crucial. The dura is carefully peeled off the inside to study the inner surface of the skull and the skull-cap is examined closely for fractures.

The dura is cut around the site of the skull removal, and two fingers are inserted beneath each frontal lobe to remove the brain. The optic chiasma and anterior cranial nerves are visible when the frontal lobes are gently pulled upward. To release the brain, it might be necessary to cut the falx. After that, the cranial nerves, carotid arteries, and pituitary stalk are divided along the floor of the skull with a scalpel or blunt-pointed bistoury until the free edges of the tentorium are reachable. Each side of the tentorium is cut, and the lateral wall of the skull is reached by following the path of the petrous temporal bones. The knife severs the remaining posterior cranial nerves by pulling on the brain while being cautious not to hit the upper surface of the posterior saw-cut. It then descends into the foramen magnum and crosses the spinal cord as far down as it can. Now, the hand is slid beneath the base of the brain, which is rotated backwards to be removed, severing any attached dura if needed. Before being fixed or dissected, the brain is weighed in a scale pan.

In order to detect any basal fractures, the floor of the skull is now inspected and the basal dura removed using a strong forceps. Used dental forceps can be helpful in this situation. An incision is made in the venous sinuses to check for thrombosis. When necessary, and always in infants, the petrous temporal bones are cut, chiseled, or sawed with bone forceps to check for infections in the middle and inner ears.

6.3.11.10. Removal and Examination of the Spinal Cord

At autopsy, the spinal cord is not always removed unless there are signs suggesting the presence of a lesion. Nonetheless, the autopsy should always be expanded to include the region of the spinal canal, the blood vessels that supply it or the vertebral column itself if there is even the remotest chance of damage to any of these structures. There are a few different ways to remove the cord; for comprehensive information, refer to Ludwig (2002) or Knight (1983). In short, there are two primary methods for accessing the spinal canal: anterior and posterior.

Using the anterior method, the vertebral bodies are extracted following the full evisceration of the body by making a lateral cut down each side of the pedicles and sawing through them. The advantages are that there is no need to turn the body over onto its face and there is no need for a large dorsal incision that needs to be repaired afterwards. However, the author finds this method more laborious, particularly in the thoracic region where the approach is complicated by the heads of the ribs.

In the more common posterior approach, the paraspinal muscles and subcutaneous tissues are reflected through a midline incision from the occiput to the lumbar region. The left and right laminae are then divided, and the spinal canal is made accessible, by making two parallel saw-cuts along the length of the spine. The best tool for this is an electric oscillating saw; be careful not to cut through the spinal dura too deeply. The spinal canal can be seen by cutting the bone strip away from below upward.

The incisions should be made far enough laterally to make it easy to remove the cord. Once the canal is open, the dura is removed while still inside its dural sheath by cutting across the nerve roots and dural attachments and gradually peeling it out from below upwards. It is then checked for hemorrhage, infection, or other abnormalities. After that, the dura is gently opened using scissors and forceps so that the cord can be examined. Similar to the brain, it can be fixed in formalin before being cut, or it can be immediately dissected, with samples being taken for histology. In a forensic context, the primary lesions are crushing, infarction, infection, hemorrhage, and degeneration. A thorough examination of the empty spinal canal is necessary to rule out tumors, fractures, hemorrhage dislocations, disc protrusions, and vertebral collapse.

A useful initial examination in cases of suspected spinal damage during autopsy is to place your hands beneath the eviscerated body's back on the autopsy table and raise the dorsolumbar spine while observing the internal vertebral bodies. Smooth bending will give way to abnormally acute angulation in the event of a fracture or dislocation. Manual manipulation can be used to test the cervical spine. An electric or handsaw can be used to cut through the vertebral bodies and discs, along with the anterior spine, if there is any suspicious angulation. This will expose the interior of the spine and show any signs of disc tearing, hemorrhage, or crushing; in the event that any of these are discovered, the cord needs to be cut.

6.4. DEATH INVESTIGATION

The three stages of a death investigation are the preliminary investigation, the examination of the body (which might or might not involve a full autopsy), and the subsequent investigations. There will be a description of various death investigation systems along with an analysis of the responsibilities of death investigators concerning non-autopsy aspects such as the investigation of the scene and the subsequent follow-up (Haglund & Ernst, 1997).

The United States has a wide range of death investigation systems, including hybrids of the coroner and medical examiner (ME) systems, which differ significantly from state to state and jurisdiction to jurisdiction. Deaths that are sudden, unexpected, violent, or unrelated to a natural disease are usually the ones that need to be investigated. Which cases should be referred to a local investigator will be explained in the most detail by the state's specific laws. Death investigators must be able to function impartially and independently of other agencies, regardless of the kind of death investigation system in place in a given jurisdiction. In order for an office to function impartially and professionally, it needs the resources, independence, and support of all other branches of government, regardless of where it is located within the organizational structure of the government (Hanzlick, 1996).

Usually, the location of the body's discovery or the person's official death certificate determines which agency is in charge of the death investigation. This is not the case for deaths that occur in aircraft or on ships at sea, where the bodies fall under the purview of the death investigation team in the next port. Furthermore, in some Federal Government cases, there are unique circumstances that give federal agencies and investigators the authority to take legal action. The passing of the President or military personnel slain in the course of duty are two examples of such cases. Native American deaths on reservations constitute yet another unique circumstance.

Many US states have coroner systems, which usually consist of a death investigation system based in the county, with a coroner assigned to each county, parish, or sometimes even district. Typically elected, the coroner may or may not have deputy coroners as assistants. The coroner, or deputy coroner in some cases, is officially in charge of conducting death investigations, choosing which cases will undergo autopsies, and filling out death certificates. The majority of coronial jurisdictions have minimal requirements for candidates seeking to be coroners; however, some jurisdictions occasionally have more stringent requirements, like having a medical degree. Additionally, formal training in death investigation is mandated by certain coroner systems for coroners and deputy coroners, and some even call for ongoing education in this field. However, there is still a lot of variation in US coroner systems quality as well as organizational structures.

The official death investigator for the state, region, district, or county, appointed individuals are usually in charge of determining whether or not to perform an autopsy and certify death in medical examiner (ME) systems. Medical examiner systems are in place in about half of the US states. There are sporadic exceptions to the rule that the medical examiner must be a doctor in the majority of systems. It is required in certain jurisdictions that the medical examiner be a forensic pathologist or pathologist. A forensic pathologist oversees most large-city medical examiner systems, with multiple assistant medical examiners holding similar credentials. Most of the non-autopsy portions of the death investigation are also typically handled by a number of non-pathologists, non physicians, or "lay death investigators." There are differences in the organizational structure of medical examiner offices; some have a clear hierarchy where a forensic pathologist is in charge of the entire state. Others, however, might be arranged at the regional, district, or county level, with county medical examiners operating similarly to coroners. Medical professionals with little to no formal training in death investigation may serve as county medical examiners instead of pathologists. There is a lot of variation in the types of investigations conducted and even in the definition of the term "medical examiner" as a result of the disparity among medical examiner systems."

A sizable portion of US states combine their medical examiner and coronial systems. For instance, in certain states coronial (or comparable) offices are situated in rural counties, while medical examiner offices are restricted to metropolitan areas. In other states, coroners may be assigned to each county, and forensic pathologists working in one or more medical examiner offices may perform autopsies on behalf of the coroners.

Systems for investigating deaths exist throughout the world in even greater diversity, with varying levels of governmental and political influence. A lawyer appointed as a judicial officer is the cornerstone of the coronial system in the United Kingdom and other nations, including Australia. The coroner gives the forensic pathologists instructions on how to conduct autopsies. A part of the coronial investigation comprises police, medical, and autopsy reports.

The coroner is the one who decides whether or not to hold a formal inquest in addition to conducting an autopsy.

6.4.1. Duties of Death Investigators

The term "death investigator" can be used generically, as there is no recognized title for a person tasked with conducting death investigations. The American Board of Medicolegal Death Investigators (ABMDI) is a nonprofit, independent professional certification board that operates nationally and requires continuing education requirements for recertification in order to maintain high standards in death investigation.

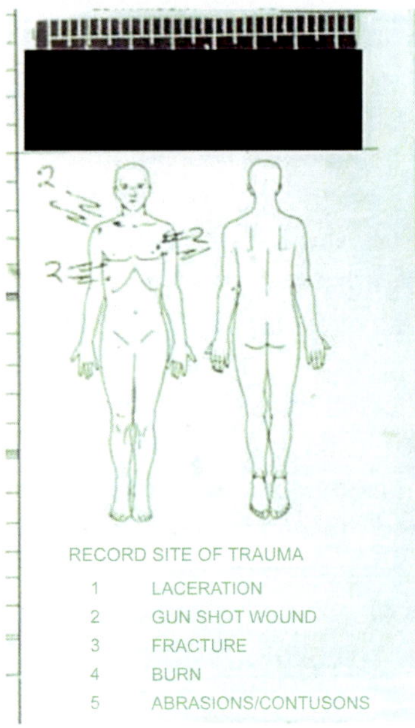

Figure 6.26. *Investigators should obtain copies of all medical records associated with a decedent's death. These can be particularly helpful to the forensic pathologist when medical therapy introduces artifacts that can be confused with true injuries. In the example shown, an emergency department diagram shows the exact location of injuries observed prior to implementation of medical therapy, which introduced numerous artifacts.*

Source: Joseph A. Prahlow and Roger W. Byard. Atlas of Forensic Pathology. Springer. doi: 10.1007/978–1-61779–058–4.

It is mandatory for individuals who become aware of a death that falls under the purview of a local death investigation agency to report the case. An official death investigation will begin as soon as the pertinent agency receives notification. Local statutes will determine whether the agency has jurisdiction over the death, which is the first issue to be resolved. These agencies have jurisdiction over deaths that are not caused by natural diseases, but they may not have jurisdiction over deaths caused by natural causes, depending on the situation, history, and scene findings.

In cases of these deaths, the name, date of birth, gender, race, social security number, address, and legal next-of-kin of the deceased must be obtained as soon as possible. The past medical history, illicit and therapeutic drug use, psychiatric history, tus, recent activities, relationship problems, and mental state could all be important pieces of information. Further information is needed, such as the time and place of the person's last known to be alive, the place of death, whether or notwhether injuries were sustained, the body's position and condition, any signs of postmortem modifications, and environmental details. Investigators looking into deaths must also be attempting to identify the deceased during the preliminary stages of the investigation (Figure 6.26).

In cases of odd or suspicious deaths, a scene examination might be necessary and could provide valuable information, especially if the body has not been taken to a hospital while resuscitation attempts have been made. Ensuring the safety and security of the scene is a prerequisite for conducting a death scene investigation. In order to control access and cordon off the area of interest, police involvement is typically required. Under certain conditions, this process may also involve other professionals like utility workers or members of the fire department. It is crucial that the scene remain uncontaminated and undisturbed after it has been secured. The general scene conditions (indoors versus outdoors, temperature, wet versus dry, etc.) should be noted by investigators. details such as the deceased's precise location, body posture, rigor mortis, livor mortis, and body cooling; the existence or non-existence of significant trace evidence on or near the body; the presence or non-existence of drugs or drug-taking paraphernalia; and the presence of weapons, electrical devices, or other relevant objects or materials. To find out if the body or clothing has been moved, investigators should speak with witnesses, the person who found the body, and emergency first responders. When a death occurs, other government agencies are usually also going to be involved. The police, emergency medical services, fire department, health department, and possibly social services, child protective services, and the prosecutors' office are some examples of this, but it's not the only list. These additional organizations might offer helpful details relevant to the general inquiry into a specific death.

While conducting a thorough initial investigation and, if feasible, a scene investigation is essential, it's also critical to understand that further follow-up data may be needed. It is always important to review all available information, even if it takes days or even weeks to obtain, as pertinent information surrounding deaths may not be known prior to autopsy. Because of this, it is common for the majority of an investigator's questions to come up following an autopsy (Figures 6.27–6.49).

Figure 6.27. *A very important part of the initial investigation of a death is the scene investigation. In this scene photograph, the exact location of the decedent's body is documented prior to moving the body.*

Source: Joseph A. Prahlow and Roger W. Byard. Atlas of Forensic Pathology. Springer. doi: 10.1007/978–1-61779–058–4.

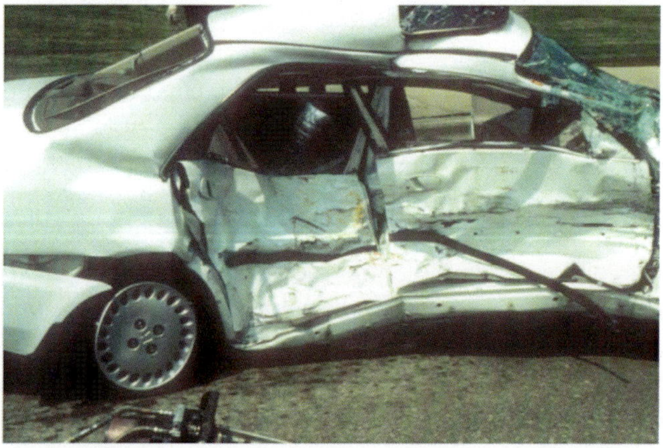

Figure 6.28. *A scene photograph showing the condition of a motor vehicle following a fatal collision. Photographs such as this can be very helpful in understanding the forces involved and the injuries sustained.*

Source: Joseph A. Prahlow and Roger W. Byard. Atlas of Forensic Pathology. Springer. doi: 10.1007/978–1-61779–058–4.

Figure 6.29. *Overall scene photographs are useful in providing documentation of the general conditions of the scene of death. Even though the death in this instance occurred inside the house, the photograph of the outside of the home provided important information about the death scene.*

Source: Joseph A. Prahlow and Roger W. Byard. Atlas of Forensic Pathology. Springer. doi: 10.1007/978–1-61779–058–4.

Figure 6.30. *A photograph showing the decedent before his body was moved. Also visible is a container of a toxic substance on the top of the bookshelf. Toxicologic analysis for the specific substance within the blood of the decedent confirmed that the death was dueson.*

Source: Joseph A. Prahlow and Roger W. Byard. Atlas of Forensic Pathology. Springer. doi: 10.1007/978–1-61779–058–4.

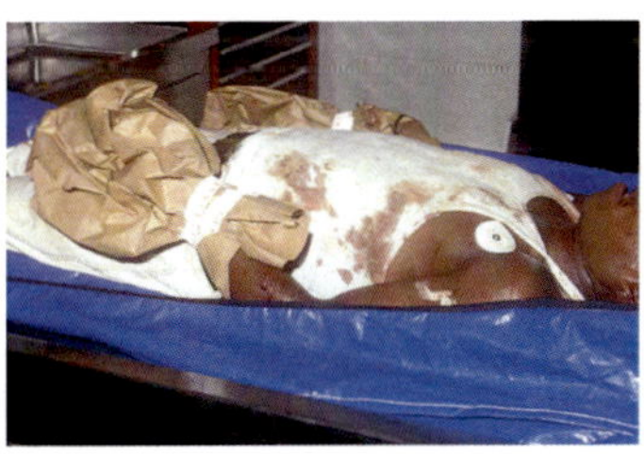

Figure 6.31. *Paper bags were placed on the hands of this homicide victim by the death investigator at the scene in order toto preserve any trace evidence present on or about the hands.*

Source: Joseph A. Prahlow and Roger W. Byard. Atlas of Forensic Pathology. Springer. doi: 10.1007/978–1-61779–058–4.

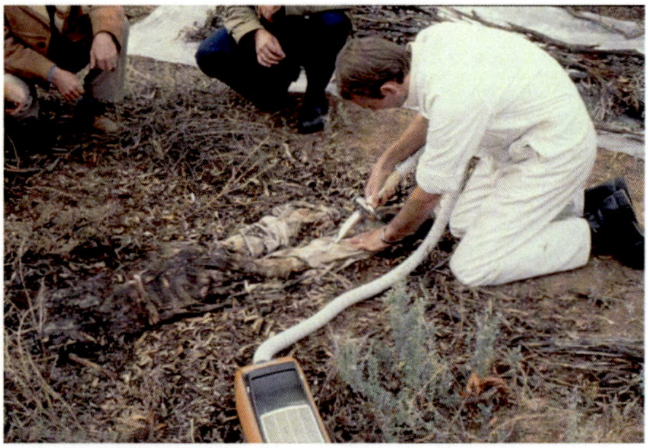

Figure 6.32. *Gently vacuuming a body at the scene may ensure that important trace evidence has been secured prior to moving the body.*

Source: Joseph A. Prahlow and Roger W. Byard. Atlas of Forensic Pathology. Springer. DOI: 10.1007/978–1-61779–058–4.

Figure 6.33. *The presence of a blood-soaked area on the pavement adjacent to the decedent (seen at the top of the photograph) at this scene indicates that, at one time, the gunshot wound victim was probably facedown on the pavement at that location. The death investigator was able to confirm with emergency medical services (EMS) personnel that the victim was in fact facedown at that location when they arrived. The decedent is in his present location as a result of EMS workers rolling him onto his back to certify life extinct.*

Source: Joseph A. Prahlow and Roger W. Byard. Atlas of Forensic Pathology. Springer. DOI: 10.1007/978–1-61779–058–4.

Figure 6.34. *Trace material at a scene may include blood on the ground or on bushes and vegetation. All of this may be lost if there is rain or with the passage of time, hence the need for early securing, protection, and evaluation of possible crime scenes.*

Source: Joseph A. Prahlow and Roger W. Byard. Atlas of Forensic Pathology. Springer. DOI: 10.1007/978–1-61779–058–4.

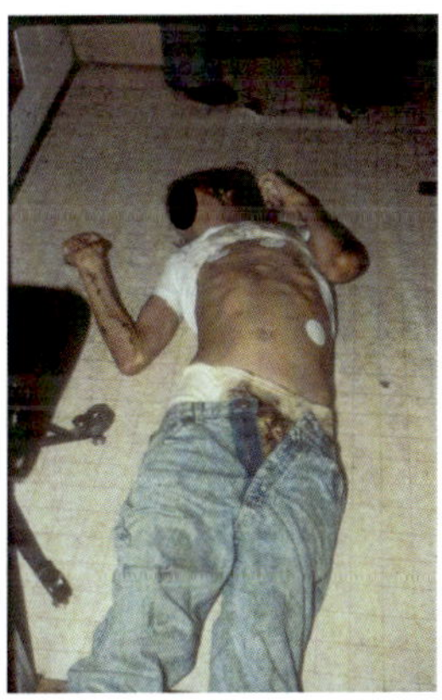

Figure 6.35. *A photograph showing the appearance of a decedent as first seen by the investigator at a death scene. In this case, it was important for the death investigator to interview the family members who discovered the body, as well as police and emergency medical workers in order to determine if the body had been moved, if the shirt was already raised when the decedent was found, and if the pants were partially down as they appear in this photograph.*

Source: Joseph A. Prahlow and Roger W. Byard. Atlas of Forensic Pathology. Springer. DOI: 10.1007/978–1-61779–058–4.

Figure 6.36. *Scene evaluation shows a decedent lying on her back with lethal stab wounds. The knife in her hand had been placed there in a clumsy attempt to make a homicide look like a suicide.*

Source: Joseph A. Prahlow and Roger W. Byard. Atlas of Forensic Pathology. Springer. DOI: 10.1007/978–1-61779–058–4.

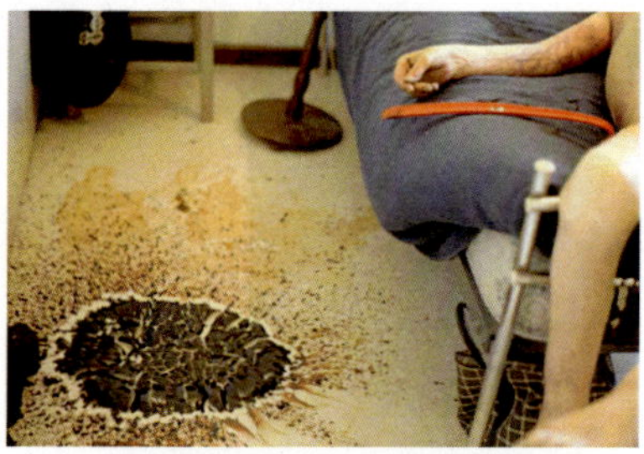

Figure 6.37. *A large collection of blood next to a decedent was associated with self-inflicted rectal trauma from the shoe horn that was found next to the body.*

Source: Joseph A. Prahlow and Roger W. Byard. Atlas of Forensic Pathology. Springer. DOI: 10.1007/978–1-61779–058–4.

Figure 6.38. *When at a death scene, it is important for investigators to observe areas away from the body. This is a photograph of the bathroom of a decedent found dead in another room. The dried red fluid in the bathroom was not blood, but was vomitus (gastric contents) containing abundant medication, leading investigators to suggest the possibility of an overdose.*

Source: Joseph A. Prahlow and Roger W. Byard. Atlas of Forensic Pathology. Springer. DOI: 10.1007/978–1-61779–058–4.

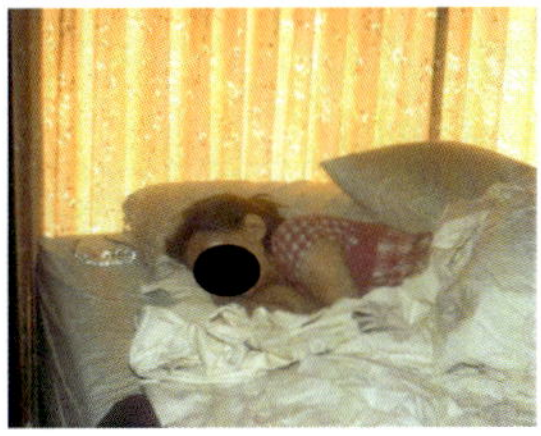

Figure 6.39. *A young female decedent found dead in bed with her deceased mother.*

Source: Joseph A. Prahlow and Roger W. Byard. Atlas of Forensic Pathology. Springer. DOI: 10.1007/978-1-61779-058-4.

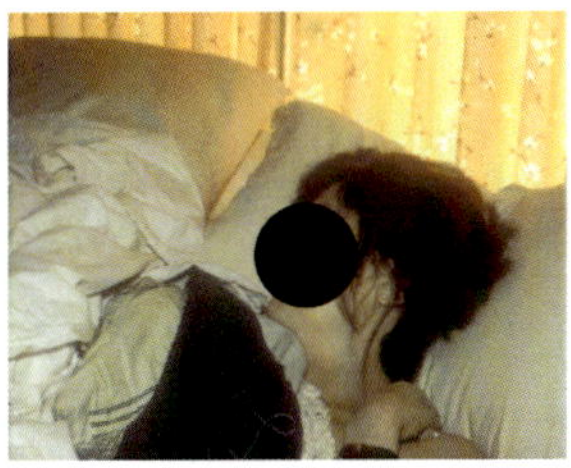

Figure 6.40. *A woman found dead in bed with her deceased daughter.*

Source: Joseph A. Prahlow and Roger W. Byard. Atlas of Forensic Pathology. Springer. DOI: 10.1007/978-1-61779-058-4.

Figure 6.41. *Initially, it was feared that the mother and her daughter were killed by another person; however, there were no signs of injury to either body and no signs of forced entry or disturbance at the scene. Another thought was that they may have succumbed to carbon monoxide poisoning or some other environmental hazard, which would possibly put others in the apartment complex at risk of injury or death. Examination of the refrigerator contents at the scene, however, revealed a "milkshake" in a glass jar, which had a "medicinal" odor. Further examination of the mother's computer revealed that she had concocted the "milkshake" and given it to her daughter to kill her, prior to committing suicide. Autopsy toxicology results revealed lethal levels of barbiturates in each decedent. The case thus represented a familial murder suicide.*

Source: Joseph A. Prahlow and Roger W. Byard. Atlas of Forensic Pathology. Springer. DOI: 10.1007/978-1-61779-058-4.

Figure 6.42. *The discovery of medications at a death scene (shown on a table) should prompt the death investigator to collect the medication containers, record the information on the containers, count and record the contents of each container, and secure the containers until final disposition. In some cases, final disposition will involve analysis of the contents by a drug laboratory. In most cases, final disposition involves eventual safe, proper, witnessed, and documented destruction of the contents.*

Source: Joseph A. Prahlow and Roger W. Byard. Atlas of Forensic Pathology. Springer. DOI: 10.1007/978–1-61779–058–4.

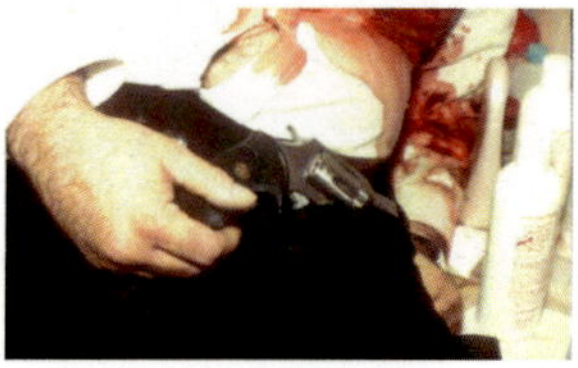

Figure 6.43. *If a weapon, such as a gun, is present at a death scene, it is important that the weapon be secured and made safe, while maintaining any evidence that may be present on or near the weapon.*

Source: Joseph A. Prahlow and Roger W. Byard. Atlas of Forensic Pathology. Springer. DOI: 10.1007/978–1-61779–058–4.

Figure 6.44. *Postmortem animal predation may cause significant damage to bodies left outdoors and make the assessment of antemortem wounds difficult. Note especially the absence of tissue around the face and the left leg, the result of animal feeding. Also of note are other significant decompositional changes, including dark discoloration and mummification of the skin.*

Source: Joseph A. Prahlow and Roger W. Byard. Atlas of Forensic Pathology. Springer. DOI: 10.1007/978–1-61779–058–4.

Figure 6.45. *Bodies that have been dumped outdoors in isolated locations may be skeletonized prior to discovery. During the process of decomposition animal predation may result in body parts and bones being scattered over considerable distances.*

Source: Joseph A. Prahlow and Roger W. Byard. Atlas of Forensic Pathology. Springer. DOI: 10.1007/978–1-61779–058–4.

Figure 6.46. *Serial killers may choose isolated areas to dispose of bodies as in this case from South Australia where the bodies of a number of young women were dumped in an area of featureless saltbush plain.*

Source: Joseph A. Prahlow and Roger W. Byard. Atlas of Forensic Pathology. Springer. DOI: 10.1007/978–1-61779–058–4.

Figure 6.47. *A body in a hidden location may not always indicate concealment after a homicide. In this case, the decedent had taken a cab to an isolated beach where he had crawled under a rock overhang and then shot himself in the head.*

Source: Joseph A. Prahlow and Roger W. Byard. Atlas of Forensic Pathology. Springer. DOI: 10.1007/978–1-61779–058–4.

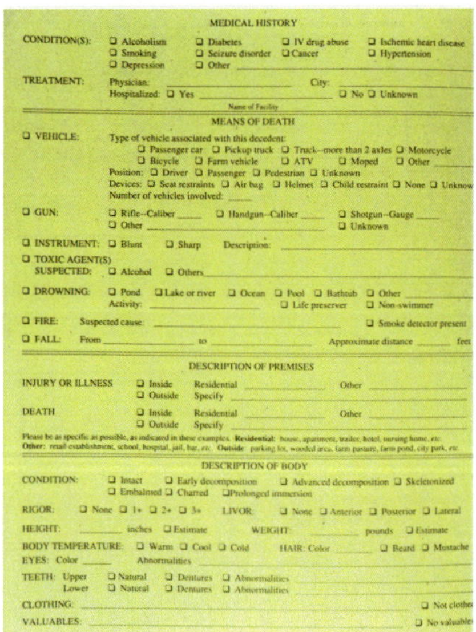

MEDICAL HISTORY

CONDITION(S): ☐ Alcoholism ☐ Diabetes ☐ IV drug abuse ☐ Ischemic heart disease
☐ Smoking ☐ Seizure disorder ☐ Cancer ☐ Hypertension
☐ Depression ☐ Other ________

TREATMENT: Physician: ________ City: ________
Hospitalized: ☐ Yes ________ ☐ No ☐ Unknown
Name of Facility

MEANS OF DEATH

☐ VEHICLE: Type of vehicle associated with this decedent:
☐ Passenger car ☐ Pickup truck ☐ Truck--more than 2 axles ☐ Motorcycle
☐ Bicycle ☐ Farm vehicle ☐ ATV ☐ Moped ☐ Other ____
Position: ☐ Driver ☐ Passenger ☐ Pedestrian ☐ Unknown
Devices: ☐ Seat restraints ☐ Air bag ☐ Helmet ☐ Child restraint ☐ None ☐ Unknow
Number of vehicles involved: ____

☐ GUN: ☐ Rifle--Caliber ____ ☐ Handgun--Caliber ____ ☐ Shotgun--Gauge ____
☐ Other ________ ☐ Unknown

☐ INSTRUMENT: ☐ Blunt ☐ Sharp Description: ________

☐ TOXIC AGENT(S) SUSPECTED: ☐ Alcohol ☐ Others ________

☐ DROWNING: ☐ Pond ☐ Lake or river ☐ Ocean ☐ Pool ☐ Bathtub ☐ Other ____
Activity: ________ ☐ Life preserver ☐ Non-swimmer

☐ FIRE: Suspected cause: ________ ☐ Smoke detector present

☐ FALL: From ________ to ________ Approximate distance ____ feet

DESCRIPTION OF PREMISES

INJURY OR ILLNESS ☐ Inside Residential ________ Other ________
☐ Outside Specify ________

DEATH ☐ Inside Residential ________ Other ________
☐ Outside Specify ________

Please be as specific as possible, as indicated in these examples. **Residential**: house, apartment, trailer, hotel, nursing home, *etc.* **Other**: retail establishment, school, hospital, jail, bar, *etc.* **Outside**: parking lot, wooded area, farm pasture, farm pond, city park, *etc.*

DESCRIPTION OF BODY

CONDITION: ☐ Intact ☐ Early decomposition ☐ Advanced decomposition ☐ Skeletonized
☐ Embalmed ☐ Charred ☐ Prolonged immersion

RIGOR: ☐ None ☐ 1+ ☐ 2+ ☐ 3+ LIVOR: ☐ None ☐ Anterior ☐ Posterior ☐ Lateral

HEIGHT: ____ inches ☐ Estimate WEIGHT: ____ pounds ☐ Estimate

BODY TEMPERATURE: ☐ Warm ☐ Cool ☐ Cold HAIR: Color ____ ☐ Beard ☐ Mustache

EYES: Color ____ Abnormalities ________

TEETH: Upper ☐ Natural ☐ Dentures ☐ Abnormalities ________
Lower ☐ Natural ☐ Dentures ☐ Abnormalities ________

CLOTHING: ________ ☐ Not clothe

VALUABLES: ________ ☐ No valuable

Figure 6.48. *An example of a portion of a four-page death investigation form used in one jurisdiction.*

Source: Joseph A. Prahlow and Roger W. Byard. Atlas of Forensic Pathology. Springer. DOI: 10.1007/978–1-61779–058–4.

Figure 6.49. *An example of the size of medical records that sometimes require review by a forensic pathologist.*

Source: Joseph A. Prahlow and Roger W. Byard. Atlas of Forensic Pathology. Springer. DOI: 10.1007/978-1-61779-058-4.

REFERENCES

1. Asnaes, S., & Paaske, F. (1980). Uncertainty of determining mode of death in medico-legal material without autopsy–A systematic autopsy study. *Forensic Science International, 15*(1–2), 3–17.
2. Byard, R. W. (2009). The value of death scene examination in the recognition of unsafe sleeping conditions in the young. *Australian Journal of Forensic Sciences, 41*(2), 147–153.
3. Byard, R. W., & Chivell, W. (2005). The interaction of death, sorcery and coronial/forensic practices within traditional indigenous communities. *Journal of Clinical Forensic Medicine, 12*(5), 242–244.
4. Byard, R. W., Gilbert, J. D., & Tsokos, M. (2007). Forensic issues in cases of diogenes syndrome. *American Journal of Forensic Medicine and Pathology, 28*(2), 177–181.
5. Collins, K. A., & Lantz, P. E. (1994). Interpretation of fatal, multiple, and exiting gunshot wounds by trauma specialists. *Forensic Science International, 65*(3), 185–193.
6. Dix, J., & Calaluce, R. (1998). *Guide to Forensic Pathology*. Boone County, MO: Jay Dix, MD.
7. Gordon, I., Shapiro, H. A., & Berson, S. D. (1988). *Forensic Medicine: A Guide to Principles* (3rd ed.). Edinburgh: Churchill Livingstone.
8. Graham, M. A., & Hanzlick, R. (1997). *Forensic Pathology in Criminal Cases*. Carlsbad, CA: Lexis Law Publishing.
9. Haglund, W. D., & Ernst, M. F. (1997). The lay death investigator: In search of a common ground. *American Journal of Forensic Medicine and Pathology, 18*(1), 21–25.
10. Hanzlick, R. (1996). On the need for more expertise in death investigation (and a National Office of Death Investigation Affairs?). *Archives of Pathology & Laboratory Medicine, 120*(4), 329–332.
11. Hanzlick, R. (2006). Death investigation systems. In *Basic Competencies in Forensic Pathology–A Forensic Pathology Primer*. Northfield, IL: College of American Pathologists.
12. Hanzlick, R. (2007a). *Death Investigation System and Procedures*. Boca Raton, FL: CRC Press.
13. Hanzlick, R. (2007b). The conversion of coroner systems to medical examiner systems in the United States: A lull in the action. *American Journal of Forensic Medicine and Pathology, 28*(4), 279–283.
14. Hanzlick, R., & Combs, D. (1998). Medical examiner and coroner systems: History and trends. *JAMA, 279*(10), 870–874.

15. Hanzlick, R., & Parrish, R. G. (1994). Death investigation report forms (DIRFs): Generic forms for investigators (IDIRFs) and certifiers (CDIRFs). *Journal of Forensic Sciences, 39*(3), 629–636.

16. Jentzen, J. M., & Ernst, M. F. (1998). Developing medicolegal death investigator systems in forensic pathology. *Clinics in Laboratory Medicine, 18*(2), 279–322.

17. Ludwig, J. (2002). *Handbook of Autopsy Practice* (3rd ed.). Totowa, NJ: Humana Press.

18. *Oxford English Dictionary* (2005). Oxford, United Kingdom: Oxford University Press.

19. Payne-James, J., Byard, R. W., Corey, T. S., & Henderson, C. (2005). *Encyclopedia of Forensic and Legal Medicine*. Amsterdam: Elsevier/ Academic Press.

20. Peterson, G. F., & Clark, S. C. (2006). Forensic autopsy performance standards. *American Journal of Forensic Medicine and Pathology, 27*(3), 200–255.

21. Pounder, D. J. (1985). Natural disaster potential and counter disaster planning in Australia. *American Journal of Forensic Medicine and Pathology, 6*(4), 347–357.

22. Prahlow, J. A., & Lantz, P. E. (1995). Medical examiner/death investigator training requirements in state medical examiner systems. *Journal of Forensic Sciences, 40*(1), 55–58.

23. Prinsloo, I., & Gordon, I. (1951). Post-mortem dissection artefacts of the neck and their differentiation from ante-mortem bruises. *South African Medical Journal, 25*(11), 358–361.

24. Randall, B., & Randall, L. (1999). Initiation of formal death investigation procedures among the Northern Plains Indians: A necessary adjunct in the study of American Indian sudden infant deaths. *American Journal of Forensic Medicine and Pathology, 20*(1), 22–26.

25. Sheaff, M. T., & Hopster, D. J. (2004). *Post Mortem Technique Handbook* (2nd ed.). New York: Springer.

26. Shemonsky, N. K., Reiber, K. B., Williams, L. D., & Froede, R. C. (1993). Death investigations on military installations. *Military Medicine, 158*(8), 585–587.

27. Vanezis, P., & Busuttil, A. (1996). *Suspicious Death Scene Investigation*. London: Arnold.

CHAPTER 7

FORENSIC PSYCHOLOGY AND PSYCHIATRY

Contents

Introduction 270

7.1. The Science of Forensic Psychology 270

7.2. Psychological Profiling and Criminal Behavior Analysis 282

7.3. Forensic Psychiatry 289

7.4. Forensic Psychiatry: Contemporary Scope, Challenges, and Controversies 296

7.5. Clinical Characteristics and Self-Harm in Forensic Psychiatric Patients 304

References 315

INTRODUCTION

The area of psychology known as "forensic psychology" focuses on creating and utilizing psychological concepts and knowledge in legal proceedings. Since the beginning of recorded history, psychology and law have been intertwined, despite the fact that forensic psychology is a relatively new field. There is hardly a field of law these days where psychological expert testimony is not used, and there is no denying that forensic psychology has greatly aided in the administration of justice. As such, the forensic psychologist is frequently called upon to testify as an expert in court. Forensic psychologists do a variety of tasks, such as evaluating a defendant's capacity to stand trial and criminal responsibility, evaluating the viability of defenses (such as intoxication, amnesia, dissociative identity disorder, and PTSD), forecasting violent behavior, evaluating the credibility of eyewitness accounts and personal injuries, offering testimony regarding appropriate sentencing, profiling, and participating in custody decisions. The forensic interview and psychological testing are the two most crucial steps in the forensic assessment process, though forensic hypnosis is also occasionally employed. Because of doubts about reliability, the polygraph is rarely used. By conducting high-quality research, presenting impartial and persuasive evidence, and acknowledging that there are certain fields in which forensic psychologists' contributions are dubious, forensic psychology can rise in stature.

7.1. THE SCIENCE OF FORENSIC PSYCHOLOGY

The application of psychology to the legal system is known as forensic psychology. The use of scientific knowledge and techniques to address legal issues in criminal, civil, contractual, or other judicial proceedings is known as forensic psychology. Research on a variety of psychology-law topics, such as jury selection, minimizing systemic racism in criminal law, assessing the fitness of eyewitnesses, determining a person's eligibility for a trial, or evaluating military veterans for compensation for service-connected disabilities, is included in the field of forensic psychology. Numerous psychology subdisciplines, including social, clinical, experimental, counseling, and neuropsychology, are mentioned in the American Psychological Association's Specialty Guidelines for Forensic Psychologists.

7.1.1. History

Criminal profiling first surfaced in the 19th century when forensic surgeon and physician Thomas Bond used it to investigate the Jack the Ripper case. Hugo Münsterberg, a pupil of Wilhelm Wundt, an early experimental psychologist, and the first director of Harvard's psychological laboratory, wrote On the Witness Stand in the early 1900s. Münsterberg made an effort to show how psychological research could be used in court cases in the publication. Sigmund Freud also talked about the connection between psychopathological processes and criminal behavior. Other notable pioneers in the field of forensic psychology are William Healy and Lightner Witmer. William Marston, a psychologist, invented the lie detector in 1917. Marston brought his lie detector to court in the Frye v. Marston case six years after it was invented. United States at James A's request. The lawyers for Frye were hoping that Marston's gadget would establish their client's innocence. Since the scientific community does not generally accept lie detection, the results were not considered admissible. As a result, the Frye standard was developed, stating that scientific evidence can only be accepted if it is well-regarded by other scientists.

In 1954, the Brown v. The Supreme Court of the United States first cited expert psychological opinions in the Topeka Board of Education case. Following this, the prevalence of psychological mechanisms in courtrooms started to be seen as advantageous. Judge David Bazelon of the D.O.T. ruled several years following the Brown decision. The Circuit Court of Appeals determined that psychologists could legally testify about mental illness as medical professionals. The American Psychology–Law Society was established in 1969 and became Division 41 of the American Psychological Association in 1980. An increasing number of organizations backed the use of psychology in the legal system as the field expanded. The American Board of Forensic Psychology was established in 1976, and in 1985 it merged with the American Board of Professional Psychology. Later, conferences and organizations like the American Academy of Forensic Psychology and the National Invitational Conference on Education and Training in Forensic Psychology contributed to the strengthening of the field's development. The American Psychological Association officially acknowledged forensic psychology as a professional specialty in 2001.

A landmark case in 1993 was Daubert v. Merrell Dow Pharmaceutical established the admissibility standard for expert witness testimony. The lawsuit was brought by the parents of Jason Daubert and Eric Schuller against Merrell Dow Pharmaceuticals after the drug Bendectin caused their children to be born with severe birth defects. Merrell Dow filed a motion for summary judgment after the case was transferred to federal court. The documents they submitted indicated that there was no published scientific study proving a connection between Bendectin and birth defects. Then, using pharmacological research, reanalysis of previously published studies, and *in vitro* and *in vivo* animal studies, Daubert and Schuller provided expert testimony demonstrating that Bendectin did, in fact, cause birth defects. These evidence-gathering methodologies were not deemed appropriate at the time of the case. Merrell Dow was awarded summary judgment, and the parents filed an appeal with the Ninth Circuit. The Ninth Circuit only granted summary judgment due to the plaintiffs' presentation of evidence that was acknowledged by scientists as a trustworthy method. Merrell Dow was given it because, at the time of the case, the Frye standard was regarded as the appropriate standard of proof. Eventually, the Daubert standard was adopted as the one by the U. S. Supreme Court. The Federal Rules of Evidence, which also govern evidence admissibility, are thought to contain the standard. The case was remanded to the Ninth Circuit Court of Appeals by the Supreme Court after it had reversed. After reviewing the evidence under the new standard through the remand, the court determined to sustain the district court's initial summary judgment award to the defendant. The U.S. considered the Daubert standard as a result of this case ruling. S. Although most states still use the old Frye standard, the Supreme Court has gradually overturned it and no longer makes reference to it.

Current forensic psychology research employs legal contexts to apply psychological methodology. A number of papers on false confessions were published in the 1980s by Saul Kassin, a psychology professor at the John Jay College of Criminal Justice in New York. Five boys who were wrongfully convicted of raping a jogger were able to have their convictions overturned thanks in large part to one of Kassin's articles. At Liverpool University, David V.

The term "investigative psychology," which refers to forensic psychology's subspecialty of criminal behavior and the investigation process, was coined by Canter. Canter contributed to the killings by helping to identify the killers through psychological profiling of the Railway Rapists. William Stern, a psychologist from the 20th century, carried out a number of studies on the reliability, consistency, and impact of leading questions on eyewitness testimony in court. Forensic psychology has become more well-known in the media lately. Forensic psychological content can be found in a number of recent Netflix docuseries, such as Making a Murderer and Sins of Our Mother. The practice of criminal profiling has gained widespread popularity thanks to other TV shows and films like Criminal Minds, Manhunter, Mindhunter, and Silence of the Lambs. This is especially true within the FBI's Behavioral Analysis Unit (BAU). Ted Bundy's sentencing is one well-known instance of a forensic psychology case. Before his trial in 1980, he underwent evaluations from several psychologists to establish his capacity to testify in court. Based on the findings of the numerous psychological assessments, Ted Bundy was deemed competent to testify in court.

7.1.2. Training and Education

Basic and applied psychology are both involved in forensic psychology. Some forensic psychologists have doctorates. D. or Psycho. D. in accredited institutions in the fields of clinical psychology, counseling psychology, social psychology, organizational psychology, school psychology, or experimental psychology. It also requires two years of supervised experience in their field. The United States does not have any particular licensing requirements for forensic psychologists, but U.S. S. Psychologists must hold a license in the state in which they plan to practice in order to work in any state, territory, or the District of Columbia. There are also options for forensic psychology-specific certification. In the US, there are 65 forensic psychology degree programs available. In-state tuition is $9,475 and out-of-state tuition is $25,856 on average. The field of forensic psychology offers a wide range of compensation to its practitioners. Clinical-forensic psychologists in the US make between $125,000 and $149,999 annually on average, with entry-level salaries starting at $50,000 and going up to over $355,000. By 2022, the U.S. S. According to the Bureau of Labor Statistics, there has been a 6 percent increase in psychologist employment and 196,000 new positions in this field.

7.1.3. Practice and Research in Forensic Psychology

The application of forensic psychology can be found in two sub-areas (family and schools) and five major areas (crime and delinquency, victimology and victim services, law, and police and public safety) (Dalby, 1997).

7.1.3.1. Practice/Direct Service

To determine a person's psychological condition for legal purposes, forensic psychologists perform evaluations and assessments. In order to obtain information for criminal court cases (like insanity or incompetence), family court cases (like child custody or parental termination), civil court cases (like personal injury, competence to manage one's financial affairs, and psychological autopsies particularly as they relate to testamentary capacity), or criminal sentencing or parole hearings (like a potential intellectual disability that prevents sentencing or one's risk of recidivism), these evaluations may be completed. These experts are also capable of doing assessments on school threats. In addition, forensic psychologists frequently have to testify in court and support judges, lawyers, and other court employees in legal matters. This offers them the chance to lend a hand as much as they can. There is a lot of discussion regarding whether or not these forensic psychological assessments qualify as medical treatment, with the majority of viewpoints holding that they do not. It is crucial to remember that although forensic psychologists are in charge of evaluating and summarizing evaluation findings, they do not decide on crucial matters like a defendant's ability to stand trial or whether they are disabled due to their military service. S. veterans of the armed forces. Rather, the court that commanded the evaluation reviews and rules upon the data submitted by the expert evaluator.

7.1.3.1.1. Treatment

In both criminal and civil cases, individuals in need of and requesting psychological interventions may be asked to see forensic psychologists. Forensic psychologists can assist those who have already received a sentence in criminal cases to lessen the possibility that they will commit the same crime again. In these situations, additional treatments are usually combined, particularly for anger management, mental illness, sex offenders, and substance use disorders. Regarding civil proceedings, forensic psychology assists families dealing with cases involving divorce, child custody, and psychological harm resulting from traumatic experiences. Private practices, mental health facilities, and forensic and state psychiatric hospitals are common places for treatment.

7.1.3.1.2. Consultations

By offering consultations, forensic psychologists are able to use their knowledge of psychology and research to better understand human behavior for law enforcement, lawyers, and other legal professionals or proceedings, (e.g., criminal, witness, victim, juror), trauma's aftereffects, civil proceedings, and so forth. When employed as a consultant, a forensic psychologist may be involved in court proceedings by reviewing court records (which may include a defendant's psychosocial history or an assessment of mitigating or aggravating factors in a case); acting as a consultant for juries (convening focus groups, shadow juries, mock juries, or assisting with voir dire proceedings); and providing assessment without testimony (in which the defense team develops a strategy for a defendant's evaluation without knowing the results of the defendant's evaluation being revealed to the prosecution team). In general, consultations can take many different forms, such as the typical ones listed below:

1. **Law Enforcement Consultations** can be in the form of helping with hiring practices and procedures, creating criminal profiles, assessing returning officers' psychological fitness, or just providing knowledge on specific criminal behaviors. Although there are many techniques and strategies associated with criminal profiling, the effectiveness and precision of criminal profiling as a whole are frequently questioned and criticized. A few popular methods are

the intuitive method, which includes Tukey's Behavioral Evidence Analysis, and the scientific method, which includes the FBI's Crime Scene Analysis and Canter's Investigative Psychology.

2. Psychologists who assist lawyers and other legal professionals with case preparation are known as trial consultants. This covers witness preparation, case strategy development, and jury selection. When providing trial consulting services, forensic psychologists rely on research to determine the best course of action for their clients. These psychologists deal with a lot of ethical challenges because trial consultants are frequently employed by one side in a case. It is the psychologist's duty to maintain objectivity during consultations. Stated differently, the consultant is prohibited from endorsing a position and then leaving out or fabricating data that would favor that position. The forensic psychologist considers the ethical guidelines established for the field of forensic psychology alongside the responsibilities of consulting on a case before agreeing to work on it.

Focal psychologists are also actively involved in providing expert testimony concerning psychological matters. Expert witnesses, as their name implies, are presumed to be experts in a particular topic and possess specialized knowledge about it, unlike fact witnesses, who are limited to testifying about what they know or have observed. As such, expert witnesses can express further knowledge of a situation or topic. Clinical psychology experience and familiarity with the laws governing the court in which forensic psychologists are to testify are prerequisites for their status as expert witnesses. Expert testimony is governed by procedural and legal rules, which include the requirements that the evidence be pertinent to the case, the expert's methodology be valid and trustworthy, and the evidence support the fact-finder. Opposing counsel may depose an expert to find out what they intend to say in court. If there are concerns about the expert's validity, reliability, or relevance, attorneys have the opportunity to challenge the expert's admissibility (in the United States, the rules vary by country and jurisdiction). The judge uses a voir dire procedure to qualify the expert witness and decides whether or not to accept them, regardless of who summons them.

7.1.3.2. Research

Researchers in forensic psychology occasionally testify as expert witnesses and produce scientific findings that are pertinent to psychology and the law. These experts typically hold a Ph.D. or other advanced psychology degree. These experts could work in academic institutions, research centers, commercial or public organizations, and mental health services (Melton, et al., 2017), among other places. In the areas of jury duty, mental health law, and policy evaluation, among other areas of psychology and law research, researchers test theories through empirical means. Their work may be published in basic psychology journals as well as forensic psychology journals like Law and Human Behavior or Psychology, Public Policy, and Law. Famous psychologists in the field include Michael Saks, who is well-known for his contributions to jury research and improvements to forensic science, Barbara Spellman, who is well-known for her open science leadership and her work on cognitive psychology-law, Saul Kassin, who is well-known for studying false confessions, Jennifer Skeem, who is well-known for studying people with mental illness involved in the justice system, and Elizabeth Loftus and Gary Wells, who are both well-known for their studies on eyewitness memory.

7.1.3.3. Education

Among other things connected to education, academic forensic psychologists train, supervise, conduct research, and instruct students. Additionally, these professionals hold a graduate degree in psychology—a Ph. D. They work mostly in colleges and universities forensic psychologists can teach in addition to being professors by giving research presentations, organizing talks on specific topics, or interacting with the public and teaching them about pertinent forensic psychology issues.

7.1.3.4. Advocacy

Forensic psychologists can use psychological research to impact laws and policies through advocacy. These could be connected to movements like Me Too or Black Lives Matter, or they might even have something to do with underappreciated civil rights.

7.1.4. Forensic Psychological Evaluations

7.1.4.1. Common Types of Evaluations

7.1.4.1.1. Forensic Assessments of Competencies

In a legal context, competence pertains to the defendant's capacity to comprehend and acknowledge the accusations made against them, the judicial process, and their ability to assist their attorney in comprehending and presenting their case. The psychologist is responsible for determining the defendant's level of competence, but the judge has the final say in the matter. The psychologist is then required to make a recommendation regarding whether the defendant can be treated back to competence or whether the charges should be dismissed altogether on the grounds of incompetence if it is determined that the defendant is not competent to stand trial. A mental illness, developmental disability, psychotic episode, or brain damage are among the possible causes of incompetence. Competency has been defined in multiple cases. Regarding Dusky v. US (1960), the case maintained the Youtsey v. US decision and established particular standards for proficiency. These include being able to speak with an attorney sensibly and comprehending court procedures on a factual and rational level.

7.1.4.1.2. Forensic Assessment of Insanity

Unlike competence, insanity relates to a person's mental state at the time of the offense rather than the time of the trial. Legal theories of insanity dictate that a defendant may only be found guilty of a crime and sentenced to prison if they were not insane when the crime was committed. The defendant needed to have demonstrated both mens rea and actus reus in order to be deemed sane. Mens rea, which means guilty mind, denotes the presence of free will and some degree of malice at the time of the offense. The term "actus reus" describes the willful commission of an illegal act. The defense of insanity admits that although the defendant committed an illegal act, they lacked mens rea. The defense has the burden of proof when it comes to proving a defendant is insane. One well-known case involving this kind of evaluation is Ford v. In Wainwright, it was determined that forensic psychologists needed to be hired in order to evaluate a prisoner's suitability for execution in situations involving the death penalty.

Different definitions of insanity are recognized by the legal system. As per the M'Naghten/McNaugton rule (1843), an individual is considered insane if they are unable to comprehend the nature and quality of their actions or if they believe that their actions were wrong because of a mental illness or defect. This is also known as the test of cognitive capacity. In the interim, the Durham Test—which was developed in Durham v. United States, 1954) specifies that if an individual's actions are attributable to a mental illness, they may be deemed insane. This definition is limited to use in the state of New Hampshire due to its ambiguous nature. The Brawner Rule (U.S.) is the last definition that the courts have accepted. S. v. Known as the American Law Institute Standard (Brawner, 1972). According to this definition, someone is deemed insane if they are unable to recognize the wrongness of their actions and cannot change their behavior to comply with the law because of a mental illness or defect. Assessing insanity entails interviewing the defendant and any other pertinent witnesses, confirming the defendant's impressions, establishing a diagnosis, and using crime scene analysis to ascertain the defendant's mental state at the time of the crime.

7.1.4.1.3. Violence Risk Assessment

A violence risk assessment determines a person's level of danger as well as their likelihood of recidivism, or the return of crimes. Risk assessments are used in sentencing and have an impact on whether or not an inmate is granted parole or is allowed to leave prison. Risk assessment can be very important when considering future danger, as it is often necessary when considering the death penalty. While many people support the use of risk assessment in sentencing, others doubt that risk assessments are reliable enough to be used as a basis for such important legal decisions. Like any attempt to predict future behavior, risk assessment is exceedingly enging, particularly because risk isn'tis not always defined in the same way in various legal contexts. Although there is a large body of research on risk assessment, bias may be present and the data can be inconsistent and erratic.

- **Types of Violence Risk Assessments:** The five primary methods of risk assessment are structured professional judgment, actuarial assessment, anamnestic assessment, unstructured clinical assessment, and adjusted actuarial assessment. There are other methods as well.
  - Unstructured clinical assessment, the forensic examiner or clinician uses their clinical judgment to determine risk and chooses what information to use and how to use it. These assessments typically rely on data from historical records, psychological test results, and in-depth interviews with the examinee in addition to collateral interviews with known personal contacts. This method of risk assessment has a low interrater reliability because it heavily relies on the judgment of the individual clinician. The majority of predictive validity research indicates that other, more structured approaches are more accurate at predicting risk than unstructured clinical assessment (though some questions have been raised regarding the data substantiating this assertion).
  - Another kind of clinical risk assessment is anamnestic assessment, which focuses on risk factors unique to the person being evaluated. This kind of risk assessment is typically used to evaluate the risk of violence. Rather than focusing on risk factors for violence generally, it places a great deal of emphasis on an examinee's history of violent behavior to determine the risk factors for that person acting aggressively once more. These risk assessments can be helpful in identifying strategies to lower an individual's risk of violence because they are customized and grounded in clinical interviews. However,

their interrater reliability is limited, just like that of general unstructured clinical assessments.

- Although the examiner still has the final say when determining risk, structured professional judgment (SPJ) is more structured than unstructured clinical assessment because these tools provide the examiner with particular, empirically supported factors to consider. Some claim the accuracy is higher than other types of assessment, including actuarial methods, but there are doubts about the validity of these claims. The interrater reliability of risk assessments conducted using these tools tends to be higher than that of those conducted using completely unstructured clinical assessment because of the more structured nature of these assessments. Furthermore, SPJ tools are typically better at identifying dynamic risk factors (which can be changed) than actuarial assessments because most actuarial risk assessment tools are based on static (or unchanging) risk factors. As a result, SPJ tools may be more helpful in treatment settings than actuarial assessments.
- A more objective approach to risk assessment is actuarial risk assessment, which uses structured tools and algorithms to combine specific risk factors and generate a risk score or rating. The algorithm instructs assessors on which variables to consider and how to combine and weigh them to get the risk score. The risk factors found in actuarial tools are typically more static (permanent, unchanging) than dynamic (changeable), and they are empirically linked to the risk of violence or recidivism. Actuarial risk assessment tools tend to be more accurate and have higher interrater reliability than unstructured clinical assessment because they involve the least amount of clinician judgment and offer the greatest guidance. The Classification of Violence Risk (COVR) and the Violence Risk Appraisal Guide (VRAG) are two actuarial examples of tools for evaluating violence risk. The Static-99 Revised is an example of an actuarial tool used to evaluate the risk of sexual recidivism (Static-99R).
- Actuarial risk assessment and unstructured clinical assessment are combined to create adjusted actuarial risk assessment. In adjusted actuarial assessment, risk is assessed using an actuarial method, and the score generated by the algorithm is then modified by the evaluator using their own clinical

judgment. The goal of this kind of risk assessment is to increase the flexibility and adaptability of actuarial instruments to the particular facts of a case. However, proponents of the actuarial technique often argue that by reintroducing clinician judgment after a risk assessment score has been calculated, this method forgoes the primary advantage of actuarial risk assessment—the lack of subjectivity.

7.1.4.1.4. Other Types of Evaluations

There are various other types of criminal assessments used in the legal system, but the most popular ones are the competency and insanity assessments. A few of these are evaluations of death penalty cases, evaluations of child sexual abuse cases, evaluations for divorce or child custody cases, evaluations from civil courts, and evaluations related to immigration and asylum.

- **Immigration/Asylum Evaluations:** Forensic psychologists may be called upon by the court or the parties involved in removal proceedings to provide support to those who qualify for different types of immigration benefits. An individual may apply on eight grounds: risk of torture, hardship, asylum, domestic abuse, ANAC (abuse, neglect, or abandonment of children), risk assessment, discretionary decisions, and competence to proceed. Since every removal proceeding is as distinct as the defendant, mental health specialists are essential in recording their experiences because many of them may or may not have supporting documentation. When someone files an application for relief or protection from removal, a forensic psychologist evaluates the applicant psychologically to help the court decide whether the applicant qualifies for the relief they are seeking. A series of interviews with the person and their family members are frequently used in immigration evaluations. These interviews cover a wide range of topics, including the person's life story, the reasons behind their migration, medical history and physical examination results, social background, and current cognitive and psychological functioning.

7.1.4.2. Distinction Between Forensic and Therapeutic Evaluation

The relationships and ethical obligations a forensic psychologist has to a client are very different from those of a psychologist working with a client in a clinical context.

- **Scope**: Rather than the broad set of issues a psychologist addresses in a clinical setting, a forensic psychologist addresses a narrowly defined set of events or interactions of a nonclinical nature.
- **Voluntariness**: Usually, in a clinical setting, a psychologist is dealing with a voluntary client. A forensic psychologist evaluates clients by order of a judge or at the behest of an attorney.
- **Autonomy**: Clients who voluntarily participate have greater flexibility and control over the goals of the evaluation. Their concerns are usually taken into consideration in any assessment. The applicable statutes or common law provisions that are relevant to the legal matter at hand limit the goals of a forensic investigation.
- **Threats to Validity**: Although unconscious distortion may occur when the client and therapist are working toward a common goal, intentional and conscious distortion is much more likely to occur in a forensic context.
- **Relationship and Dynamics**: The goal of therapeutic interactions is to create a trusting and empathic therapeutic alliance. However, because forensic evaluators have conflicting interests and can only guarantee a limited amount of confidentiality to their clients, forensic psychologists may not act in an ethically nurturing or helpful manner. When working in the adversarial context of a legal setting, forensic evaluators need to be on the lookout for manipulation. This is different from a therapeutic interaction in that these concerns require an emotional detachment.
- **Pace and Setting**: In contrast to therapeutic interactions, which can be influenced by various factors, the forensic setting imposes significant time constraints on the evaluation without providing opportunities for reevaluation. This is due to court schedules, resource limitations, and other external factors. The forensic examiner emphasizes the value of precision and the finality of court decisions.

7.1.5. Ethics in Forensic Psychology

The APA's Specialty Guidelines for Forensic Psychology contains a list of the ethical standards and recommendations that are particular to forensic psychology. Reminders of the importance of integrity, impartiality, and fairness as well as the necessity of avoiding conflicts of interest when working with forensic psychologists are included in these guidelines. These conflicts of interest may occur when a psychologist is needed to testify or evaluate something that conflicts with their own beliefs or values, when the psychologist is working as a consultant to one side or the other in a court case, or when the psychologist must decide whether to act as the person's evaluator or treatment provider in a case. The ethical rules concerning maintaining multiple relationships with clients are also related to this last conflict of interest. Forensic psychologists are required by ethics to provide a certain amount of pro bono or reduced fee services to people who might not otherwise be able to afford hiring a psychologist for a court case. Other ethical rules include getting clients' informed consent before sharing information about their evaluations or treatments, honoring and acknowledging client privilege, privacy, and confidentiality, remaining neutral and unbiased during legal proceedings, and assessing the moral and ethical implications of following any court orders that might be at odds with professional standards. Working within the bounds of their expertise—which are established by their education, training, supervised experiences, consultation, research, or professional experience—is a requirement for forensic psychologists.

7.2. PSYCHOLOGICAL PROFILING AND CRIMINAL BEHAVIOR ANALYSIS

In order to comprehend and forecast criminal behavior, forensic psychology and criminology have integrated the fields of psychological profiling and criminal behavior analysis. Creating a thorough psychological profile of an offender using victimology, crime scene data, and other relevant information is known as psychological profiling, or criminal profiling. It is an investigative instrument mainly employed to help law enforcement locate, detain, and prosecute criminal suspects. Profilers build a profile that can help identify potential suspects by examining motivations, personality traits, and patterns of behavior. In order to determine details about the offender, including age, gender, occupation, habits, and potential psychological disorders, this procedure usually entails analyzing the crime scene, the nature of the crime, and any forensic evidence that may be available.

Criminal behavior analysis looks at more than just profiling; it also looks at the larger picture of what influences criminal behavior. This field combines ideas from sociology, psychology, and criminology to comprehend the motivations and underlying causes of criminal behavior. It examines both individual characteristics like personality traits, mental health conditions, and developmental history, as well as the effects of society factors like peer relationships, family dynamics, socioeconomic status, and cultural background. Criminal behavior analysis integrates these different components in order to find trends and risk factors that could lead someone to become a criminal, giving insights for intervention, prevention, and rehabilitation.

Criminal behavior analysis and psychological profiling have many real-world uses. Profiling is used in criminal investigations to assist law enforcement in creating interviewing techniques, making predictions about future crimes, and comprehending the behavior of repeat offenders. It is especially helpful in situations involving violent crimes where the offender frequently exhibits recognizable patterns of behavior, like arson, sexual assault, and serial killings. Working closely with detectives, profilers offer a psychological viewpoint to help direct the investigation and reduce the pool of potential suspects. Psychological profiling can also be applied to threat assessment and management, assisting individuals and organizations in recognizing and averting possible threats before they materialize into violent acts. Beyond the investigative stage, criminal behavior analysis is vital to the criminal justice system. It influences risk assessment and management choices, including parole hearings and the creation of treatment programs for criminals. Rehabilitative programs that address the underlying causes of criminal behavior with the goal of reducing recidivism can be more successful when they take into account the psychological and social factors that influence criminal behavior. Additionally, by informing public policy and crime prevention tactics, this analysis can support a more complex approach to addressing crime and its underlying causes.

7.2.1. Criminal Justice Ethics

The academic study of ethics in the context of law enforcement is known as criminal justice ethics. Candidates for law enforcement positions typically need to complete an ethics course in order to be hired. The content of these courses is primarily determined by the demands of society values and social institutions. To preserve public trust while carrying out their duties, law enforcement agencies adhere to ethical standards and established police practices that are in line with community norms. Effective crime control techniques are made possible by the fundamental components of the law enforcement system, namely police ethics and integrity. Laws, training, and standards all work together to support police officers in upholding moral conduct while they are on duty. Police personnel must uphold the highest ethical standards in order to prevent contentious or dishonest misuses of their authority while simultaneously possessing the legal right to use force. Ethical situations that may include, but are not limited to, criminal investigations, procedural justice, racial profiling, early intervention systems, internal affairs, citizen complaints, mediation, recruitment, and use of force are frequently taken into account when policing the community. The study and application of laws pertaining to criminal behavior is known as criminal justice. The police, judges, and attorneys who either represent or prosecute criminal defendants are among those who study criminal justice. Others, like Supreme

Court justices who make decisions about current laws, strive to advocate for changes to the criminal justice system as it stands. The word justice is crucial to the criminal justice system because the laws that are applied to people who are accused of crimes should be just. Justice also encompasses just retaliation for victims of crimes, such as the imprisonment of the offender, in addition to the fair trial that most nations grant their citizens. The goal of criminal justice is constant. Everyone involved in a suspect's arrest, prosecution, defense, or verdict wants to be fair. This objective isn't always achieved, though, because of the judiciary's interpretive authority, the flexibility with which laws are applied, and the modifications made to unjust laws.

Most people who work with areas of the law that deal with behavior that is classified as criminal will pursue a degree in criminal justice. Criminal justice is a common term used to describe police officer certification and training. Attorneys who have a particular interest in prosecuting or defending suspected offenders may also decide to major in criminal justice during their four years in college. In order to pursue justice in the legal and law enforcement systems, it is imperative that one is aware of the laws, rights, and privileges that apply to both suspects and victims. An additional option for those interested in training with the FBI or CIA is to pursue a four-year degree in criminal justice. With this kind of degree, one studies the law in its current form as well as evaluating it. Universities that offer a criminal justice major may offer a wide range of subjects.

These might cover subjects like sociology, ethics, criminal justice history, and forensic psychology. Police personnel receive specialized training on the powers they possess and lack in relation to a suspect. As law enforcement officers, they acquire knowledge on the legal aspects of enforcing criminal justice. They also receive training in the use of force in appropriate and capable ways, such as shooting a gun or using pepper spray. It takes a specific set of skills to apprehend an evading criminal. The majority of people who want to work in law enforcement major in criminal justice before attending special academies to further their education. Criminal justice is not always just, even with training. Judges can be too strict or too lenient, and there are great cops and terrible cops. There are also very exceptional and talented lawyers as well as incredibly disorganized lawyers. Many specifically contend that because minority populations typically lack the resources to hire elite attorneys, US laws appear to be especially unfair to them. There are countless instances where the criminal justice system goes wrong. In this field, there's always room for improvement. Many people are still devoted to achieving true criminal justice and serving as models of fairness in this area of study and practice.

7.2.2. Aspects of Police Ethics Training

Police officers deal with difficult situations involving intense emotions and unstable conditions on a regular basis. Officers and other law enforcement professionals can benefit from ethics training by learning how to respond morally in unforeseen circumstances.

Training can include ethical guidance such as:

- Quickly recognize ethical issue or problem
- Identify options and alternatives to address the problem
- Make rational and ethical decisions
- respond with actions based on the ethical decisions made to solve the issue or problem
- Accept the responsibility of the outcomes in the situation

Law enforcement personnel need to behave and think morally. There are two components to any given situation response: the action and the reaction. The action describes how a professional police officer responds to the situation, while the reaction is an emotional response. Ethics education places a strong emphasis on acting in a way that not only complies with the law but also takes motivation into account. When an officer acts morally upright but for the wrong motive, it is not regarded as ethical behavior. In a 2009 report titled "Building Trust between the Police and the Citizens" they serve, the US Department of Justice described how ethical training can contribute to the establishment and upkeep of trust between the people who police a community and the professionals who work in it. The establishment, demonstration, and promotion of moral behavior and equity within and outside the department by the police chief is one facet of training. In addition to creating an ethical culture, ethical training for new police professionals should start at the beginning of their careers and continue until retirement.

7.2.3. Profiling, Ethical Issues

Numerous terms are used to describe profiling, such as behavioral evidence analysis, crime scene analysis, criminal investigation analysis, psychological profiling, bio-psychosocial profiling, psychosocial profiling, investigative process management, criminal behavioral profiling, criminal profiling, criminal personality profiling, and criminal profiling. Profiling can provide depth to crime scene investigations as part of the criminal investigative process because an offender's behavior is indicative of their underlying psychological processes. A crime scene's appearance can also provide crucial details about the psychopath's underlying psychopathy, sociopathy, psychopathology, or ingrained character traits. Profiling can also be helpful in the search for minute similarities between serial killers. Profiling has evolved to be a tool for adding depth to an investigation, not for the purpose of identifying a specific offender in a given case. In cases of equivocal death, profiling helps investigators determine the likelihood that the death was caused by a natural, accidental, suicidal, or homicidal origin. Profiling also helps with psychological examination. Profiling can lead to fresh lines of inquiry, validate the working theories of the investigating authorities, establish a structure for questioning once the suspect is apprehended, help the prosecution or defense prepare a case plan for the court, or open the door for plea negotiations.

Numerous typologies and definitions exist for profiling, probably as many as there are names for the collection of activities that come under this umbrella. In the United States, the Federal Bureau of Investigation's (FBI) involvement with serial killers and their victims led to the widespread use of profiling. Beginning in the 1970s, the FBI's Behavioral Science Unit (BSU) promoted its formal use as part of an endeavor to integrate behavioral science concepts into the legal system. The media has focused a lot of attention on profiling. It has been the focus of multiple television series and shows, the subject of novels and nonfiction crime books (many of which were authored by former FBI BSU employees), and it has been included in motion pictures. The field of profiling has lost credibility in the legal and frequently public spheres due to the abundance of labels and definitions. Furthermore, the concept of profiling as a whole has a great deal of ethical problems due to the lack of consistency. Currently, there are two main approaches to profiling: deductive, which builds from general theories to specific case findings, and inductive, which is typically employed by the FBI and goes from specific case findings to general theories.

As a result, there is curren the wide range of professions where profiling is used by professionals (and paraprofessionals)professionals (and paraprofessionals) use profiling. By its very nature, the concept of profiling entails the interaction of multiple disciplines. The practice of profiling needs to reach a number of developmental milestones in order to become somewhat homogeneous. These milestones include having an infrastructure, or set of norms, procedures, guidelines, and standards of practice, as well as a vocabulary and set of ethical guidelines that are widely, if not unanimously, accepted. The concepts of standardizing and professionalizing profiling have encountered significant opposition within the field, for which several explanations have been offered. The inability of profilers from various disciplines to come to a consensus when discussing the fundamentals of practice has been demonstrated (a police detective has different mandates than a forensic psychiatrist or an FBI Special Agent, forensic nurse, forensic anthropologist, and so on). Due to confidentiality concerns, profilers frequently refuse (or are forbidden from doing so) to publicly discuss the specifics of cases (this can be circumvented by de-identifying case materials). A vocal group of diverse profilers opposes standardization on the grounds that it might stifle their creativity. The practice of profiling can be compared to a niche market in many respects, where professionals have developed their (typically local) expertise to the point where they are deemed somewhat indispensable in the field of law enforcement. A proposal to standardize the field would be to propose that any qualified profiler—by whatever definition of qualified would be used—could be hired by any jurisdiction to come in, carry out the required profiling procedures, and then depart. It is possible that this scenario will result in a loss of revenue for small, local, and private organizations.

The lack of professionalization in profiling raises a great deal of ethical concerns. It is not necessary to have completed any particular schooling or training to identify as a profiler. The absence of prerequisites for education or training also implies that there are no minimal standards for assessing competency, which makes it difficult to penalize or discipline practitioners who lack responsibility or competence. There is no consensus regarding the contents of a profile, the steps involved in creating one, or a jury- or peer-reviewed system of measuring practices. Moreover, there is no established protocol for carrying out the profiling process. This indicates that there is no scientific foundation for profiling because it is not analytically testable and thus cannot be replicated. The application of psychological and personality theories to guide the conclusion of a criminal investigation raises ethical questions regarding the practice of profiling itself. The media's romanticized and heroic portrayal of profiling may have led to a false impression of the work and lifestyle of profilers. This means that people who are not well-suited to competent practice may be drawn to the field. When done credibly, profiling can lead to inappropriate investigation directions, which can delay a case's resolution or cause serious harm. Pursuing suspects who fit a profiler's suggested typology that differs significantly from the real offender's could potentially implicate or arrest innocent people. Lastly, the practice of profiling is not subject to official ethical guidelines.

Established in 1999, the Academy of Behavioral Profiling (ABP) is a globally renowned non-profit corporation that underwent incorporation in 2004. Part of the reason the ABP was developed was to address some of the ethical issues brought up by the absence of standards in the field of profiling. Its mission statement outlines a dedication to advancing the ideas of peer review, interdisciplinary education and training, and common professional standards for practitioners of evidence-based criminal profiling in order to raise the bar for profilers as professionals. Its initial objectives included: developing written guidelines for multidisciplinary practice and an ethical code of conduct; creating easily accessible, uniform educational and continuing professional education opportunities; creating and implementing a general knowledge exam for profiling in order to establish common competency standards; encouraging research opportunities to advance the field's understanding of evidence-based profiling and ensure that results can be replicated; creating an informative database for profiling; developing the peer review process in order to professionalize the practice of profiling; and raising positive public awareness of behavioral profiling. The ABP's ethical guidelines and code of professional conduct indicate that profilers should adopt a more professional demeanor. By requiring impartiality, independence, and objectivity, they support the need for an impartial approach to the profiling and reporting process and advocate for a global mindset that embodies integrity. Because of this, they establish guidelines for maintaining the privacy of case information in order to protect the honor of crime victims and their families. In order to prevent bias, they also stipulate that the interpretations and conclusions drawn from the profiling process must be strictly restricted to the data and supporting documentation that have been examined and found. The ABP ethical code of conduct prohibits the use of conjecture and the expression of opinions regarding the guilt or innocence of a suspect in a specific crime, and it limits expert witness testimony to the facts of the case. Lastly, the ethical guidelines establish the procedures for notifying the proper authorities connected to the professional associations that oversee the offending profession of unethical behavior or ethical code violations.

If a member of the ABP violates the ethical guidelines for professional conduct, they may face three levels of sanctions: (1) advisement, in which case the offending individual receives written notice instructing them to stop their unethical behavior. A member will automatically receive a warning after receiving two of these advisements; (2) the member responsible for the ethical violation will receive a written warning stating that failure to immediately cease the unethical conduct could result in expulsion from the ABP. All ABP members are notified of warnings in a public manner. If a member receives two warnings, they will automatically be expelled from the ABP; (3) the member who committed the ethical transgression will receive written notice of their expulsion from the ABP. Public access is granted to these notices of expulsion. The sanction process's fundamental goal is to raise membership awareness of the value of upholding the strictest norms of moral conduct in the workplace. All of the ABP's initial objectives have been met, and the organization is still expanding globally. This suggests that it might be possible to bring together the professionals who work in the field of profiling and eventually standardize and adhere to the highest ethical conduct standards while preserving the art of the multidisciplinary process.

7.2.4. Analyze the Relevance of Victimology to Criminal Profiling

During the investigation process, law enforcement uses criminal profiling as a tool to lighten the workload. It helps law enforcement to create a hypothesis about the perpetrator, which helps to reduce the "rog gallery" of potential offenders. This educated estimate is the outcome of a behavioral profile created for the offender through a process known as "reverse-engineering," or "retro-classification," based on the behaviors (or "Modes Operandi") of the offender. In actuality, law enforcement typically provides only crime scene modes of operation and signatures to criminal profilers in order to create a profile. The most crucial element missing from a comprehensive profile is usually the victimology, which explains "why" the victim was singled out. Forensic victimology is the scientific study of victims with the goal of resolving forensic and investigative issues. Criminal profilers have found it especially helpful when examining crime scenes to determine the traits of the offender profile. It is possible for the victim (S) to have a feature, attribute, location, or even social accessibility that makes it possible to add details to the criminal profile. What makes these "victims" comparable to one another helps to explain why the perpetrator chose them as a target (victim) because of a shared characteristic.

Victimology is a rigorous and analytical field, much like the broader picture of the crimin behavioral profiling it supports. It is inconsistent, working sometimes and not always. Ultimately, it 'sis merely an estimate, derived from either deductive or inductive procedures. An increasing amount of computers may be heralded as a breakthrough in modernization. You believe that while technology can help classify data quite well, it does not have the cognitive analytical side that humans do, and that this is "art" rather than science. Data is data, and facts are facts. People are not as predictable as you might think. The garbage in, garbage out phenomenon of the computer sciences is another factor you believe will restrict the use of computerized profiles. Without the right data, the results in the field of behavioral profiling will be different and possibly ambiguous.

7.3. FORENSIC PSYCHIATRY

A branch of psychiatry that is associated with criminology is called forensic psychiatry. It includes the area where psychiatry and law meet. It is described as a subspecialty of psychiatry in which scientific and clinical expertise is applied in legal contexts involving civil, criminal, correctional, regulatory, or legislative matters, as well as in specialized clinical consultations in areas like risk assessment or employment, by the American Academy of Psychiatry and the Law. A forensic psychiatrist helps courts with adjudicative processes by providing services like determining a defendant's competency to stand trial and treating offenders with medicine and psychotherapy.

7.3.1. Court Work

In their collaboration with courts, forensic psychiatrists assess a person's capacity to stand trial, as well as any mental health defenses (e.g., the defense of insanity), and suggested sentences. Competency to stand trial (CST) and mental state at the time of the offense are the two main components of criminal evaluations in forensic psychiatry (MSO).

7.3.1.1. Competency to Stand Trial

The competency assessment used to establish whether a defendant is mentally capable of comprehending the charges against them and cooperating with their attorneys is known as competency to stand trial (CST). The Fifth Amendment to the US Constitution, which guarantees the right to face one's accusers, be present at one's trial, and receive legal assistance, is the foundation for this in the US. Three goals are achieved by CST, also known as adjudicative competency: it protects defendants' right to make their own decisions, maintains the integrity of the criminal justice system, and lowers the possibility of incorrect convictions. The United States Supreme Court ruled in Dusky v. in 1960. The United States created the federal court standard, deciding that the defendant must be able to consult with his attorney at this time with a reasonable level of rational understanding and a factual and rational understanding of the actions taken against him. Evaluations must determine whether the defendant is competent to support their attorney, which means that they comprehend the charges against them, the consequences of being a defendant, and the adversarial nature of the legal process, which includes the roles that defense attorneys, prosecutors, judges, and juries play. They have to be able to understand information that their attorney provides them and convey pertinent information to them. Lastly, they have to be capable of making critical choices, like accepting a plea deal or not.

In England, Wales, Scotland, and Ireland, a similar legal concept is that of "fitness to plead."

7.3.2. As an Expert Witness

Expert witness testimony is frequently requested of forensic psychiatrists in both criminal and civil proceedings. Expert witnesses share their thoughts on a particular topic. The psychiatrist will frequently have written a thorough report before testifying. The principal responsibility of the expert witness is to offer the court an unbiased opinion. When the issues in question are not typically understood by the fact finders, such as a jury or judge, an expert may testify in court regarding matters of opinion. Because of this, eminent figures in the field of forensic psychiatry, such as Thomas Gutheil, Robert Simon, Liza Gold, and others, have recognized that teaching is an essential component of the expert witness position. In addition to being asked to form an opinion and testify about it, the expert will be required to explain the reasoning behind it, outlining key ideas, strategies, and techniques from the field of psychiatry.

7.3.3. Mental State Opinion

When determining whether a defendant was able to understand what he or she was doing at the time of the crime, the court is given an opinion—and only an opinion—by the mental state opinion (MSO). Although this has been rejected in some states and interpreted differently in others, the intent to commit a crime and the knowledge that the act is criminal have an impact on how the case is ultimately resolved in every situation. These three standards, along with other important court decisions and laws pertaining to this field, serve as a major guide for forensic psychiatry.

- M'Naghten rules: Excuses a defendant who, by virtue of a defect of reason or discasc of thc mind, does not know the nature and quality of the act, or, if he or she does, does not know that the act is indeed wrong.
- Durham rule: Excuses a defendant whose conduct is the product of mental disorder.
- ALI test: Excuses a defendant who, because of a mental disease or defect, lacks substantial capacity to appreciate the criminality (wrongfulness) of his or her conduct or to conform his conduct to the requirements of law.

One possible result in this kind of trial is not guilty by reason of insanity (NGRI). Crucially, the term "insanity" is not medical; rather, it is legal. Psychiatrists frequently provide testimony for both the prosecution and the defense. In addition to treating mentally ill people who have committed crimes, forensic psychiatrists also work with prisoners in jails and prisons (such as those who have been found not guilty by reason of insanity).

7.3.4. Forensic Psychiatry vs Psychology

- **Forensic Psychiatry:** Psychiatrists who specialize in forensics concentrate on the biological aspects of law. They pay more attention to diagnosing and treating mental health issues in addition to the scientific facts. Legally speaking, they evaluate patients, offer diagnoses, and write prescriptions for drugs as needed. They are licensed physicians (MDs) with yearly incomes of about $190,000.

- **Forensic Psychology:** The application of various disorders and conditions in court is examined by forensic psychologists. Typically, they work as probation officers and research assistants. They frequently evaluate an inmate's risk, decide trial competency, and assist in jury selection. To support individuals who are mentally ill, forensic psychologists can utilize knowledge they have gained about criminal justice systems and mental health. They can work as forensic psychologists after receiving a master's and doctoral degree in psychology, or a Doctor of Psychology, PsyD. They don't have to be medical professionals in order to be licensed by the state. They are therefore unable to write prescriptions for drugs. The average salary for forensic psychologists is $67,000 per year.

7.3.5. Risk Management

A number of individuals with mental health disorders, intellectual or developmental disabilities, and past offenders who have committed crimes against others are under the supervision of community-based forensic psychiatric teams, which consist of a diverse range of professionals such as psychologists, psychiatrists, nurses, and care workers.

These teams have twofold duties: they have to advance public safety as well as the well-being of their clients. Through risk management, the goal is not so much to predict as it is to prevent violence. In the forensic field, risk assessment and management is a developing field, with a large amount of academic research being conducted in British Columbia and Ontario. Initially, the aim was to forecast the probability of a specific type of offense recurring by merging offense details and static indicators from personal history into actuarial tools like the Static-99 and RASOR.

The results demonstrated that this method was more accurate than using independent professional judgment. Dynamic risk factors, including attitudes, impulsivity, mental health, family and social situations, substance use, and the acceptance and availability of support, are also being used more recently to inform structured professional judgments. The objective is to shift from prediction to prevention through the identification and subsequent management of risk factors. Depending on the availability of funds and legal authority, this may involve victim safety planning, monitoring, treatment, rehabilitation, and supervision.

In forensic psychiatry, structured professional judgment tools—standardized assessments—are frequently used for risk management. The HCR-20 and the more recent SAPROF, both created in the late 2010s, are two examples of such instruments. These instruments are used to calculate the probability of recidivism and pinpoint elements that shield offenders from harm.

7.3.6. United Kingdom

The majority of forensic psychiatrists in the United Kingdom are employed by the National Health Service, providing specialized secure units for mentally ill offenders and individuals whose behavior has rendered them unmanageable in other hospitals. These can be classified as either high security hospitals (also called special hospitals), of which there are three in England and one in Scotland (the State Hospital, Carstairs), the most well-known of which is Broadmoor Hospital, or medium secure units, of which there are numerous throughout the nation. The other "specials" are the Nottinghamshire-based Rampton Hospital and the Ashworth Hospital in Maghull, Liverpool. Also, a number of private-sector medium secure units sell their beds exclusively to the NHS, as not enough secure beds are available in the NHS system. In addition to treating patients suspected of having mental illnesses, forensic psychiatrists frequently work in prison outreach programs.

A large portion of these psychiatrists' daily workloads involves caring for extremely seriously mentally ill patients, particularly those who suffer from schizophrenia. Individuals with severe personality disorders or learning disabilities are also treated in certain units. Due to varying mental health laws, the areas of assessment for courts in Britain also differ somewhat. While consideration is given to factors such as mental state at the time of the offense and fitness to plead, another important factor is the mental state at the time of trial. Based on this assessment, mental health legislation is frequently used to detain individuals in hospitals rather than sending them to prison.

Learning-disability hospitals (or specialized community-based units with a similar regimen, as the hospitals have mostly been closed) may house learning-disabled offenders who pose a continuing risk to others. This encompasses individuals who perpetrate severe violent offenses, such as sexual assault and arson. Learning disability psychiatrists and registered learning disability nurses would be responsible for their care. Some psychiatrists who work in this field have received dual training in adolescent or forensic psychiatry (Simon, Robert and Liza Gold, ed. 2010) as well as learning disabilities. A few nurses would also have received training in mental health. Psychiatrists (usually forensic psychiatrists) and clinical and forensic psychologists, who typically work in the NHS, typically handle court work (medicolegal work) on a private basis.

Usually, the Legal Services Commission (formerly known as Legal Aid) provides funding for this work.

7.3.7. United States

Typically, forensic psychiatrists collaborate with lawyers and magistrates. Their role is to mediate mental-legal disputes that call for a more expert viewpoint. As part of their practice, they assist clients in achieving better mental health. A forensic psychiatrist's typical responsibilities include assessing a client's suitability for parole, evaluating injuries and their impact on the client, and performing assessments to rule out any mental health concerns. One thing unites all of these tasks: assessing competence and capacity is their primary objective. These employees are crucial in the fight against the practice of hospitals and prisons having double revolving doors. Because they are not receiving the necessary assistance, a large number of mentally ill patients will alternate between hospitals and prisons. Legal choices that have an impact on mental health patients are serious matters that necessitate careful consideration of all parties. Psychiatrists with expertise in forensics are trained in both the medical and legal facets of mental health.

7.3.8. Canada

7.3.8.1. Criminal Law Framework

In Canada, certain credentialed medical practitioners may, at their discretion, make state-sanctioned investigations into and diagnosis of mental illness. Appropriate use of the DSM-IV-TR is discussed in its section entitled "Use of the DSM-IV-TR in Forensic Settings".

Concerns have been expressed that the Canadian criminal justice system discriminates based on DSM IV diagnosis within the context of Part XX of the Criminal Code. This part sets out provisions for, among other things, court ordered attempts at «treatment» before individuals receive a trial as described in section 672.58 of the Criminal Code. Also provided for are court ordered «psychiatric assessments». Critics have also expressed concerns that use of the DSM-IV-TR may conflict with section 2(b) of the Canadian Charter of Rights and Freedoms, which guarantees the fundamental freedom of «thought, belief, opinion, and expression».

7.3.8.2. Confidentiality

According to the Canadian Psychiatric Association, there have been significant infringements on people's right to privacy in recent years by governments, large corporations, law enforcement, and the courts. It continues by saying that violations or possible violations of confidentiality in the context of therapy gravely jeopardize the accuracy of the information shared between the patient and the psychiatrist as well as the mutual confidence and trust required for successful therapy to take place.

The Centre for Addiction and Mental Health in Toronto published The Forensic Mental Health System. In Ontario: An Information Guide, which provides an overview of the forensic psychiatric procedure as it is implemented in the province. As per the Guide, any information disclosed to a forensic psychiatrist and other evaluating professionals is not private. The Guide goes on to say that the forensic psychiatrist will provide a report to the court based on whatever information that is available, including records from the police and hospital, statements from friends, family, and coworkers, and observations made while you were in the hospital. The Guide further states that you have the option to decline to participate in all or part of the assessment. Your friends and family may occasionally be questioned for personal information. They are also free to decline to respond to inquiries.

It's noteworthy that the guide emphasizes the freedom to decline participation. This might seem strange considering that, much like the insanity defense in the US, a verdict of Not Criminally Responsible due to Mental Disorder is frequently presented as desirable to the defense. The Criminal Code refers to a finding of not guilty by crime as a defense. Differentiating it from many other legal defenses, however, is the possibility that the Crown or the court itself may raise the question of the accused's mental state in addition to the defense team.

7.3.8.3. Treatment/Assessment Conflict

When a court orders an inpatient forensic assessment for criminal responsibility in Ontario, the accused is usually treated and assessed by a single multidisciplinary team for a duration of 30 or 60 days. There have been concerns raised about the possibility that an accused person may provide assessors with information, whether it be medical or otherwise, for ethical, medical, or legal reasons in an effort toto permit and guarantee safe and appropriate treatment during that time of custody. A few online resources discuss treatment/assessment conflicts in relation to different legal systems, especially international civil litigation. It may seem contradictory, but the American Academy of Psychiatry and the Law states in its ethics guidelines that the standard physician-patient responsibilities apply in situations where a treatment relationship exists, such as in correctional settings.

7.3.9. South Africa

In South Africa, when there are doubts about CST and MSO, the courts will refer patients for observation for a duration of 30 days. A panel is necessary for serious crimes, and it may consist of two or more psychiatrists. In the event that the court rules that the defendant is not guilty of a crime, the defendant might be admitted to a forensic mental health facility as a state patient. Although they are referred for treatment for an indefinite amount of time, the majority returned to their communities three years later.

7.3.10. Educational Requirements

A psychiatrist is a medical professional who has finished residency training, medical school, and undergraduate studies. Typically, forensic psychiatrists have additional training pertinent to their position (e.g., specializing in addiction, geriatrics, or child/adolescent medicine). Many forensic psychiatrists will finish specialized training in a related field following their residency. Usually, this training takes an additional year or two. They are qualified to diagnose and treat mental health disorders because they hold a doctorate in medicine (MD). They can also write prescriptions for drugs.

7.3.11. Training Standards

Certain forensic psychiatrists have completed additional training in that particular field. In the US, psychiatrists who have finished their training in general psychiatry are eligible to apply for one-year fellowships in this field. After that, these psychiatrists might be qualified to take the forensic psychiatry board certification exam. After completing general psychiatry training, individuals in Britain must complete a three-year subspecialty program in forensic psychiatry in order to obtain a Certificate of Completion of Training as a forensic psychiatrist. In certain nations, forensic psychiatry is also practiced by general psychiatrists. But in other nations, like Japan, doing this kind of work necessitates a particular government certification.

7.4. FORENSIC PSYCHIATRY: CONTEMPORARY SCOPE, CHALLENGES, AND CONTROVERSIES

The area of psychiatry known as forensic psychiatry addresses problems that emerge at the intersection of mental health and the legal system as well as the movement of mentally ill criminals through various social systems. Four major developments have contributed to the growth of modern forensic psychiatry: the public's evolving attitudes and perceptions of mental illness; the evolution of legal tests to define legal insanity; new approaches to treating mental illnesses that offer alternatives to custodial care; and the understanding and appreciation of the relationship between mental illness and criminality. This essay examines the present state of forensic psychiatry and the moral conundrums that this subspecialty is dealing with across the globe. Forensic psychiatrists began as a small, obscure group of psychiatrists who focused on studying the mental health conditions of prisoners and treating them; they also occasionally appeared in legal proceedings. Today, however, forensic psychiatrists are a well-known and respected group of super-specialists who have a significant impact on the legal system and are changing the practice of psychiatry. This status hasn't come without reservations regarding the fundamental nature of forensic psychology as well as issues with its applicability and morality.

Four major developments have benefited modern forensic psychiatry: the development of the legal tests to define legal insanity; the evolution of the medico-legal understanding and appreciation of the relationship between mental illness and criminality; the new approaches to treating mental conditions that offer alternatives to custodial care; and the shifts in public attitudes and perceptions about mental conditions in general. These four points serve as the foundation for the recent growth of forensic psychiatry, which has expanded to include many other areas of law and mental health policy in addition to issues solely pertaining to criminal prosecutions and the treatment of mentally ill offenders. According to standard definitions, the subspecialty of forensic psychiatry is the area of psychiatry that addresses problems that emerge at the intersection of psychiatry and the legal system (1). This definition, however, is a little limited because forensic psychiatry spends a significant amount of its time assisting mentally ill people who are in legal trouble in navigating three totally opposed social systems: the criminal justice, correctional, and mental health. Hence, the definition needs to be changed to reflect the area of psychiatry that addresses problems that emerge at the intersection of mental health and the legal system as well as the movement of mentally ill criminals along a spectrum of social systems. The field of forensic psychiatry addresses problems that arise in the assessment of civil law cases, in the creation and implementation of mental health laws, and at the intersection of criminal and penal law.

7.4.1. Penal Law

A greater understanding of the connection between criminal behavior and mental health has resulted in a global increase in the use of forensic experts in courts at various stages of the legal process. Three main areas need to be taken into account when entering the legal system: applications for dangerousness, regulations regarding insanity, and fitness to stand trial. The main developments in the case law regarding fitness to stand trial concern the decisions made to commit defense attorneys found incompetent to stand trial to mental health facilities, where it is hoped that their capacity to stand trial will be restored. The challenge facing clinicians is determining what criteria to use to assess restorability of competence, which should be predicated on a satisfactory response to treatment. The term "insanity regulations" refers to the legal standards that determine whether the effect of a mental illness on one's ability to comprehend or appreciate the nature of a crime could be used to declare a person not guilty by reason of insanity, not criminally responsible due to a mental condition, or any other phrase used in various countries. Applications to designate an individual as a dangerous offender typically require forensic experts to possess a high degree of expertise because they are expected to give courts technical and scientific data regarding risk assessment and violence prediction in the future. One of the main responsibilities of forensic psychiatrists after an offender has been found guilty is determining the degree of systemic interface with various receiving and treatment facilities. The mental health system includes hospitals for the criminally insane, mental hospitals for patients with civil commitments, penitentiary hospitals for mentally ill prisoners, and hospital wings in local jails. It is necessary to recognize the interdependency of these facilities for the purposes of budgeting and system integration. Concerns about the treatment of mentally ill inmates in jails are also very real. A few of the options that are currently available are displayed in Table 7.1.

Table 7.1. *Models for the Delivery of Mental Health Care to Mentally Disordered Offenders*

Ambulatory treatment within prison
Mental patients remain with other inmates in the regular cells and tiers of the prison and come for visits to the infirmary during psychiatric clinic
Special wing within the prison
Mental patients are transferred to this wing for the duration of the episode or duration of their incarceration
Specialized security hospitals (penitentiary hospitals)
Mental patients or those with special criminal pathology such as sexual offenders are transferred out to these hospitals, usually for the duration of their incarceration

Contractual arrangements with outside psychiatric facilities
Mental patients are transferred out to these hospitals or psychiatric units for the duration of the episode
Forensic community corrections
Every effort is made to prevent that mental patients enter the prison system or, if released from prison, to ensure that they not go back

Source: https://www.ncbi.nlm.nih.gov/pmc/articles/PMC1525122/.

Finally, on exit from the legal-correctional system, forensic psychiatrists are expected to provide expert knowledge on matters such as readiness for parole, predictions of recidivism, commitment legislation applicable to exiting offenders, and the phenomenon of double revolving doors for the mentally ill in prisons and hospitals.

7.4.2. Civil Law

It is frequently necessary for psychiatrists and other mental health professionals to perform assessments in order to ascertain whether one of the parties is experiencing mental or emotional issues. These kinds of evaluations are required in a variety of circumstances. These include tests to determine the effects of injuries on a third party in a car accident, assessments of the ability to make contracts or write a will, psychological autopsies to determine testamentary capacity in cases of suicide or sudden death, assessments of fitness to work, and, more recently in many nations, assessments to determine eligibility for benefits considered in disability insurance. In the majority of these cases, determining someone's ability and competence to carry out a certain task or assessing an impaired person's capacity for independent decision-making are the pertinent issues. A finding of incompetence resulting from an incapacity determination becomes a social control issue that is used to justify imposing social restrictions on a specific person. This places a greater ethical burden on physicians to ensure that the best available clinical evidence has served as the foundation for all of their decisions.

There is typically an assumption of competence and, consequently, of capacity. Until the contrary is demonstrated, it is considered that a person is capable of making decisions. A significant physical or mental illness does not by itself result in generalized incapacity or incapacity for particular functions. Furthermore, even in the case of a condition that may impair capacity, an individual may still be able to perform certain tasks due to the fact that capacity is not a binary concept but rather depends on the particular choice or task that needs to be completed. A determination of incapacity should also have a time limit, meaning it will need to be reviewed periodically. For instance, a person may still be able to sign contracts and handle their own finances even though a stroke has left them unable to operate a motor vehicle. In this case, the person will be considered incompetent to drive. The individual might be able to recover the ability and competence to drive with enough time and rehabilitation. Generallytoto proceed with gathering information in any other way or to force someone to cooperate with an assessment of incapacity, legal authority must be obtained. A screening test of capacity should be used, and a full assessment should only be conducted in the event that the test taker fails. If the screening test is easily passed, this will avoid placing an excessive burden on the person being assessed.

7.4.3. Mental Health Legislation and Systems

Forensic psychiatrists have become acutely aware of the relationships within the mental health system and the connections between it and the justice and correctional systems as a result of the double revolving door phenomenon, which sees mental patients moving between mental health facilities and prisons. Because of their involvement in the legal system, forensic psychiatrists have become highly interested in the creation and implementation of mental health laws. This is particularly true when it comes to issues like involuntary commitment, which is often based on a determination of dangerousness rather than a just need for treatment, managing mentally ill offenders, and providing legal protections for people who are incapable of making decisions for themselves. Psychiatrists who specialize in assessing violence and the likelihood of violent behavior in the future are often called upon to determine the risk associated with violent patients who have committed civil acts. Laws, the creation of functional mental health systems, and the provision of care—in facilities or in the community—interact closely. A sense that the mental health system is adrift has been created in many countries by mental health legislation with unduly restrictive commitment clauses, even for short-term commitment; deinstitutionalization as a result of the closure of old mental hospitals; changes in health care delivery systems toward short admissions to general psychiatric units and subsequent treatment in the community; and the high number of mental patients who wind up in jails. Changes in the law and a broader acceptance of psychiatric explanations for behavior may have contributed to the growth of forensic psychiatry, but the sheer volume of mental patients housed in jails, prisons, and penitentiaries is a more pressing cause. Therefore, the increasing significance of forensic psychiatry could be attributed to shortcomings in the general mental health system.

Governments' deinstitutionalization policies over the past 50 years have been cited as one of the main explanations for the high number of mental health patients who end up in the criminal justice or correctional systems. Deinstitutionalization generally refers to legislative actions taken to close large mental hospitals and reintegrate patients into the community, offering services such as outpatient treatment, alternative housing, psychosocial rehabilitation, short-term admissions to general hospital psychiatric units, and other community services. On occasion, though, these choices were made without consideration for any kind of planning or needs analysis for the patients who were about to be deinstitutionalized or relocated. The kind of services to be rendered and the features of the communities to which patients were to be transferred were also unclear. Therefore, rather than being based on sound scientific reasoning, the decisions were primarily based on rhetorical and political beliefs. Deinstitutionalization as an idea and set of policies has garnered both praise and criticism. Deinstitutionalization has been viewed by some as a progressive, humane, and enlightened set of policies that have brought the needs of the mentally ill to the forefront of many communities. Deinstitutionalization has proven to be quite successful in this sense. Deinstitutionalization is credited with the following: it has increased patient involvement in their own care and rehabilitation; it has prompted research and learning; it has raised questions that challenge the therapeutic nihilism prevalent in a bygone era; it has increased the visibility of mental patients in the community and in general hospitals and academic centers; it has improved our understanding of the disease process, which had previously been distorted by the detrimental effects of prolonged institutionalization; and it has raised awareness of anguish and civil rights.

However, deinstitutionalization has also been linked to a number of drawbacks. Legal activism and deinstitutionalization have both been held accountable for igniting litigation and driving expensive over-legalization and over-regulation of psychiatric practices. The plight of the mentally ill in society has been directly impacted by a number of harmful social effects. These have included accounts of "revolving door" patients—that is, patients who require recurrent admissions—and the rise in the percentage of homeless people who are at least 30% mentally ill. Even in cases where housing is available, it is frequently found in dilapidated tenements in inner cities or in the psychiatric ghettos of large urban centers, where mentally ill and destitute patients wander aimlessly and talk to themselves. These vulnerable places make them easy targets for robberies, rapes, abuse, and physical violence. Some people simply pass away on cold winter nights from exposure on the streets. The criminalization of mental health patients, their migration from the mental health system to the justice or correctional system, and the violent behavior of some mental health patients in the community have all been attributed to deinstitutionalization.

However, the most scathing critiques of deinstitutionalization now focus on the manner in which the concept has been carried out rather than the notion of placing the patients back into their communities. The fact is that, in many communities, mental hospitals have been closed more quickly than the development of sufficient community resources and community alternatives as they were intended to be in the original policies, whether this is due to budgetary constraints or the actions of visionless administrations. The realization that there are treatment options other than custodial care, such as improved drugs with increased efficacy and effectiveness that are becoming more widely available and psychosocial treatment strategies that offer new, tried-and-true methods for managing mentally ill people in the community, should counteract these regrettable effects of deinstitutionalization. In this regard, the emergence of mental health courts in certain nations, alternatives to incarceration such as diversion, assertive community treatment and intensive case management techniques, the use of community treatment orders, improved housing policies, and other measures suggest a social movement to address the injustices associated with deinstitutionalization and stabilize community tenure for the mentally ill. Evaluations of anti-stigma programs appear to suggest that some of these efforts are contributing to a shift in public perceptions of mental illness and a greater understanding of the human rights concerns surrounding the care and treatment of the mentally ill in many nations.

7.4.4. Ethical Controversies

Worldwide, the practice of forensic psychiatry is rife with moral conundrums due to its dual roles in medicine and law. A forensic psychiatrist is first and foremost a medical professional with expertise in both general and forensic psychiatry, as well as theory and practice, and a track record of reasoned decision-making grounded in well-defined scientific evidence. Forensic psychiatrists are required by law to be knowledgeable about legal definitions, policies, and procedures, as well as legal precedents pertinent to the issue or case at hand. In addition to being familiar with courtroom procedures, forensic psychiatrists need to be able to express their conclusions succinctly and clearly, especially during the challenging cross-examination phase. The subspecialty of forensic psychiatry is defined by the dual knowledge of psychiatry and law, which also gives its practitioners the ethical groundwork. The way a forensic psychiatrist approaches the subject of the evaluation, how they initially agree to participate in the evaluation, and the warnings that must be given should all be indicative of this dual knowledge. At this point, the forensic psychiatrist's primary concern is ensuring that the person being evaluated is not misled into thinking that, as a medical professional, the relationship between the two of them will be one of physician and patient, where the doctor is expected to act in the patient's best interest and to always act to maximize the patient's benefit while assuring the patient that privacy and confidentiality are protected. The relationship in forensic psychiatry is one of evaluation, where the evaluator is expected to maintain a foundation of objectivity. Additionally, because the evaluator cannot reassure the patient regarding matters of confidentiality or privacy, negative findings may jeopardize the patient's interests and cause harm, even in cases where the patient is well and the evaluator is a doctor. As a result, forensic psychiatrists might even be held accountable for the criminalization of people with mental illnesses.

According to some observers, forensic psychiatrists' social control role distinguishes them from medical and psychiatric ethics. Regarding the controversial question of whether forensic psychiatrists are practicing medicine in their legal capacity, these pundits are unsure. From the beginning to the end, the forensic psychiatrist's power to act stems from the fact that they are first and foremost medical professionals, and as such, they must respect medical ethics. However, the consequences of forensic assessments are typically the result of other people's actions.

This places an ethical duty on forensic psychiatrists to carefully consider their own motivations as well as the motivations and potential outcomes of those who engage them for assessments. This duty includes examining how data are collected, how the evaluator forms opinions, how legal documents like reports, memos, and expert testimony are prepared, and—above all—what the intended application of their findings will be. A significant dispute arising from the dual responsibilities of forensic psychiatrists and other psychiatrists, including those in the armed forces, concerns the utilization of psychiatric judicial hospitals in the Soviet Union and, more recently, China, as well as psychiatrists' involvement in questioning detainees and prisoners that may result in accusations of torture, particularly in light of the current terrorist environment.

This can involve giving interrogators access to private psychological information that could be used to identify the prisoner's weaknesses and vulnerabilities, offering advice on effective interrogation strategies, or actively engaging in deception to obtain intelligence. It is in this context that forensic psychiatrists, or doctors in general, cannot overlook the ultimate goals of those requesting evaluations. Engaging in any activity that could result in torture would constitute a serious violation of medical ethics. This should serve as a stark reminder to forensic psychiatrists that medical ethics are rules that cannot be broken, regardless of the master's demands.

7.5. CLINICAL CHARACTERISTICS AND SELF-HARM IN FORENSIC PSYCHIATRIC PATIENTS

Self-harm, which includes both suicidal and non-suicidal self-harm, is a severe and potentially fatal behavior that has been linked to a lower quality of life and a higher risk of suicide. Suicide is one of the main causes of death in forensic populations, and there have been reports of higher rates of self-harm. There is little information available on self-harm in forensic psychiatric populations, aside from links between self-harm and mental illnesses. 800,000 people worldwide take their own lives each year. In forensic populations, this translates to one suicide every 40 seconds, i.e., Suicide is one of the main causes of death for criminals, regardless of the severity of their mental illnesses. It has been noted that the suicide rate in prisons is 5 to 10 times higher than in the general community. According to studies conducted in prisons, certain environmental factors (e.g., being housed in a single cell), criminological factors (being on remand, having received a life sentence, and having committed a violent index offense), and psychiatric factors (prior suicide attempts, recent suicidal ideation, mental illness) are particularly significant in identifying individuals with a high risk of suicide. A primary risk factor for suicide in prison populations is a history of non-suicidal self-harm behavior. Individuals who exhibit non-suicidal self-harm behavior have a 30-fold increased risk of completing suicide compared to those who do not.

Self-harm is a general term that encompasses both self-inflicted harm with the goal of committing suicide (suicide attempt) and non-suicidal self-injury (NSSI). This behavior, which is prevalent in the general population (2.9–41.5%), is regarded as a global public health concern. It has been reported that non-suicidal self-harm and suicide attempts range from 7 to 47.6% in prison environments. The true lethal intention of apparent suicide attempts was found to be as low as 6 percent in a Swedish prison cohort. Few studies, as far as we know, address the intention behind suicide attempts. One study did discover, however, that people with personality disorders intended to commit suicide with much less frequency than people with substance abuse issues or unidentified psychiatric disorders. All things considered, self-harm poses a serious problem for both the general public and forensic environments like jails. Determining the frequency of such a problematic behavior is vital, but so is knowing why some people hurt themselves in order to develop and carry out prevention and treatment plans. Forensic psychiatry is one particular context in which there is a dearth of information regarding self-harm. In Sweden, about 350 people are sentenced to forensic mental health treatment annually. The number of forensic mental health patients in Sweden is approximately 1,800, which is a relatively small number when compared to the 5,000+ individuals who are imprisoned there annually. It has been shown that there are notable differences between countries in terms of the quantity of forensic beds available, the duration of care, and the characteristics of the patient group [e.g., gender distribution], but all forensic mental health settings have one thing in common: forensic mental health patients demand a lot of work and expertise in terms of medical attention and intervention. Clinical presentations of these patients include a wide range of complex mental disorders, comorbid psychosocial issues, antisocial behaviors, and traumatic early experiences. The small number of research on non-suicidal self-harm and attempted suicide in forensic mental health patients reveals startlingly high rates (~61%). These populations exhibit wide variations in the severity of self-harm, which begs the question of why this behavior occurs. Although this hasn't been investigated in forensic mental health patients before, theoretical and clinical research in other populations suggests that self-harm could serve as a coping mechanism for emotions.

This population is particularly vulnerable in this regard, as evidenced by the clinical presentations and high prevalence of self-harm among forensic mental health patients. These patients need forensic mental health care immediately, but there is a lack of information to support evidence-based practice.

7.5.1. Prevalence, Characteristics, and Function of Self-Harm in Forensic Psychiatric Patients

67 individuals, or 68.4% of the sample, reported having attempted suicide or engaged in non-suicidal self-harm at some point in their lives. Of those, men made up n = 54 (55.1%). Thirteen of the study's female participants (n = 13) disclosed a history of NSSI or attempted suicide. Of the participants, 57 (58.2%) had attempted suicide at least once, and seven (12.5%) had done so in the preceding half-year. Among the female participants, only one (n = 1) had never tried suicide. The average age at the time of the first attempted suicide was 21.5% of the total age (median 19 years; range 9–53, SD = 9.0). The majority of recent suicide attempts used multiple techniques. The most common alternative (n = 14, 26.4%) was hanging. Other options included self-poisoning (n = 12, 22.6%), cutting (n = 9, 17%), self-strangulation (n = 5, 9.4%), choking/swallowing objects (n = 3, 5.7%), jumping from heights (n = 2, 3.8%), and attempts related to traffic (n = 2, 3.8%). Six participants, or 11.3%, had attempted suicide using a different method that was not offered. When asked to describe their process, they said they "started a fire in a prison cell," "ran out on an iced lake," "caused infection," "injected air into blood," and "tried to overdose." The most severe attempts at suicide that the participants experienced had no or very minor physical effects for 20 (40%), minor effects

for 8 (16%), moderate effects for 11 (22%), moderately difficult effects for 6 (12%), and severe or almost fatal effects for 5 (10%). For both male and female participants, the most popular means of attempting suicide were hanging or strangling (n = 13, 15:3% of male participants) and cutting (n = 6, 46:2% of female participants).

With a mean age at onset of 18 years, SD = 8.3, range 4–41, more than half of the participants (n = 56, 59%) had participated in NSSI. 28.25 years old was the average age at the last episode (SD = 8.03, range 13–45).

Although more information on the specifics of the NSSI episode was not gathered, many participants frequently informed the data collector that these episodes had taken place during their arrest or early in their admission to forensic psychiatry. Of those who had self-harmed with non-suicidal intent, the majority (n = 31, 66%) had not done so while under the influence of drugs. Banging or hitting oneself (M = 31 times) and cutting (M = 30 times) were the most popular NSSI techniques. Of the participants (n = 13, 14:9%) who reported cutting as an NSSI, the majority had only done so once. While female participants primarily reported repeated instances of cutting, male participants reported more single instances. Of the seven female participants (n = 7), the lowest frequency of cutting (50–1,000 times) was reported by three of them.

The remaining female participants (n = 7) reported higher frequencies. Many individuals who achieved high scores on the NSSI frequency reported an estimate because they claimed the frequency could not be counted. About half of the participants (n = 21, 45.7%) who had self-harmed said "yes," 14 (30.4%) said "sometimes," and 11 (24%) said "no" when asked if they had ever experienced pain while doing so. The majority said they preferred to be by themselves when self-harming (n = 38, 82.6%). The time interval between the participants' initial thoughts of self-harm and their actual self-harm act was also asked to be estimated. 9 percent (n = 4) answered "3–6 h," the majority (n = 31, or 70%) reported "<1 h," 11% (n = 5) answered "1–3 h," and 6% (n = 3) answered "6–12 h" or "more than 1 day." 81.8% (n = 36) of the participants said "yes" when asked if they wanted to stop self-harming. "

In general, the participants indicated that the more pertinent NSSI functions were the intrapersonal ones. Table 7.2 shows that affect regulation and self-punishment were the two most frequently mentioned NSSI functions, followed by distress signaling. The large SD for some of the scales in Table 7.2 can be explained by the fact that the distribution of the participants' self-reported NSSI functions was positively skewed for the majority of the scales.

Table 7.2. *Functions of NSSI (Mean ISAS Values) in Forensic Psychiatric Patients*

ISAS Scale	Function	*M (SD)*	Range
Intrapersonal			
	Affect regulation	3.04 (2.02)	0–6
	Anti-dissociation	1.55 (1.80)	0–6
	Anti-suicide	1.48 (2.02)	0–6
	Marking distress	2.23 (1.84)	0–6
	Self-punishment	2.48 (1.84)	0–6
Interpersonal			
	Autonomy	0.40 (1.07)	0–5
	Interpersonal boundaries	0.86 (1.35)	0–4
	Interpersonal influence	1.50 (1.53)	0–5
	Peer bonding	0.21 (0.51)	0–2
	Revenge	0.44 (0.88)	0–4
	Self-care	1.97 (2.07)	0–6
	Sensation seeking	0.60 (1.25)	0–6
	Toughness	0.90 (1.21)	0–4

Source: https://www.ncbi.nlm.nih.gov/pmc/articles/PMC8365140/.

7.5.2. Psychosocial and Clinical Risk Factors of Self-Harm in Forensic Psychiatric Patients

Table 7.3, which displays a few significant associations with wide confidence intervals, illustrates the effects of various psychosocial and clinical characteristics on self-harm when tested using chi-square analysis. Comparable outcomes were shown when examining just male subjects.

Table 7.3. *Psychosocial and Clinical Risk Factors of Self-Harm (NSSI & Suicide Attempts)*

Psychosocial and Clinical Characteristics*	Self-Harm (*n*)			X^2	*P*	CI	OR
	No	Yes	Expected Yes-Count				
Female gender	0	13	8.9	6.95	0.008	1.10–1.40	1.20

Neurodevelopmental disorders	8	38	31.4	8.13	0.004	1.47–9.63	3.77
Schizophrenia spectrum and other psychotic disorders	24	46	47.9	0.79	0.372	0.24–1.72	0.64
Depressive disorders	5	19	16.4	1.71	0.190	0.69–6.15	2.06
Anxiety disorders	5	23	19.1	3.44	0.064	0.92–8.02	2.72
Trauma- and stressor-related disorders	3	15	12.3	2.28	0.131	0.72–10.09	2.69
Disruptive, impulse-control, and conduct disorders	1	16	11.6	6.31	0.012	1.19–74.58	9.41
Substance-related and addictive disorders	21	42	43.1	0.23	0.627	0.32–1.97	0.80
Personality disorder clusters A, B, and C	13	29	28.7	0.01	0.900	0.45–2.50	.90
Cluster B personality disorders	11	27	26	0.20	0.649	0.51–2.79	1.23
Other personality disorders	8	17	17.1	0.002	0.963	0.37–2.59	0.98
Parents absent during childhood	11	29	27.3	0.53	0.465	0.57–3.35	1.39
Institutionalization during adolescence	6	30	24.6	5.89	0.015	1.23–9.30	3.38
Foster care placement during childhood	6	22	19.1	1.89	0.17	0.73–5.69	2.04
Truancy	21	53	50.6	1.48	0.224	0.69–4.69	1.80
Bullying others	11	18	19.8	0.75	0.385	0.27–1.66	0.67

*Due to low representation in some diagnostic categories, bipolar syndrome, obsessive-compulsive and related disorders, paraphilic disorders, and other mental disorders and mental illness could not be analyzed in a chi-square analysis.

Source: https://www.ncbi.nlm.nih.gov/pmc/articles/PMC8365140/.

7.5.3. Psychosocial, Criminological, and Clinical Characteristics of Forensic Psychiatric Patients

The study's results support earlier conclusions that people with forensic mental illnesses are a particularly vulnerable group who have endured traumatic experiences since they were young. Many of the participants had difficult educational histories with repeated truancy (61%) and school failures; one in five had not completed compulsory primary school. Their childhoods were also characterized by seemingly complex relationships with peers and family. Nearly two out of every five children did not spend a significant portion of their childhood with both parents present. Foster care or institutionalization of children, typically for extended lengths of time, was also prevalent. Researchers have talked about how some children's temperaments are negatively correlated with their parents' bad parenting styles over the years, and how this affects the child's ability to adjust behaviorally as they get older and into adulthood. Some children are inherently more aggressive, easily irritated, and find it difficult to express themselves in a prosocial way. This can annoy parents, who may then stop being a parent or act inconsistently and sporadically toward the child, which unfortunately exacerbates the child's already harmful development. All of the participants in our study were once children, and many of them bullied their peers, struggled to complete their basic education, and were truant frequently for unknown reasons. Some spent extended periods of time in foster care or institutions as a result of their early circumstances. When considered collectively, the results point to a severe lack of parental support, which requires further study. In terms of gender disparities, the findings indicate that male forensic mental patients had higher externalizing childhood behaviors (e.g., bullying others), as well as the female patients' lower levels of work experience and more intimate partner relationships. Given that male and female patients may have different needs, these findings are significant for the rehabilitation of forensic mental health patients back into society. However, more research on this is required using a sample of patients who are more female.

According to reports from the Swedish National Registry of Forensic Psychiatry, the criminal histories of the study participants included sexual offenses, property crimes, arson, theft, threats, and repeated assault ofConsidering potential gender disparities, the male patients showed a more varied background in criminology than the female patients, and their younger onset age supported the notion that male forensic psychiatric patients tend to exhibit more externalizing childhood behaviors. In contrast to female participants, male participants were overrepresented in instances of repeated lethal violence; however, the percentage of female participants who committed lethal violence on one occasion (30.8%) was higher than the percentage of male participants (18.8%). A Swedish study indicates that the difference in the number of crimes committed by gender is closing. The authors contend that there are a number of plausible explanations for this, but there is unquestionably agreement that the number of female criminals has increased. The current study was carried out in a forensic mental health clinic with strict admission standards and high levels of security. Had the study recruited participants from clinical settings with lower security, the outcomes could have been altered.

The mean age of onset within the various crime categories is in line with earlier research on the development of criminal behavior in various forensic populations, including violent offenders. Drug-related crimes have the youngest mean ages of onset (15.9 years) and theft or robbery (16.4 years), while lethal violence has the oldest mean age of onset (27.6 years). In certain instances, the age at which these crimes began was as young as five years old. When considered collectively, the participants' criminal histories appear to be marked by a concentration on violent crime, but they also exhibit some adaptability that needs to be considered in the context of the recruitment process—a high-security forensic mental health clinic. This pattern may therefore be unique to patients who are referred to high-security care facilities rather than being applicable to all forensic mental contexts. Nonetheless, the findings unequivocally show that further research into the gender variations in criminological traits is necessary, as is the need for early childhood interventions and support to avert the criminological trajectory of some forensic psychiatric patients.

The sample's gender representation, which was primarily male, was consistent with data from the Swedish National Registry of Forensic Psychiatry (Howells et al., 2004). At the time of participation, schizophrenia spectrum and other psychotic disorders were the most prevalent primary psychiatric diagnoses. Although the most prevalent primary or secondary diagnosis in this sample was schizophrenia (paranoid and unspecified), over 64% of the participants had been diagnosed with an addictive or substance-related disorder at some point in their lives. Prior studies have shown that patients in the forensic mental health field are more likely than those in the general mental health population to be treated with a mix of various antipsychotic drugs at higher dosages. Pharmacological treatment for the current cohort of forensic psychiatric patients with high comorbidity of substance use disorders and psychotic disorders may present significant challenges for clinicians. It's interesting to note that this sample's lifetime prevalence of neurodevelopmental disorders was higher than its prevalence at the time of participation. While neurodevelopmental disorders may eventually lead to a reduction in symptoms for some individuals, psychotic disorders, particularly when more severe, may obscure other mental disorders and thus not be sufficiently considered in forensic psychiatric care. As symptoms of many other mental illnesses, like personality disorders, may be more difficult to identify in a comprehensive clinical picture, this raises legitimate concerns about those illnesses as well. It is well known that women report higher lifetime prevalence of mood and anxiety disorders as well as BPD, and that women in forensic psychiatry are disproportionately overrepresented in BPD, raising the possibility of gender differences in psychiatric morbidity. Even though we discovered that BPD was prevalent among female participants, the small number of women in the sample prevented us from drawing any such conclusions. Before any conclusions can be made, samples with a higher percentage of female patients must be examined because the results show different psychiatric (co)morbidity between male and female forensic psychiatric patients. The current research on complex psychiatric comorbidity in forensic psychiatric patients highlights the necessity of forensic psychiatric care that takes gender differences and comorbidity into account when customizing interventions.

7.5.4. Prevalence, Characteristics, and Function of Self-Harm in Forensic Psychiatric Patients

The current study's high rate of self-harm was consistent with earlier research on forensic samples. Over 50% of the participants said they had at least once attempted suicide or self-harmed. Self-harm has serious consequences that extend beyond the individual's personal suffering and health care costs. It is a behavior that can result in death or other severe physical injuries. The expenses, necessity, and duration of hospitalization, as well as any medical care and psychosocial evaluation associated with the self-harm incident, are frequently used to describe the societal costs of self-harm. Three particularly intriguing aspects of self-harm were identified by this study: (1) the most common method of attempting suicide was hanging; (2) the most serious type of suicide attempt typically had little to no physical consequences; and (3) the most common form of NSSI was cutting or banging one's head against a wall.

Findings showing that hanging is the most popular method for successfully completing suicide among men in Europe are in good alignment with the notion that hanging is the most commonly used method for suicide attempts. Researchers contend that the likelihood of completing the suicide successfully and staying undetected frequently influences the method of suicide that is selected. Our study's findings indicate that while the majority of participants did select a deadly method for their most serious attempt at suicide, they survived with little to no physical harm. We speculate that this could be because the individual attempted suicide in a forensic or care setting, where they were unable to be left alone unsupervised for an extended period of time. Therefore, the suicide attempt might not have been made with the intention of killing someone, but it might have served another purpose. However, this needs to be looked into more in future research because no comprehensive information about the circumstances surrounding the suicide attempt was gathered. Our results can be compared to those of patients with severe depressive disorders, of whom 32% had attempted suicide at some point in the past. The most common NSSI techniques (banging fists, head against wall, or cutting) were not further documented, but participants frequently informed the data collector that these episodes of NSSI and/or suicide attempts had taken place during their arrest or early in their admission to forensic psychiatry. This lends more weight to the idea that staff members should be particularly watchful for the possibility of self-harm in situations involving mentally ill offenders since these individuals are particularly susceptible to it during the crucial period following their initial deprivation of liberty as a result of criminal activity. While male participants reported hanging or strangulation more frequently, all female participants reported some form of self-harm (NSSI and/or suicide attempt) and high frequencies of the NSSI behavior cutting. Previous research suggests that self-harm behavior varies depending on a person's gender, but more recent research indicates that men's rates of self-harm do not differ significantly from women's rates. Despite the fact that there was a statistically significant difference in self-harm between male and female participants in the current study, the small number of female participants prevents general conclusions about gender differences from being made from this research.

Prior research on the NSSI's functions has tended to focus on either intrapersonal or interpersonal functions. The study's findings suggest that the NSSI's functions have an intrapersonal focus, with regulation, self-punishment, and distress signaling being its most notable applications.

This was particularly noticeable in the case of the female participants, though they also reported higher interpersonal functions in terms of self-care and interpersonal influence. The functions of NSSI in forensic psychiatric patients, despite the influence of severe mental disorders, are comparable to those in other clinical and non-clinical groups, and gender differences need to be taken into consideration. This pattern is similar to the discussions that currently dominate the research field of self-harm. Decisions about interventions aimed at preventing self-harm in forensic psychiatry depend heavily on this data, which provides a unique perspective on the views of forensic mental health patients on the issue. As previously shown and supported by the current study, patients in forensic psychiatry frequently have severe mental illnesses and have had traumatic childhood experiences.

7.5.5. Psychosocial and Clinical Risk Factors of Self-Harm

None of the psychosocial variables under investigation showed any statistically significant correlations with self-harm (NSSI and/or suicide attempts). Moreover, no clear correlations with any particular psychiatric diagnosis were found. Though the large confidence intervals should be noted, self-harm was linked to disruptive impulse-control and conduct disorder ($p = 0.012$, CI = 1.19–74.6, OR = 9.41) and neurodevelopmental disorders ($p = 0.014$, CI = 1.23–8.02, OR = 3.14). Self-harm has been linked to BPD in a number of prior studies; however, the bulk of those clinical studies' participants were female, and BPD is known to over represent women. Because the specific diagnosis was not very common in the sample, we were unable to test the relationship between self-harm and BPD in this study. However, a number of other diagnostic groups reported high rates of self-harm. 45 of the 67 individuals who reported self-harm showed signs of a psychotic disorder, including schizophrenia. Despite the fact that female gender increased the risk of self-harm by a factor of 1.2, when the males in this sample were examined separately, no gender-specific differences were found.

The NSSI functions that the participants reported may indicate that they saw NSSI as a means of venting their frustration and distress. Nonetheless, inferences regarding the role of NSSI in this specific group need to be made cautiously and require additional research. Although self-harm has been extensively studied, it has not been studied in forensic populations. It is important to consider the variations in the environmental and psychosocial backgrounds of forensic samples and general population samples.

7.5.6. Strengths and Limitations

Given the previously documented challenges in enlisting participants from forensic psychiatry, the total number of forensic psychiatric patients in Sweden (approximately 5% of the total population), and the characteristics of the total population, the sample size in this study was substantial. However, for analyzes involving self-harm as a dependent variable, there was insufficient variation in the distribution of psychiatric diagnoses. Therefore, it was not possible to conduct in-depth analyzes of self-harm in relation to potential risk factors. Furthermore, because the current sample was drawn from a high-security forensic mental health clinic, it might not be applicable to other forensic mental health settings. Legal context variations must also be taken into account, as different jurisdictions may have different legal definitions for forensic mental health patients. Additionally, we recognize that sample size limits can have an impact on the opportunities for statistical analysis. Furthermore, no conclusions on causality can be made from the current findings because the study was cross-sectional in nature. The instrument used to gather NSSI self-report data has never been used in a forensic sample, which is another study limitation. Even though the instrument's psychometrics had respectable results, more research needs to be done on this. Participants in the ISAS report the total number of NSSI incidents in the first section. Reliability issues arise when the number increases, as it did in our sample. Several participants reported anywhere from 100 to a 1,000 NSSI incidents. This result begs the question of whether this instrument is appropriate for a sample with a significant NSSI, without casting doubt on the veracity of their information. Prior studies have identified this as problematic. Lastly, because of the exploratory nature of the study, we did not adjust for multiple comparisons.

REFERENCES

1. Buchanan, A. (2001). HCR-20: Assessing risk for violence, version 2. By C. Webster, K. Douglas, D. Eaves, and S. Hart. Mental Health, Law and Policy Institute, British Columbia. 1997. 98 + vii pp. *Criminal Behavior and Mental Health, 11*(S1), S77–S78. https://doi.org/10.1002/cbm.437.
2. Dalby, J. T. (1997). *Applications of Psychology in The Law Practice: A Guide to Relevant Issues, Practices, and Theories*. Chicago, IL: American Bar Association. ISBN 0-8493-0811-9.
3. Howells, K., Day, A., & Thomas-Peter, B. (2004). Changing violent behavior: Forensic mental health and criminological models compared. *Journal of Forensic Psychiatry & Psychology, 15*(3), 391–406. https://doi.org/10.1080/14788940410001655907.
4. Jones, L. M., Cross, T. P., Walsh, W. A., & Simone, M. (2005). Criminal investigations of child abuse: The research behind 'best practices'. *Trauma, Violence, & Abuse, 6*(3), 254–268. https://doi.org/10.1177/1524838005277440.
5. Melton, G. B., Petrila, J., Poythress, N. G., Otto, R. K., Mossman, D., & Condie, L. O. (2017). *Psychological Evaluations for The Courts: A Handbook for Mental Health Professionals and Lawyers* (4th ed.). New York, NY: Guilford. ISBN 9781462532667.
6. Neal, T. M. S., Martire, K. A., Johan, J. L., Mathers, E. M., & Otto, R. K. (2022). The law meets psychological expertise: Eight best practices to improve forensic psychological assessment. *Annual Review of Law and Social Science, 18*(1), 169–192. https://doi.org/10.1146/annurev-lawsocsci-050420-010148.
7. Ogloff, J. R. P., & Finkelman, D. (1999). Psychology and law: An overview. In R. Roesch, S. D. Hart, & J. R. P. Ogloff (Eds.), *Psychology and Law: The State of The Discipline*. New York, NY: Springer. ISBN 0-306-45950-7.
8. Simon, R., & Gold, L. (Eds.). (2010). *American Psychiatric Textbook of Forensic Psychiatry*. Washington, DC: American Psychiatric Publishing. ISBN 978-1585622641.

CHAPTER 8

DIGITAL FORENSICS

Contents

Introduction 320
8.1. Basic Concept of Digital Forensics 320
8.2. Digital Forensic Investigation Models 340
8.3. Research Methodology in Digital Forensics 344
8.4. Challenging Aspects of Digital Evidence 351
References 354

INTRODUCTION

The recovery, investigation, examination, and analysis of material found in digital devices are all included in the field of digital forensics, a subfield of forensic science that frequently deals with mobile devices and computer crime. Originally used as a synonym for computer forensics, the term "digital forensics" now refers to the investigation of any device that can store digital data. With origins in the personal computing revolution of the late 1970s and early 1980s, national policies did not emerge for the discipline until the early 1990s, during which time it evolved haphazardly. There are many uses for digital forensics investigations.

The most typical is in front of criminal or civil courts, where one can prove or disprove a hypothesis. Criminal cases deal with the alleged violations of legal statutes, such as murder, theft, and assault against an individual, that are enforced by law enforcement agencies and prosecuted by the state. Contrarily, civil cases deal with defending the rights and property of individuals (often related to family disputes). They can also involve contractual disputes between commercial entities, in which case electronic discovery (ediscovery), a type of digital forensics, may be used.

In the private sector, forensics may also be used in situations like corporate intrusion investigations or internal investigations (a specific look into the type and scope of an unauthorized network intrusion). Depending on the kind of digital device being investigated, the technical part of an investigation can be broken down into several sub-branches, such as computer forensics, network forensics, forensic data analysis, and mobile device forensics. Digital media seizure, forensic imaging (acquisition), and analysis are all common steps in the forensic process. A report summarizing the evidence gathered is then produced. Digital forensics can be used not only to find concrete proof of a crime but also to link evidence to particular suspects, verify statements or alibis, ascertain intent, locate sources (such as in copyright cases), and authenticate documents. Compared to other forensic analysis fields, where the primary goal is to provide answers to a series of simpler questions, investigations have a far wider scope and frequently involve intricate timelines or hypotheses.

8.1. BASIC CONCEPT OF DIGITAL FORENSICS

The assessment of a digital artifact's condition that might be relevant to any computer system inquiry is the main goal of digital forensics. An investigator can gather digital evidence, examine it, and present the results of that examination by using digital forensics methods. Governments and private businesses should be able to successfully examine the digital trail left by suspects or other persons of interest associated with suspected illegal cyber activity thanks to the development of digital forensic tools and other even more sophisticated techniques. A subfield of forensic science known as "digital forensic science" is dedicated to the recovery and examination of evidence linked to cybercrime that is discovered on digital devices.

At first, computer forensics and digital forensics were used interchangeably. Subsequently, it has broadened to encompass the examination of all gadgets capable of storing digital information. A taster of how to conduct investigations to properly gather, analyze, and present digital evidence to both business and legal audiences is given by digital forensics, an introduction to computer forensics and investigation. It also describes how to stay current with evolving technologies, digital forensics laws and regulations, and tools for locating and analyzing digital evidence on a range of devices (Figure 8.1).

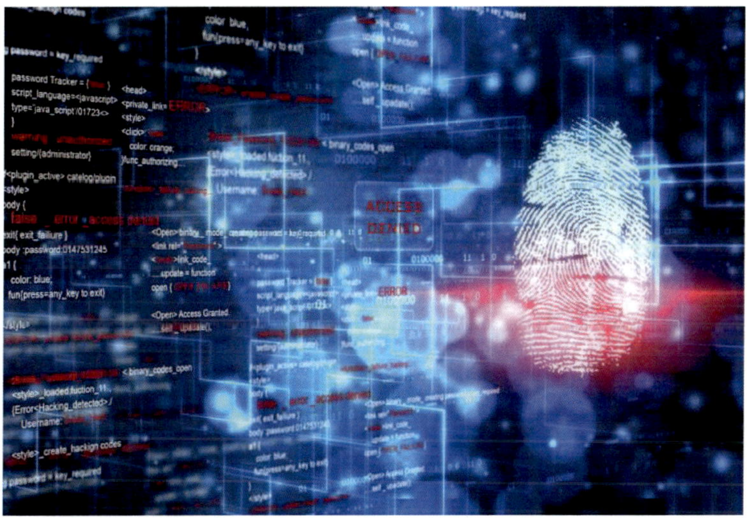

Figure 8.1. *The principal purpose of digital forensics.*

Source: https://media.licdn.com/dms/image/C4E22AQEMNb03MIiXCA/feed-share-shrink_2048_1536/0/1644910933586?e=2147483647&v=beta&t=qeKt0sYHCeHex0qfcvCRMZw9CA4OnA9qfuH-v8_zDxk.

Depending on the kind of digital devices being examined, the technical portion of an investigation can be broken down into several sub-branches, including computer forensics, network forensics, forensic data analysis, and mobile device forensics. A typical forensic procedure includes digital media seizure, forensic imaging (acquisition), and analysis, as well as the creation of a report summarizing the evidence gathered. Most people believe that digital forensics is only applicable in digital and computing environments. However, its impact on society is actually far more extensive. Given the pervasiveness of computers and other electronic devices in modern life, digital evidence has emerged as a vital tool for resolving legal disputes and a variety of criminal cases, both online and offline. Massive volumes of data are generated by all connected devices. Numerous gadgets record everything that their users do in addition to the autonomous tasks that they carry out, like network connections and data transfers. This covers a wide range of both public and private electronics, such as traffic lights, automobiles, cell phones, routers, and personal computers.

Digital evidence can be used as evidence in investigation and legal proceedings for:

- **Data Theft and Network Breaches**—digital forensics is used to understand how a breach happened and who were the attackers.
- **Online Fraud and Identity Theft**—digital forensics is used to understand the impact of a breach on organizations and their customers.
- **Violent Crimes Like Burglary, Assault, and Murder**—digital forensics is used to capture digital evidence from mobile phones, cars, or other devices in the vicinity of the crime.
- **White Collar Crimes**—digital forensics is used to collect evidence that can help identify and prosecute crimes like corporate fraud, embezzlement, and extortion.

Digital forensics can be used within an organization to locate and look into physical security incidents as well as cybersecurity incidents. Digital evidence is most frequently utilized in incident response procedures to identify breach activity, track down threat actors and its source, neutralize the threat, and supply legal teams and law enforcement agencies with proof.

Organizations must centrally manage logs and other digital evidence, make sure they keep it for a sufficient amount of time, and safeguard it against alteration, unauthorized access, or unintentional loss in order to enable digital forensics.

1. **Methodologies:** Digital forensic techniques are used in many different contexts, but are most commonly employed by law enforcement, other official authorities, or private companies to support internal investigations or gather evidence in criminal or civil court cases. Depending on the specific area of inquiry, the term "digital forensics" can be used to describe a wide range of specializations. For instance, mobile-device forensics focuses primarily on recovering digital evidence from smartphones and tablet computers, whereas network forensics analyzes computer network traffic. Digital

forensic techniques can be applied in countless ways, but the most widely employed ones involve recovering deleted files, examining unallocated space, conducting keyword searches throughout digital media, and extracting registry information (e.g., through the use of linked USB devices). It is crucial to make sure that the integrity and authenticity of the data and metadata are preserved throughout the investigation stages when working with digital evidence.

Therefore, it is imperative to prevent any tampering of the evidence resulting from the investigators' work and to confirm that the data gathered are "authentic"—i.e., exactly the same as the original information in every manner. Cybercrime fighters in movies and TV shows may deftly figure out a target's password and then log in to their computer or other smart device; however, in real life, such direct action could change the original in a way that renders anything found on the device inadmissible in court, if not unusable.

Acquiring an image of the contents of the computer or other device is the goal of the acquisition phase, also known as the "imaging of exhibits." The primary issue with digital media is that it's easy to change their state; this can happen even when trying to access files or content stored in a computer's memory. Therefore, it is essential to prevent direct access by accurately imaging the system under analysis's disks and volatile memory.

Figure 8.2. *Digital forensic methodologies.*

Source: https://s.yimg.com/ny/api/res/1.2/MoWUdx0ZjJ1VF09BoSUtsA--/YXB-waWQ9aGlnaGxhbmRlcjt3PTk2MDtoPTY0MDtjZj13ZWJw/https://media.zenfs.com/en-US/homerun/ccn_656/ebc3bd5bdb3d914cdb394abf73718711.

This can be accomplished by employing specialist write-blocking tools to create a "bit copy," or an exact bit-by-bit replication, of the media. These tools "mirror" the data and prevent any alterations to the media's original content. New acquisition techniques are required because of the increasing size of storage media and the spread of paradigms like cloud computing. These techniques enable investigators to take a "logical" copy of the data instead of a complete picture of the physical storage device. Investigators employ "hashing" mechanisms, which produce shorter, fixed-length values that represent the longer or more complex original, in a focused effort to assure the integrity of the data. Researchers can conduct faster searches and assess the consistency of the digital content they are examining at every instant thanks to the hashed values. Any changes made to the digital artifact's content would result in a change in its hash, making it easy to identify them without having to search the entire database (Figure 8.2).

2. **Practical Applications:** Seoul hosted the seventh annual International Conference on Digital Forensics and Cyber Crime, organized by the European Alliance for Innovation (EAI), in October 2015. Those leading the charge in the investigation and prevention of cybercrime include members of the European Association of Investigators (EAI), an international organization founded by a range of corporate, research, and educational entities with the goal of developing cutting-edge Web tools. Government agencies could be able to track foreign intelligence agents and assist law enforcement in their investigations of criminal activity by analyzing the digital dust left inside a device.

In virtually all of these investigations, digital forensics is becoming increasingly important. Law enforcement and major security companies report that the number of cybercrimes is rapidly increasing, drawing in both organized crime and both professional and amateur hackers. According to some sources, in 2011 over 430 million adults across 24 countries fell victim to cybercrime, primarily via hacking and accidentally downloading malware, which is malicious software that infects a computer by introducing viruses, worms, or other pernicious programs. Cybersecurity is predicted to cost more than $120 billion by 2017.

In order to detect and stop cybercrime, the FBI's National Cyber Investigative Joint Task Force (NCIJTF), which was founded in 2008 and is composed of almost two dozen federal intelligence, military, and law enforcement agencies, collaborates covertly with regional law enforcement and the private sector. Additionally, the organization is in charge of over a dozen Regional Computer Forensics Laboratories (RCFLs), which offer digital forensic training and equipment locally. Even though cyber espionage is thought to be the main cyberthreat facing governments and commercial enterprises, victims and investigators can resolve the issue of cyberattack attribution and provide evidence that is admissible in a court of law thanks to digital forensic methodologies. By examining the attack's evidence, digital forensic science is also crucial for profiling cyber threat actors—those who actually carry out threats. It is feasible to identify the techniques, tactics, and procedures (TTPs) used by the main attackers and stop additional attacks by using established and shared techniques.

Digital forensic specialists can help with private security issues or law enforcement by offering vital data or proof. Tracing a person of interest's movements and activities through the use of GPS coordinates stored in their cell phone or other portable device can verify or refute an alibi. Even damaged and deleted files, such as emails, text messages, and images, can frequently be sufficiently reconstructed to access data or metadata thanks to advanced technology.

Digital traces that remain in the memory or hard drive of a computer can reveal details about earlier iterations of a file, such as whether it was originally created on the device under study or was copied over from another locatios also possible to assess hidden metadata, those changes would indicate such as proof of changes made to a device's internal clock.

Regrettably, threat actors are rapidly implementing updated methodologies to be used as forensic cyber analysis countermeasures and new tactics meant to evade digital forensics. These methods most frequently rely on steganography, which is the process of embedding hidden information within an image, video, or other file, and encryption to evade detection and analysis by digital forensic specialists, whose processes they must constantly improve and expand. Both private investigations and criminal law frequently use digital forensics. It has historically been connected to criminal law, wherein evidence is gathered to bolster or refute a theory put forth by the courts.

Similar to other forensic specialties, this one frequently forms a portion of a larger inquiry involving several different academic fields. Sometimes the gathered evidence is used for intelligence gathering outside of court proceedings, such as finding, identifying, or stopping other crimes. Because of this, intelligence collection is occasionally subject to laxer forensic standards. Digital forensics is a procedure used in corporate or civil litigation as part of electronic discovery, or eDiscovery. Although they frequently have different legal restrictions and requirements, forensic procedures resemble those used in criminal investigations. Digital forensics can be used as part of corporate internal investigations conducted outside of court. The act of responding to an unauthorized network intrusion is a typical example. As part of a damage limitation exercise, a forensic specialist investigates the nature and scope of the attack in an effort to determine the extent of any intrusion and to identify the perpetrator. In the 1980s, these attacks were frequently carried out over phone lines; however, in the present day, they are typically spread via the Internet. The primary goal of digital forensics investigations is to locate objective proof of criminal activity, or what lawyers refer to as actuaries. On the other hand, the wide variety of data stored on digital devices can support further research.

8.1.1. History of Digital Forensics

Computer-related crimes were prosecuted under existing laws prior to the 1970s. The 1978 Florida Computer Crimes Act, which forbade the unauthorized alteration or removal of data from a computer system, recognized the first computer crimes.

In the ensuing years, a wider variety of computer crimes were perpetrated, leading to the passage of legislation addressing copyright, privacy/harassment (e.g., child pornography, cyberbullying, happy slapping, cyber stalking, and online predators). The inclusion of computer offenses in federal legislation did not start until the 1980s. In 1983, Canada was the first nation to enact legislation. The US Federal Computer Fraud and Abuse Act of 1986, the British Computer Misuse Act of 1990, and the Australian amendments to their respective crime acts of 1989 came after this (Figure 8.3).

Here, are important landmarks from the history of Digital Forensics:

- Hans Gross (1847–1915): First use of scientific study to head criminal investigations
- FBI (1932): Set up a lab to offer forensics services to all field agents and other law authorities across the USA.
- In 1978 the first computer crime was recognized in the Florida Computer Crime Act.
- Francis Galton (1982–1911): Conducted first recorded study of fingerprints
- In 1992, the term Computer Forensics was used in academic literature.
- 1995 International Organization on Computer Evidence (IOCE) was formed.
- In 2000, the First FBI Regional Computer Forensic Laboratory established.
- In 2002, Scientific Working Group on Digital Evidence (SWGDE) published the first book about digital forensic called "Best practices for Computer Forensics."

- In 2010, Simson Garfinkel identified issues facing digital investigations.

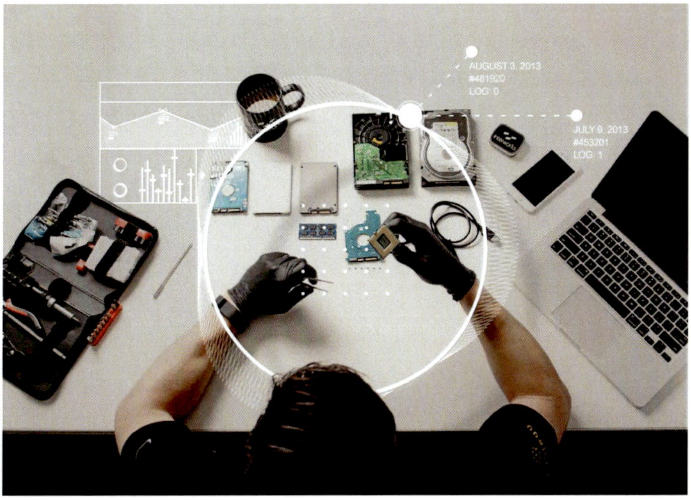

Figure 8.3. *History of digital forensics.*

Source: https://blog.ccasociety.com/how-to-do-packaging-labeling-and-transportation-of-digital-evidence/.

8.1.1.1. 1980s–1990s: Growth of the Field

Law enforcement agencies started creating specialized groups, typically at the national level, to handle the technical aspects of investigations in response to the rise in computer crime during the 1980s and 1990s. For instance, the British Metropolitan Police fraud squad established a computer crime department the following year, while the FBI established a Computer Analysis and Response Team in 1984. Many of the early members of these groups were not only law enforcement professionals but also avid computer users who took on the role of spearheading the field's initial research and direction. Cliff Stoll's 1986 pursuit of hacker Markus Hess was one of the first uses of digital forensics, at least in the public eye. Stoll was not a specialized examiner, even though his investigation used forensic techniques related to computers and networks. This was the pattern followed by many of the first forensic investigations.

Tsignificant demand for these novel and fundamental investigative resources throughout the 1990s. In order toTo help manage the burden on central units, regional and even local level groups are formed. To provide a national infrastructure for computer crime, for instance, the British National Hi-Tech Crime Unit was established in 2001. Its personnel are spread across the various regional police forces as well as a central location in London. In 2006, the unit was merged into the Serious Organized Crime Agency (SOCA). During this time, the impromptu tools and methods created by these hobbyist practitioners gave rise to the field of digital forensics. This is not the case for other forensics specialties, which grew out of scientific research.

The term "computer forensics" was first used in academic literature in 1992, though it had previously been used informally. Collier and Spaul's paper attempted to defend this new field within the forensic science community. Due to the rapid development, training and standards were lacking.

In his book High-Technology Crime: Investigating Computer-Related Cases, published in 1995, K. Rosenblatt stated that the biggest forensic issue facing law enforcement in the 1990s is finding, preserving, and evaluating evidence kept on computers. While most forensic tests, like DNA and fingerprinting, are carried out by highly qualified professionals, patrol officers and detectives are frequently tasked with gathering and examining computer evidence.

8.1.1.2. 2000s: Developing Standards

Since 2000, a number of organizations and agencies have released guidelines for digital forensics in response to the need for standardization. Best practices for Computer Forensics, a 2002 paper from the Scientific Working Group on Digital Evidence (SWGDE), was followed in 2005 by the release of an ISO standard (ISO 17025, General requirements for the competence of testing and calibration laboratories).

The Convention on Cybercrime, an international treaty led by Europe, was put into effect in 2004 with the intention of balancing national computer crime laws, investigative methods, and international cooperation. 43 countries—including the US, Canada, Japan, South Africa, the UK, and other European countries—have signed the treaty, and 16 countries have ratified it. There was also discussion about training.

Commercial organizations (typically forensic software developers) started to offer certification courses, and the UK's Centrex, a specialist investigator training facility, added digital forensic analysis to its list of topics. The late 1990s saw the widespread availability of mobile devices, which went beyond basic communication tools and were discovered to be rich information sources, even for crimes not typically linked to digital forensics. Despite this, issues with proprietary devices have caused digital analysis of phones to lag behind traditional computer media.Focus has also shifted onto internet crime, particularly the risk of cyber warfare and cyberterrorism. A February 2010 report by the United States Joint Forces Command concluded the following:

- Through cyberspace, enemies will target industry, academia, government, as well as the military in the air, land, maritime, and space domains. In much the same way that airpower transformed the battlefield of World War II, cyberspace has fractured the physical barriers that shield a nation from attacks on its commerce and communication.

Digital forensics is still plagued by unsolved problems. A bias towards Windows operating systems in digital forensics research was noted in a 2009 paper by Peterson and Shenoi titled Digital Forensic Research: The Good, the Bad, and the Unaddressed. In 2010, Simson Garfinkel outlined the problems that digital investigations would face in the future. These problems included the growing volume of digital media, the widespread accessibility of encryption to consumers, the expansion of operating systems and file formats, the rise in the number of people who own multiple devices, and the legal restrictions placed on investigators. The unaffordably high costering the field and ongoing training issues were also noted in the paper.

8.1.1.3. Development of Forensic Tools

There weren'twere not many specialized digital forensic tools available in the 1980s. As a result, investigators frequently conducted live analysis on media, looking through computers from within the operating system and extracting evidence with the help of pre-existing sysadmin tools. This procedure increased the possibility of accidentally or intentionally altering data on the disk, which could give rise to accusations of tampering with evidence. To solve the issue, several tools were developed in the early 1990s. The Federal Law Enforcement Training Center initially identified the need for such software in 1989, which led to the development of IMDUMP (by Michael White) and SafeBack (by Sydex) in 1990. Other nations also produced software of a similar nature; in 1991, the UK commercially released DIBS, a hardware and software solution, and Rob McKemmish gave Australian law enforcement free access to Fixed age. Examiners could produce an identical duplicate of a digital media file using these tools, keeping the original disk in tactintact for validation. As the need for digital evidence increased by the end of the 1990s, more sophisticated commercial tools like EnCase and FTK were created, enabling analysts to examine media copies without the need for live forensics.

8.1.2. Evidence Exchange

Any investigation's primary objectives are to track the tracks criminals leave behind after committing a crime and connect them to the victims and crime scenes. Even though witnesses might be able to identify a suspect, concrete proof of a person's involvement is typically more convincing and trustworthy. In order to find strong connections between the perpetrator, victim, and crime scene, forensic analysts are used.

In principle, there will be an exchange when two items come into contact. This rule applies to all interactions that take place at a crime scene, such as those involving a weapon, victims, and the crime scene itself. In summary, there will always be evidence of the interaction, even though it might not always be obvious (keep in mind that the lack of evidence does not imply its absence). As shown in Figure 8.4, this transfer takes place in both the digital and physical domains and can create connections between them. In the real world, an offender may unintentionally remove a fiber from the scene and leave their hair or fingerprints behind. For example, in a homicide case, the perpetrator might try to lead investigators astray by leaving fingerprints on the victim's computer while writing a suicide note. Investigators can prove that there is a good chance the criminal was present at the crime scene with the help of one such piece of evidence. The connection between the criminal and the crime scene is strengthened and made easier to prove when there are two pieces of evidence. Digital evidence adds a digital dimension to the investigation by revealing online activities during critical periods, communications between suspects and the victim, and other details.

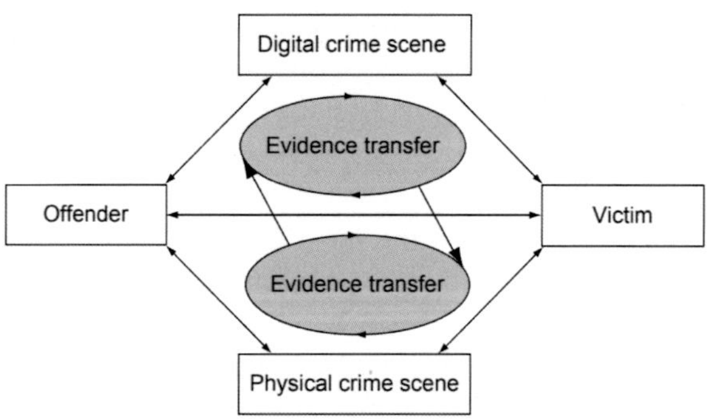

Figure 8.4. *Evidence transfer in the physical and digital dimensions helps investigators establish connections between victims, offenders, and crime scenes.*

Source: https://encrypted-tbn0.gstatic.com/images?q=tbn:ANd9GcSLUwaHc5KtLMOxyCSI7a-0uvpnFmbawrXWIA&s.

The attackers in a computer intrusion will leave behind various signs of their presence in the system, such as registry entries, file systems, system logs, and network-level logs. Also, the attackers might take items from the crime scene with them, like user passwords they stole or personally identifiable information stored in a file or database. Such proof may be helpful in connecting a specific person to an intrusion. Sending threatening emails using a web-based email service like Hotmail can leave a lot of evidence in an email harassment case.

Together with date-and-time-related data, the Web browser used to send messages will save files, links, and other data on the sender's hard drive. As a result, the offender's hard drive may contain a wealth of information about the sent message, including the original message contents, according to forensic analysts. Furthermore, investigators might be able to get relevant data from Hotmail, such as IP addresses, Web server access logs, and maybe the full message in the offender's email account's sent mail folder.

8.1.3. Forensic Soundness

Digital evidence needs to be preserved and analyzed in a way that adheres to forensic best practices in order to be helpful in an investigation. According to some digital forensics professionals, a technique for maintaining or analyzing digital evidence is only valid from a forensic standpoint if it doesn't modify the original source of evidence in any way. This is just untrue. Conventional forensic fields like DNA analysis demonstrate that maintaining the original is not necessary for determining forensic soundness. The process of gathering biological material samples typically smears or scrapes the original evidence. Since DNA testing is destructive, forensic analysis of the evidentiary sample modifies the sample even more. DNA evidence is frequently admitted as evidence, and these procedures are regarded as forensically sound despite the alterations that take place during preservation and processing.

Even with a hardware write-blocker, the routine task of extracting data from a hard drive in digital forensics modifies the hard drive's initial state. These changes may involve updating data kept by Self-Monitoring, Analysis, and Reporting Technology (S.) or opening a hidden section of the hard drive, (M.A.R.T.) on contemporary hard disks. The majority of techniques for retrieving memory contents from active computer systems and mobile devices also modify or erase memory, although this is a widely recognized standard in the field of digital forensics.

Digital investigators must actually preserve data on live systems because courts are beginning to order the preservation of volatile computer data in certain cases. In the Indian Columbia Pictures. v. Bunnell, It is risky to apply an unwavering standard that says to "preserve everything but change nothing" in a legal setting in addition to being incompatible with other forensic disciplines. It may not always be possible to comply with such a standard, so declaring it to be the "best practice" and using digital evidence to support this claim only exposes it to criticisms unrelated to the problems being looked into. Documentation is one of the cornerstones of forensic soundness.

Supporting documentation that details the origins of the evidence and its handling forms the foundation of a strong case. From a forensic perspective, the acquisition procedure ought to minimize any alteration to the original evidence, and any modifications ought to be recorded and evaluated in light of the analysis's conclusions. It is usually regarded as forensically sound as long as the acquisition process maintains a full and accurate representation of the original data and its authenticity and integrity can be verified. Digital investigators must record the date and time of volatile data preservation, the tools utilized, and the MD5 hash value of each output when preserving data. When working with computers, it's imperative to record the computer's date and time and contrast it with a trustworthy time source.

8.1.4. Authentication

Digital evidence authentication, but it's critical to start with a fundamental comprehension of this idea. Although the idea is more nuanced, some texts on digital forensics state that authentication is the process of making sure the evidence that has been recovered is identical to the data that was originally seized. Comparing the acquired data with the original is not always feasible from a technical perspective. A computer that is operating constantly has different contents in its RAM. The contents of captured memory are merely a moment in time of the computer's operating state, and the copy cannot be compared to the original. In a similar vein, network traffic is fleeting and needs to be recorded while it is moving. After network traffic is captured, the original data is no longer available for comparison—only copies remain. Authentication is the process of evaluating the admissibility of evidence from a legal perspective (Figure 8.5).

Figure 8.5. *Authentication of digital evidence.*

https://www.loginradius.com/blog/static/6d170d83a7074847494831a6df861d3c/d3746/cover-auth.jpg.

8.1.5. Types of Digital Forensics

Types of digital forensics are:

8.1.5.1. Disk Forensics

The recovery, examination, and preservation of data from computer storage devices, such as hard drives, solid-state drives, and external storage media, are the focus of the specialized field of disk forensics within digital forensics. Disk forensics' main goal is to retrieve, analyze, and interpret data in a way that makes it admissible in court—often in connection with criminal investigations or legal prongs.

The first step in the procedure is to create a forensic image, which is a bit-by-bit copy of the storage device. This copy guarantees that the data won'twill not change while being analyzed by maintaining the precise condition of the original disk. To produce these images and carry out preliminary analyses, programs like EnCase, FTK Imager, and X1 are frequently utilized. After that, the forensic image is examined to find any pertinent evidence, which might include hidden partitions, system logs, or erased files. Expert methods like file carving are used to recover data that has been intentionally destroyed or erased. File carving is the process of reconstructing files from data fragments.

Examining file systems is another aspect of disk forensics that is essential to comprehending the arrangement and storage of data on a disk. Experts in forensics examine metadata, including file attributes and timestamps, to reconstruct a timeline of system events and user behavior. This can be essential for establishing a timeline or confirming statements made by subjects of an inquiry.

Disk forensics also entails finding and examining usage-related artifacts on the system, like temporary files, registry entries, and browser histories. These artifacts can reveal information about software usage, user behavior, and possibly malicious activity. Network forensics, which examines data pertaining to network activity to comprehend the larger context of the disk findings, is frequently used in conjunction with analysis.

Making sure the evidence is kept safe and handled in compliance with legal and procedural requirements is a major challenge in disk forensics.

This entails upholding the chain of custody, recording every stage of the procedure, and guaranteeing the reproducibility and verifiability of the results. Experts in forensics also need to stay up to date on new developments in encryption and technology, as these can affect the accessibility and interpretation of data. Disk forensics, which offers a thorough and systematic method for locating digital evidence, is essential to contemporary investigations. Its importance in the digital age is highlighted by the range of applications it has in criminal justice, corporate security, and civil litigation.

8.1.5.2. Network Forensics

The analysis of network traffic for the purpose of gathering data for both legal and internal investigations is known as network forensics. Network forensics is a tool for intrusion detection and interception used for system security in addition to being used for investigations. Many methods exist for intercepting data, utilizing different devices to either gather all data passing through a network or pinpoint specific data packets for additional analysis. Accurate and efficient forensic analysis of a network requires computers with fast processing speeds and large amounts of storage. Interest in network forensics grew as computer systems migrated more and more toward networks in the 1990s and home Internet became widely available in many communities. As a result, a large number of businesses started producing goods and providing services in the network forensics sector. These tools are used by law enforcement, security firms, internet service providers, and information technology personnel for security purposes in locations handling private data. In network forensics, information is recorded and examined as it flows through a network. Analysts search for any odd or suspicious activity and are able to pinpoint specific computers or individuals to look into further. In the case of law enforcement, investigations may be carried out in order to obtain information that will be presented in court. Network forensics can be used by internal investigations to find the origins of data leaks and possible security flaws in a system. Network forensics-based intrusion detection can be a component of an organization's security plan. Automated systems search for unusual activity and notify security staff. In certain situations, these systems may also automatically take action to prevent access to private data or to remove users from the network entirely. This proactive security strategy enables computer networks and systems to react to threats in real time. In the 2000s, governments began to press for greater access to computer networks so that data could be accessed and analyzed. Some law enforcement agencies promoted the development of wire-tap compliant devices and systems in order to use network forensics to identify potential security threats, which could include anything from terrorist activity over computer networks to evidence of criminal activity. In the 1990s, criminals began using the Internet to plan offline activities and launch network attacks. As a result, many governments felt helpless to respond or censor information in the absence of a comprehensive framework for information interception.

8.1.5.3. *Wireless Forensics*

A branch of network forensics is called wireless forensics. Providing the methodology and instruments necessary to gather and examine (wireless) network traffic that can be admitted as genuine digital evidence in a court of law is the primary objective of wireless forensics. The evidence gathered may be in the form of unstructured data or, given the widespread use of Voice-over-IP (VoIP) technologies, particularly wirelessly, voice conversations.

8.1.5.4. *Database Forensics*

A subfield of digital forensic science called database forensics studies databases and the metadata that goes along with them. The field follows the standard forensic procedure and applies investigative techniques to database contents and metadata, much like computer forensics. A server's RAM may also contain cached data, necessitating the use of real-time analysis methods. In order to confirm the actions of a database user, a forensic examination of a database may pertain to the timestamps that correspond to the update time of a row in a relational table that is being examined and validated. As an alternative, a forensic investigation might concentrate on finding transactions in a database system or application that point to evidence of fraud or other wrongdoing. Data can be manipulated and analyzed using software tools. Additionally, these tools have audit logging features that offer documented evidence of the tasks or analysis a forensic examiner completed on the database.

8.1.5.5. *Malware Forensics*

Malware forensics has become more and more important as the cybercrime community destroys technology, financial institutions, and retail. Governmental and private organizations are both vulnerable to cybercrime, and malware is a common tool used by cybercriminals to infect devices with Trojan horses, worms, and botnets.

Organizations handling sensitive data must react quickly and accurately to malware in order to protect client and company information.

There are different types of malware that cybercriminal uses to infect user and get credential and access to critical and valuable information. The list of Malware types focuses on the most common and the general categories of infection which include:

- **Adware:** The slightest dangerous and most beneficial Malware for attackers regarding redirecting the user to the desired Adware shows ads on your computer.

- **Spyware:** Spyware is software that aims to gather information about a person or organization without their knowledge or that asserts control over a device without the consumer's knowledge.
- **Virus:** A virus is an infectious program or code that appends itself to a different piece of software, and then utilizes system's resources each time the software is executed.
- **Worm:** A program that replicates itself to spread to other computers and wipes out data and files on the computer. Worms destroy the operating system's files and data files until the drive is empty.
- **Trojan:** It is the most hazardous Malware that creates a backdoor on your computer that gives malicious users access to your system, possibly allowing confidential or personal information to be compromised.
- **Rootkit:** Rootkits allow viruses and malware to "hide in plain sight" by disguising as necessary files that your antivirus software will overlook. It is the hardest to detect Malware and therefore to remove.
- **Backdoors:** Backdoors are much the same as Trojans or worms, apart from that they open a "backdoor" onto a computer, providing a network connection for hackers or other Malware to penetrate or send more viruses.
- **Keyloggers:** Records everything you type on your PC to glean your log-in names, passwords, and other sensitive information, and send it on to the source of the keylogging program.
- **Browser Hijacker:** This dangerous Malware will redirect your regular search activity and give you the results the developers want you to see. It intends to make money off your web surfing.
- **Ransomware:** It is the most brutal type of malware that is the most effective in harming victim's data and for financial gain. Ransomware is a sort of noxious programming from cryptovirology that threatens to distribute/publish the victim's data or block access to it unless a ransom is paid. Some of the most critical and famous ransomware includes Golden Eye, Crypto Locker, Wanna Cry, Locky, Petya, Crysis, HydraCrypt, etc.

8.1.5.6. Email Forensics

Deals with recovery and analysis of emails, including deleted emails, calendars, and contacts.

1. **Email Header Analysis:** Important information can be found in email headers, such as the sender and recipient's names, the servers

and other devices the message traveled through, etc. The highlighted email header fields are some of the most crucial ones. Email investigators and forensics specialists can benefit from the crucial information found in email headers.

For example, the recipient's email address is contained in the Delivered-To field, and the IP address, SMTP ID, and time and date of the email's receipt are contained in the Received-By field. Similarly, important information like the sender's IP address and host name may be provided in the Received: from field. This kind of information can be very helpful in locating the offender and gathering proof.

2. **Email Server Investigation:** Email servers are examined to determine an email's origin. Since email servers typically save copies of messages after delivery, they are scanned if an email is removed from a client application, sender's, or recipient's. Additionally, servers keep logs that can be examined to determine the computer address from which an email originated.

   It is important to remember that big ISPs regularly archive their HTTP and SMTP (common messaging initiation protocol) logs. Tracing pertinent emails from an archived log can be very time-consuming and complex, requiring methods for extraction and decompression. In order to avoid having the logs archived, it is best to review them as soon as possible.

3. **Investigation of Network Devices:** Server logs are occasionally unavailable. This can occur for a variety of reasons, including servers that aren't set up to keep logs or ISPs that won't share the log files. When this happens, investigators can track down the email message's origin by looking through the logs kept by network equipment like switches, firewalls, and routers.

4. **Sender Mailer Fingerprints:** Email headers called X-headers are appended to messages in addition to the standard headers, such as Subject and To. These are frequently added to provide authentication results, spam filter information, etc., and can be used to determine which program—Outlook or Opera Mail, for example—is managing the client's email. The original sender, i.e., can be located using the X-originating-IP header. e. computer's IP address that sent the message.

5. **Software Embedded Identifiers:** Email software used by the sender may occasionally contain extra information about the message and any attachments. It appears as a custom header or Transport Neutral

Encapsulation Format (TNEF) in MIME content. A thorough examination of these can provide important information about the sender, including PST file names, MAC addresses, and Windows logon usernames.

6. **Bait Tactics:** Bait tactic is an email investigation technique that's used when the location of a suspect or cybercriminal is unknown. In this, the investigators send an email that contains a *http: "<img src>"* tag to the suspect. The image source is at a computer that's monitored by the investigators. When the suspect opens the email, the computer's IP address is registered in a log entry on the HTTP server that hosts the image. The investigators can use the IP address to track the suspect.

   Sometimes, suspects take precautionary measures like using a proxy server to protect their identity. In that case, the IP address of the proxy server is recorded. However, the log on the proxy server can be analyzed to track the suspect. If the log isn't available either, then the investors can send an email that contains either of the following:

- HTML page with an Active X Object
- Embedded Java Applet that's configured to run on the recipient's computer

8.1.6. Developing Digital Forensics Resources

You need to be knowledgeable about multiple computing platforms in order to be a successful digital forensics investigator. You should be conversant with Macintosh, Linux, and the most recent versions of Windows in addition to more antiquated ones like DOS, Windows 9x, and Windows XP. But nobody can be an authority on every facet of computing. Similarly, you are unable to be an expert on every aspect of the technology you are researching. You should establish and keep in touch with experts in computing, networking, and investigation to augment your knowledge. Participate in public and private computer user groups.

For instance, the Computer Technology Investigators Network (CTIN) in the Pacific Northwest convenes to deliberate on issues that digital forensics examiners face. Additionally, this nonprofit organization offers training. IACIS is a great organization for law enforcement professionals, but it isn't local. In most major cities, professionals can access local chapters of organizations like the International Information Systems Security Certification Consortium (ISC), Infra Gard, and the High Technology Crime Investigation Association. Create your own network of knowledgeable people in digital forensics and stay in contact via email. Build professional connections with individuals who have different areas of expertise than you. For example, if you are an expert on Windows, stay in touch with experts on Linux, UNIX, and Macintosh. When interacting with experts on social media, use caution and sound judgment when corresponding with individuals you haven't met in person or whose backgrounds you are unfamiliar with.

User groups are especially useful if you're looking for information on rare operating systems. For instance, in Pierce County, Washington, in 1996, a user group assisted in the conviction of a child molester. The accused put cameras all over his home, gave young ladies alcohol to get them tipsy, and then surreptitiously recorded them while they played strip poker. His computers and other tangible evidence were taken by the police after he was charged with child molestation. The computers were running Coco DOS, an operating system that had been discontinued years earlier, the investigator found. After reaching out to a local user group, the investigator received the standard commands and additional details required to gain access to the system. The investigator discovered a diary on the suspect's computer that described his actions over a 15-year period, including the molestation of over 400 young women. The suspect was consequently given a lengthier sentence than he would have if he had only been found guilty of abusing one child (Figure 8.6).

Figure 8.6. *Developing digital forensics resources.*

Source: https://cisomag.com/wp-content/uploads/2021/07/digital-forensics-640x414.png.

You can also get the specific information you need to recover digital evidence from outside specialists. For instance, a husband and wife who ran a Macintosh store were the subject of a recent murder case. Investigators discovered that the wife had wanted to leave her husband but had refrained due to her religious beliefs. She was found dead, seemingly murdered. With a search warrant in hand, the police seized the computers from the home and workplace. Upon examining the home system, the case detective discovered that the hard drive had been compressed and erased. After reaching out to a Macintosh engineer, he discovered the two software applications that were utilized to compress the disk. With this information, the detective was able to recover data from the hard drive, including text files showing that the husband had used $35,000 of company funds to pay for prostitution services and cocaine. The husband's murder conviction was made possible in large part by this evidence.

8.2. DIGITAL FORENSIC INVESTIGATION MODELS

The majority of largs rely significantly on the use of technology in both operations and other business areas. Because of our growing reliance on and use of technology, there is a greater chance that cybercrime will occur. In order toTo mitigate this risk, companies that specialize in digital forensic investigation offer support in carrying out forensic analysis following the commission of any cybercrime. To increase the effectiveness of this investigation, the forensic investigation process has also evolved over time and been divided into several phases. Each stage affects the investigation process differently.

Since information technology was introduced to the business world, all IT-related organizations have begun to reap its benefits. This is accomplished by gaining a competitive edge over other market players, by offering new features to clients following the integration of technology, particularly in the operational domain, by boosting operational velocity and lowering the likelihood of any operational error. IT helps senior management with decision-making as well.

There are, as we all know, always opportunities for advancement and progress toward perfection in every aspect of life, and in the same way, information technology, which is becoming an indispensable component of today's business world, has few gaps. Aside from the entire physical infrastructure, which includes buildings, machinery, and human resources, etc. Information, which is closely related to the organization, has emerged as one of the most valuable resources for any company using IT in its operations. It serves as a platform for connecting with other partners in the business world in addition to supporting IT operations.

Since information technology heavily depends on and operates with information, it is crucial to protect that information by making sure that no unauthorized person can access it and that its integrity and confidentiality are maintained. Make sure that the data is timely made available for related operations, and protect these from various threats. g. For the technical staff in their company, phishing is an essential task.

Even though businesses are investing in launching, updating, and securing the security of their technology-related infrastructure and operations, there is still a risk of cybercrimes, which could not only take advantage of data breaches but also ruin their entire company or have a significant impact. The biggest threat of this kind comes from insider threats, who are always looking for the perfect opportunity to commit cybercrime in order to further their illegal goals.

Threat identification thus becomes a critical component that must be watched over and managed. Along with an annual external audit, many organizations have begun hiring digital forensic firms to deal with these types of criminals. To offer their clients or organizations a comprehensive solution to their cybercrime-affected scenarios, these digital forensic firms consist of both forensic experts and technical personnel. Since these companies don't have any affiliations or connections to insiders in any organizations, the investigations conducted on their behalf continue to be reliable.

Depending on the target organization and the kind or extent of the loss caused by the cybercrime, various models are used by forensic firms.

These models are based on distinct phases that each have their own set of steps to collect important and potent evidence against the offender. These phases also carry out legal and time constraints in linear course control and forensic administration throughout the entire forensic process. In addition, forensic companies make sure that the evidence they produce complies with all national and organizational legal requirements.

This allows the evidence to be admitted into court if it is necessary to present it there. The many models of digital forensic investigations have been developed year after year and their phases have been explained in accordance with the order in which they occur. This has demonstrated how digital forensic investigation has developed globally and how important it is to various business industries. Every model that has been described has the same main goal.

In addition to the roles and methodologies employed by digital forensic companies, we have also outlined a number of addressable components in various Pakistani organizational types with the aim of facilitating and supporting the companies in their efforts to obtain relevant evidence when needed. If these factors are appropriately taken care of, forensic companies may have an increasing number of options when it comes to selecting the best platform for gathering the most evidence possible from the crime scene.

8.2.1. Forensic Models

In the field of information technology, particularly in the corporate business sector, people working in digital forensics began putting up effort to address the audit and research challenges related to digital forensics of the organizations as much as they could. Organizations began investing in this area after realizing the profound impact it could have on their business and economy, which was partly attributed to their appreciation of the field's importance in IT governance.

Because most businesses are unaware of corporate forensic, they are seen squandering valuable time, energy, and resources on digital forensic investigations. It is advised by experts that the process of digital forensic investigations be carried out by professionals with complete objectivity in order to establish their credibility and establish a negative reputation for the organizations where the investigation will take place.

There is still uncertainty surrounding the internal investigator's ability to conduct forensic investigations, and the evidence gathered through internal channels may not have the necessary impact to identify any of the parties involved in a criminal case. The various models that were introduced in various years with the intention of giving digital forensic investigation companies guidelines. Each model is broken down into distinct steps, and these steps continued to grow over time as the significance of the digital forensic investigation process was recognized.

8.2.2. Forensic Process

A digital forensic investigation commonly consists of 3 stages:

1. acq imaging of exhibits;
2. analysis; and
3. Reporting.

A picture of the computer's volatile memory (RAM) is typically not taken during acquisition unless it is required for an incident response investigation. In order toTo avoid altering the original, the task usually entails making an exact sector level duplicate, also known as a forensic duplicate, of the media. This is frequently accomplished by using a write blocking device. However, the use of "live" acquisitions—in which a "logical" copy of the data is acquired rather than an entire image of the physical storage device—has increased due to the growth in size of storage media and technological advancements like cloud computing. To ensure the accuracy of the copy, the original media or data and the acquired image (or logical copy) are hashed (using an algorithm like SHA-1 or MD5) and the values are compared.

Digital forensics and eDiscovery procedures are combined in an alternate (and patented) method known as "hybrid forensics" or "distributed forensics." This method was implemented in a commercial tool named ISEEK, which was showcased at a conference in 2017 along with test findings. An investigator gathers evidence during the analysis phase by employing various techniques and instruments. This step is known as an extensive, methodical search of the evidence linked to the suspected crime, according to a 2002 International Journal of Digital Evidence article.

Forensics researcher Brian Carrier outlined a logical process in 2006; after identifying clear evidence, thorough searches are carried out to begin filling in the blanks. The actual analysis process can differ depending on the investigation, but common approaches include recovering deleted files, extracting registry information (for instance, to list user accounts or attached USB devices), and performing keyword searches across digital media (within files as well as unallocated and slack space). In order to reconstruct events or actions and draw conclusions, the recovered evidence is analyzed—work that is frequently capable of being completed by less skilled personnel. Once an investigation is finished, the data is presented in plain language, typically as a written report.

8.2.3. Attribution

Meta data and other logs can be used to attribute actions to an individual. For example, personal documents on a computer drive might identify its owner.

- **Alibis and Statements:** Information provided by those involved can be cross checked with digital evidence. For example, during the investigation into the Soham murders the offender's alibi was disproved when mobile phone records of the person he claimed to be with showed she was out of town at the time.
- **Intent:** As well as finding objective evidence of a crime being committed, investigations can also be used to prove the intent (known by the legal term mens rea). For example, the Internet history of convicted killer Neil Entwistle included references to a site discussing *How to kill people*.
- **Evaluation of Source:** A specific piece of data can be traced back to its original source using file artifacts and meta-data. For instance, in previous iterations of Microsoft Word, files contained a Global Unique Identifier that identified the machine on which they were created. Demonstrating whether a file was created on the analyzed digital device or if it was downloaded from another source (e.g., the Internet) can have a significant impact.

- **Document Authentication:** Related to "Evaluation of source," meta data associated with digital documents can be easily modified (for example, by changing the computer clock you can affect the creation date of a file). Document authentication relates to detecting and identifying falsification of such details.
- **Limitations:** The use of encryption is one of the main drawbacks to forensic investigations; it interferes with the preliminary keyword search process that may be used to locate relevant evidence. Legislation requiring people to reveal their encryption keys is still comparatively new and contentious. However, there are always more often ways to get around encryption or brute force passwords. For example, on PCs or smartphones, bootloader techniques can be used to obtain the device's content first, then force it to reveal the password or encryption key. An estimated 60% of cases involving encrypted devices are thought to go unprocessed due to the inability to obtain possible evidence.

8.3. RESEARCH METHODOLOGY IN DIGITAL FORENSICS

The questionnaire-based survey research methodology was used in this study because it yields objective feedback of various kinds.

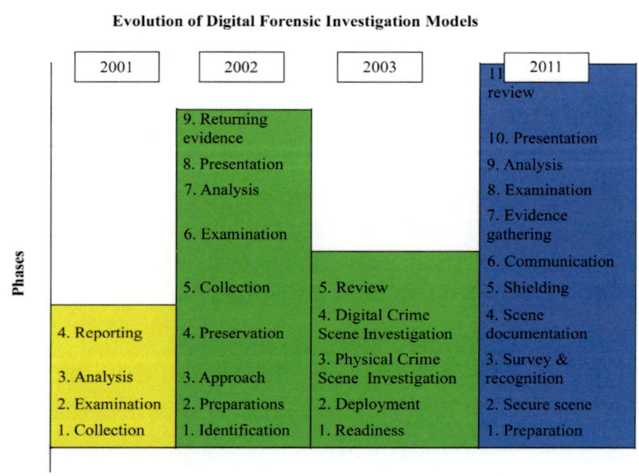

Figure 8.7. *Forensic models.*

Source: https://minio.scielo.br/documentstore/1807–1775/QvqXxDdsP3H73f9WQZFcnTq/781ff4e3cdca30daa65f8f8986a75efc10d568ba.jpg.

Once information is gathered, a valuable analysis addressing a specific topic of interest can be produced. This analysis uld become significant for future decision making in that particular field. A digital forensics-related questionnaire comprising 72 items was created and disseminated among 80 distinct categories of sizable businesses. T. We learned a great deal from the feedback regarding the state of technology and other matters pertaining to the forensic investigation process in these organizations. Later, this collected data was examined from several angles to conduct a critical analysis and identify the elements that large businesses could address in this regard (Figure 8.7).

In 2001, the first digital forensic model was unveiled. This project's originator was Ashcroft, a member of the U.S. National Institute of Justice, S. This model included the electronic crime scene investigation process and served as a manual for responders who were very inexperienced with it. Subsequently, the law enforcement and other agencies used this model as well to identify and secure digital evidence.

The gathering of evidence following a careful search of the area surrounding the crime scene is the focus of the first (of four) phases of this model. The examination process for the second phase involved assembling the transparent evidence gathered from the first phase and determining its source. The analysis of the examination phase's results is done in the third phase. Following the analysis, the final step consists of summarizing and reporting the findings from each of the earlier stages as well as the data gathered during the entire process.

The only limitation of this model, though, is not fully explained and is still unclear. Carr, Reith, and Gunsch attempted to further elucidate the 2001 model of digital forensic investigation in 2002 by incorporating a few more stages into the procedure. In order toTo simplify, they integrated the conventional method of gathering evidence into this model.

The first stage of this model identifies the incident that has occurred, what kind it is, and offers all the support needed to accomplish this phase's objective. The second step involves preparing for the techniques and processes that will be applied in the remaining stages of this forensic model. It also provides guidance on how to prepare various search warrants in case they are needed to obtain evidence. The third stage involves creating suitable methods and procedures that will be used in the evidence-gathering phase five.

Preserving every part and gadget that might hold pertinent evidence is the fourth stage of preservation. Following the acquisition of evidence comprising devices and components, the fifth phase of collection is employed to standardize the protocols for documenting the actual scene. The sixth stage is examination, which deals with identifying the pertinent suspect in the perpetrated crime.

Analyzing the significance of the items that have undergone inspection is the seventh phase. The phase that follows the analysis phase is the presentation of all the phases involved in this model.

The process of returning the devices and sources of digital evidence to their rightful owners follows the completion of the forensic investigation. This is the ninth and final phase. The fact that the third phase is somewhat similar to the second phase is the only weakness or area for improvement in this phase that has been found. Digital forensic investigators Spafford and Carrier introduced the third model in 2003. The Integrated Digital Investigation Process model was created and is now used as an additional set of guidelines by forensic examiners to conduct digital forensic investigations and collect relevant evidence.

This model underwent five phases of resizing once more. The first phase, referred to as the readiness phase, had as its goal making sure that the infrastructure and actions in place were sufficient to support and facilitate the investigation process. As a result, the purpose of this phase is limited to preparation for the subsequent stages of the investigation. The forensic examiners receive a system in the second phase of deployment, which enables them to identify an incident and subsequently validate it.

The third stage involves collecting and analyzing tangible evidence from the crime scene and closely observing the actions that were connected to the incident as it happened. The fourth phase is a follow-up to the third and focuses on reviewing and compiling digital evidence that was gathered during the physical crime scene investigation phase. The third phase of this model is comparable to the remaining process used in phase. The fifth and final step of the digital forensic investigation process involves reviewing all of the analysis completed in the earlier stages and emphasizing any areas that still require improvement. The deployment phase of this model deals with the certification of the occurred incident; however, it is practically impossible to endorse the digital crime before appropriate investigation, which is why it is not the most widely used and recognized model for digital forensic investigation.

A Ciardhuain proposed a model for digital forensic investigation in 2004, but it lacked clear phases and guidelines, making it less recognizable and useful than earlier models. Comparably, Ruibin Yun and Perusal presented their models for research and evidence gathering in 2005 and 2009, respectively, but they lacked a clear and comprehensive description of their methodology and failed to divide their models into distinct stages.

As a result, these models were also unable to receive the recognition and credit that they deserved. The investigation process model, which evolved into the most recent guideline, has the most comprehensive phase descriptions and entire process into distinct phases. The investigation process was carried out through 11 phases of this model, which was named the Systematic Digital Forensic Investigation Model (SRDHM).

As it must be in the early stagespreliminary stages of an investigation process, the first phase of this model was preparatory. During this stage, the forensic investigator learns what kind of crime was committed and what activities were connected to it at the time of its occurrence. The examiner then makes plans regarding the material gathered in order to pack the evidence sources. During this stage, the examiner may also obtain the appropriate search warrants, obtain various authorizations from upper management with their full support, and send legal notices to all relevant parties or segments connected to the crime that was committed.

Creating a suitable policy that will be followed during the investigation is another essential task completed in this phase. In order to maintain the f all the devices and evidence at the crime scene, the second crucial stage is to secure the crime scene. At any point during the investigation, these gadgets could turn out to be the primary sources of evidence. In order toTo prevent unauthorized individuals from accessing these devices once the investigation process has begun, the examiner makes sure of this. At this stage, the evidence's quality is also determined.

However, maintaining the integrity of the crime scene and its infrastructure is the primary focus of this phase. Following the successful completion of the first two phases, the examiner conducts an initial survey at the crime scene with the goal of determining the sources of evidence and developing a plan for where to look for evidence. In order to handle the crime scene during the examination of electronic devices, the examiner may also need assistance from other specialists. Another preliminary function of this phase is interviewing the pertinent individuals following identification.

Asking the various users, administrators, or even the owners of the devices can yield important and efficient information gathering that can lead to the production of important evidence for analysis. The examiner should plan how to evaluate the evidence in later stages of the process at various phases after gathering and developing it during this phase. Another crucial step in this investigation process model is documenting the entire scene. It involves recording every visible piece of information that has been gathered, such as various photos, etc. Reviewing the entire process at any point could be beneficial. The date and time of every entry and departure from the crime scene must be noted in all logs and records. The examiner enumerates all potential communication channels for the connected devices in the fifth phase of the current model and disables these channels so that information cannot be changed, updated, erased, or overwritten once the examination process has begun. One way to achieve this would be to fully isolate these devices from any other linked devices. Gathering the evidence is the sixth phase, and it may be the most crucial of all.

This is the main goal of the entire investigation model, including all of its stages. This stage necessitates careful thought and attention to detail in order to create the best possible system for gathering the needed evidence, which could then be presented in court and granted admissibility in order to identify the guilty party.This phase involves the expert forensic examiners reviewing the evidence that has been successfully packaged and transported.

Following this stage, the team of experts examines the evidence, defining the connections between various data segments, revealing the data that was concealed, and ultimately providing the outcomes of every stage of the entire forensic model. Following the effectction and analysis of the evidence by the forensic specialists, the evidence must be produced before any authority, including a court of law or the higher management of the targeted organization.

As a result, these evidencesevidence must be provided in a way that makes it abundantly evident that the individual identified as the culprit is, in fact, the culprit, and that all of the evidences offered bolster this assertion. The last step in this model is reviewing the outcome. Every action taken in the earlier stages is carefully examined and evaluated. One can learn a lot and identify areas for improvement by going over each step one by one. Examiners may find it easier to apply these lessons in the upcoming investigations.

8.3.1. Findings

- In our findings of current, we have highlighted the different important security elements that need to be addressed by enterprises of Pakistan as effectively and appropriately that it assists the digital forensic examination process towards collecting the evidences and establishing the actual culprit behind the committed cybercrime.
- Every element highlighted here is equally importance as it possesses capability to provide evidence or hint or even provides the path the reach out the oe and then prove in the court of Law as legitimized matter.
- Only 55% of recipients are fully aware about the Domain of Cyber Forensics. It means that 45% organizations have employed the I.T persons who are considered to beare most responsible and considered as reliable I.T person don't even know anything about the Domain of Cyber Forensics, it is really alarming addressable too.

- 58% organizations don't have a formal, institutional plan that outlines Digital Forensics for the institution as a whole. It means that if any situation arises to conduct a Digital Forensic InvestigationsInvestigations, then the employees may deny any responsibility since this is not addressed by the institutional plan at all.
- 50% of the organizations may collapse by single incident in the absence of Cyber Forensic Policy and procedure. It shows the significance of this domain needs to be addressed at enterprise level and also reveals the flaws in the I.T security level in these organizations.
- 79% of organizations don't even acquire the service of cyber forensic firms.
- 46% of organizations' I.T operations is being spoiled mostly affected by cybercrime.
- 51% or organizations don't conduct any awareness training programs for employees to educate them about cybercrime and forensics. It is quite shocking situation because if we don't educate our employees to face any such situation or avoid or prevent it, then how may we expect that our security measure are up to the mark.
- 47% enterprises don't contain any clause addressing the cybercrime in their hiring terms and conditions document. It needs to be addressed to ensure the function of accountability against the employees.
- % organizations don't employ any tool to record the key strokes of client. It eliminates another effective element of collecting evidences therefore must be addressed.
- 28% organizations don't use cameras as per requirement of recording the physical activities. Physical evidences are often undeniable in the court of law therefore need to work on it as well to rectify it.
- 25% companies store the recorded videos forever, while only 15% perform it for
- 1 year. The requirement of these durations may vary organization to organization by considering its nature of business, but still this sector should be improved.
- If the primary media of recorded videos is lost then backup of these videos becomes essential. 25% organizations don't opt to take backups of videos is not reckoned as fool proof scenario.
- If we allow employees to use their blue-tooth service freely, especially in the financial institution like Banks which contain extremely

confidential information of customers then it will be mentioned as a vulnerable part of I.T security as well. 57% of organizations don't restrict their employees or other to use blue-tooth inside the organization, which is highlight able matter.

- 33% of organizations allow their employees to download freeware on their computers. This percentage is worry because freeware downloading may cause some security or monitoring tools troubles to record or collect the appropriate evidences.
- 28% of enterprises don't adopt any mechanism and monitor the downloading or installing new applications in the client systems. This ought to be addressed to prevent clients doing it by them and this may also create hurdles in the forensic process.
- 51% organizations have permitted employees to store the critical data directly to their storage devices. This issue is seriously addressable as well because often it doesn't leave any evidences of data being stolen or used illegitimately.
- The percentage of organizations that let their employees to execute (.exe) files directly from the web or emails. 28% is the percentage which needs to be reduced as much as possible as well.
- 26% companies have not employed policies that prohibit users from disclosing their passwords to anybody else. This situation may create ambiguity in the process of accountability in terms of forensic; therefore it also needs to be addressed.
- 19% of organizations have not yet implemented polices that require users to lock their workstations when they leave their desks.
- 32% organizations have not implemented policies that prohibit users from allowing anyone else to use the computer after they've logged in.
- 53% is huge number of those organizations that don't employ any snapshot tool to collect the evidences and monitor the client screens. It is an effective tool to collect the evidences therefore this matter need to be addresseority basis.

Finally, another addressable issue needs to be highlighted here is that 42% of organizations have allowed employees to erase the web browser's history and temp files. It may also cause serious damage and obstacleobstacles in the process of evidence collection, therefore mentioned here.

8.4. CHALLENGING ASPECTS OF DIGITAL EVIDENCE

Forensic analysts dealing with digital evidence face various difficulties since it is a type of tangible evidence. First of all, it is a disorganized, slick type of evidence that can be exceedingly challenging to manage. For example, a hard drive platter holds a disorganized collection of data that has been accumulated over time and mixed together. The useful pieces must be taken out of this amalgam, put together, and translated into a format that can be understood because only a small percentage of it may be pertinent to a given case. Second, digital evidence typically consists of an abstract representation of a digital object or event. When someone gives a computer instructions to do something, like send an email, the activities that follow produce data remnants that only provide a portion of the actual event.

The email message and server logs are the only remnants of the activity that provide us with a partial picture of what happened. In addition, there are multiple levels of abstraction involved in using a forensic tool to recover a deleted file from storage media, from the magnetic fields on the disk to the characters and numbers we see on the screen. As a result, we only ever see a representation of the data and errors may be introduced by successive layers of abstraction. The circumstances here are comparable to those of a conventional crime scene investigation. Similar to piecing together a puzzle, there may be hints in a homicide case that can be utilized to reconstruct what happened. However, it is impossible to reconstruct the crime in its entirety because not all of the puzzle pieces are available. explains different digital evidence sources and shows how a more comprehensive picture of the related crime can be created by utilizing these numerous, independent sources of corroborated information. Third, it is challenging to link specific computer activity to an individual because digital evidence is typically circumstantial. Digital evidence can therefore only be one part of a thorough investigation. A case is unacceptably weak if it depends only on one type of digital evidence, such as date-and-time stamps on computer files. It could be legitimately argued that someone else was using the computer at the time in the absence of further details. For example, many computers do not require a password, making them accessible to anybody, and some computers have password protection mechanisms that can be circumvented. In a similar vein, if a defendant claims that some incriminating digital evidence was not gathered from one system, this will only have an effect on a feeble case that lacks additional proof of guilt. Fourth, digital investigators face new difficulties because digital evidence is so easily altered or destroyed. Digital evidence can be destroyed or altered without leaving any visible traces of distortion, either purposefully by criminals or unintentionally during collection.

Fortunately, digital evidence has several features that mitigate this problem;

- Digital evidence can be duplicated exactly and a copy can be examined as if it were the original. It is common practice when dealing with digital evidence to examine a copy, thus avoiding the risk of altering or damaging the original evidence.
- With the right tools, it is very easy to determine if digital evidence has been modified or tampered with by comparing it with an original copy.
- Digital evidence is difficult to destroy. Even when a file is "deleted" or a hard drive is formatted, digital evidence can be recovered.
- When criminals attempt to destroy digital evidence, copies and associated remnants can remain in places that they were not aware of.

The ease with which digital evidence can be altered or destroyed creates challenges in many investigations in the form of evidence dynamics.

8.4.1. Evidence Dynamics and the Introduction of Error

It is rare for investigators and digital evidence examiners to witness a digital crime scene in its original condition, so they should be prepared for certain evidence dynamics: any influence between the time evidence is transferred and the time the case is resolved that modifies, relocates, obscures, or obliterates evidence, regardless of intent. Evidence dynamics can be caused by criminals, victims, first responders, digital evidence examiners, and anybody else who had access to digital evidence before it was preserved.

Some examples of evidence dynamics encountered in past cases:

- A system administrator attempted to recover deleted files from a hard drive by installing software on an evidential computer, saving recovered files onto the same drive. This process overwrote unallocated space, rendering potentially useful deleted data unrecoverable.
- Consultants installed a pirated version of a forensic tool on the compromised server. In addition to breaking the law by using an unlicensed version of digital forensic software, the installation altered and overwrote data on the evidential computer.
- Responding to a computer intrusion, a system administrator intentionally deleted an account that the intruder had created and attempted to preserve digital evidence using the standard backup facility on the system. This backup facility was outdated and had

a flaw that caused it to change the times of the fi les on the disk copying them. Thus, the date-time stamps of all fi les on the disk were changed to the current time, making it nearly impossible to reconstruct the crime.

- During an investigation involving several machines, a first responder did not follow standard operating procedures and failed to collect important evidence. Additionally, evidence collected from several identical computer systems was not thoroughly documented, making it very difficult to determine which evidence came from which system.

Digital evidence-containing media may degrade over time or in response to fire, water, jet fuel, and harmful chemicals. Inaccuracies may also occur when analyzing and interpreting digital evidence. Digital evidence examiners may misinterpret data, and digital evidence examination tools may have bugs that lead them to represent data incorrectly.

For instance, while a digital evidence examiner was examining several log files, transcribing relevant entries for later reference, he transcribed several dates and IP addresses incorrectly; for example, he misread 03:13 A.M. as 3:13 P.M., resulting in the wrong dial-up records being retrieved, implicating the wrong individual. Similarly, he transcribed 192.168.1.54 as 192.168.1.45 in a search warrant and implicated the wrong individual.

REFERENCES

1. Brinson, A., Robinson, A., & Rogers, M. (2006). A cyberforensics ontology: Creating a new approach to studying cyber forensics. *Digital Investigation, 3S*, S37–S43. https://doi.org/10.1016/j.diin.2006.08.011.
2. Carnegie, H. H., Carnegie, T. V., & Cranor, L. (2011). Usability of forensics tools: User study. In *Proceedings of the 6th International Conference on IT* (pp. 1–10).
3. Carrier, B. D., & Spafford, E. (2004). *An Event-Based Digital Forensics Investigation Framework*. Center for Education and Research in Information Assurance and Security.
4. Chaikin, D. (2007). *Network Investigations of Cyber-Attacks: The Limits of Digital Evidence*. Springer Science and Business Media.
5. Hewling, M. O., & Sant, P. (2011). Digital forensics: The need for integration. In *Proceedings of Digital Forensics & Incident Analysis (WDFIA 2011)*.
6. Hildebrandt, M., Kiltz, S., & Dittmann, J. (2011). A common scheme for evaluation of forensic software. In *Proceedings of the 6th International Conference on IT Security Incident Management and IT Forensics*.
7. Kenneally, E. K. (2005). The Internet is the computer: The role of forensics in bridging the digital and physical divide. *Digital Investigation, 2*(1), 41–48. https://doi.org/10.1016/j.diin.2005.09.006.
8. Kruse, W., & Heiser, J. G. (2001). *Computer Forensics: Incident Response Essentials* (1st ed.). Addison-Wesley Professional.
9. Mason, D., Carlin, A., Ramos, S., Gyger, A., Kaufman, M., & Treichelt, J. (2007). Is the open way a better way? Digital forensics using open-source tools. *The Computer Society*, 1–10.
10. Naqvi, S., Dallons, G., & Christophe, P. (2010). Applying digital forensics in the future Internet enterprise systems—European SMEs' perspective (CETIC). In *Proceedings of the 5th International Workshop on Systematic Approaches to Digital Forensic Engineering*.
11. Pollitt, M. (1995). Principles, practices, and procedures: An approach to standards in computer forensics.
12. Reith, M., Carr, C., & Gunsch, G. (2002). An examination of digital forensic models. *International Journal of Digital Evidence, 1*(3). Archived from the original on October 15, 2012.
13. Salemat, S. R., Yusof, R., & Sahib, S. (2008). Mapping process of digital forensic investigation framework.

14. Yang, C. H., & Yen, P. H. (2010). Fast deployment of computer forensics with USBs. In *Proceedings of the International Conference on Broadband, Wireless Computing, Communication and Applications*. Conference held in Fukuoka, Japan.

CHAPTER 9

FORENSIC DOCUMENT EXAMINATION

Contents

Introduction 358

9.1. Questioned Document 358

9.2. Handwriting Comparisons 360

9.3. Printed Documents: Typewriters, Computer Printers, Electrostatic Copiers 366

9.4. Other Examinations Performed by Document Examiners 369

References 380

INTRODUCTION

Forensic Document Examination (FDE) is a specialized field within forensic science that focuses on the analysis and comparison of documents to determine their authenticity, origin, and possible alterations. Forensic document examiners, also known as questioned document examiners, employ a variety of techniques to scrutinize handwriting, signatures, typewritten documents, printed materials, and even digitally produced documents. They often work with legal professionals and law enforcement agencies to provide expert testimony in court cases involving disputed documents.

One of the primary tasks of FDE is to verify the authenticity of a document. This involves examining the paper, ink, printing methods, and any signs of forgery or tampering. Handwriting analysis is a significant aspect of FDE, where examiners compare known writing samples with questioned documents to identify the author. They look for unique characteristics in handwriting, such as pressure patterns, stroke formations, and letter spacing.

FDE also plays a crucial role in detecting alterations in documents. Examiners use various tools and methods, such as magnification, ultraviolet light, and infrared imaging, to reveal erasures, overwriting, and other modifications that may not be visible to the naked eye. Additionally, they analyze the sequence of strokes to determine the order in which elements were added to a document.

The expertise of forensic document examiners is essential in a wide range of cases, including fraud investigations, forgeries, contested wills, and anonymous threatening letters. Their detailed analysis can help establish the authenticity of documents, uncover fraudulent activities, and provide critical evidence in legal proceedings. Through meticulous examination and advanced technology, FDE contributes significantly to the pursuit of justice by ensuring the integrity and reliability of documentary evidence.

9.1. QUESTIONED DOCUMENT

A document under question doesn't have to be a piece of paper; it can be any object. A document is defined as one that has linguistic or numerical markings applied by handwriting, typing, copying, computer printing, or some other method. If there is any uncertainty as to the authenticity of the document (e.g., If the document is questioned, it is a questioned document (for example, a real draft card or passport) or the identity of the author. For instance, approximately 25 years ago, in a Virginia case, a man used spray paint to write a large, menacing note on a woman's home's exterior wall. The wall is a disputed document because it was unclear who wrote on it and their identity. Bills, wills, letters, checks, contracts, passports, lottery tickets, driver's licenses, and other similar documents are typically the kinds of questioned documents. The crucial aspect to note is that these documents have signatures, letters, or numbers whose origin or veracity are uncertain. Even though authorship is frequently the examiner's concern, the examiner is frequently asked to assess the authenticity of a "official" document, like a driver's license. Furthermore, there are instances where an authentic document has been modified through the addition of additional markings, erasure, obliteration, or destruction.

9.1.1. The Questioned Document Examiner

Photographers were the first document examiners to be questioned. Curiously, although being a skilled photographer is by no means a prerequisite for becoming a questioned document examiner, it is an area in which they must be extremely knowledgeable. The Dreyfus treason case is among the most well-known instances where a photographer testified as an expert in a case involving a questioned document. Alphonse Bertillon was a photographer who also invented the "science" of anthropometry, which claims to be able to measure a person's body in a way that is specific to them. Bertillon stated in court that the case's key document was written by Alfred Dreyfus. Later, Dreyfus' innocence was established, casting doubt on Bertillon and the nascent field of questioned document examination. Questioned document analysis and testimony were not commonly accepted in courts until the 20th century. Common law in England held that handwriting standards which were not previously in evidence could not be admitted into evidence if their only function in the case was to be compared with a document that was under question. As a result, questioned documents could not be introduced into court and could not be compared to known samples. As most of the early U. S. law was founded on English common law. As a result, forensic document examination was not used in the US until 1913, when Congress passed a rule permitting the use of document standards as evidence in court thanks to the efforts of renowned document examiner Albert Osborne. Before this point, the only way a disputed document could be verified was if a witness could attest in court to having seen the writer actually write the document. The field of questioned document examination advanced quickly after 1913. A comprehensive set of rules was created to regulate the methods for obtaining handwritten samples that were known to be comparable.

9.1.2. Training and Education of Questioned Document Examiners

It is doubtful that there will be any official college-based education programs in questioned document analysis in the United States in the near future. Though questioned document analysis, like that of firearms, tool marks, and fingerprints, is essentially a traditional apprenticeship field, there are some college courses that can offer a theoretical foundation for the field. The trainee might work with an experienced professional in the field for a number of years. The trainee may advance to the position of journeyman questioned document examiner after successfully completing a series of exams and exercises. The American Society of Questioned Document Examiners oversees a certification program for questioned document examiners in the United States.

A questioned document examiner trainee's typical training program would include formal coursework, if any is available, reading and studying pertinent basic and advanced books and journals that cover all facets of document examination, as well as studying and examining real questioned documents under the trainer's supervision. In addition, there are materials for quality assurance and control, such as blind tests and exercises requiring the successful completion of mock trials. It would also be expected of the trainee to become familiar with the pertinent statutes and legal issues that control document review, reporting, and expert testimony. The training program for questioned document examiners is very lengthy, and there is a severe shortage of qualified candidates. Universities may be able to create courses so that a prospective document examiner can complete all of the required "book learning" regarding practice and history as part of the training process, and then they can work as an apprentice with a journeyman examiner. This method may drastically cut the price and duration of the apprenticeship program.

9.2. HANDWRITING COMPARISONS

Children are given model letters for every alphabet letter when they first learn to print or write, and they are instructed to copy the letters as neatly as they can. After that, they are instructed on how to form words by joining the letters. Most children's handwriting at this time would be fairly similar. Teachers start focusing on content when students apply their newly acquired word-formation skills to written work. This indicates that the writers start to pay less attention to the structure of their letters and more attention to what they are writing. Individual traits emerge as a result of writing habits internalization and subconscious writing, many of which the writer is unaware of. Handwriting develops into a kind of automatic habit over time, but this habit is dynamic. Over time, handwriting varies. An individual's handwriting gradually changes over years, taking on distinct characteristics. These modifications may have a significant impact on the body of known handwriting samples. Changes in one's physical or emotional state can also affect one's handwriting. Handwriting can be impacted by physical illnesses, drug abuse, and depression. Additionally, handwriting differs depending on the kind of writing tool and surface (e.g., paper) employed. When known handwriting samples are acquired, many of these variables are taken into consideration.

Both the presence of sufficient individual characteristics in the unknown sample and the availability of sufficient samples of the purported writer's authentic handwriting are necessary for a questioned document examiner to be able to identify the author of a handwritten document by comparison with exemplars, or known, authentic writing samples. Questioned document examiners feel that it is possible to identify an unknown handwriting exhibit as belonging to a specific individual if both of these requirements are satisfied. It might be necessary to draw the ambiguous conclusion that the unknown writing could have originated from the suspect's writing if one of the aforementioned requirements is not met. Of course, another option is to rule out a suspect as the author of the questioned handwriting based on personal traits or class. Similar to other forms of comparative evidence like fingerprints, gunshots, and shoe prints, etc., the minimal amount of handwriting traits that must exist in both known and unknown handwriting samples in order to determine individuality is not standardized. The size of the exemplar and questioned samples, the type of characteristics, and the examiner's experience all influence the minimum number.

A questioned document examiner might need to look for fewer anomalies in a handwriting sample with a lot of unusual characteristics than in one with a more "normal" handwriting. In any event, the individual examiner needs to discover enough similarities between the exemplar and the questioned document to reach a reasonable level of scientific certainty regarding the identity of the writer of the questioned document. It is never appropriate to give a pwritten by the suspectthe suspect wrote the questioned document. That is to say, claiming, "I am 95% certain that the suspect wrote the will," would not be acceptable.

This is a crucial idea that also holds true for other kinds of evidence, like tool marks and fingerprints. In order for an examiner to provide numerical probabilities regarding the probability that known and unknown evidence share a common source, studies that provide data on the prevalence of a specific set of characteristics in a given population are required. While this method is effective for DNA, where there is a limited range of DNA types, it is not feasible to draw similar conclusions for handwriting because features do not fit neatly into categories. This leads to two perceived weaknesses in the conclusions of individuality that document examiners frequently draw: there are no established criteria by which to judge when authorship has been established, and there are no conclusions that can be drawn with any degree of probability from a document comparison analysis.

9.2.1. Handwriting Comparison Characteristics

A large number of handwriting characteristics, both class and individual, can be used for comparisons of questioned and exemplar specimens. A few of the more common ones are as follows:

- Spacing between letters
- Spacing between words
- Relative proportions between letters and within letters
- Individual letter formations
- Formations of letter combinations
- The overall slant of the writing
- Connecting strokes
- Pen lifts
- Beginning and ending strokes
- Unusual flourishes
- Pen pressure

Figure 9.1 shows a questioned document and several known samples for comparison.

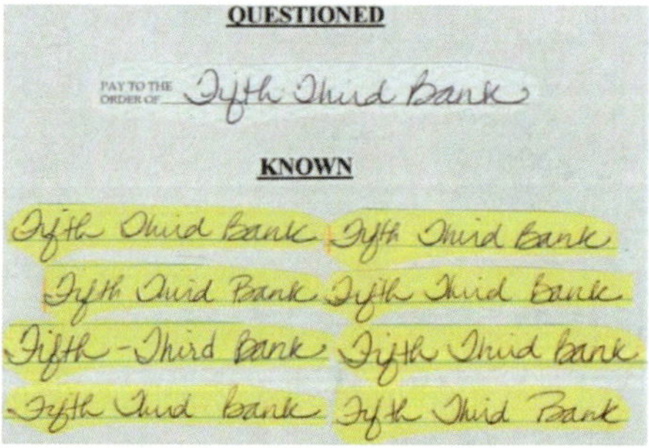

Figure 9.1. *A handwriting comparison. The questioned document is a bank check.*

Source: Max M. Houck, Jay A. Siegel; Fundamentals of Forensic Science; ISBN: 978–0-12- 374989–5.

9.2.2. Collection of Handwriting Exemplars

Examiners and investigators of questioned documents have little to no control over the quantity and caliber of the questioned writing samples, but they do or ought to have control over the exemplars. A successful handwriting comparison requires well-known writing samples. Acquiring the entire spectrum of variation in the subject's writing is crucial, as is the quantity of exemplar material.

But the kinds and caliber of exemplars matter just as much. For meaningful comparisons to be possible, there needs to be some similarity between the known and unknown writings. Exemplars come in two varieties: writings that are requested and those that are not. Writing samples obtained from someone in order to compare them with a document under question are known as requested writings. These writings are typically obtained through several dictations of a section containing terms and phrases found in the document in question. This kind of data collection reduces the possibility that the participant is attempting to purposefully change the style of their handwriting. The writing frequently consists of a few general phrases or paragraphs, either entirely or partially followed by the precise document in question. Because the person reviewing the document in question has considerable control over the content, paper, writing instrument, etc., requested writings are frequently preferred. , that are utilized in the writing, and you can ask for an adequate amount of writing samples to reduce the likelihood that the writer will be able to conceal their work and to take into consideration handwriting variations that occur naturally. Requested writings have one major drawback: if a lot of time has passed between the time the questioned document was written and the requested writing was collected, the examiner of the questioned document might not be able to make a valid comparison because the handwriting might have changed significantly in that time.

9.2.3. Proper Collection of Requested Writings

Successful comparison of known and unknown handwritings depends in part on the quality and quantity of the exemplars. Following are some of the more important considerations that must be kept in mind when collecting these known samples:

- The most crucial factor to keep in mind is that there needs to be enough writing to guarantee that all of the typical variances in handwriting are represented. Although there isn't a set quantity of writing that is required, some examiners feel that 10 to 20 examples of similar writing should be adequate.
- Each writing sample should be on a separate sheet of paper and should be removed from the sight of the writer before collecting the next sample.
- It is best to collect requested writings by dictation rather than copying. Because the subject of dictation must focus on listening to the dictation, the likelihood of intentional handwriting alteration is reduced.

- Dictated passages should be long. This will also help uncover attempts to deliberately alter handwriting because the longer someone is forced to write, the harder it is to make deliberate alterations to what is essentially a subconscious process.
- The requested writing should contain some words and phrases that are present in the questioned document. If there are misspelled words in the questioned document, they should also be given in the exemplar. The same holds true with mistakes in punctuation.
- the extent possible, the subject should be supplied with the same type of writing instrument and paper used in the questioned document. The subject should also be made as comfortable as is practical and there should be adequate lighting.

Using non-requested writing exemplars can occasionally get around the temporal restriction of requested writings. These are samples of the subject's writing that were obtained during casual or professional interactions. They could consist of banknotes, invoices, a journal, deeds, etc. Efforts ought to be made to acquire non-requested writings that were composed concurrently with the document under investigation. Establishing the authenticity of non-requested writings is the main challenge.

There must be evidence that the subject of the writings wrote them in order for them to be admitted in court.

Having a witness who witnessed the subject writing the exemplar, having the subject available to testify that the subject wrote the exemplar, or obtaining an exception to the hearsay rule under the business records exception are some methods to accomplish this proof. Evidence like non-requested handwriting would typically be considered hearsay and be excluded from court proceedings.

In this case, the handwriting sample is an example of a statement made outside of court by an unindicted witness that is now being used to support its assertions.

Defendants are shielded from the issue of unsponsored testimony in court and the absence of a cross-examination regarding the veracity of the testimony by the hearsay rule. The hearsay rule does not apply to "business records." This is a document that was produced in the regular course of business, and since it is crucial to the operation, it would be pointless to forge it. Sometimes a non-requested exemplar made during regular business operations is accepted as a true example of the writer's handwriting. In other cases, a questioned document examiner has demonstrated that two pieces of writing—one admitted, the other non-requested—were written by the same hand. It is best to have both requested and non-requested exemplars in most questioned document examinations.

9.2.4. Signatures

Questioned document examiners may encounter unique issues when it comes to signatures. A person's signature does not always rble typical handwriting or havehas all of the same individual traits. This happens frequently. On the whole disputed document, a single signature might be the only handwriting, raising concerns that the sample size might not be sufficient to draw a firm conclusion.

Ultimately, context often has a significant impact on signatures. Think about the various circumstances in which someone is required to provide a signature. A will or property deed is an official document that most people would carefully sign, making name verification impossible.

This signature is official in nature. In regular correspondence, like personal letters and other documents where you want the reader to recognize your signature but don't care about the name's exact spelling, you would use an informal signature. Lastly, there is the stylized or shortened signature that is used to sign documents such as credit card receipts and checks.

This is comparable to the well-known "physician's signature" found on prescriptions. It frequently has a very stylized appearance and resembles a scrawl with nothing that would be recognized as a signature. There are guidelines for gathering signature exemplars because of how context affects signature sensitivity. The conditions under which the exemplar is gathered ought to be as close as feasible to the conditions under which the document in question was composed. As such, context is always considered when gathering signatures. The subject might be asked to fill out 10 to 20 blank checks for different amounts and sign them, for instance, if the document under investigation is a forged check signature.

9.2.5. Forged Signatures

Many times, attempts to forge signatures are made. There are several ways to carry out the forgery, depending on the specifics. There are two ways in which a forger would try to pull off a forgery if the signature needs to be provided immediately, like in the case of a stolen check. Either the person would write the check freehand without attempting to forge the signature, or they would practice it from a copy of the authentic signature beforehand and then try to duplicate the check owner's signature on the check. The counterfeiter may have hoped that the buyer would overlook the signature. Figure 9.2 displays both questioned and known signatures.

There are various methods for forging a document that doesn't need to be signed in front of another person. It could be tracked, for instance. Transmitted light or tracing—writing the signature indented on a piece of paper and then retracing it—could be used for this. The trained questioned document examiner may be able to discern the majority of tracings, regardless of type, due to their artificial appearance. Finding a sufficient number of exemplars is crucial to identifying a forged signature, just like with other questioned documents.

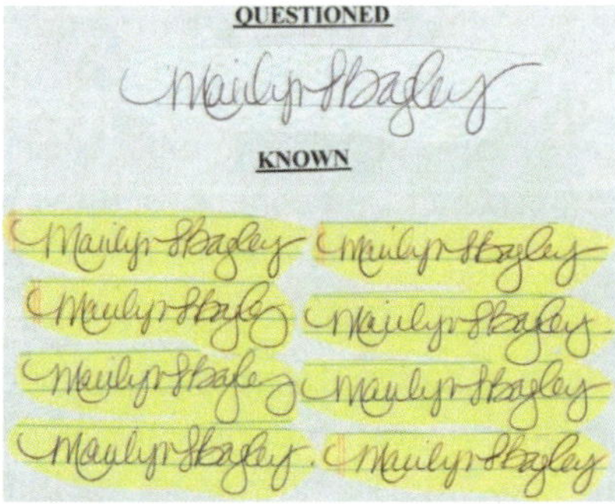

Figure 9.2. *A signature comparison.*

Source: Max M. Houck, Jay A. Siegel; Fundamentals of Forensic Science; ISBN: 978–0-12- 374989–5.

9.3. PRINTED DOCUMENTS: TYPEWRITERS, COMPUTER PRINTERS, ELECTROSTATIC COPIERS

Documents that are printed must be treated differently than ones that are handwritten. Individualization of a document to a specific machine is not possible due to mass production of machines like copiers, printers, and typewriters, unless there are exceptional circumstances. This rule is only exempted in the event that a printing or copying mechanism flaw causes an odd or distinctive characteristic—preferably multiple such characteristics—to repeatedly appear. Compared to other printing devices, typewriters have a higher likelihood of exhibiting these flaws.

9.3.1. Typewriters

Two common questions posed to forensic document examiners regarding typewritten documents are: Can the document be lin to a specific machine, and Cancan the typewriter's make and model be identified? The first question necessitates some understanding of typewriter functionality and the likelihood of distinctive features emerging. Standard keyboards are typically used with older style typewriters. The matching raised metal character, affixed to a long stem, is struck by a key, striking a ribbon that subsequently imprints the letter in ink on paper. The metal character may eventually get bent, chipped, worn out, or misaligned. This results in repeatable flaws that can be used to identify the specific typewriter. The IBM Selectric® models are prime examples of newer typewriter models that use a metal sphere with all of the characters raised on the surface. The sphere aligns itself with the ribbon when a character is pressed on the keyboard, lining up the character's portion with it. When the sphere hits the ribbon, the paper is imprinted with ink. Individualization is made more difficult by the fact that these Selectric typewriters are less likely to develop wear or misalignments in the typefaces because all of the characters are held more rigidly and on a single sphere as opposed to individual stems. This issue is made worse by the fact that the spheres are replaceable, which means that the original sphere used to type the document must be included in any comparison of a typewritten document with a specific machine. The examiner must have access to a comprehensive library of sample writings from every make and model of typewriter in order to identify the make and model of the typewriter that created a document. The font type and size are typically distinctive to specific manufacturers' typewriter models; therefore, the make and model of a typewritten document under suspicion can be ascertained by comparing it with library entries. Figure 9.3 compares typewriting styles.

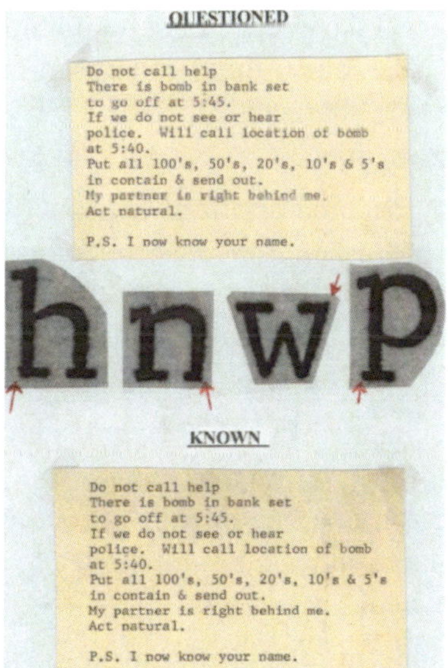

Figure 9.3. *A typewriter comparison. The arrows point to unusual features of certain letters made by the typewriter in question. The features show up in both the known and questioned type writings.*

Source: Max M. Houck, Jay A. Siegel; Fundamentals of Forensic Science; ISBN: 978–0-12- 374989–5.

9.3.2. Typewriter Exemplars

It is best practice to give the questioned document examiner access to the actual, suspect typewriter when a questioned document was created on one of these machines.

The document examiner must maintain control over a number of typewriter-related variables that can alter how the text appears on paper. For instance, a lot of typewriters allow the typist to change the font's color by varying the keystroke pressure. Furthermore, having the typewriter allows the examiner to inspect the ribbon and all of the typefaces.

The typeface ball that was purportedly used to create the contested document must also be turned in for Selectric models. It will be required to obtain a full set of all characters at all pressure set typewriter cannot be turned in. In order forFor the examiner to make direct comparisons, it is also advisable to type the exact document in qewriter. The ribbon should, if at all possibleif possible, be turned in for analysis.

9.3.3. Laser Printers and Copiers

Xerography© laser printers and copiers do not require ink to print characters on paper. Rather, binders, a laser, and a toner composed of finely divided carbon powder are used to create the characters. Characters have almost no chance of developing deformities over time.

The print quality may become erratic if the toner cartridge begins to run low, but this will probably not help much as time goes on. However, in some cases, until the machine is cleaned or repaired, unnecessary marks or toner blotches may appear repeatedly in the same spot.

The exemplars and the questioned document may reveal specific details about the questioned document's source if they display the same markings in the same place on the copy. The examiner wouldn't require access to a printer or copier. Rather, the person conductingation should ensure that a sufficient number ofenough exemplars—at least 12—are taken to demonstrate the degree of consistency of the extraneous markings.

It might still be possible to identify the make of the copier or printer by chemical analysis and comparison of the toners with known samples if there are no repeatable extraneous markings on the paper and the source of the copy is unknown. However, this evidence is not unique; typically, it is impossible to establish beyond a reasonable doubt that a specific machine was the author of a disputed document.

9.3.4. Ink-Jet Printers

Typically, ink-jet printers spray ink onto paper to create images and characters. Similar to laser printers and copiers, misalignment of specific characters is typically not a problem, and there is no problem with user-defined pressure or darkness of the characters. Furthermore, similar to laser printers or copiers, there's a possibility that the copy will have unintentional, repeatable markings on it that could be used to identify where it came from. As the ink cartridge depletes, the typescript might become crooked and fade. This feature is particularly noticeable when using color cartridges, as the absence of one-color ink causes the colors to appear distorted on the page. But once more, this issue persists until the user changes cartridges or until there is no more ink. Chemical analysis of the ink may still be able to identify the printer manufacturer if there are no repeatable flaws with the printer. Of course, a document can also be linked to a computer and printer using other class attributes, like font type.

9.3.5. Fax Machines

Fax machines are comparable to the machines covered in the sections above in terms of ink or toner and the potential for random, extraneous markings on the paper. Fax machines, however, also have an additional header that lists certain details about the fax, like the date and time, the sender and recipient's fax numbers, etc. An acronym for this header is Transmitting Terminal Identifier (TTI). As known and unknown facsimiles are compared, the TTI can be a crucial feature. Attempts to forge TTIs and place them on a document are typically detectable by document examiners because they are typically in a special font that differs from the text font.

9.4. OTHER EXAMINATIONS PERFORMED BY DOCUMENT EXAMINERS

Questioned document examiners are occasionally asked to carry out a range of additional relevant examinations in addition to comparing handwritings, and printed writings. Document alterations are one broad category. They consist of burned documents, additional markings, erasures, obliterations, and indented writings. Pencil leads, paper, and inks are examples of tools used in another important area of analysis. And lastly, there's the new problem of the age of documents, particularly those written by hand in ink. Few document examiners worldwide are currently conducting this kind of examination, which requires a great deal of chemistry knowledge and skill. Several investigators are currently working on developing new techniques for ink dating.

9.4.1. Document Alterations

9.4.1.1. Obliterations

Overwriting a writing sample or printing with another writing instrument is called obliteration. It might be intentional or unintentional. The task of identifying the content of the writing beneath the obliteration may fall to the document examiner. Writing instruments such as pens, pencils, and others can be used to make obliterations. It is dependent upon the original writing and the means employed to determine what is written beneath an obliteration. The obliteration may be partially or completely dissolved, or a light source that passes through the obliteration but not the original writing may be used. With this method, the original writing underneath the obliteration can be read by the examiner. The paper may occasionally be treated with a unique transparent liquid that alters its refractive index, allowing the original writing to be seen on the reverse of the document. A powerful backlighting source may occasionally be able to read through the obliteration to the underlying writing. Figure 9.4 displays an example of erasure handwriting.

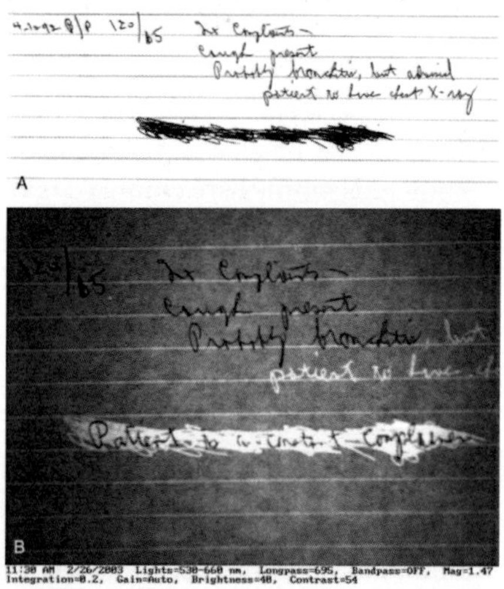

Figure 9.4. *Obliteration. (a) A portion of a patient's medical record with an entry obliterated. (b) The same record photographed with infrared light.*

Source: Max M. Houck, Jay A. Siegel; Fundamentals of Forensic Science; ISBN: 978–0-12- 374989–5.

In the last 10 years, one of the book's authors has come across instances where people have used black markers to completely destroy portions of printed documents. In one instance, the document was sufficiently cleaned of the marker by soaking it in methyl alcohol so that the printing underneath remained intact. The same thing was done in another instance by ethyl alcohol. If the original writing was created with ink rather than toner, these soaking methods might not work because the ink might be dissolved by the same solvent that was used to dissolve the obliterating agent. It is possible to see underlying handwriting that has been erased by using infrared or ultraviolet light. The light's wavelength is selected so that it can reach the ink below through the obliteration. The ink will appear dark if it absorbs the light at that point. The ink may occasionally fluoresce in the visible or infrared spectrum when exposed to light, making it visible with a camera and specific film or filters or even with the unaided eye.

9.4.1.2. Erasures

Erasures can happen in several ways. Using an abrasive eraser material, the common abrasive erasure method involves erasing writing, typically created with a pencil. Chemical erasures include whitening or dissolving ink to make it invisible.

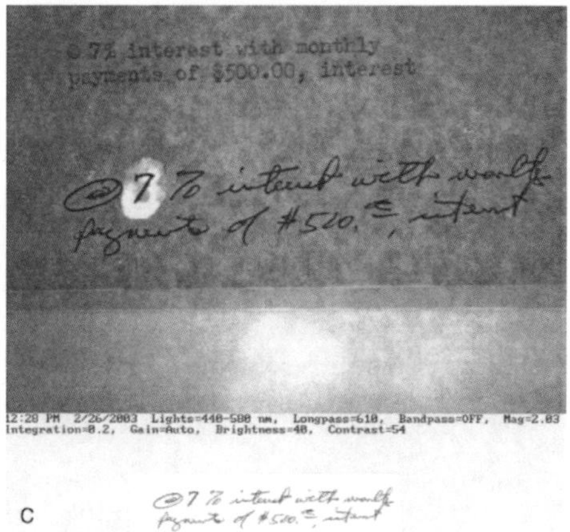

Figure 9.5. *Erasures. Original documents read "6% interest." (a) A pencil erasure. (b) A typewriter erasure. (c) A chemical erasure.*

Source: Max M. Houck, Jay A. Siegel; Fundamentals of Forensic Science; ISBN: 978–0-12- 374989–5.

A ribbon is used in typewriter erasures to remove typewritten images from paper. It is theoretically possible to detect all of these erasure types. Erasures using abrasives are the simplest to identify. They almost always entail disruption of the paper's fibers and coatings at the erasure point, which is visible under a low-power microscope. Chemical erasures can be identified by variations in the paper's color due to bleaching effects or by the way the chemicals react to UV or infrared light. By looking for the typewriter's indentations on the paper, one can identify typewriter erasures. Low-power microscopy and oblique-angle photography can be used for this analysis. It's usually harder to figure out what was erased than it is to detect that an erasure has occurred. It might be impossible to reverse an effective erasure, and the writing might never be recovered. As shown in Figure 9.5, partial erasures may allow the examiner to read all or part of what was erased.

9.4.1.3. Indented Writings

There are numerous circumstances where a writing instrument, like a ballpoint pen, is used to write on a document that presses against the top sheet of a pad of paper. This could produce a picture of the writing developing on one or more pages underneath. This indented writing can be viewed in several ways. The easiest and most common way to read indented writings is in indirect lighting. The writing may be visible on the page if enough shadow is cast by the indentations when light is shining at an angle across the page. If a high-resolution digital camera is used to take the picture, this might work for a few pages underneath the top sheet. On TV or in movies, indented writing is occasionally demonstrated by rubbing the indented area with the side of a pencil. This will typically result in the indented portion of the writing not being visible, as well as the destruction of the evidence, making it impossible to employ practical solutions. Additionally, an instrument known as the Electrostatic Detection Apparatus (ESDA) can be used to record indented writings. This device uses a toner that gathers inside the indented writings so that they can be seen, much like an electrostatic copy machine. ESDA's application is demonstrated in Figure 9.6.

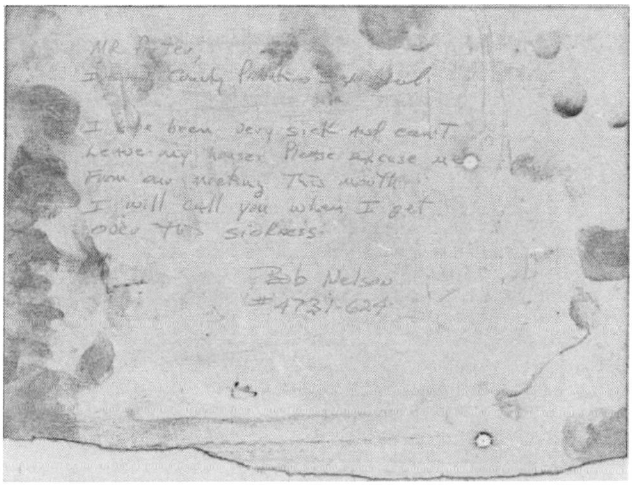

Figure 9.6. *The use of an Electrostatic Detection Apparatus (ESDA). This is a note given to a bank teller during a robbery. ESDA reveals what was written on the piece of paper above the note in the pad of paper on which the note was written.*

Source: Max M. Houck, Jay A. Siegel; Fundamentals of Forensic Science; ISBN: 978–0-12- 374989–5.

9.4.1.4. Charred Documents

The perpetrator of many crimes or civil infractions attempts to destroy documentary evidence that might otherwise be used against them. The documents can be conveniently burned in order to accomplish this. There is a possibility that some of the writing can be identified if the documents are found before being destroyed entirely. The reason is that while the paper might burn, the pencil or ink might not burn as quickly. The fact that burned documents are so delicate is one of their issues. Occasionally, misting them with water, alcohol, or lacquer can strengthen them. The document may be sufficiently strengthened by this misting to allow the examiner to keep it between glass or plastic sheets. The process of analyzing burned documents is similar to that of analyzing obliterations.

The ink or toner must be kept intact, and the next step is to create as much contrast as you can between the ink and the burned, darkened paper. If the ink fluoresces when exposed to UV or infrared light, then photography with specific films and the right lighting conditions may be used. On occasion, even bright incandescent light sources have given the necessary contrast to make the writing easier to see. For an illustration of the analysis of burned writing, refer to Figure 9.7.

Figure 9.7. *Charred writing. Through the use of infrared light, the figures made with the ink fluoresce against the charred background.*

Source: Max M. Houck, Jay A. Siegel; Fundamentals of Forensic Science; ISBN: 978–0-12- 374989–5.

9.4.2. Ink Analysis

Forensic document examiners have grown more accustomed to doing chemical analyzes as part of their daily duties in recent years. Research on the makeup of inks has facilitated this kind of analysis by resulting in the creation of simpler techniques for describing and contrasting inks. Comprehending the composition of an ink sample and the chemical transformations it experiences during the drying process can be crucial in various document scenarios. An examiner might be asked to decide, for instance, whether two documents were written with the same writing instrument—say, a specific ballpoint pen—in a number of questioned document cases. In other situations, it becomes unclear if a document could have been changed by adding writings after it was first created. An example of this would be a check that was changed by adding zeros to the amount on it. In other cases, the question of whether a document could have been altered by appending extra writings and then backdating them to give the impression that they were added earlier is raised. The chemical analysis of an ink sample and the comparison of two or more writings are required for the first two of these questions. It is possible to demonstrate that a suspect pen, for example, could be included in the population of pens that could have written a document, or that it could not have written a document, even though it is impossible to match an ink sample to a specific writing instrument. The final question asks you to estimate the age of the ink sample or determine its age in relation to other writings on the document. Understanding how the ink dries is necessary to make this decision.

9.4.2.1. Analyzing and Comparing Ink Samples

The vast array of pens on the market today is proof that there are numerous varieties of inks. These pens include the well-known rollerball, ballpoint, gel, fiber, and porous tip pens in addition to the age-old India ink and fountain pens. Certain computer printer cartridges also contain ink-jet inks. For every type of pen and printer, there is an ink designed specifically for the ink delivery system. Inks may consist of highly intricate substances. For instance, dyes and a solvent like ethylene glycol are ingredients in contemporary ballpoint pen inks. In an ink formulation, additional additives and drying agents might be present. The type of writing instrument an ink sample originated from can be inferred from its composition.

9.4.2.1.1. Sampling

Sampling ink from a disputed document poses special challenges because the handwriting's or printing's legibility needs to be preserved in order to preserve its characteristics. This implies that very small ink samples must be taken for analysis. Typically, a blunt-point syringe needle is used for sampling, and tiny plugs are taken from individual letters in the writing. As long as there are enough writings available to maintain legibility, a writing sample may be used for numerous plugs. The quantity and kind of testing that can be conducted will inevitably depend on the size and quantity of plugs.

9.4.2.1.2. Thin Layer Chromatography

Thin layer chromatography is the most widely used and straightforward technique for analyzing and comparing inks (TLC). Typically, 10 ink plugs are dissolved in a small amount of a solvent, like methanol, and then spotted at the plate's bottom. Since multiple dyes may have been used to create that specific color of the ink, there will typically be multiple spots from the dyes when the plate is developed. Seeing the plate is not required because the dyes have already taken on color. There might be additios from some of the other ingredients in the ink in addition to the dye peaks. Since these wouldn'twould not be colored, a visualization of some kind would be required. Some ink samples are shown in a TLC in Figure 9.8.

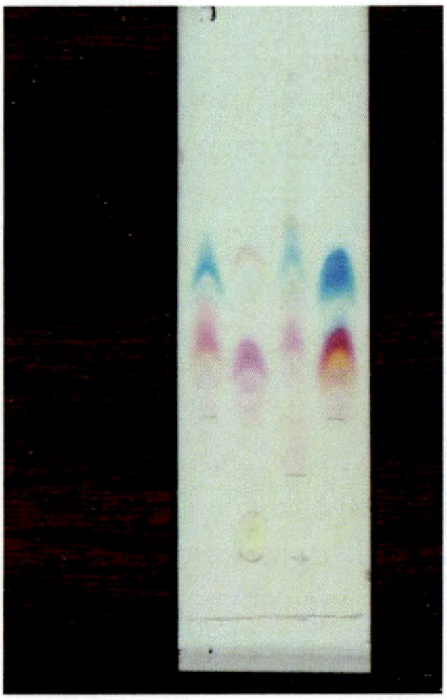

Figure 9.8. *Thin layer chromatography of inks. Lanes one and three are standard black, ballpoint pen inks. Lanes two and four are each different black inks.*

Source: Max M. Houck, Jay A. Siegel; Fundamentals of Forensic Science; ISBN: 978–0-12- 374989–5.

9.4.2.1.3. Other Types of Chromatography

Ink analysis and comparison have successfully used both liquid and gas chromatography techniques. They have two advantages over TLC: they produce both qualitative and quantitative data, and they are usually more sensitive than TLC, requiring fewer ink plugs. Furthermore, gas chromatography-mass spectrometry (GC-MS) is frequently employed, enabling the identification of every ingredient in the ink. Although there hasn't been much research done on it yet, capillary electrophoresis, a more recent chromatography technique, has also been used for ink analysis. Similar to HPLC, capillary electrophoresis uses tiny columns for separation, allowing analysis to be performed with as few as one or two plugs. When the sample size is small, this has a lot of benefits.

9.4.2.1.4. *Infrared Spectrophotometry*

Characterizing inks has also been done using infrared spectrophotometry. This method displays absorption peaks simultaneously for the solvent, dyes, and additives that make up the ink. For this reason, when comparing two ink samples to determine whether they could have come from the same source, infrared spectroscopy (IR) can be very useful. The fact that IR requires more sample than other chromatographic methods generally is one of its drawbacks. Micro plugs are challenging to use for infrared sampling. With varying degrees of success, several sampling techniques have been tried, such as focusing a microscope on microplugs.

9.4.2.1.5. *Mass Spectrometry*

Ink analysis has been done with and without gas chromatography using mass spectrometry. "Laser desorption," a more recent kind of MS, involves using a laser to remove ink from paper surfaces before analyzing them.

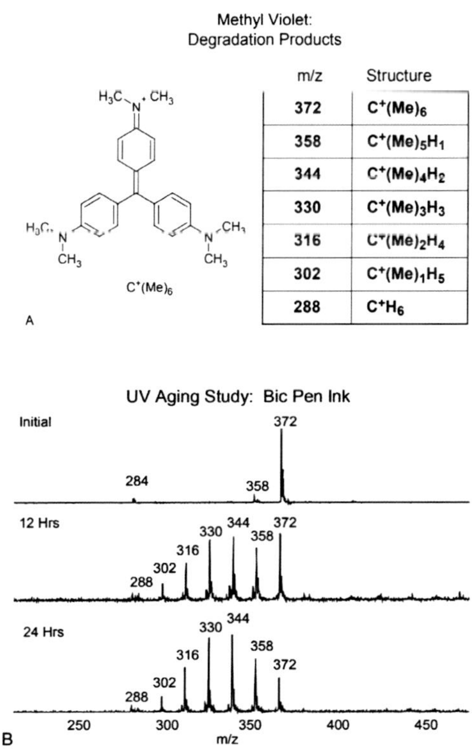

m/z	Structure
372	$C^+(Me)_6$
358	$C^+(Me)_5H_1$
344	$C^+(Me)_4H_2$
330	$C^+(Me)_3H_3$
316	$C^+(Me)_2H_4$
302	$C^+(Me)_1H_5$
288	C^+H_6

Figure 9.9. *(a) The degradation of methyl violet. Each degradation causes the replacement of a methyl group with a hydrogen atom, resulting in the loss of 14 mass*

units. (b) An artificial aging study of methyl violet dye in a blue, ballpoint pen, by tracking with laser desorption mass spectrometry.

Source: Max M. Houck, Jay A. Siegel; Fundamentals of Forensic Science; ISBN: 978–0-12- 374989–5.

This kind of mass spectrometry has the benefit of not requiring the ink to be taken out of the paper beforehand. You can insert a piece of paper with ink writing on it straight into the device. Furthermore, it is practically non-destructive. An ink dye's aging can be monitored using laser desorption. Dyes experience chemical deterioration with age. Methyl violet, a common dye for ballpoint pens, deteriorates when CH_3 groups are lost and are replaced with hydrogen atoms. The molecule loses fourteen mass units as a result of this. Figures 9.9a, 9.9b, and an aging study on a standard ballpoint pen illustrate the degradation of methyl violet.

9.4.2.1.6. Microspectrophotometry

Determining whether the ink from a suspect pen and a writing sample have the same color is one of the trickier ink analysis problems. Although the human eye is a very good color discriminator, it is clear that it is unable to provide precise information regarding an ink's color. The precise color of an ink, or any other colored material, is determined by the visible light wavelengths that the ink's dyes either absorb or transmit. A visible microspectrophotometer is the perfect tool if an examiner of questioned documents is handling very small ink samples. It establishes the dyes' absorption or transmission spectrum. Two inks with the same color will have identical visible spectra.

9.4.2.2. Document Dating

Questioned document examiners are occasionally asked to ascertain whether a document's age is consistent with its claimed age in addition to examining and comparing inks. One scenario that comes to mind is when a document has some writing on it that was not done when the document was dated. In these situations, establishing the document's age is necessary. The most popular method for doing this is to figure out how old the document's ink is. For instance, there was a Michigan case a few years ago where a doctor was charged with recording information about a specific medical procedure in a patient's file after the patient passed away. To ascertain whether the notes were written at the time that the date on them indicated, a questioned document examiner was called upon.

An ink sample's age can be estimated in a variety of methods. The most widely used technique involves monitoring the ink's chemical changes as it dries. Several chemical reactions occur simultaneously when ink dries, such as the constant evaporation of the ink's solvent. While this is going on, some of the ink's constituents might form polymers (e.g., resins). Furthermore, the chemical makeup of the ink's dyes will alter with time. Finding out how quickly ink will dissolve again in an appropriate solvent while it dries is one method of monitoring the ink's drying process over time. As ink dries, its solubility decreases. Thin layer chromatography can be used to monitor this process. This drying procedure can also be monitored using infrared spectrophotometry. A portion of the IR peaks will become less intense as the solvent evaporates. Some new peaks will show up in the ink as polymers begin to form. Inks' chemical compositions alter with aging dyes. Certain types of chromatography or mass spectrometry can be used to monitor this process. For instance, a dye's mass spectrum will alter when its molecular weight varies due to compositional changes in the dye. These methods can be applied to ascertain whether a document is as old as claimed or whether a particular set of writings on it is noticeably older or younger than others. Remember that these processes that cause documents to age occur over an extended period of time, so measuring these changes might not be totally precise. Several weeks or months may pass before an ink change is consistently noticeable.

9.4.2.2.1. Artificial Aging of Inks

Since inks deteriorate slowly over time, it's essential to have a dependable way to accelerate the aging process so that drying processes can be easily researched. Heating the document in an oven is the only technique that has received any significant research. Research has generally demonstrated that a document can be aged by several months by heating it to 100 °C for a few minutes or hours. Alternative techniques for creating artificial aging are being investigated, as heating could result in undesired interactions between ink and paper. These techniques include the use of oxygen-rich environments and UV light. Whatever method is employed, it must cause the ink to age chemically in the same way that aging occurs naturally.

REFERENCES

1. ASTM International. (2009). *Standard Guide for Scope of Work of Forensic Document Examiners* (ASTM Standard E444). West Conshohocken, PA. https://doi.org/10.1520/E0444-09.
2. Kam, M., & Lin, E. (2003). Writer identification using handprinted and nonhandprinted questioned documents. *Journal of Forensic Sciences, 48*(6), 1391–1395. https://doi.org/10.1520/JFS20080J.
3. Kam, M., Feilding, G., & Conn, R. (1997). Writer identification by professional document examiners. *Journal of Forensic Sciences, 42*(5), 778–786. https://doi.org/10.1520/JFS13992J.
4. Kam, M., Feilding, G., & Conn, R. (1998). The effects of monetary incentives on document examination by non-professionals. *Journal of Forensic Sciences, 43*(5), 1000–1004. https://doi.org/10.1520/JFS15158J.
5. Kam, M., Gummadidala, K., Feilding, G., & Conn, R. (2001). Signature authentication by forensic document examiners. *Journal of Forensic Sciences, 46*(4), 884–888. https://doi.org/10.1520/JFS15262J.
6. Kam, M., Westein, J., & Conn, R. (1994). Proficiency of professional document examiners in writer identification. *Journal of Forensic Sciences, 39*(1), 5–14. https://doi.org/10.1520/JFS14951J.
7. Kelly, J. S., & Lindblom, B. S. (2006). *Scientific Examination of Questioned Documents* (2nd ed.). CRC Press.
8. Sita, J., Found, B., & Rogers, D. K. (2002). Forensic handwriting examiners' expertise for signature comparison. *Journal of Forensic Sciences, 47*(1), 11–17. https://doi.org/10.1520/JFS15045J.
9. Srihari, S., Cha, S. H., & Lee, S. (2002). Individuality of handwriting. *Journal of Forensic Sciences, 47*(4), 856–872. https://doi.org/10.1520/JFS14967J.
10. Srihari, S., Huang, C., & Srinivasan, H. (2008). On the discriminability of the handwriting of twins. *Journal of Forensic Sciences, 53*(2), 430–446. https://doi.org/10.1520/JFS16639J.
11. Yaraskavitch, L., Graydon, M., Tanaka, T., & Ng, L. K. (2008). Controlled electrostatic methodology for imaging indentations in documents. *Forensic Science International, 177*(2), 97–104. https://doi.org/10.1016/j.forsciint.2008.02.010.

CHAPTER 10

THE INTERFACE OF FORENSIC SCIENCE AND THE LAW

Contents

Introduction 382

10.1. The Role of Forensic Experts in Court 382

10.2. The Role of an Expert Witness in a Trial 394

10.3. Admissibility of Forensic Evidence (Daubert and Frye Standards).. 399

10.4. Ethical Issues in Forensic Science 408

10.5. Criminal Justice and the Law 418

10.6. Future Trends in Forensic Science and its Impact on the Legal System 420

References 426

INTRODUCTION

The interface of forensic science and the law represents a crucial convergence of scientific methodology and legal principles, playing a fundamental role in the administration of justice. Forensic science applies rigorous scientific methods to analyze physical evidence, helping to uncover facts that can substantiate or refute legal claims. This intersection encompasses a variety of scientific disciplines, including biology, chemistry, physics, and digital technology, which collectively contribute to the resolution of legal issues.

In the legal context, forensic science is indispensable for criminal investigations and civil litigation. It aids in the accurate identification of perpetrators, the exoneration of the innocent, and the provision of critical evidence that supports legal arguments. For instance, DNA analysis, one of the most potent tools in forensic science, can definitively link a suspect to a crime scene or victim, or conversely, can exclude individuals as possible perpetrators. Similarly, forensic toxicology can determine the presence of drugs or poisons in biological samples, influencing cases ranging from DUIs to suspicious deaths.

Legal professionals rely on forensic evidence to build their cases, presenting scientific findings in a manner that is understandable and compelling to juries and judges. This necessitates a robust framework for ensuring the reliability and admissibility of forensic evidence in court. The landmark case of Daubert v. Merrell Dow Pharmaceuticals established criteria for the admissibility of expert testimony, emphasizing the importance of scientific validity and peer-reviewed methodologies.

Challenges at this interface include maintaining the integrity of evidence, the potential for misinterpretation of complex scientific data, and the evolving nature of both scientific techniques and legal standards. As forensic science advances with new technologies and methodologies, legal systems must continually adapt to ensure that these innovations are integrated in a way that enhances, rather than compromises, the pursuit of justice.

Ultimately, the synergy between forensic science and the law underscores a commitment to truth and justice, where scientific rigor informs legal decision-making, ensuring fair and equitable outcomes in both criminal and civil matters.

10.1. THE ROLE OF FORENSIC EXPERTS IN COURT

With their expert testimony, forensic experts play a vital role in the legal system, having the power to dramatically impact a trial's verdict. These experts are called upon to make difficult scientific concepts understandable to the jury and judge, as well as to present their findings.

Critical facts, like the existence of a substance, the reason for an injury, or the identity of a suspect, can be established with the aid of their testimony. Experts in forensics have to remain unbiased, concentrating only on the evidence and not letting the interests of either side in the case influence them. To determine their credibility, their credentials—which include their education, training, and experience—are frequently examined. The purpose of opposing counsel's cross-examination is to evaluate the credibility and dependability of the witness. Proficiency in communication is imperative for experts, as they must effectively and convincingly communicate technical information.

10.1.1. Admissibility of Evidence: Standards for Admitting Forensic Evidence

Rules governing the admissibility of forensic evidence in court are intended to guarantee the presentation of only trustworthy, legitimate scientific evidence. The Daubert and Frye standards are the main ones used in the US. The 1923 case Frye v. established the Frye standard. The relevant scientific community must deem scientific evidence to be "generally accepted" in the United States. Consensus and established acceptance are highlighted by this standard. As opposed to this, the Daubert standard was developed by the Supreme Court in the 1993 case Daubert v. Dow Pharmaceuticals, Merrell, Inc. affords a framework that is more adaptable. Judges function as gatekeepers under Daubert, evaluating a number of criteria to decide whether or not a theory or method is testable, whether or not it has undergone peer review and publication, the known or potential error rate, and the level of acceptance within the pertinent scientific community. Thus, a more thorough scientific examination of forensic evidence is encouraged by the Daubert standard.

10.1.2. Ethics in Forensic Science: Ethical Considerations and Professional Conduct

Since forensic evidence's integrity can have a big influence on justice, ethics in forensic science are extremely important. Strict ethical rules must be followed by forensic scientists in order to preserve their impartiality, accuracy, and objectivity. Steer clear of conflicts of interest, make sure evidence is handled and analyzed properly, and give objective testimony, among other ethical considerations.

It is expected of forensic experts to stay up to date on developments in their field and to pursue ongoing education and training to improve their abilities. Honesty in reporting outcomes, openness in procedures and conclusions, and a dedication to maintaining the profession's standards are all components of professional conduct. Any type of misconduct, including data fabrication and false qualification claims, can erode public confidence and result in incorrect convictions or the exoneration of guilty individuals. Professional associations' (like the American Academy of Forensic Sciences) codes of ethics offer comprehensive recommendations to help forensic scientists resolve moral conundrums and uphold the highest standards of conduct in their field.

Many organizations, including federal, state, or local laboratories and academic institutions, can hire forensic experts.

They might be asked to testify as expert witnesses or employed as consultants to offer their specialized knowledge and counsel on matters pertaining to science or technology. To aid the judge or jury in a criminal or civil case, to support an impoverished criminal defendant, or to offer a third opinion on material and evidence that has already been examined by the prosecution and defense experts, the court may subpoena or appoint forensic experts.

Expert witnesses need to be ready to testify, regardless of the circumstances or method of summoning them. They have to collect technical data relevant to the case or test the evidence.

They have to adhere to standard lab procedures and protocols when testing evidence. They must gather the data, facts, and test results that serve as the foundation for their conclusions by going step-by-step in a systematic and logical manner.

Expert witnesses are required to gather information, process it, and write clear, concise reports using the scientific method and appropriate supporting documentation. In order to keep each other's attention on the most crucial aspects of the case and to ensure that each other understands technical and legal jargon, expert witnesses and the lawyers or courts that request them must collaborate. Expert witnesses can enhance their credibility by presenting a polished and well-organized testimony.

It also aids in learning the fundamental facts pertaining to a matter in dispute during the important and occasionally taxing pretrial discovery process that opposing attorneys undertake. Giving requested information to the other side so they can use it to support their case is known as discovery. It is organized and guided by procedural rules or deadlines set by the court.

10.1.3. Tips for Testifying in Court

Expert witnesses must convince the judge or jury that their testimony is sound and truthful. They must be highly knowledgeable, organized, alert, unflappable and ethical:

- **Knowledgeable**: Show that you are up to date, have command of the subject matter in your field, and are knowledgeable about the Federal Rules of Evidence and any state or jurisdictional laws relevant to the case. Know how to use such things as demonstrative evidence (an item not from the crime scene that is used to illustrate a point).
- **Organized**: Be able to easily reference and locate key pieces of evidence. Reports should always be updated to include results of retesting, further testing of previous evidence or testing of new evidence.
- **Alert**: Answer questions promptly and intelligently. How you respond could affect your credibility. Recognize the unauthorized appearance of evidence denied through motion in limine (a pretrial motion that bans evidence from trial for various prejudicial, irrelevancy or constitutional reasons).
- **Unflappable**: Do not appear combative or annoyed during questioning, especially during cross-examination (questioning by the opposing attorney).
- **Ethical:** Know the ethical standards of conduct. Do not be persuaded into presenting false testimony. Display objectivity, not advocacy.

10.1.4. Forensic Science in the Courtroom

In a court of law, forensic science is comparable to a detective's secret weapon. It's the study of deciphering clues from even the smallest pieces of evidence to solve mysteries and crimes.

Forensic science assists legal systems in obtaining evidence, such as DNA and fingerprints. In today's courts, forensic science—the application of scientific principles to criminal investigations and legal proceedings—plays a crucial role. It has a significant impact because it helps to achieve justice by bridging the fields of science and law.

Because forensic science is an impartial, objective arbiter of truth, it is essential to justice. Through the analysis of physical evidence, it offers vital answers to questions regarding crimes and incidents, frequently uncovering hidden details that human accounts alone are unable to uncover.

Forensic science provides highly reliable assistance in determining guilt or innocence by using rigorous methodologies and empirical data. Its accuracy and objectivity guarantee the administration of justice, safeguarding the innocent and holding the guilty accountable. A crucial cornerstone of the legal system in the search for justice and the truth is forensic science.

Forensic evidence frequently serves as the voice of the silent witness, providing an unbiased account of events that might have otherwise remained hidden. This is especially important in cases where human reports are contradictory or untrustworthy. Thus, forensic science is the cornerstone of justice, guaranteeing that the guilty bear the consequences of their deeds and that the innocent are not falsely convicted.

10.1.5. Producing Forensic Evidence in the Courtroom

Forensic evidence in Indian courtrooms is typically produced and presented through the following process:

1. **Evidence Collection:** The process begins with collecting physical evidence from crime scenes by law enforcement agencies. This can include fingerprints, blood samples, DNA, firearms, and documents.
2. **Preservation:** Proper preservation of collected evidence is crucial to maintain its integrity. The chain of custody is maintained to ensure evidence is not tampered with or contaminated.
3. **Examination:** The collected evidence is then sent to forensic laboratories for study. Trained forensic experts conduct various tests and analyzes to determine the nature and significance of the evidence.
4. **Forensic Reports:** Forensic experts prepare detailed reports outlining their findings after examination. These reports include methodologies used, results, and interpretations.
5. **Expert Testimony:** Forensic experts are often called to testify in court as witnesses. They present their findings, explain the significance of the evidence, and provide expert opinions when necessary.
6. **Cross-Examination:** Lawyers representing both the prosecution and defense can cross-examine forensic experts to challenge their findings, orensic evidence is determined by the judgeThe judge determines the admissibility of forensic evidence. The judge assesses whether the evidence is relevant, reliable, and meets legal criteria for admissibility.
8. **Bench Assessment:** In bench trials, the judge assesses the evidence and reaches a verdict.
9. **Verdict:** Based on the presented forensic evidence and other factors, the court reaches a verdict, either finding the accused guilty or not guilty.

10.1.6. Challenges Faced to Present Forensic Evidence in Courtrooms

Presenting forensic evidence in Indian courtrooms, while crucial for ensuring justice, comes with several challenges:

- **Lack of Standardization:** Forensic practices and protocols in India often lack standardization. Different laboratories and experts may employ varying methods, leading to discrepancies and challenges to the credibility of evidence.
- **Resource Constraints:** Many forensic laboratories in India are under-staffed and underfunded, leading to backlogs in evidence processing and delays in court cases.
- **Quality of Evidence:** The quality and preservation of evidence collected at crime scenes can be suboptimal due to inadequate training of law enforcement personnel and forensic experts.
- **Chain of Custody Issues:** Maintaining a transparent chain of custody for evidence is essential. However, lapses can occur during evidence handling, raising doubts about its integrity.
- **Admissibility Challenges:** Indian courts can be stringent about the admissibility of scientific evidence. Ensuring that evidence meets the legal criteria for admissibility can be a challenge.
- **Limited Awareness:** Judges and lawyers may have little awareness of complex forensic techniques, making it challenging to effectively present and cross-examine forensic evidence.
- **Backlogs and Delays:** Overburdened court systems and forensic laboratories can lead to significant delays in cases involving forensic evidence, affecting timely justice delivery.
- **Ethical Concerns:** Issues related to privacy, consent, and ethical practices in collecting and analyzing biological evidence, such as DNA samples, can arise.

10.1.7. Role of Forensic Sciences in Criminal Prosecution

Crime has existed in one form or another since the dawn of human history. Criminal behavior and the idea of crime have changed significantly as science and technology have advanced. This made it harder for police investigators to rely on their traditional methods of surveillance, questioning, and investigation to find crimes since criminals exploited their intelligence to use technology to their advantage.

In the current situation, the traditional approach of detecting crime through painful methods is no longer applicable. The police investigators in this case also rely on science to complete their investigations. This is where forensic science has saved the day and is now a potent tool in the hands of the legal system and law enforcement agencies.

The word "forensic" comes from the Latin word "forensicus," which denotes participation in a court of law or public discourse. "Forensic science" refers to the science applied in justice courts. The scientific field of forensic science addresses the identification, individualization, assessment, and recognition of tangible evidence through the application of natural science procedures in the context of criminal justice administration.

All scientific disciplines, including medicine, surgery, biology, physics, chemistry, and photography, are included in forensic science. But over time, it has branched out into other fields as well, including toxicology, entomology, anthropology, ballistics, hairs and fibers, pathology, fingerprint odontology, and questioned documents.

At the moment, it has been expanded to include forensic engineering, forensic neuropathology, forensic accounting, and fraud auditing. The second lie detection test that involves the interaction of the mind and body is the polygraph. Using this technique, the subject of the expert's cross-examination has a variety of polygraph machine sensors and components affixed to their body. 5 Any variations in the subject's electrical resistance at the skin, blood pressure, respiration rate, or pulse rate indicate a deliberate attempt to withhold information.

The third kind of lie detection test involves attaching test sensors to the subject's head, called brain mapping. Later, using the linked computer, some images are displayed or sounds are produced. The sensors watch for any kind of electrical activity or response and record P300 waves. This kind of reaction takes place when someone connects with the displayed image or audible sound.

This demonstrates unequivocally that the person is connected to the incident in some manner. The biological blueprint of life is tested using DNA fingerprinting, which is the fourth test type. This approach is regarded as essential in the field of forensic science in our nation. Compared to other forensic science techniques or branches, this is a more thorough scientific investigation.Any kind of crime, including murders, hit-and-run incidents, assaults, sexual assaults, encounters, rapes, and other body offenses against people, can be found using DNA fingerprinting. Numerous substances, such as hair roots, saliva, blood, semen, etc., can be used for this. The offender unintentionally leaves any of these items where they are. Every living cell in our body has DNA, which aids in identity tracing.

10.1.7.1. Main Functional Elements of Forensic Science in Crime Investigation

The prime functional components of forensic science are as follows:

a. **Corpus Delicti:** The cause of death could be homicidal, suicidal, accidental, or natural. Forensic Science ascertains the cause and nature of death to establish whether the death was homicidal or non-homicidal. It can also differentiate a fake incident from the real one.

b. **Modus Operandi:** The inspection of the corpus delicti, crime scene, evidentiary clues, and the surrounding condition indicates the possible modus operandi.

c. **Criminal Identity:** The identity of the offender could be discovered with the help of many clues that include mobile phone records, personal details like SMS, emails, transactions which provide some relevant information about his participation in the crime. The culprit may also leave some traces behind like footprints, fingerprints, hair, blood drops, saliva, semen, or other body fluids on the victim's body or on weapons at the place of crime. In certain circumstances, a series of chain is created all of which when linked together connects a suspect with the crime.

d. **Victim Identity:** Forensic Science through a detailed study of personal clues helps to find out the unknown deceased person, any mutilated dead body, or any skeletal remains. There are other clues as well that help in the identification of the victim's body, but DNA profiling and fingerprints give major hints in this respect.

e. **Forensic Scientists:** Forensic scientists assist the criminal justice system in many ways. They apply the principles of the physical or natural sciences for the analysis of distinct evidence which can prove the guilt or innocence of the suspect during investigation and trials. A forensic scientist takes the lead of investigation; he distinguishes the real crime scene from the fake one. The sequence of events relating to any incident is established by him that aids in further investigation.

10.1.7.2. Forensic Evidence and its Analysis in Crime Investigation

Any information or data that is presented in court and has the potential to establish the guilt or innocence of the suspect can be considered evidence. By bringing forensic evidence into the legal system, forensic science made a significant contribution. Scientific procedures are used to gather forensic evidence, which is then presented in court. It establishes tee of a person's involvement in crime and serves as evidence for the prosecutionoffense or defense.

To reveal the modus operandi and provide information about the corpus delicti, forensic evidence is gathered, handled, examined, analyzed, and presented. It can be used to establish connections between crimes that are thought to be connected.

The police are able to identify patterns of crime and reduce the pool of potential suspects by linking crimes, which aids in the identification and prosecution of the accused. Physical evidence, transfer evidence, trace evidence, pattern evidence, and transient evidence are some of the categories used to classify common forensic evidence.

- Physical evidence is usually found at crime scenes and contributes in understanding the case by perceiving these evidences. Example – fingerprints, footprints, handprints, cut marks, tool marks and such other marks.
- Transfer evidence refers to that evidence which is exchanged as a result of contact between two objects.
- Trace evidence exists in small traces or are very minute in size that usually goes unnoticed and can be transferred or exchanged between two surfaces, example – dust, soil, hair, fiber and other materials.
- Pattern evidence includes finger impressions, foot impressions, gunshot residue, and other impressions that are later interpreted to discover the evidence.
- Transient evidence is temporary evidence and can be easily altered or lost that must be recorded at the crime spot as soon as possible, which includes odors, temperature, and certain imprints that do not last for a longer period.

10.1.7.3. Statement of problems associated with Forensic Analysis and Services

We cannot deny that there are imperfections in this world and that science has some of them since nothing is perfect. Regrettably, forensic science disciplines and methodologies suffer from a number of drawbacks. To be successful, forensic analysis must overcome a number of obstacles and difficulties. Numerous flaws have undermined the scientific basis of forensics by jeopardizing its services.

Some of the common problems that are faced quite often are mentioned below:

- A surprisingly high rate of errors in the laboratories is one of the emerging problems which includes cross contamination and mix up of DNA samples, these errors seem to be persistent in forensic labs.
- The results of the test conducted are often falsified by dishonest DNA Analysts. They manipulate the test outcome to cover up errors.
- Scientific analysis is a tedious task and consumes a lot of time and as a result the judgment is delayed. The interpretation of analysis varies from person to person which may cause difference in opinions.
- Analysis needs to be precise and accurate as much as possible and if not might show ambiguous figures.
- In reality evidence is not always easily available.
- Forensic evidence can be manipulated, altered, or moderated which may end up in unjust verdict.
- Forensic analysis can be averted by strong influences (political or financial factors).
- There is no specific manner to validate the results of experiment, it requires broad knowledge and deep study.
- Last but not the least any kind of inefficiency and misinterpretation can mislead the scientific analysis.

10.1.7.4. Dimensions of Forensic Science Tests

- **Lie Detection Tests:** During the early years of 20th century Psychosomatic disorders received a great deal of study by psychologists, psychiatrists, and physiologists. What is meant by this phrase 'Psychosomatic disorders' is simply that certain disorders at the body, or some, may be covered by emotions. The modern lie detector technique is also based on the principle of psycho so Matic interaction which means that emotional experiences, as felt by the individual, causing certain type of psychological disturbance are always found to go together and that the evidence for the occurrence of one can be used as evidence for the occurrence of the other.
- **Narco-Analysis Test:** The term 'narco-analysis' derived from the Greek word "Narke" means 'anesthesia or torpor' and is used to

describe a diagnostic and psychotherapeutic technique that uses psychotropic drugs, particularly barbiturates, which act as central nervous system depressants, and by virtue of this they produce a wide spectrum of effects, from mild sedition to anesthesia. It is also known as drug hypnosis or truth serum or a combination of hypnosis and narcosis.

10.1.7.5. Polygraph Test

It's well known that when someone lies, their body exhibits visible signs, like a spike in blood flow to the face, twitching of the lips, toe movements, movement of the "Adam's apple," etc.

Scientists have created devices in the modern era that can record lying or telling the truth. The introduction of new lie detection techniques has created a volcano in the age of established laws of evidence and criminal jurisprudence, as well as old laws of crime detection. The polygraph operates under the premise that any alteration in an individual's conscious feelings or perceptions triggers a defensive mechanism that manifests as psychological changes i.e., in the skin's electrical resistance, blood pressure, respiration rate, and pulse rate G. S. R. (Galvanic Skin Response).

The polygraph is a test that uses a variety of parts or sensors of a machine that are attached to the subject's body while they are being questioned by an expert. It is based on the idea that there is a relationship between the mind and body. There are several reasons why polygraphs are administered. In addition to being used for pre-employment testing on potential hires, it is also used for arrests in criminal investigations in the United States and Japan.

10.1.7.6. Brain Mapping

The brain produces a specific kind of electrical wave known as P300, or brain mapping, when it detects a sound or a person. These days, the government acknowledges it as a trustworthy forensic instrument for factinvestigations.

The neurologist Dr. Lawrence A. Goodbye developed and patented this test in 1995.Goodbye, Chief Scientist and Director of "Brain Wave Fingerprinting"; the accused is first questioned and interviewed to determine if he is withholding any information.

These tests, which aim to correlate changes in the cognitive evoked potential with the patient's clinical changes, are typically used in cases of white-collar crime or heinous crime.

10.1.7.7. Brain Fingerprinting

Despite receiving a lot of attention, Dr. Lawrence Farwell's "Brain Fingerprinting" method has not been the focus of a thorough independent investigation. A significant objection, aside from this initial skepticism, is focused on the inherent challenge of creating suitable "probes" for the examination.

A subject may have previously been exposed to the material probes, even if the "probes" are created by the examiner, who is fully conversant with all the details of the case under investigation. If the subject has such prior exposure, it won't matter in the grand scheme of the investigation even if it is discovered that they are familiar with the probes.

For instance, there are numerous ways in which the subject can be exposed to the test stimuli following crimes that garner significant media attention. One could become aware of the crime through reading about it in periodicals or newspapers, watching TV, hearing about it on the radio, or through hearing about it from others.

Scientific advancements have established the irreversible need for such studies by elevating modern investigations' stature in terms of outcomes. In today's advanced world, scientific technology is undergoing a revolution that is spreading like wildfire. Scientific progress also casts a shadow over the legal profession. Science's progress has not escaped the judicial system, especially in the area of criminal justice.

In light of this, forensic science is essential to the detection of criminal activity. It can be characterized as a science that is used to gather, examine, present, and utilize tangible evidence in court, particularly when it comes to criminal cases. It incorporates all scientific disciplines and applies them to legal issues. Even though it draws inspiration from many scientific fields, including chemistry, medicine, surgery, biology, physics, photography, and mathematics, it has also developed its own branches over time, such as anthropology and D. N. A., Fingerprint Odontology, Fingerprinting, etc.

The 20th century saw a revolution in the modern investigative system thanks to forensic science tests like DNA fingerprinting, lie detection, and fingerprint comparison. There are three different kinds of lie detection tests. First, there is the narco-analysis test, which entails giving a patient a drug intravenously to induce hypnosis and reduce inhibition.

Investigators can benefit from the drug-induced hypnotic stage because it increases the subject's likelihood of providing information. Sodium pentothal, the medication used in this test, is frequently used in large doses to induce general anesthesia during surgical procedures. This test is a scientific method designed to elicit information from an accused person while they are naturally dozing off. The polygraph test is the second exam. The polygraph operates under the tenet that altering an individual's perception or intentionally held emotions triggers a defense mechanism that manifests as psychological alterations i.e., in the skin's electrical resistance, blood pressure, respiration rate, and pulse rate—known as G. S. R.

A trans duct attached to the thumb measures blood volume, which reflects pulse rate, and electrodes attached to the palm or fingers measure the electro dermal response. During the polygraph test, a corrugated rubber tube tied around the subject's chest measures respiratory changes and an inflated cuff wrapped around the upper arm measures cardiovascular changes.

By posing queries with known answers, investigators can establish a baseline. When a suspect lies, there are noticeable behavioral and psychological changes that go along with it. The graph's sensors and wave pattern show this. A departure from the baseline is interpreted as a lie sign. Brain Mapping, or P300. When a person is emotionally connected to those images or sounds, waves are typically reflected back to them.

A computer controls the entire system. The accused is thought to have some connection to the incident if the stimulus elicits a positive resp fingerprinting is tested in the fourth forensic science test. The acronym for Deoxyribonucleic Acid is DNA. It is the life'slife's biological blueprint. Almost all body materials can be used for DNA fingerprinting, and they are used in a wide range of horrific crimes, including murders, sexual assaults, encounters, and other body offenses against people.

10.2. THE ROLE OF AN EXPERT WITNESS IN A TRIAL

A person who possesses a great deal of knowledge or experience and is able to provide an unbiased opinion based on the evidence presented is called an expert witness. Experts are used in courts, tribunals, and arbitrations for a variety of purposes.

A view on the evidence supporting the case becomes essential in order to resolve a dispute. In court proceedings, an expert witness testifies to support the evidence with their technical analysis.

10.2.1. Expert Witness in a Trial

An itness is a person with specialized knowledge, education, training, experience, and/or skills that surpass the average person'spersons. Expert witnesses are allowed to testify in federal and state courts to help the judge or jury reach a verdict. An expert witness with skill will use complex situations and technical terms to further explain them so that the jury and other members can underst An expert witness's duties may also occasionally include assessing possible cases.

In an advisory capacity, an expert witness'switness' advice to clienthe best ways to calculate can be helpful. They make initial estimates of the high and low ranges of losses in a case that has tomust be handled. They offer thorough and essential case advice that has the power to change the dynamic of court proceedings.

10.2.2. When to Ask for Expert Witness Services?

Just as there are many different subjects on which attorneys can file a lawsuit, so too do the experts that attorneys can hire. An expert witness's main goal is to offer insight into a skill or body of knowledge that could be further useful to the case.

It is more likely that an expert witness will be needed to provide assistance or an opinion on specific judicial matters in complex cases. Keep in mind that, depending on the case and the circumstances, an expert witness for a class action may be needed.

10.2.3. Expert Witness in a Trial Affect the Results of a Case

The case can be made or broken by expert witnesses. Their testimony is an essential component of a litigation strategy designed to give the jury a clearer understanding of the case's facts. Poor expert testimony can weaken your case, and at worst completely destroy it, whereas strong expert witnesses can bolster your case and give credibility to your arguments.

Consequently, it is crucial to have knowledgeable specialists who can withstand the most intense cross-examination. Maintaining your expert's credibility and identifying any flaight cast doubt on their advice requires you to be assertive at all times.

10.2.4. Types of Expert Witnesses

An expert witness'switness' job is to offer advice that may be needed in a variety of legal contexts, including adoption proceedings, child custody disputes, medical malpractice cases, personal injury lawsuits, product liability, criminal law, divorce, and financial and securities issues.

In order to find an expert witness, we must first know their types and the services which they can cater. The types of expert witnesses that may be required in order to assist your case are:

- Medical Experts
- Vocational Experts
- Engineering Experts
- Forensic Experts
- Financial Experts
- Securities Experts
- Mental Health Experts
- Parenting Experts

Experts are needed in various circumstances based on those specific facts to a given case.

1. **Medical Experts in a Trial:** Physicians, nurse practitioners, physical therapists, and other individuals with medical training who are referred to as professionals are examples of medical experts. Medical expert witnesses may provide testimony in lawsuits involving medical malpractice or plaintiffs' personal injuries.

   In certain criminal cases, medical experts may testify during a trial to provide insight into the type and severity of injuries suffered by a victim of criminal assault.

2. **Financial Experts in a Trial:** Financial specialists are communicators as well as technicians in their industry. If they are ill-prepared to present their findings clearly and succinctly, even the most technically skilled specialists will collapse on their faces. This needs to be communicated verbally and in writing to the fact-finder, opposing attorneys, and clients.

   A forensic accountant can ascertain the different possible facets of a court proceeding, and financial experts in a trial might help in a divorce case. By estimating the value of various assets, such as rental property, a family business, antiques, artwork, jewelry, and gun collections, forensic experts can also provide assistance in probate court.

   3. **Engineering Experts in a Trial:** In a court of law, an engineering expert offers the legal profession thorough engineering analysis within their area of expertise and acts as a consultant.

   When it comes to product liability cases, engineers can use their knowledge to help the jury decide whether a product was made or designed safely.

4. **Vocational Experts in a Trial:** Professionals in the field can provide advice on a person's ability to return to work and, if so, in

what capacity. They might also provide professional advice on how long it might take for an individual with a certain skill set or job to become independent.

5. **Forensic Experts in a Trial:** The role of an expert witness in a trial may be involved in one of any number of areas of scientific pursuit. They may be:

- an anthropologist
- a biochemist
- a chemist
- a dentist
- a medical examiner
- a psychologist
- a psychophysiologist
- a toxicologist

They may even be an expert in areas such as:

- Ballistics
- Computers
- Crime scene reconstruction
- Fingerprints
- Firearms
- Explosives
- Handwriting
- Textiles
- Toolmarks

Most pcoplc associate forensic expert witnesses with criminal cases, furthermore, they can also assist in civil court proceedings.

6. **Security Expert Witness in a Trial:** Expert witness services are provided by security specialists on a wide range of risk management and security-related matters, ranging from evaluating inadequate security and carelessness to anticipating potential threats, training security guards, and their operations. A securities expert may be crucial in cases involving white-collar fraud.

   When determining whether or not there has been intentional fraud, a securities expert can assist in reviewing the available data and the status of the market. They can also determine whether a financial institution's actions or inactions constitute a breach of its fiduciary duties.

7. **Mental Health Expert Witness in a Trial:** There are many different circumstances where one or more parties' mental health is in doubt. Mental health professionals can assess a person and provide an opinion on any number of issues, including: Was the person criminally insane at the time the criminal act was committed? Has the person been brought back to competency so they can resume managing their financial affairs?
8. **Parenting Expert Witness in a Trial:** Experts in parenting frequently provide their advice in matters involving adoption, divorce, and the relinquishment of parental rights. A few situations where a parenting expert could be useful are when assessing whether's addiction recovery is sufficiently under control or when assessing a child's emotional capacity to handle a once-every-other-week schedule.

10.2.5. QualifiesQualified as an Expert Witness to Prepare for a Trial

Making sure that experts are suitably qualified to testify in court through the Voir Dire procedure is one of the most important aspects of being an expert witness.

The method used to qualify an expert witness is called voir dire. This includes a cross-examination as well as a direct examination by the person calling the witness as an expert. Introducing the expert to the judges and going over their resume will help to establish their extensive experience, background in education, and work history.

10.2.6. Admissibility of Expert Evidence

Generally speaking, witnesses should only testify about things they are familiar with. Opinion or belief-based evidence is not admissible. Only during the expert's deposition as a witness in court does the expert's opinion become admissible. An expert's report is not admissible unless the opposing party tests the expert's evidence through cross-examination and the expert provides justification for the opinion formed. However, the law has waived the need to examine some scientific experts in order to reduce the time and costs associated with obtaining their assistance.

10.2.7. Expert Report

An expert's report serves to provide their opinion on subjects under their purview that they have been asked to report on. The report's main purpose is to educate the court on subjects outside of its purview, subjects on which it must make decisions in order to settle the conflict at hand. The report will be used by the court, but it will also provide technical information to the parties so they can assess the merits of their case further.

10.2.8. Expert Witness Prepare for a Trial

In court, expert witnesses are a necessary component of many legal proceedings. Make sure the expert you have chosen is ready to testify in court if you are getting ready for litigation and you need one on your side.

- Thorough preparation on the facts of the case
- Brushing up on vital legal concepts
- Practicing examination and deposition
- Refreshing themselves on their own qualifications
- Prepare demonstrative aids (verbal testimony)

10.2.9. Choose an Expert Witness

In today's commercial litigation, the role of an expert witness in a trial has become crucial. With the world becoming more and more specialized, a growing number of cases involve aspects that experts can help counsel, judges, and juries understand and process.

Selecting the appropriate experts to assist you in effectively communicating your client's story is crucial, especially given the constant demand for experts. A thorough expert witness plan is less common than you might think, despite this.

Take a deeper dive to learn about choosing the right expert witness to assist your case with these potential steps:

- Define a pool of potential expert candidates
- Communicate the question you need your expert to answer
- Final selection—trust your instincts in identifying the ideal expert witness services provider.

10.3. ADMISSIBILITY OF FORENSIC EVIDENCE (DAUBERT AND FRYE STANDARDS)

Science has become an essential aspect of our lives in the modern world. Everything in our lives is intimately tied to science, either directly or indirectly. Additionally, science is now a crucial component of the legal and criminal justice systems. The courts have repeatedly held in a number of rulings that the scientific evidence is always relevant to the legal proceedings. Every time there is a challenge in court, forensic evidence comes up as a crucial factor. They are now an essential component of our criminal justice system, and as technology advances, it has also made it easier for the courts to handle complex cases. The use of forensic evidence has become a necessary component of the criminal justice system, making it necessary for the courts to proceed with their proceedings. These pieces of evidence consistently yield precise outcomes and are consistently trustworthy. These forensic techniques can be used to verify the credibility of an evidence. The ever-evolving field of forensic science presents a challenge to both the advocates and the honorable courts. One of the well-established rules of criminal jurisprudence is that the courts must verify the validity of any material before accepting it as evidence and determine the basis for its introduction. Their admissibility occasionally gives rise to legal disputes in the courts. The primary factor determining an evidence's quality is its legal relevance. The courts have introduced the legal reliability of forensic evidence in court proceedings by relying on a variety of different types of forensic evidenEvidence

One kind of item that has been brought before the court to support or refute a claim is called evidence.It is also made after some investigation has taken place. It contains a variety of items, including testimonies, documents, fingerprints, DNA, photos, and CCTV footage. These are referred to as proof. The legal professionals' statements will not be regarded as evidence. Neither attorney is permitted to testify in a case that they were opposing. The arguments put forth by legal professionals always attempt to interpret the evidence and suggest that it is reliable. The Indian Evidence Act of 1872, which is a legal framework rather than an act in and of itself, provides further insight into this definition of evidence.

Forensic evidence is the type of evidence gathered via scientific observations or experiments. They are also referred to as scientific proofs. It encompasses a variety of items, such as DNA testing and fingerprints.

10.3.2. DNA Testing

DNA Testing is itself an important part of forensic evidence. It can be described here as follows:

DNA, or deoxyribo nucleic acid, is the full name for this widely used term. It is a specific kind of necessary component that varies depending on the body. This kind of substance is organic. Although it can be extracted in other ways, the human body mostly contains it in the blood. Since these DNAs are specifically identical, each individual has unique expectations for other identical individuals, which gives them enormous significance. The fact that it is unbreakable by humans and eternal in nature is one of its best features. These kinds of DNA tests are typically performed to gather information regarding children, in cases of rape, among many other purposes. It is impossible to overstate their significance in the criminal justice system, and they can occasionally be helpful in civil disputes as well. As a result, they greatly aid the court in its decision-making.

Given that DNA testing is now a common practice in courts, its significance in the legal system is also clear. It is crucial to the functioning of the criminal justice system. Because of their precision and specificity, the results have a significant impact on the court's decision. Even though it has only been introduced with positive thinking, it also has some negative effects in addition to opening up new avenues for scientific evidence. However, they have not yet been found. In order to find this aspect of DNA testing, a thorough investigation must be conducted, and technological advancements must be embraced in order to identify and minimize the technology's flaws. Even so, these aspects are still unknown. New avenues for the evidence in our criminal justice system have been made possible by the development of forensic science. A new era of evidence has begun. Blood is one of the primary sources used in DNA testing, but there are numerous other sources as well, including bones, fingerprints, and hair.

Although DNA testing has a limited application, there are still undiscovered aspects of the technology. However, it can also be used negatively. For example, although it is required of executives to collect samples from rape victims within 96 hours of the incident, most of the time the samples are either not collected or cannot be processed in time. This is due to the fact that there is no authority for check and balances and the executives are unable to enforce the law on a timely basis. The main causes of these occurrences are also the lack of laboratories and time-consuming factors. Practically speaking, the courts are unable to hear every case, so responsible machinery must operate effectively.

These issues can be solved thanks to technology improvements. By creating additional labs and teams for the same goal and having a suitable system for gathering evidence, the situation can be improved. Because more organized crime-scene teams and formalized evidence collection protocols have been established in many jurisdictions, the initial collection of evidence is improving. Just in the last few years, significant advancements have been demonstrated by adhering to a comparable mechanism. Because they are likewise one-of-a-kind, another breakthrough in the field of fingerprints is also greatly assisting the criminal justice system.

10.3.3. Admissibility of Forensic Evidence in the Court of Law

In cases of sexual assault, forensic evidence is crucial because it gives the court precise information and aids in delivering justice to the accused. The term "forensic evidences" refers to any information gleaned from the accused in the case, including clothing, test results, and other items. The court of law has access to a variety of forensic evidence types that can help them. The significantly aids the legal system in dispensing justice in an open and honest manner.

In order to give the accused justice in a more precise and open way, forensic evidence is essential. In a set amount of time, the court can reach a better decision with the help of these evidences. Every time forensic evidence is presented to the court, the evidence is constantly evolving, making it challenging for the judge to assess scientific evidence. Only after thoroughly assessing each piece of evidence during the trial will the court take it into consideration. The admissibility of evidence is a complex issue in our nation. The application of forensic evidence is not consistent over time because its reliability is constantly subject to the whims of the court. When a new kind of technology is introduced into society, the situation gets more complicated because judges and legal professionals need to be aware of it. Admissibility of forensic evidence in a court of law is contingent upon its presentation alongside pertinent case facts. A court of law has verified the legitimacy, transparencyuracy of any evidence before it is deemed relevant. The evidence must uphold its integrity and adhere to the standards established by the court.

10.3.4. Admissibility Standards of Forensic EvidencesEvidence in Cr

The accuracy, dependability, and relevance of forensic evidence are the three funrs that determine its admissibility. The evidence must meet these fundamental requirements in order forfor it to be admitted in a court of law. The court found it challenging to assess the scientificscientific evidence because it is constantly evolving with the times. Only the evidence that has undergone a thorough evaluation of its validity during the trial will be taken into consideration by the court. The admissibility of evidence is a complex issue in our nation. The application of forensic evidence is not consistent over time because its reliability is constantly subject to the whims of the court. The Indian Evidence Act makes no mention of the necessary requirements that the court must meet when reviewing forensic evidence, which is one of the fundamental issues that the law has with the admissibility of forensic evidence. The only reference to the act is found in section 45, which states that evidence provided by someone who becomes an expert in a particular field shall be deemed relevant for legal purposes. Comparably, section 51 of the Evidence Act states that if evidence is provided by a subject-matter expert, it will become relevant. Aside from this, the legislature has not established any rules addressing the admlity of forensic evidence or verifying its dependability.

Forensic evidence is the type of evidence gathered via scientific observations or experiments. They are also referred to as scientific proofsproof. Its admissibility is the primary query that comes up in court. Assessing the precision or dependability of forensic evidence can occasionally become a contentious issue in front of the court and attorneys. It is challenging for judges and attorneys to accept forensic evidence as a reliable source that will influence the legal proceedings since they are not as familiar with the day-to-day workings of science. For forensic evidence to be accepted in court, it must meet the fundamental requirement of accuracy. When there is a dispute over forensic evidence, the courts typically value an expert's opinion more than the validity of the evidence. It disregards the different hypotheses put forth in relation to the forensic evidence. Judges have the discretion to decide whether or not to rely on forensic or scientific evidence; in most cases, it makes no difference what specific guidelines have been issued regarding the reliability of forensic evidence. Usually, it is determined by the case's specific facts. Since jury trials were not permitted in our nation, judges are the only ones who can decide the case's legal and factual issues. Therefore, the court's judges ought to be informed about the most recent scientific technologies and their dependability and accuracy. Regarding the use of these forensic technologies and the evaluation of their dependability and accuracy in court proceedings, no specific guidelines have been released. The fundamental Indian Evidence Act of 1872 law does not establish any particular standards for evaluating the authenticity and dependability of evidence.

10.3.5. Admissibility of Expert Evidence

The courts in our nation have generally upheld the principle that they require expert assistance when handling forensic evidence. As a result, specialists in a given field serve as the amicus curii. i.e., a court friend. Experts' opinions are important because they possess the necessary knowledge in their fields. The courts have called for assistance, and forensic evidence plays a crucial role in this process. When a decision must be based on specific forensic evidence and the courts are unsure of the evidence, they have consistently acted in an unwilling manner. When the courts feel that they need expert assistance, they will always seek it out. The evidence will not be considered by the courts until their confidence in its accuracy and dependability has been fully establis the admissibility of forensic evidence, the courts in our nation have adopted the check and balances method. Transparency, accuracy, and dependability have always been used to determine whether or notwhether forensic evidence is admissible. The courts will only consider the evidence if it is consistent with the facts of the case law. There are situations where the courts will not admit facts unless they are relevant. In the event that the facts are pertinent in any way but not in accordance with the legislative process i.e., Courts will not admit evidence if it does not comply with the requirements of the Indian Evidence Act of 1872. As a result, in our nation, forensic evidence is always evaluated according to its accuracy, dependability, and transparency. Only forensic evidence will be taken into consideration by the court of laws if it successfully satisfies all of these requirements.

When a decision must be made exclusively based on forensic evidence without the appropriate counsel of subject-matter experts, the courts have consistently exhibited a lack of enthusiasm in this regard. Similar characteristics were noted in the historic Magan Bhiarilal vs. In the case of the State of Punjab, our nation's highest court has maintained the verdict rendered by the Punjab and Haryana High Court. The expert's opinion will only be considered very cautiously, the court has noted. In addition to being against the rule ofnsistently upheld by all nations, the conviction shouldn't have been rendered solely on the basis of forensic evidence. Regarding Forest Range Officer v. P. Thntry's highest courtt, Mohhammad Ali, ruled that forensic evidence should only be considered admissible if expert assistance is sought. Any conclusion should only be drawn after that. However, it won'twill not change the court's interpretation. The court has established the rule that seekrt's opinion is required before proceeding with the case. However, there is no mention of this in the Indian Evidence Act. However, the courts have established this idea in earlier rulings.

In oe court of law, forensic evidence is presented. Many academics have conducted numerous studies on forensic evidence, but these studies have only ever looked at the results. This is due to the fact thatbecause conducting an in-depth analysis of every stage—from the first stage of arrest to the last stage of jurisdiction—requires analyzing enormous volumes of data. The studies arrive at varying conclusions depending on the stage, but they all emphasize the significance of forensic evidence. The fact that forensic evidence offers an accurate, transparent, and reasonable thing that is based upon logical aspects is one of its most important characteristics. It makes a clear connection between the accused and the case law victim. The aforementioned arguments make it evident that forensic evidel to the criminal justice system, but they also present challenges to the court regarding its interpretation and dependability from a legal standpoint. The victims of the case are becoming more and moreincreasingly in demand for the forensic evidence because it yields clear and precise results.

10.3.6. The Frye Standard

The US made its first attempt in 1923 to create a logical standard for determining whether scientific evidence can be admitted into court by issuing a significant ruling in the Frye v. 293 F. United States. 1013 (D. C. Cir. 1923). Because the technology was not widely accepted at the time, the Columbia (US) district court rejected the Lie Detector (polygraph) test's scientific validity. The District of Columbia Circuit rendered a decision in this in 1923.

The Frye case decision addressed the admissibility of testimony that predated the contemporary polygraph test and was based on the systolic blood pressure test. The court ruled that in order forfor a novel scientific technique to be widely accepted in the relevant scientific field, it must be sufficiently established. Therefore, in accordance with Frye's standards, the mere qualification of an experen technique. However, the unique requirement of the Frye standard was that specific scientific evidence could only be admitted into court if it was widely acknowledged by the relevant scientific communitythe relevant scientific community widely acknowledged it.

10.3.7. The Federal Rules 702 of Evidence

Following Frye, the US Federal Rules of Scientific Evidence were established in 1975 to provide guidelines for both criminal and civil cases filed in federal courts. The Federal Rule of Evidence (702) was originally worded as follows:

"A witness qualified as an expert by knowledge, education or training, skill, and experience may testify thereto in the form of an opinion or otherwise if scientific, technical, or other specialized knowledge will assist the trier of fact in understanding the evidence or determining a fact in the issue."

Following the enactment of Rule 702, disputants, judges, and legal experts disagreed about whether the regulation adopted the Frye standard or created a new one. The application of Rule 702 of the evidence in civil cases was also highly contentious. For instance, when courts accept dubious expert testimony to bolster tort claims.

The testimony in a case where the lie detector was used was rejected, leading to the development of the Frye Test, also known as the General Acceptance Test. It was predicated on the idea thans to be accepted in court must be grounded in scientific principles that have received widespread recognition from colleagues in that specific field (Frye v. US, 1923).

This assumption was made in order toto prevent the admission of evidence, and the conclusions drawn from that evidence are founded on erroneous and unsupported scientific theories. The Federal Rule of Evidence, which took a more liberal stance and was published in 1975, states as follows.

"if scientific, technical, or other specialized knowledge will assist the trier of fact to understand the evidence or to determine a fact in issue, a witness qualified as an expert by knowledge, skill, experience, training or education, may testify thereto in the form of an opinion or otherwise if...

1. The testimony is based upon sufficient facts or data,
2. The testimony is the product of reliable principles and scientific methods,
3. The witness has applied the principles and methods reliably to the facts of the case.

The purpose of this rule was to clarify the experts' ability to select relevant facts, trustworthy procedures, and appropriate uses in that specific field in order to form an expert opinion.

10.3.8. The Daubert's Standard

The 1993 decision by the U.S. Court of Appeals in Daubert v. Dow Pharmaceuticals, Merrell, Inc. , also referred to as The Daubert Ruling, offered judges a thorough framework to assist them in assessing the significance and dependability of the expert testimony that they are required to present in court. In this instance, two children who were born with severe birth defects claimed that the teratogenic combination of dicyclomine hydrochloride and doxylamine succinate, which is present in Benedictine (a medication manufactured by Merrell Dow Pharmaceuticals Company), which is used as an anti-nausea medication during pregnancy, was the cause of the birth defects.

Documents provided by Merrell Dow's expert indicated that there was no published scientific study proving a connection between Benthine and birth defects.

Conversely, because their methods were not yet widely accepted by the scientific community at that time, the plaintiffs were unable to present any evidence that bendectine causes birth defects. As a result, the Supreme Court outlined the following rulings which must be followed by experts in order to produce the expert testimony in the court of law, these are:

1. The empirical testability of a particular scientific theory or a technique.
2. The study or theory has been subjected to peer- review or published.
3. The acceptance of known or potential rate of errors of theory or technique and the existence and maintenance of standards.
4. The general acceptance of theory or technique in a scientific community.

The Daubert Court further noted that doubtful evidence could be addressed with forceful cross-examination, the introduction of opposing evidence, and meticulous guidance regarding the burden of proof. This Daubert standard now applies to scientific expert testimony in many states. However, a variation of the Frye standard is still in use in some states.

10.3.9. Influence of Daubert's Standard

10.3.9.1. On Forensic Science

The way the courts have examined expert testimony has been completely changed by Daubert's ruling. Reevaluating the evidence led to a rejection or acceptance decision. The Court in Kumho made it clear that the trial judges' gatekeeping role extended to all expert testimony, not just testimony based on science. In Daubert, the trial judges were held accountable for acting as gatekeepers to exclude untrustworthy expert testimony. Therefore, the admissibility of non-scientific expert testimony based on fingerprint analysis, handwriting analysis, etc., was diminished by the application of some of the Daubert factors. due to the highly subjective nature of the analysis performed with these evidences.

10.3.9.2. Fingerprints with Respect to Daubert' Standard

Following the Daubert rulings, the admissibility of fingerprints as scientific evidence is under dispute. The first case challenging fingerprint evidence occurred in 1999 and was United States v. Byron Mitchell, in Pennsylvania's Eastern District. In this instance, the District Court accepted the fingerprint evidence because it believed witness to be trustworthy. The 3rd Circuit Court of Appeals declared in 2004 that fingerprint identification satisfies the reliability requirements set forth in the Daubert and Kumho Tire cases.

In an anotheranother case United States v. Llera Plaza, the ACEV (analysis, comparison, evaluation, and verification) method of fingerprint id partially admissible as the method was failed to fulfill the following parameters of Daubert Ruling:

1. Impossibility of accurate peer review due to non-alienation of fingerprints to any particular scientificscientific community.
2. Testability element as the analysis which is subjective in nature varying within the fingerprint expert community,
3. Insufficient harmony regarding obligating the exact number of points between the two fingerprints to be matched before considering final 'match,'
4. In-adequate control standards in context to specific qualifications or certifications mandatory to be a fingerprint expert.

While presenting testimony in the court, the fingerprint experts need to:

1. Explain the methodology used in taking fingerprints and/or in developing the latent prints,
2. To show the enlargements of prints depicting ridge minute details and points of similarities and dissimilarities between the given prints.

Experts in fingerprints from all over the world are currently working to substantiate the scientific basis of this vital evidence, which is the permanence and individuality of every skin area determined after hundreds of years of study.

10.3.9.3. DNA After Daubert

Due to its unique properties, durability, reproducibility, polymorphism, and reliability, DNA is an important piece of scientific evidence that can be used in criminal investigations and paternity cases. Blood typing has already been superseded by DNA matching as a means of identification. Andrews v. was the first criminal case in which DNA was used as a key piece of evidence. State took place in the U. S.

DNA evidence has been contested in various U.S. courts on a number of grounds, including improper techniques, broken chains of custody, inadequate laboratory accreditation, contamination, and improper use of st presenting it as scientific evidence. S. and additional nations. The scientific community is trying to find answers for all these problems surrounding this extremely important evidence, since it shows whether or notwhether a specific person was present at a crime scene.

10.4. ETHICAL ISSUES IN FORENSIC SCIENCE

A profession is distinguished from a trade by having an established code of conduct that its members are expected to abide by. Members of each profession voluntarily abide by these codes because they are typically ethical in nature and are not mandated by external laws. It is imperative that each profession develop its own set of codes, or a self-regulation system. When there are no such self-regulatory codes, governments step in and impose laws that are far less suitable and have significant flaws. Compared to professionals in other fields like law and medicine, the number of forensic science professionals is comparatively low. Since forensic scientists serve as the link between science and the criminal justice system, many of them have affiliations with other professional associations (Knight, 1989; Holmes & Murdock, 1991). Because they provide results and conclusions that assist law enforcement officials, attorneys, judges,delivering justice, forensic scientists work in forensic science laboratories connected to law enforcement or other governmental agencies that have developed specific ethical codes for their organizations. The majority ofMany of the individuals working at that agency find importance in the areas of professional behavior covered by these codes. Ethical codes will be created for police officers and prosecutors, respectively, regardless of the agency that oversees law enforcement. There is a need to create codes that are unique to forensic scientists because ethical standards are organization-specific and partially applicable to forensic scientists. These codes will serve as a guide for them in situations where the criminalist's line of work raises ethical questions. These codes may help forensic scientists choose the best course of action in such circumstances because what is morally right for one may not be for another and yet another. Furthermore, according to Barnett (2001), these ethical codes represent the pinnacle of professional standing.

The standard courtroom dictum, which is "to tell the truth, the whole truth, and nothing but the truth," has been recognized by many pundits as being difficult to implement in real life. Does the obligation to tell the whole truth mean that all possible, all probable, all reasonably probable, all highly probable, or only the most probable alternatives must be given in response to a question? In any given situation, what does the whole truth include? If the whole truth includes all the possible alternatives for a given situation, what should a forensic expert witness do when the prosecutor fails to ask a crucial question? (Barnett, 2001).

Since there is no regulatory body overseeing forensic science, it lacks official recognition and registration, which ought to grant forensic scientists certain obligations and rights. People from a variety of fields who meet the necessary qualifications are employed in forensic science without having to obtain any official certification or registration. Membership in a craft organization of this kind is the only way for a forensic scientist to be restrained from engaging in professional misconduct (Knight, 1989). As a result, there is a great need to create these codes; however, this does not mean that they cannot be modified; r should be updated frequently to keep up with the rising demands of forensic laboratory standards.

It is never acceptable to falsify, trim, tailor, or alter laboratory results or the expert's interpretation of them in order toto serve the interests of a third party, whether for financial, racial, political, or military reasons. Threats of physical harm to themselves or their families, as well as financial or professional penalties, are real possibilities for forensic scientists. A robust and well-publicized code of conduct can fortify the resolve of a scientist who feels threatened, particularly if he is aware that a large group of highly esteemed colleagues worldwide are prepared to reveal any wrongdoing or oppression.

Inappropriate behavior in the forensic science field encompasses ongoing drug or alcohol addiction, violent or dishonest criminal convictions, defamation of colleagues in the field, etc., and is unsuitable for people who regularly interact with law enforcement. It is necessary to discourage the use of deceptive advertising techniques and false claims of expertise in private, unfair client acquisition practices.

10.4.1. Professional Vs Personal Ethics

The intersection of science and law where scientific ideas are applied to legal matters is known as forensic science. Therefore, the ethics surrounding the application of science to law are the ethics of forensic science. There are many contentious ethical aspects to forensic science, and forensic scientists are frequently surrounded by perplexing ethical disputes. They are able to avoid many ethical conundrums because there is still an arbitrary distinction made between ethics and morals. In forensic science, "the concerns a forensic scientist has, that are based on personal ethics (morals) or religious considerations which are not derived from professional and/or scientific roles" is what is meant to be understood when one speaks of personal ethics or morals. In contrast, professional ethics refer to the more fundamental codes or guidelines that govern scientific and professional conduct than personal ethics or morality (Weinstock et al., 2013).

10.4.2. Ethical Dilemmas in Forensic Science

Siegal (2012) has classified ethical dilemmas broadly into six categories.

10.4.2.1. Professional Credentials

Among them is the fabrication of one's qualifications in front of a judge. Among the falsehoods are claims of having earned a degree (e.g., asserting an undeserved Ph.D. or that a degree was obtained from a specific university when it wasn't, professional certifications or licenses (e.g., employment history, information about prior testimonies, such as the frequency, locations, and other details, and fraudulently claiming certification as a forensic pathologist from the American Board of Pathology (a common tactic that equates having attained actual certification with being board "eligible"). The majority of the time, this is done to dazzle the client, the jurors, or the judge in order to avoid awkward situations like cross-examination by inflating the credentials. Such exaggerations are rarely discovered due to a lack of resources and fact-checking techniques; nevertheless, such actions are immoral and ought to be discouraged.

10.4.2.2. Laboratory Analytical Procedures

The majority of laboratories have established and validated protocols that must be adhered to when performing analysis tests and documenting the tests' outcomes. The implementation of such protocols is prioritized in laboratories; however, it is unethical when forensic scientists fail to follow these protocols. Analyzing insufficiently or indiscriminately, as well as tailoring analysis to the written law, are unethical practices. "Dry-labbing" is the term for when forensic scientists report the findings without even cracking open the containers. The findings and recommendations made by forensic scientists have to be precise and understandable.

10.4.2.3. Interpretation of Analytical Data and Presentation of Testimony in a Court of Law

When giving testimony in court, forensic scientists must navigate a number of moral conundrums. The interpretation of analytical data and the presenting of testimony in a court of law can present ethical challenges. These can include bias on the part of forensic scientists, the use of scientific jargon, the use of testimony that is unclear or misleading, excessive equivocacy, and advocacy. An additional concern regarding forensic laboratories pertains to the reporting of findings and conclusions. Certain laboratories provide minimal findings without providing relevant or helpful context. Furthermore, it frequently happens that the forensic scientist who carried out the analysis need not even be present in court to give testimony.

10.4.2.4. Privately Employed Forensic Scientists

The ethics of forensic science were seriously jeopardized by the growing number of private consulting practices. Such private consultants are not subject to any disciplinary measures. A member's professional integrity may be less of an issue in forensic science than in other professions because we have the strictest quality control mechanism possible—cross-examination in court—where any misconduct, omissions, or fudging is almost certain to come to light. The highest risk of malpractice is found in private consulting because there is less financial incentive, less peer review, and less supervision.

10.4.2.5. Publicly Employed Forensic Scientists

It is important to remember that public forensic laboratories are not run or a part of local governments or law enforcement organizations. As a result, the common belief that these labs are a component of a nearby law enforcement organization grows. Under such circumstances, it is imperative that these laboratories' autonomy be preserved in order to uphold the highest ethical standards.

10.4.2.6. Obligations to the Forensic Science Profession and Professional Skill Maintenance

All forensic scientists have an inherent duty to uphold the highest ethical standards and values within the forensic science profession as researchers, practitioners, and scientists. Three categories of ethical dilemmas exist: continuing the incorrect educational practice, using proficiency tests improperly, and not keeping up with new developments and updated knowledge.

10.4.3. Objectivity in Forensic Science

In his paper on ethics in forensic psychiatry, Applebaum (1997) made the distinction between objective and subjective truth-telling and stated that telling the truth is the fundamental ethical precept. While the goal is to acknowledge the limitations of the methods used to reach conclusions, subjective truth telling involves stating what we believe to be true. It involves acknowledging the gaps in our professional and scientific knowledge, which have resulted in inferences. In order to employ the explanatory framework that is generally acknowledged by the scientific community, it is objective to include literature in reports that both supports and contradicts our conclusions. Jasper (1997) distinguished between objective and subjective phenomena in his book on general psychotherapy. He defined the objective as anything that can be observed by a trained observer and is felt by our senses, while the subjective is imperceptible to our sense organs. According to Norko (2005), an expert's honesty is a subjective component of truth telling, while his knowledge and testimony are an objective component.

In a similar vein, forensic scientists have to maintain objectivity while drawing conclusions that can be determined by training and adherence to accepted ethical standards. A scientist who aspires to draw conclusions from investigations conducted impartially and without going above and beyond their call of duty is an ethical forensic scientist (Murdock & Holmes, 1991). They must remember that their primary quality is objectivity and that they must consider all options before drawing a conclusion. They must be responsible and unbiased in their examinations and analyzes because they owe the public an explanation (Murdock & Holmes, 1991).

10.4.4. Ethical Dilemmas in Forensic Psychology

Shapiro (2016) underlined the following ethical issues after reviewing various ethical codes present across the world.

10.4.4.1. Misuse of Work

Various ethical codes around the world have attempted to clarify that the practice of psychology should not be abused by both organizations and psychologists. The practice of the profession must never involve violating fundamental human rights (American Psychological Association, 2010). When unethical behavior is detected, one should work to either minimize the impact of the violation or find a solution. According to the Canadian Psychological Association (2000), psychologists must refrain from engaging in activities that violate the legal, civil, or moral rights of others. They must also refuse to help anyone who might use their expertise to counsel, instruct, or provide information to someone in violation of human rights.

10.4.4.2. Competence

According to the American Psychological Association (2010), psychologists are required to practice to the best of their abilities within the parameters of their education, training, supervised experience, consultation, research, and professional experience. They either have a reasonable understanding of the legal or administrative guidelines dictating their roles, or they acquire one. The relative complexity and nature of the service to be rendered, pertinent training and experience, the amount of time and effort they were able to put into the subject, and the availability of consultation in a specific field are all important factors to consider when assessing competence (American Psychological Association, 2010). Forensic psychologists have an ethical obligation to advise the referral source if there is a recognized foundation in research or practice to address the specific inquiry being posed. They have to be careful not to misrepresent research in any way. In addition to being sensitive to and informed about individuals, awareness of legal and professional standards, law, rules, and procedures involved must not result in a threat to or impairment of the rights of the affected person (Canadian Psychological Association, 2000).

10.4.4.3. The Basis for Scientific and Professional Judgments

According to the American Psychological Association (2010) and the Canadian Psychological Association (2000), these must be founded on current research, established scientific and professional knowledge, pertinent literature, and ongoing education.

10.4.4.4. Delegating Work to Others

The idea of supervision—where the supervisor is accountable for the work of those under his supervision—is legally referred to as vicarious liability. He must take appropriate precautions to prevent assigning the work to individuals who have a close relationship with the clients, as this could result in exploitation or a lack of objectivity (Canadian Psychological Association 2000; American Psychological Association, 2010).

10.4.4.5. Avoiding Harm

While it is uncommon for a psychologist to intentionally hurt someone with their superior professional skills, accidents do happen occasionally. Before providing any assessment, forensic psychologists have to take long-term harms into account. A situation where a forensic psychologist has to examine a criminal's execution is one instance of unintentional harm. If the offender is determined to be competent for execution, he will be endangering life. Many will counter that he is also saving a life if the offender is deemed incompetent to be executed (Shapiro, 2016).

10.4.4.6. Multiple Relationships

According to Shapiro (2016), it is described as having a professional relationship with someone while also having a relationship with them or someone closely related to them, or as pledging to have a relationship with them in the future. The American Psychological Association (2010) states that psychologists must be clear about their role expectations and the extent of confidentiality from the beginning of the process and as circumstances change if they are called upon to serve multiple roles in legal proceedings due to legal requirements, institutional policies, or unusual circumstances. Furthermore, according to the American Psychological Association (2010), forensic psychologists are prohibited from taking on a professional role if they have any other interests that might compromise their competence, objectivity, or efficacy in providing psychological services. Shapiro (2016) gave a case study that vividly demonstrated the problem of having multiple relationships. The court ordered the concerned psychologist to treat a child who had been sexually abused and to report back to the court on a regular basis about the same case. She always thought of herself as a therapist, not a forensic investigator. Subsequently, the alleged abuser lodged a complaint alleging the psychologist's incompetence due to noncompliance with ethical guidelines. The psychologist clarified that she did not have to adhere to the guidelines because her role was therapeutic rather than forensic. She had not, however, addressed this matter until the complaint was lodged. Put another way, she neglected to explicitly state that she was only offering therapeutic services and that her reports would not be taken into consideration for a forensic examination when she took the child under her supervision.

10.4.4.7. Exploitation

In order to further political or commercial interests, as well as the best interests of research participants, students, or employees, forensic psychologists are not allowed to take advantage of people they supervise or in which they have an authority role, such as clients, patients, students, supervisees, and employees. This kind of exploitation could involve approaching potential clients, having sexual relations with them, or intimidating them into accepting services.

10.4.4.8. Informed Consent

Both the individual in question and the council that is representing them must give their consent. If the person is legally unable to give their own consent, legal counsel must be sought. The person must be informed by the forensic psychologist of all the various guidelines pertaining to the expected services, including the extent of confidentiality. In situations where written consent cannot be obtained, oral consent may be obtained. But in this instance, the examination's intervention needs to be made explicit and explained to the person (Shapiro, 2016).

The psychologist has a strong duty to inquire as to whether or not the client is represented by a council. It is important to resolve any issues at the outset that may have an impact on the relationship later on, such as fees, past personal or professional relationships, or any other similar factors (American Psychological Association, 2013). The forensic psychologist needs to be aware of factors that could lead to bias, such as conflicts of interest, examiner competence, and limitations or the scientific basis. According to the American Psychological Association (2010), informed consent also covers information from unrelated sources that could have an impact on the individual's decision to engage.

10.4.4.9. Confidentiality

A forensic psychologist's primary responsibility is to safeguard their clients' confidentiality by taking appropriate measures and communicating any limitations. According to the American Psychological Association (2010), disclosures can only be made with the client's consent or the consent of a legally authorized individual. A lawful order or the psychologist using the information for client protection or consultation may require disclosures without the client's consent.

10.4.4.10. Forensic Methodology

The forensic practitioner's obligation is to avoid obfuscating or modifying any relevant information, misinterpreting the evidence that is already available, and trying to suppress any contradicting evidence. The forensic psychologist is not allowed to draw any hasty judgments. After coming to a conclusion, the psychologist needs to vigorously and forcefully defend his conclusions (American Psychological Association, 2013). He must maintain competence in his areas of practice and specialization, avoid misrepresenting his credentials, and accurately represent his credentials (Canadian Psychological Association, 2000). Reporting of information must be as accurate as possible to prevent the formation of competing theories (Meta code of Ethics, 2005).

10.4.4.11. Documentation

To support the provision of research, institutional requirements, billing accuracy, and legal compliance, proper records must be kept. Of course, maintaining their records does not mean sacrificing confidentiality. Nonetheless, if necessary in an emergency, these records can be consulted (American Psychological Association, 2010). Enough records must be kept to ensure that activities are carried out continuously and suitably coordinated with those of others (Canadian Psychological Association, 2000).

10.4.4.12. Assessment

Unless it is impractical, it must be founded on adequate information, including a personal examination. The assessment's tests need to be valid and dependable. It is also necessary to talk about the test data's advantages and disadvantages.

10.4.5. Ethical Dilemmas in Forensic Genetics

Wallace (2014) and Cordner (2001) outlined the ethical issues related to the forensic database.

10.4.5.1. Collection and Storage of DNA Samples

Getting samples for the DNA database is one of the most important and hotly contested topics. First, who will supply the samples for the criminal investigation? Secondly, who will be obligated to supply a sample, the profile of which will be kept in the DNA database (Cordner, 2001)?

The first forensic DNA database was created in 1995 and is called the UK National DNA database. Millions of innocent citizens' DNA profiles were added to the database, but this move was heavily criticized because it was seen as an invasion of privacy. The European Court of Human Rights' Grand Chamber considered the case of Marper v. The United Kingdom unanimously determined that the permanent storage of DNA profiles, fingerprints, and samples belonging to innocent individuals violated their right to privacy (Wallacl., 2014). The requirements for whose DNA sample must be obtained vary amongst nations. In Australia, for example, samples of people suspected of committing crimes carrying sentences longer than five years are taken. In the event that chargessheets are not filed, the prosecution is dropped, or the accused is found not guilty, the samples and profile must be destroyed within 12 months. However, in the event that the defendant is found guilty, the database will still contain his profile. In the United Kingdom, the database contains the profiles of all those charged with recordable offenses, which include those for which a jail sentence may be imposed upon conviction. The database in France is exclusive to people who have been charged with sexual offenses (Cordner, 2001). It's also essential to have an audit system in place to keep an eye out for and stop unethical database use.

10.4.5.2. Testing the Samples/ Using the Results

Appropriate sample gathering, security, transportation, storage, processing, and analysis are all necessary prerequisites for excellent database management. Fulfilling these requirements leads to a high degree of confidence, which in turn leads to a high degree of credibility and dependability. Issues with contamination pose a serious threat and are a compelling argument against credibility. Analytical processes, including sample collection, securing, transport, storage, and analysis, can all be contaminated. Contaminations can never be completely eliminated, but they can always be reduced, and estimation errors can always be computed (Cordner, 2001).

10.4.5.3. Access and Retention of DNA Samples

Databases are used to store DNA profiles. Numerous writers assert that physical traits and DNA markers are correlated. Additionally, DNA may disclose a medical history. Researchers frequently use these databases excessively in their quest to find and examine these correlations. This will increase the pressure on other databases to supply data so that researchers can work with them (Cordner, 2001).

10.4.5.4. Misuse of Genetic Research in Application of Genetics to Forensic Sciences

One of the subjects of discussion is the assignment of racial and ethnic labels to genetic samples. Forensic scientists frequently attempt to assign racial and ethnic labels to samples found at crime scenes by using the findings of genetic research. Nonetheless, a lot of writers think that cultural factors, not biological or genetic, are what really cause racial and ethnic differences. The usefulness of racial classifications from a scientific standpoint has been questioned by many.

10.5. CRIMINAL JUSTICE AND THE LAW

Laws have been put in place to control interactions between people and between groups or agencies and people. These norms of behavior are based on what a specific society considers important and have existed in one form or another since the dawn of civilization. A long history of accepted social norms, regulations, practices, court rulings, and customs has resulted in the laws of today.

The United States Constitution is the ultimate charter that governs individual rights laws, the authority of the government to enact laws, and the extent to which penalties may be meted out. There is no comprehensive list of all the laws that govern our nation in the Constitution itself. It must be interpreted in light of our fundamental democratic values when determining whether new or existing laws are acceptable. State laws are superseded by federal laws.

There are a number of different types of law in the U.S. criminal justice system:

- Statutory law, or written or codified law, is the "law on the books" as enacted by a governmental body or agency having the power to make laws (such as Congress). Statutory law is based on the Constitution.
- Common law or case law is made by judges. Precedents are decisions made in previous cases or superior courts that are used as a basis to justify later decisions made in similar cases. They must be followed, and become a part of the law itself. The U.S. Supreme Court carries the greatest influence, as decisions it makes are incorporated into the process by which lower courts make their decisions. The principle of recognizing previous decisions as precedents is called stare decisis, "to stand by the decision." Once a decision is made in court, it is written down and becomes law. This makes for predictability and consistency in how the law is applied.
- Civil law, sometimes referred to as private law, deals with relationships between individuals involving such matters as property or contracts. It provides a formal means for regulating noncriminal relationships among individuals, businesses, agencies of government, and other organizations. Contracts, marriages, divorces, wills, property transfers, negligence, and products manufactured with hidden hazards are all civil concerns. It is up to an individual to bring the suit to court. Civil law is more concerned with assigning blame than with

establishing intent. In civil cases, a "preponderance of evidence" is required to convict. Violations of civil law are generally punishable by fines or transfer of property.

- Criminal law, sometimes referred to as public law, deals with regulation and enforcement of rights. It is concerned with offenses against an individual that are deemed offensive to society; the state becomes the plaintiff (as in U.S. v. Toby or State of Michigan v. Smith). The roots of our law come from medieval England, where offenders who violated the "King's Peace" were thought to be offending not just an individual, but the order established under the rule of the monarch. A misdemeanor is a minor crime such as theft, minor assault and battery, or possession of small amounts of illegal drugs. A felony is a major crime such as murder, rape, armed robbery, serious assault, dealing in illegal drugs, fraud, auto theft, or forgery. In criminal cases the prosecution must prove guilt "beyond a reasonable doubt" to convict the suspect. Violations of criminal law are punishable by fines, community service, probation, incarceration, or, in extreme cases, life in prison or capital punishment (death).
- Equity law is remedial or preventive (such as an injunction or a restraining order). These laws are for cases not covered by common law.
- Administrative law includes rules or laws established by agencies such as the Internal Revenue Service (IRS), Social Security Administration, or branches of the military.

Experts in forensic science can review evidence related to any and all of the categories of laws mentioned above. Every person who handles or gathers evidence needs to be aware of the rights outlined in the United States Constitution's Bill of Rights. U. S. Constitution, to ensure that all evidence is gathered legally and without infringing on the rights of any individual. The following list includes some of the personal freedoms protected by the U.S. Constitution during a period of regularity.

10.5.1. Individual Rights Guaranteed by the Bill of Rights

- The right to be presumed innocent until proven guilty
- The right not to be searched unreasonably, either on one's person or in one's home
- The right not to be arrested without probable cause
- The right against unreasonable seizure of personal property
- The right against self-incrimination

- The right to fair questioning by police
- The right to protection from physical harm throughout the justice process
- The right to an attorney
- The right to trial by jury
- The right to know any charges against oneself
- The right to cross-examine prosecution witnesses
- The right to speak and present witnesses
- The right not to be tried again for the same crime
- The right against cruel and unusual punishment
- The right to due process
- The right to a speedy trial
- The right against excessive bail
- The right against excessive fines
- The right to be treated the same as others, regardless of race, gender, religious preference, country of origin, or other personal attributes

According to the Patriot Act of 2001, actions labeled as presenting a "clear and present danger" to the national security of the country may lead to the suspension and/or limitation of these rights.

10.6. FUTURE TRENDS IN FORENSIC SCIENCE AND ITS IMPACT ON THE LEGAL SYSTEM

The complex fusion of law and science known as forensic science is constantly at the forefront of criminal investigations. It has always aided forensic specialists in unraveling the mysteries surrounding crimes, helping to bring the victims' rights to justice. The future of forensic science is looking bright, with limitless potential driven by changing forensic trends and driven by advances in science and technology. We have covered every detail regarding the future of forensic science in this blog post, along with an examination of the cutting-edge trends and technologies that are reshaping the criminal justice system and its perception.

Forensic science is the branch of study that combines the laws of the land with scientific principles to provide law enforcement with pertinent data. This field guarantees that victims receive justice without having their rights violated in the modern era, and it has a special place in the legal system of the nation. This field has seen numerous changes over the years that have benefited those involved in the legal system, and these changes will persist for years to come. Since new trends and technologies are emerging daily, the field of forensic science is seen as futuristic. Here, we provide all the information on how different technologies are changing the face of the forensic science industry:

10.6.1. Advancement in DNA Analysis

DNA analysis has always been seen as a crucial component of forensic science that has transformed how professionals investigate crimes. This field assists in identifying the perpetrators and provides hitherto untapped insights into the identities of the victims. Next-generation sequencing (NGS), one of the futuristic developments in DNA sequencing technologies, has been shown to improve forensic analysis's precision and effectiveness. Since the creation of NSG, forensic scientists have been able to quickly sequence genomes to obtain precise information from samples taken from crime scenes as evidence, which has assisted in ton of unsolved cases. The extraction of the most accurate profiles from a single cell can be achieved through single-cell sequencing, another cutting-edge method that is expanding the possibilities for DNA analysis.

10.6.2. Forensic Biometrics and Facial Recognition

In order toTo solve crimes more quickly and effectively, forensic science investigations frequently incorporate biometrics and facial recognition technology. The reason for this is that biometrics are thought to be the most reliable means of identifying a perpetrator or a victim. Biometric techniques will have worked with forensic science in the next few years to enable forensic experts to compare, analyze, and examine biometric details with the highest level of accuracy. Law enforcement agencies can track down suspects using recovered footage and social media images thanks to deep learning algorithms supporting facial recognition systems.

10.6.3. Digital Forensics and Cybercrime Investigation

The use of digital media and devices has increased, and as a result, forensics has become a crucial part of today's crime investigation tactics. Digital forensics has a vast application in cybercrime investigations, and as digital evidence is analyzed and examined, it will eventually allow investigators to precisely gather information about a given case. For the purpose of the investigation, sources such as computers, storage devices, and mobile phones are inspected. Since cybercrime cases are known to be rising quickly, cybercrime examiners are essential to the investigation of digital cases and the subsequent use of cutting-edge techniques and technologies in the prosecution of offenders.

10.6.4. Forensic Nanotechnology and Microscopy

Among all the scientific technological breakthroughs, nanotechnology is not only a new area of study in forensics. Because it makes it possible for professionals to find and examine evidence at the nanoscale level, nanotechnology is thought to revolutionize the science of criminal investigation. In the near future, materials like carbon nanotubes and quantum's will be analyzed by forensic scientists, allowing them to examine the evidence at the nanoscale and improving the sensitivity of forensic tests. Advances in transmission electron microscopy and scanning electron microscopy go hand in hand with nanotechnology. Experts will be able to see the evidence in high-resolution detail, which will aid in the identification of offenders.

10.6.5. Ethical and Legal Implications

"With great power comes great responsibility" is a true statement. Developments in the field of forensic science have the same effect. The ethical and legal dimensions of science are in danger due to new developments in forensics trends and technologies. Therefore, discussing the moral and legal ramifications of using forensic science is essential for a true investigator. Threats that are associated with the use of forensics are privacy rights, algorithm bias, data security, etc.

To preserve the public's faith in the justice delivery system, investigators in this field are required to uphold ethical standards. They should remember that by abiding by ethical and legal standards, the full potential of emerging trends and technologies in forensics can be fully realized.

10.6.6. Enhancing Efficiency Through Automation in Forensics

Automation is a significant trend and technological advancement that is changing the forensics landscape. These systems are used to gather evidence, process it, analyze it, and examine it so that experts can work as precisely and productively as possible. Here we have given how automation makes an impact in forensics:

- **DNA Analysis:** The analysis and examination of DNA is an important aspect of forensic investigations, but sometimes it can be time-consuming as well. Automated systems in forensics help in crime investigation by enabling the investigators to extract DNA from the samples collected from the crime scene and thus prepare the samples for further analysis and examination. Apart from t system also enables an examiner to separate DNA samples into fragments thus allowing the investigators to get maximum efficiency and accuracy out of it.

- **Fingerprint Analysis:** Automated fingerprint identification systems (AFIS) are another area that is benefitted from automation. It helps inhelps quickly matching the fingerprints with extensive databases present by the investigating departments. The database consists of known prints thus enabling the investigators to identify potential suspects easily. Even some of the AFIS systems can also help in pattern recognition and ridge counting, thus helping in reducing the need for manual analysis by the examiners.
- **Ballistics Analysis:** This field is used for the comparison of bullets and shell casings with those fired from a suspect's weapon. It is done so as to determine the weapon from which the ballistics fired that killed the victim. Earlier the verification task was done in a manual manner but now with the help of automated systems, this task of analysis is done at a faster pace. Through this system, the markings left on the bullet by the gun are verified.
- **Crime Scene Reconstruction:** Another important aspect of using automation in forensics is increased efficiency in the reconstruction of crime scenes. Using automation in crime site reconstruction has revolutionized the process of investigation of scenes. Through these systems detailed 3D models of the crime scene can be created hence providing investigators the ability to analyze and examine the scenes more comprehensively. It helps the investigators to identify potential clues present in evidence and scenes.

10.6.7. Forensic Science Impact on the Legal System

Forensic science has profoundly impacted the legal system by enhancing the accuracy, reliability, and efficiency of criminal investigations and legal proceedings. Here are key aspects of its influence:

1. **Improved Evidence Collection and Analysis**

- **Objective Evidence**: Forensic science provides objective and scientific analysis of evidence, such as DNA, fingerprints, bloodstains, and digital data. This reduces reliance on subjective testimonies and eyewitness accounts, which can be unreliable.
- **Trace Evidence**: Techniques in forensic science allow for the collection of trace evidence that can link a suspect to a crime scene, such as hair, fibers, or soil samples.

2. **Advancements in DNA Technology**

- **Identification**: DNA profiling has revolutionized the identification of individuals, making it possible to match suspects to biological evidence with high precision.
- **Exoneration**: DNA evidence has also played a crucial role in exonerating individuals wrongfully convicted of crimes, often many years after their convictions.

3. **Enhancement of Criminal Profiling**

- **Behavioral Analysis**: Forensic psychology and behavioral science help in profiling criminals based on crime scene evidence and psychological patterns, aiding in apprehending suspects.
- **Predictive Tools**: Advanced statistical tools and databases help in identifying patterns and predicting future criminal activity.

4. **Digital Forensics**

- **Cybercrime Investigation**: The rise of digital forensics allows for the investigation of cybercrimes, including hacking, fraud, and identity theft.
- **Evidence Recovery**: Specialists can recover and analyze data from computers, smartphones, and other digital devices, even if it has been deleted or encrypted.

5. **Crime Scene Reconstruction**

- **3D Modeling**: Modern techniques enable the creation of 3D models of crime scenes, which can be used to visualize events and present clear, comprehensible evidence in court.
- **Trajectory Analysis**: Forensic experts can analyze bullet trajectories, blood spatter, and other physical evidence to reconstruct the sequence of events.

6. **Chain of Custody**

- **Integrity of Evidence**: Forensic science emphasizes the importance of maintaining a clear chain of custody for evidence, ensuring that it is handled properly from the crime scene to the courtroom.
- **Legal Compliance**: Strict protocols for evidence collection, storage, and analysis help in complying with legal standards and avoiding contamination or tampering.

7. **Expert Testimony**

- **Specialist Input**: Forensic scientists often serve as expert witnesses, providing specialized knowledge and explaining complex scientific evidence to the court in a comprehensible manner.

- **Credibility**: Their testimonies can significantly influence the outcome of trials by providing credible, scientifically-backed evidence.

8. Cold Case Resolution

- **Old Evidence**: Advances in forensic technology enable the re-examination of old evidence, leading to the solving of cold cases that were previously unsolvable due to technological limitations.
- **Database Cross-Referencing**: National and international databases allow for cross-referencing of evidence, leading to breakthroughs in unsolved cases.

9. Impact on Legislation

- **Forensic Standards**: The integration of forensic science into the legal system has led to the establishment of standards and regulations to ensure the accuracy and reliability of forensic evidence.
- **Policy Development**: Lawmakers use forensic science findings to develop policies and laws that better address modern crime challenges, including cybercrime and terrorism.

10. Public Confidence

- **Justice Assurance**: The use of forensic science in criminal investigations and legal proceedings increases public confidence in the justice system, as it is perceived as a reliable and impartial means of uncovering the truth.
- **Deterrence**: The knowledge that sophisticated forensic techniques can be used to solve crimes acts as a deterrent to potential criminals.

11. Challenges and Considerations

- **Misuse and Misinterpretation**: There are risks of misuse or misinterpretation of forensic evidence, which can lead to wrongful convictions or acquittals.
- **Bias and Error**: Human error and bias in forensic analysis can impact the reliability of forensic evidence.
- **Resource and Training**: Adequate resources and training are essential for maintaining the integrity and effectiveness of forensic practices.

In summary, forensic science plays a critical role in modernizing the legal system, providing the tools and techniques necessary for thorough and accurate criminal investigations, ultimately leading to a fairer and more just legal process.

REFERENCES

1. American Psychological Association. (2010). *Ethical Principles of Psychologists and Code of Conduct. American Psychologist, 65*, 493–521.
2. American Psychological Association. (2013). Specialty guidelines for forensic psychologists. *American Psychologist, 68*(1), 7–19. https://doi.org/10.1037/a0029889.
3. Appelbaum, P. S. (1997). A theory of ethics for forensic psychiatry. *Journal of the American Academy of Psychiatry and the Law, 25*(2), 233–247.
4. Barnett, P. D. (2001). *Ethics in Forensic Science: Professional Standards for The Practice of Criminalistics*. CRC Press.
5. Canadian Psychological Association. (2000). *Canadian Code of Ethics for Psychologists. Canadian Psychology/Psychologie Canadienne*. https://doi.org/10.1037/h0086812.
6. Cordner, S. (2001). Ethics of forensic applications and databanks. In *Encyclopedia of Forensic and Legal Medicine* (Vol. 2). Elsevier Ltd.
7. European Federation of Psychologists' Associations. (2005). *Meta Code of Ethics*. Retrieved from: https://www.efpa.eu/sites/default/files/2023-04/meta-code-of-ethics.pdf
8. Jasper, K. (1997). *General Psychopathology*. Johns Hopkins University Press.
9. Knight, B. (1989). Ethics and discipline in forensic science. *Society News–Professional Affairs, 29*(2), 53–59.
10. Murdock, J. E., & Holmes, K. J. (1991). The conflicts between managerial responsibilities and the ethics of forensic science. *Journal of Forensic Sciences Society, 31*(2), 151–161. https://doi.org/10.1016/S0015-7368(91)73130-7.
11. Norko, M., & Commentary, A. (2005). Compassion at the core of forensic ethics. *Journal of the American Academy of Psychiatry and the Law, 33*(4), 386–389.
12. Shapiro, D. L. (2016). Ethical issues in forensic psychology and psychiatry. *Ethics, Medicine, and Public Health, 1*, 1–14. https://doi.org/10.1016/j.jemep.2016.01.015.
13. Siegal, J. A. (2012). Ethics in forensic science. In J. C. Downs & A. R. Swienton (Eds.), *Ethics in Forensic Science* (pp. 59–79). Elsevier Ireland Ltd. https://doi.org/10.1016/B978-0-12-385019-5.00003-8.
14. Wallace, H. M., Jackson, A. R., Gruber, J., & Thibedeau, A. D. (2014). Forensic DNA databases: Ethical and legal standards: A global review.

Egyptian Journal of Forensic Sciences, 4(1), 57–63. https://doi.org/10.1016/j.ejfs.2014.04.002.

15. Weinstock, R., Leong, G. B., & Silva, J. A. (2013). Ethics. In *Encyclopedia of Forensic Sciences* (pp. 175–180). https://doi.org/10.1016/B978-0-12-382165-2.00291-9.

INDEX

A

Academy of Behavioral Profiling (ABP) 287
Accidents 18, 21, 27, 90, 124, 126, 147, 180, 196, 213, 217, 223, 224, 246, 414
Actuarial assessment 278, 279
Adjusted actuarial assessment 278
Adoption proceedings 395
Advanced Light Source (ALS) 88
Adware 335
Age Determination 158, 168
Alcohol 17, 18, 32, 91, 113, 114, 128, 129, 130, 131, 132, 140, 142, 241, 242, 243, 339, 371, 373, 410
Alternative light source 88
American Academy of Forensic Sciences (AAFS) 11, 26, 160
American Board of Forensic Odontology (ABFO) 31, 181, 182, 189
American Board of Medicolegal Death Investigators (ABMDI) 252
American Board of Pathology (ABP) 204
American Dental Association (ADA) 185
Amnesia 270
Amplified fragment length polymorphism (AFLP) 97
Anamnestic assessment 278
Anomalies 27, 29, 158, 161, 240, 361
Antigen polymorphism 95, 96
Anti-Stokes bands 125
Apprenticeship program 360
Archaeology 157, 199
Arcus senilis 230
Artwork, jewelry 396
Atomic absorption spectroscopy (AAS)
Authentication 34, 332, 344
Automation 422
Automobiles 118, 322
Autopsia cadaverum 210
Autopsy dissection set 217

B

Backdoors 336
Bait tactic 338
Ballistic reports 2
Ballistics 14, 22, 25, 397, 423
Ballpoint pen 372, 374, 375, 376, 378
Behavioral Science Unit (BSU) 286
Bio-archaeology 157
Biological anthropology 157
Biological evidence 88, 90
Biology 2, 3, 15, 88, 90, 92, 95, 96, 102, 104, 139, 157, 160, 382, 388, 393
Bite marks 30, 156, 180, 185, 186, 190
Blood 6, 8, 9, 10, 11, 12, 18, 19, 32, 45, 46, 47, 48, 49, 50, 52, 53, 54, 57, 59, 60, 75, 76, 88, 90, 91, 92, 93,

94, 95, 96, 98, 99, 102, 106, 112, 114, 126, 128, 129, 131, 132, 137, 138, 139, 143, 144, 145, 146, 184, 186, 210, 217, 219, 220, 223, 224, 228, 229, 231, 234, 235, 240, 241, 242, 243, 244, 249, 255, 256, 257, 258, 305, 386, 388, 389, 392, 394, 400, 405, 424
Blood alcohol concentration (BAC) 128
Blood group systems 96
Bloodstains 2, 10, 94, 423
Body fluids 52
Bone 27, 88, 91, 92, 138, 144, 156, 163, 164, 165, 166, 168, 170, 171, 172, 175, 176, 177, 178, 179, 193, 200, 233, 240, 245, 248, 249
Bone cancer 156
British National Hi-Tech Crime Unit 327
Broken bones 156

C

Campbell de Morgan spots 230
Carboxyhemoglobin 231, 242, 243
Caucasoids 164, 170
Cell phones 322
Central nervous system (CNS) 128
Cerebrospinal fluid 244
Chelex extraction 89
Chemical analysis 369
Chemical bonds 118
Chemical erasures 371
Chemicals 52, 58, 60, 112, 132, 134, 135, 136, 137, 353, 372
Chemistry 2, 3, 20, 31, 32, 33, 58, 104, 112, 115, 117, 134, 136, 138, 203, 369, 382, 388, 393
Child custody 21, 273, 274, 280, 395
Child custody disputes 395
Child pornography 326
Chromatography 10, 12, 18, 20, 31, 32, 112, 113, 116, 117, 132, 139, 375, 376, 377, 379
Civil court cases 273, 322
Civil litigation 295, 325, 334, 382
Civil proceedings 198, 274, 290
Classification of Violence Risk (COVR) 279
Clinical psychology 273
CODIS (Combined DNA Index System) 14, 90
Colorado Bureau of Investigation (CBI) 46
Commercial organizations 328
Competency to stand trial (CST) 290
Computer crime 13, 320, 326, 327, 328
Computer forensics 320, 321, 328, 335, 354, 355
Computer-related crimes 326
Computers 194, 397
Computer science 2
Computer system 105, 320, 326
Concrete 2, 320, 329
Congestion 230
Corporate security 334
Counseling psychology 273
Court of Law 158, 402, 411
Crime investigation 4, 218, 421, 422
Crimes 2, 3, 4, 9, 22, 23, 28, 30, 32, 37, 51, 80, 90, 98, 101, 104, 106, 122, 148, 162, 180, 186, 221, 278, 283, 284, 291, 292, 296, 309, 310, 322, 325, 326, 328, 373, 385, 388, 390, 393, 394, 417, 420, 421, 424, 425
Crime scene investigation 45, 46, 85
Crime scenes 2, 23, 24, 31, 32, 44, 63, 69, 83, 88, 89, 90, 92, 99, 102, 112, 113, 114, 126, 162, 194, 218, 219, 257, 289, 329, 330, 386, 387, 390, 417, 421, 423, 424
Crime Scene Security Log 71
Criminal behavior 282, 283, 387
Criminal court cases 273
Criminal Investigation Department 218
Criminal justice 2, 3, 4, 31, 34, 37, 99, 109, 112, 113, 138, 140, 156, 173, 283, 284, 290, 292, 294, 297, 301, 334, 388, 389, 393, 399, 400, 401, 404, 408, 418, 420
Criminal justice system 2, 4, 37, 99, 109, 112, 113, 138, 140, 173, 283, 284,

290, 294, 389, 400, 401, 404, 408, 418, 420
Criminal law 5, 36, 270, 325, 395, 419
Criminal prosecution 4
Criminal sentencing 273
Cross-contamination 72, 83, 93
Crypto Locker 336
Crysis 336
CT scanning 203
cultural anthropology 157, 162
Cutting-edge technology 5
Cyanoacrylate 62
Cyberattack attribution 325
Cyberbullying 326
Cybercrime fighters 323
Cybersecurity incidents 322
Cyber stalking 326

D

Data interpretation 2
Data transfers 322
Defendants 364
Deinstitutionalization 301
Dental records 29, 198
Dental traits 189
Destructive methods 115
Detection of drugs 112, 139
Deuterated triglycine sulfate (DTGS) 118
Dictated passages 364
Digital data 2, 320, 423
Digital devices 320, 321, 326, 424
Digital evidence 322, 330, 331, 332, 351, 352, 353
Digital forensics 139, 320, 321, 322, 324, 325, 326, 327, 328, 329, 331, 332, 333, 338, 339, 342, 343, 345, 354, 421, 424
Digital media 321, 323, 329, 343, 421
Digital media seizure 321
Digital Single Lens-Reflex (DSLR) 185
Disease Processes 158
Diseases 134, 135, 156, 202, 203, 205, 212, 214, 229, 253
Disk forensics 333
Dissociative identity disorder 270
DNA 2, 4, 12, 13, 14, 16, 28, 29, 32, 33, 34, 58, 59, 60, 70, 74, 75, 76, 83, 87, 88, 89, 90, 91, 92, 93, 94, 95, 96, 97, 98, 99, 100, 101, 102, 103, 104, 105, 106, 108, 109, 139, 156, 183, 190, 191, 196, 328, 331, 361, 382, 385, 386, 387, 388, 389, 391, 393, 400, 401, 408, 416, 417, 421, 422, 423, 424, 426
DNA polymorphism 95, 96
DNA profiling 4, 13, 32, 96, 108, 139, 389, 424
DNA reference samples 91, 105
DNA testing 92, 94, 96, 97, 99, 100, 102, 105, 108, 109, 191, 331, 400, 401
DNA types 361
Document Examination 14, 357, 358
Double transmission 121
Dreyfus treason case 359
Drug addicts 143, 228
Drugs 6, 12, 15, 17, 18, 19, 31, 32, 52, 112, 113, 122, 123, 124, 126, 127, 135, 139, 143, 144, 149, 151, 253, 292, 296, 302, 306, 310, 382, 392

E

Education 20, 29, 31, 65, 205, 251, 252, 276, 282, 284, 285, 287, 288, 309, 359, 383, 394, 398, 405, 406, 413
Electric torch 217
Electromagnetic beam 120
Electronic documents 52
Electrostatic copy machine 373
Electrostatic Detection Apparatus (ESDA) 373
Elliptical Fourier analysis (EFA) 176
Email headers 337
Email servers 337
Email software 337
Engineering Experts 396
Erasures 371, 372
Ethnic group 103, 162, 163, 170
European Alliance for Innovation (EAI)

324
European Association of Investigators (EAI) 324
Experimental psychology 273
Explosives 32, 112, 113, 118, 126

F

Family court cases 273
Fax machines 369
Federal Bureau of Investigation's (FBI) 286
Federal Rules of Evidence 12, 272, 385
Fibers 8, 32, 52, 59, 60, 93, 114, 116, 118, 119, 123, 124, 125, 126, 170, 219, 220, 222, 372, 388, 423
File systems 330, 333
Financial Experts 396
Financial specialists 396
Fingerprinting 14, 392, 393
Fingerprint Odontology 393
Fingerprints 2, 8, 9, 10, 13, 14, 24, 29, 45, 46, 52, 54, 57, 58, 60, 70, 71, 74, 82, 100, 108, 326, 330, 359, 361, 385, 386, 389, 390, 400, 401, 407, 408, 416, 423
Firearms 63, 397
Firearms evidence 52
First responding officer (FRO) 44
Fixed Disk Image 329
Focal-plane array (FPA) 118
Forensic analysts 351
Forensic Anthropology 12, 14, 25, 155, 157, 159, 160, 161, 162
Forensic Chemistry 14, 31, 32, 111, 112, 113, 115, 117
Forensic data analysis 320, 321
Forensic death investigation 203
Forensic Document Examination (FDE) 358
Forensic Engineering 14, 354
Forensic Entomology 14, 15, 17
Forensic evidence 2, 199, 386, 391, 400, 403
Forensic Experts 382, 396, 397
Forensic identification 96
Forensic imaging 320, 321
Forensic Medicine 108, 160, 161, 217, 264, 265
Forensic odontology 14, 29, 30, 196
Forensic process 44, 320, 341, 350
Forensic Psychiatry 14, 20, 289, 291, 296, 309, 310, 315
Forensic science 2, 3, 108, 126, 382, 385, 388, 420, 423, 424
Forensic Toxicology 14, 17, 112, 136, 137, 138
Fourier transfer (FT) 123

G

Gas chromatography (GC) 117, 139
Gas chromatography-mass spectrometry (GC-MS) 18, 32, 376
Gender differences 165
Glass 32, 45, 52, 57, 58, 75, 91, 114, 126, 128, 145, 223, 259, 373
Golden Eye 336
Grid search 56, 82
Ground-state molecules 125
Gun collections 396
Gunshot residue (GSR) 24, 58

H

Hair 52, 59, 105, 151, 230
Hair roots 105, 389
Hair shafts 88
Hand lens 217
Handwriting 358, 360, 362, 397
Handwriting analysis 358
Happy slapping 326
Hazardous materials 112, 113, 134, 212
Hexamethylenetriperoxideamine (HMTD) 127
High-performance liquid chromatography (HPLC) 32, 116, 139
High-quality infrared spectra 123
HIV infection 228
Homicide 47, 49, 96, 100, 106, 156, 162, 180, 190, 191, 194, 204, 205, 209,

210, 216, 218, 219, 225, 232, 236, 255, 258, 262, 330, 351
Honesty 383
Human identification 95, 199
Humanity 157
Human Tissue Act 1961 215
HydraCrypt 336

I

Identification 13, 14, 26, 29, 30, 34, 44, 94, 108, 151, 158, 159, 161, 171, 172, 174, 179, 180, 191, 193, 195, 199, 200, 222, 223, 224, 424
Illegal drugs 58, 150, 419
Impressions 52, 62, 182, 185
Infrared imaging 118, 358
Infrared (IR) 121
Infrared light 115, 119, 123, 126, 370, 372, 374
Infrared microspectroscopy 123, 124
Injuries 17, 22, 25, 27, 30, 53, 134, 158, 161, 180, 182, 186, 195, 197, 198, 202, 203, 204, 205, 214, 217, 218, 222, 223, 224, 226, 231, 232, 233, 234, 235, 247, 248, 252, 253, 254, 270, 294, 299, 311, 396
Ink analysis 376, 377
Inks 116, 118, 126, 369, 374, 375, 376, 377, 378, 379
Intelligence collection 325
Internal reflection element (IRE) 121
International Organization on Computer Evidence (IOCE) 326
Intoxication 19, 129, 131, 138, 270

J

Jurisdiction 172, 203, 204, 250, 253, 262, 275, 287, 404
Jury selection 270, 275, 292

K

Keylogging program 336
Kubilka–Munk equation 123

L

Lambert–Beer's law 120
Laser desorption 377
Law enforcement 2, 12, 26, 31, 32, 34, 37, 88, 98, 99, 100, 112, 113, 114, 158, 159, 160, 196, 197, 198, 213, 217, 226, 274, 282, 283, 284, 285, 287, 289, 295, 320, 322, 324, 325, 327, 328, 329, 334, 338, 345, 358, 386, 387, 388, 408, 409, 410, 411, 420
Legal system 2, 3, 20, 21, 22, 34, 35, 37, 38, 40, 108, 162, 204, 270, 271, 277, 280, 286, 296, 297, 300, 382, 385, 388, 390, 401, 402, 420, 421, 423, 425
Light intensity 120
Linguistic Anthropology 157
Liquids 120, 130, 146
Locky 336
Low-power microscopy 372

M

Malware forensics 335
Manslaughter 19, 213
Mass grave 156
Mass spectrometry 12, 18, 20, 31, 32, 112, 113, 117, 139, 376, 377, 378, 379
Master casts 185
Medical examiners 198, 211, 251
Medical Experts 396
Medical malpractice cases 395
Medical procedures 156, 184
Mental Health Experts 396
Mental state opinion (MSO) 291
Mercury cadmium telluride (MCT) 119
Metals 24, 116, 120, 133
Methyl violet 378
Microbiological culture 243
Microbiology 203, 243
Mini-tape recorder 217
mitochondrial DNA (mtDNA) 88, 97
Mobile device forensics 320, 321

Mobile devices 320, 328, 331
Molecular fingerprint 123
Mucus 243
Multi-locus profiling 96
Murder 7, 8, 9, 12, 13, 15, 22, 30, 34, 51, 82, 85, 162, 195, 202, 211, 213, 214, 217, 259, 320, 339, 340, 419

N

National Cyber Investigative Joint Task Force (NCIJTF) 324
Natural causes 213, 217, 253
Natural sciences 3, 389
Near-infrared (NIR) 125
Necropsy 210, 211
Needles 217, 243
Negroids 164
Network connections 322
Network forensics 320, 321, 322, 334, 335
Network forensics-based intrusion detection 334
Network-level logs 330
Neuropsychology 270
Non-suicidal self-injury (NSSI) 304
Novel psychoactive substances (NPS) 139

O

Obduction 210
Oblique-angle photography 372
Obliteration 359, 370, 371
Online predators 326
Organizational psychology 273
Organizations 322, 335, 342
Overwriting 370

P

Paint residue 52, 58
Paints 32, 119, 123, 126, 150
Parental termination 273
Parenting Experts 396
Parole hearings 22, 273, 283
Past trauma 156
Paternity testing 88, 196
Pattern evidence 390
Pen pressure 362
Personal computers 322
Personal computing revolution 320
Personal injury 21, 273, 395
Personal injury lawsuits 395
Petaciae 181
Petya 336
Pharmaceutical 116, 137
Photography 4, 46, 182, 199, 217, 235, 236, 374, 388, 393
Physical anthropology 157
Physical evidence 57, 75, 77, 81, 390
Physical evidence collection 57
Physics 2, 3, 382, 388, 393
Plastic bags 127, 150, 217
Poisons 12, 17, 18, 112, 113, 114, 132, 133, 137, 138, 139, 140, 141, 142, 143, 145, 146, 147, 148, 149, 235, 382
Police investigators 198
Political society 157
Polymerase chain reaction (PCR) 13, 96, 139
Polymers 126, 379
Population-oriented methodology 157
Post-mortem examination 210, 235
Post-mortem interval (PMI) 15, 163
Pre-autopsy testing 228
Private vendors 91
Product liability 395, 396
Prosecutors 2, 37
Protein polymorphism 95, 96

Q

Quantitative polymerase chain reaction (qPCR) 89
Questioned document analysis 359
Questioned document examiners 358, 360
Questioned documents 52

R

Race 60, 156, 158, 161, 185, 194, 203, 230, 253, 420
Radiation source 118
Radiograph analysis 197
Raman spectroscopic imaging 126
Raman spectroscopy 124
Ransomware 336
Rapid spectrum acquisition 126
Rayleigh scattering 124
Reflection-absorption 121
Regional Computer Forensics Laboratories (RCFLs) 324
Restriction fragment length polymorphism (RFLP) 100
Rich information sources 328
Risk assessment 22, 278
Rootkits 336
Routers 322, 337
Rubber gloves 217

S

Saliva 18, 32, 52, 59, 88, 90, 91, 94, 180, 183, 191, 389
Scattering 124
Scene of Crime Officers (SOCOs) 218
School psychology 273
Science 2, 3, 4, 6, 8, 11, 13, 14, 15, 17, 20, 22, 25, 29, 31, 33, 45, 46, 88, 90, 99, 108, 112, 121, 126, 132, 135, 138, 139, 151, 156, 161, 194, 199, 218, 223, 243, 276, 286, 289, 320, 321, 325, 328, 335, 358, 359, 382, 383, 384, 385, 386, 387, 388, 389, 390, 393, 394, 399, 400, 401, 403, 407, 408, 409, 410, 411, 412, 419, 420, 421, 422, 423, 424, 425, 426
Scientific analysis 2, 99, 391, 423
Scientific Working Group on Digital Evidence (SWGDE) 326, 328
Securities Experts 396
Selectric typewriters 367
Self-harm 304, 311, 313
Semen 32, 52, 59, 88, 90, 91, 93, 94, 95, 98, 183, 221, 231, 237, 389
Semiconductors 120
Senile hyperkeratosis 230
Senile purpura 230
Serious Organized Crime Agency (SOCA) 328
Serous fluids 243
Server logs 337
Sex 26, 27, 91, 98, 156, 158, 159, 160, 161, 162, 163, 165, 166, 170, 171, 172, 174, 185, 194, 274
Sex Determination 158, 167
Sexual assault 91, 93, 94, 95, 97, 98, 99, 104, 106, 127, 152, 283, 293, 402
Short tandem repeats (STR) 14, 89
Short tandem repeat (STR) assays 97
Single-locus profiling 96
Single nucleotide polymorphisms (SNPs) 97
Skeletal abnormalities 156
Sketches 46, 51, 78
Social psychology 273
Social security number 203, 253
Spectral mapping 123
Spectroscopy 6, 8, 31, 32, 33, 112, 113, 115, 116, 117, 118, 119, 120, 121, 122, 123, 124, 125, 126, 127, 128, 150, 151, 152, 377
Specular reflection 121
Spermatozoa 93
Spyware 336
Standard keyboards 366
Stature 26, 156, 158, 160, 161, 162, 163, 170, 171, 172, 233, 270, 393
Steganography 325
Sterile swabs 217
Stokes band 125
Strict ethical rules 383
Structured professional judgment 278, 279, 293
Suicide 6, 52, 63, 204, 209, 217, 219, 226, 227, 258, 259, 299, 304, 305, 306, 307, 311, 312, 313, 330
Super Glue 60, 62

Supporting documentation 332
Syringes 217, 224
Systematic Digital Forensic Investigation Model (SRDHM) 347
System logs 330, 333

T

Teeth preserve information 192
Teeth roots 88
Temperature readings 221
Textiles 397
Thermometer 217, 221
Toolmarks 397
Toxicology 7, 8, 17, 18, 19, 20, 32, 88, 112, 113, 132, 133, 134, 135, 136, 137, 138, 139, 203, 226, 259, 382, 388
Trace evidence 32, 52, 390
Traffic lights 322
Trajectory determination 46
Transfer evidence 390
Transient evidence 390
Transmitting Terminal Identifier (TTI) 369
Transport Neutral Encapsulation Format (TNEF) 338
Typewriter 366, 367, 368, 372

U

Ultraviolet-visible (UV-Vis) 117
Unstructured clinical assessment 278
Urine 18, 19, 32, 59, 88, 91, 112, 129, 131, 132, 137, 138, 139, 231, 243

V

Variable number tandem repeat (VNTR) 96
Violence Risk Appraisal Guide (VRAG) 279
Violence risk assessment 278
Virus 216, 228, 229, 336
Vocational Experts 396
Voice-over-IP (VoIP) technologies 335
Vomit 52, 59, 129

W

Wanna Cry 336
Waterproof apron 217
Wavelength 116, 117, 119, 120, 121, 122, 125, 371
Wavenumber 119, 120
Weapons 52, 94
Web browser 331
Web server 331
Wireless forensics 335
World Health Organization-mandated format 228
Worms 336
Writing instruments 370
Writing samples 363
Written records 92

X

X-headers 337
X-ray 32, 175, 197, 199

Y

Y-incision 238, 247

Z

Zone search 56

MIX

Papier | Fördert gute Waldnutzung

FSC® C083411

Kolibri 360 GmbH
Ferdinand-Jühlke-Straße 7
99095 Erfurt, Deutschland
produktsicherheit@kolibri360.de